PRAYERS, VERSES, AND DEVOTIONS

PRAYERS, VERSES, AND DEVOTIONS

JOHN HENRY NEWMAN

THE DEVOTIONS OF BISHOP ANDREWES
MEDITATIONS AND DEVOTIONS
VERSES ON VARIOUS OCCASIONS

IGNATIUS PRESS   SAN FRANCISCO

The Devotions of Bishop Andrewes
was first published in 1843
by John Henry Parker, Oxford and London

Meditations and Devotions
was first published in 1903
by Longmans, Green, and Co.,
London and New York

Verses on Various Occasions
was first published in 1903
by Longmans, Green, and Co.,
London, New York, and Bombay

Permission to reproduce George Richmond's
illustration of John Henry Newman
was kindly granted by
The Friends of Cardinal Newman
The Birmingham Oratory

Cover by Roxanne Mei Lum

CONTENTS

MEDITATIONS AND DEVOTIONS

Prefatory Notice

PART I

CONTENTS

PART II

PART III

MEDITATIONS ON CHRISTIAN DOCTRINE

VERSES ON VARIOUS OCCASIONS

CONTENTS

INTRODUCTION

Newman is not what the Christians of the last few centuries have come to mean by a "spiritual writer". He does not try to move his readers to devotion by emotionally soliciting their turning to God and having recourse for this effect to analyses and suggestions based upon psychological insight. For Newman is not one of those modern theologians who have tried to nourish piety mainly with psychological—when not just emotional—considerations and devices, like Gerson at the end of the Middle Ages, who had to turn to psychology after recognizing the dessication of his own theology due to its too successful adaptation to the model of Aristotelian "science".

Of Newman, rather, must be said what was already true of those theologians of the first generation of what we call "Christian humanists"—like Erasmus, Bartolomeo Carranza, Morrone or Pole, or later Petau and Thomassin—all Catholics—or Anglicans like Hooker and his heirs, the Caroline Divines, or even Lutherans of the same period and tendencies, like Johann Gerhard: I mean that for all these as for Newman, who in this followed their example, the rediscovery of the great Fathers of the Church, especially the Greek Fathers, led to a fresher look at the Bible and created in their time a "new" way of doing theology that had in fact been that of all the early Christians. For these, theology and spirituality could never be divorced—nor even distinguished—from one another. We should even say more: Newman, along with the Christian humanists of the Renaissance, followed the vision represented by the ancient Christian thinker known as Pseudo-Dionysius. However saturated this Father might be by philosophy, for him "mystical theology" would not have meant some "scientific" theology applied to mysticism but the mystical experience itself, as constituting the highest possible knowledge of God.

In this sense we may say of Newman, as well as of all those Christian thinkers just mentioned, that it is as spiritual writer that he theologizes and as theologian that, indeed, he is a "spiritual writer", but in the sense that this phrase would have had for the Fathers themselves or for their disciples of the sixteenth and seventeenth centuries.

Among these Cardinal Bona, one of the first great liturgiologists of modern times, and Lancelot Andrewes, among the Anglicans, would have agreed with Newman's realization that all of us moderns are more or less in need of some pedagogy to restore us to the possibility of a *lectio divina* as practiced by the ancient Christians: a reading of Scripture leading us, not to a purely abstract meditation of the Word of God, but to its vital assimilation, which alone befits it as the Word of Life it essentially is. This is why Andrewes, like Bona, composed centos of scriptural, liturgical, or simply traditional sentences likely to develop devotion in us systematically, but not through largely artificial devices. Rather, these centos group together and offer us their material in a clear and coherent order, according to the different subjective reactions that the objective history of revelation—or, for that matter, the objective revelation *in* history—was intended to evoke in us.

Such is the movement that Johannes Arndt described as "proceeding from Christ *for us* to Christ *in us*". This Johannes Arndt was himself a Lutheran of the post-Renaissance period whose anonymously published *Wahres Christentum*, although the work of a Protestant, was in

fact translated and propagated by a Catholic like Cardinal
de Noailles and by a Russian Orthodox monk-bishop like
Tikhon of Zadonsk. Arndt's work is characterized by the
same inspiration and the same method as found in the
Preces privatae of Lancelot Andrewes, and it was this
common Christian spirit of authentic devotion that was
later to enthrall Newman himself, still an Anglican but
already well underway to Catholicism.

Newman was quite captivated by the very personal,
but also very catholic (in every sense of the term) style of
Andrewes' *Preces*, spiritual "exercises" of penance, confession of faith, praise, thanksgiving, and intercession,
leading to a fully conscious participation in the eucharistic
mysteries and, ultimately, to a whole life in God's presence in Christ. So taken was he, in fact, that he undertook
to translate and adapt them (the original text was in
Greek) for the general benefit of his contemporaries. It
must be added that, to the end of his long life, Newman
quite believed that in these exercises of Andrewes he had
discovered that form of prayer which springs directly
from the Word of God and leads to a life fully lived in
Christ. Not only as a priest, but later on as a cardinal of
the Roman Church, he would keep the *Preces privatae* on
his kneeler for his daily preparation and thanksgiving
before and after Mass and for his most personal meditations.

It can be said, therefore, that this work of Andrewes',
thus translated and adapted by Newman and entirely
woven of sentences from the Bible, the Fathers, and the
ancient liturgies, should be considered the fundamental
inspiration of all Newman's devotional writings. It
opened the way to the special style and character which
would be exhibited by whatever he would in the future
write in this field.

This consideration is what has led us to place at the
head of the present volume Newman's rendering and

recasting of Andrewes' Greek text in a beautiful English all his own. Such an accomplished translation and adaptation constitutes a most personal re-creation. None of his own compositions from the Catholic period would have been what they are were it not for this preliminary and ever-inspiring achievement.

The second part of this volume is composed of the *Meditations and Devotions* that Father Neville edited after Newman's death. These texts reflect a return to the sources of Christianity similar to that of Andrewes himself, but now within the forms of meditation and prayer developed by post-Tridentine Catholicism. Here we have devotions in a style familiar to the simple people who comprised the majority of the congregation of the Oratorian parish of Birmingham, as well as to the boys of the Oratory School; but here we find the same spirit that characterizes Andrewes' prayers, a spirit always conveying the breath of Bible and liturgy, the very sources of patristic devotion. This spirit is the hallmark of the simple yet so profound "Meditations on Christian Doctrine", as well as of the lighter though equally sober "Meditations for the Month of May", based on the titles applied to the Blessed Virgin by the Litany of Loretto.

Noted for this same sobriety and imbued with this same spirit, the "Meditations on the Way of the Cross and the Passion" reflect the serenity which is so engaging an aspect of the Church of the martyrs, who in this followed the example of the Apocalypse of St. John: the Cross is never seen other than in the light of the Resurrection.

The accompanying prayers, especially the litanies, are in harmony with this type of meditation. The litany and meditations centered on St. Philip Neri give the note both of simplicity and of persuasive beauty—the "beauty of holiness" which is a constant mark both of Newman's style and of his thought.

The third and final part of the volume is a reprinting of the *Verses on Various Occasions* compiled by Newman himself at the end of his life. Not everything in them can be described as precisely "devotional"; but all of it is poetry suffused with the vision of man's life so typical of Newman: a life illuminated by that "kindly Light" from above invoked by Newman in the most popular of these compositions.

Nothing could have provided a more fitting conclusion to the present book than the only long poem ever written by Newman, *The Dream of Gerontius*. Not only does it present us with a most impresssive vision of Christian death as introducing us to eternal life, but it is shot through with that sense of the invisible thriving within the visible world which is so "Newmanian". Beyond this, the *Dream* gives the most striking expression ever produced of the view first formulated explicitly by St. Catherine of Genoa in her *Treatise on Purgatory*: that all the trials of Christian life, here and now as well as in the very mysterious intermediate state of Purgatory—which is to lead us to the immediate vision of God in His glory—are but a development of that "love poured forth in our hearts by the Spirit". In other words, the trials and sufferings of Christian life are a purification of human love by that divine love which is the substance of the divine life itself, as revealed to us by the Gospel of Christ.

To this general presentation of our volume it may be good to add a few slightly more detailed explanations of its major elements.

In the *Preces* of Andrewes, what explains the fact that they adapt the meditation of the divine Word to modern minds is their principle of composition: the centos of sentences drawn from Scripture, the ancient liturgies, and the Fathers are structured as meditations on confession, prayer for grace, supplication, intercession, praise, and

thanksgiving. These devotions are a practical embodi-
ment of St. Teresa's advice that the simplest, but perhaps
the best, form of meditative prayer is achieved when we
make our own the meaning of the Word of God by
quietly applying it in faith to our needs. The thought was
perhaps best expressed in Bengel's famous dictum, still
found on the first page of Greek New Testaments printed
in Wurttemberg: *Totus te applica ad textum, totum textum
applica ad te!* And it should be observed that each of the
sections of Andrewes' prayers includes some touch of the
substance of the others, a feature which thus upholds the
organic unity of Christian prayer.

This part of our volume ends with an immediate
preparation for the celebration of the Eucharist and Holy
Communion. In this sense we may see it as an application
of Origen's view that the final aim of the whole of
Scripture is the creation in us of a proper response to the
Word. Does not St. Paul, in his Letter to the Ephesians,
dare to say that Christ, the Son and Word made man,
attains to ultimate and complete fulfilment only in the
members of His mystical body, the Church?

By identifying all the quotations and allusions in Andrewes' *Preces*, the great modern scholar F. E. Brightman
has clearly shown how Origen's consideration of the aim
of Scripture was very much present to the mind of
Newman, who in this followed Andrewes: both of them
interwove Scripture and its echoes in the liturgy with
passages from those very Fathers whose whole point is
continually to refer the Bible to its realization in the
liturgy.[1] Here we may say that we are dealing with a
form of meditation which, far from having to be put
away when divine contemplation begins, has in fact led

[1] See *The Private Devotions of Lancelot Andrewes*, translated with an
introduction and notes by F. E. Brightman (London, 1903; re-edited by
Meridian Books, 1961).

to such contemplation from the outset, preparing and disposing the believer for nothing else.

Newman's meditations for the month of May, which follow in this volume, convey to the reader the sense of that new springtime the image of which came so naturally to Newman when, having already entered the Catholic Church, he fully made his own the Spirit of Him whose body this Church is. In these meditations we have something in the genre of the "prose poem". In an unforgettable way they express the eternal youth of the one true Church throughout the course of her history—a youthful springtime that manifests itself anew every time the Church allows herself to be led back to her own sources. These May Meditations are developed along the succession of Marian feasts: Immaculate Conception, Annunciation, Seven Sorrows, and Assumption. The memorandum appended on the Immaculate Conception, as defined by Pius IX only a few years before the meditations were written, may explain why Newman's thoughts on the Blessed Virgin centered more on the perfect example of holiness Mary represents than on her divine motherhood. His considerations of the Marian mystery are dominated by the centrality of the grace of Christ and everything this grace can bring to the person He was most intimately associated with.

It is understandable that the novena to St. Philip Neri, the founder and patron saint of the Oratory, has been given a place directly after these May meditations in the volume prepared by Father Neville after Newman's death. The reader will find reproduced here Father Neville's preface, which gives his principles of organization. What above all attracted Newman in the figure of Philip Neri was his closeness to the spirit of the primitive Church and, at the same time, his astonishing openness to the needs of his contemporaries.

Beyond doubt, however, it is the "Meditations on

Christian Doctrine", the third part of the book as edited by Neville, that are at the heart of Newman's *Meditations and Devotions* and, therefore, of the whole present volume. For here we see all the positive renewal that could be accomplished once the spirit of the Church of the New Testament and the Fathers was infused into the very framework of post-Tridentine Catholic devotions. Following the order of the articles of the Creed—and, therefore, the very historical path along which the Word of God has became incarnate in the New Adam, the celestial Man—these "Meditations on Christian Doctrine" attempt to show the way toward the realization in us Christians, both individually and communally, of the very life of God's Spirit in our assumed humanity.

We may specifically take note of the structure of these meditations. Each begins with an exposition of the divine truth in its objectivity. A second paragraph then shows how the particular truth involved has come to touch the heart of our fallen human nature in order then to inspire, in a third paragraph, the efficacious surrender of the individual believer to what has been made available to all on the road of the Incarnation and the Cross.

The Meditations on the Blessed Virgin had concentrated on a single theme, a single image, which the meditator had simply to make his own to the depths of his soul, like a stone falling into a lake of pure waters, soon entirely taken into an ever-wider encircling wave. The task of the subsequent meditations on doctrine, however, is to develop fully articulated doctrinal themes in all their detailed ramifications and implications. For both sets of meditations, the very rich fullness encountered at each step requires that only one meditation should be slowly read and reread at one sitting; otherwise, instead of the intended effect of concentration on the essential, what will result from too casual and broad a perusal will be a superficial, not to say wholly confused, perception.

Climaxing the *Meditations and Devotions* are the prayers in litany form, and we have been careful to leave them at the center, where they belong. Except for the delightful litany Newman himself composed in honor of St. Philip Neri—and which distils a very peculiar grace—the other litanies were simply borrowed by Newman from that rich garden, the *Hortus animarum* of Horstius, "planted" by its author at a time not too distant from Andrewes', and in a similar spirit. They are to be used in the same manner of simple, contemplative assimilation.

If we pass from these prayers and devotions to the poetry, we must acknowledge that the best that can be said of most of Newman's verses is that they are not totally unworthy of his prose, as is generally the case with the greatest prose writers. Froude, the *enfant terrible* of the Oxford Movement, once remarked to Keble, "There is something Sternhold-and-Hopkinsey in your versification . . . ", Sternhold and Hopkins being the authors of a verse translation of the Psalms, then very popular but poetically below the level even of mediocrity. The same could not be said of Newman's poems: they are never without some distinction, but they evoke those pedestrian verses of Wordsworth where, for lack of inspiration, the great poet substitutes some gnomic considerations which are not as devoid of interest as prejudiced critics have maintained but which, admittedly, are more dignified than truly poetical in their end-product. The only exceptions occur when a genuine insight has coupled the appropriate images with a wording whose musicality in some way makes up for the neutrality of the rhythm. This is the case above all with the poems inspired by the sudden and unexpected death of Newman's younger sister, Mary (numbers IX and X, still more so XIII, and especially the conclusion of XVII). Nevertheless, more poetry than in these verses may still be found in just a few words from a letter on the same theme.

"Dear Mary seems embodied in every tree and hid behind every hill. What a veil and curtain this world of sense is! Beautiful, but still a veil!"

Despite the general weakness of Newman's poetry, however, we must say that, more so even than in the famous "Lead, Kindly Light" . . . , there certainly is something genuinely poetical in pieces like *Angelic Guidance* or that *Melchisedech* that owes something to Herbert, although their authentic poetry resides more in the idea itself than in its clothing in verse. But the fact remains that there is no poem of Newman's where some reminiscence may not be found of his vision of faith—the presence of the invisible behind the visible so characteristic of Newman's religiosity.

We conclude these few remarks by noting how deeply moving is Newman's own final disposition in his expectation of death, quite beyond the very plain method of meditation which he at the same time recommends to a sick person. But he would not, I think, have ever forgiven a commentator of this very mixed but ever so rich material if, in concluding, the reader's attention had not been drawn to the quiet humor behind Newman's own "way of perfection". . . .

Louis Bouyer
of the Oratory

THE DEVOTIONS

OF

BISHOP ANDREWES,

TRANSLATED FROM THE GREEK

AND ARRANGED ANEW.

I

DAILY PRAYERS: PREPARATION.

I. TIMES OF PRAYER

Always. *Luke* xviii. 1.

Without ceasing. 1 *Thes.* v. 17.

At all times. *Eph.* vi. 18.

Samuel among such as call upon His name.[1] *Ps.* xeix. 6.

God forbid that I should sin against the Lord in ceasing to pray for you, and shewing you the good and the right way. 1 *Sam.* xii. 23.

We will give ourselves continually to prayer and to the ministry of the word. *Acts* vi. 4.

He kneeled upon his knees three times a day, and prayed and gave thanks before his God, as he did afore-time. *Dan.* vi. 10.

In the evening, and morning, and at noon day will I pray, and that instantly, and He shall hear my voice. *Ps.* lv. 18.

Seven times a day do I praise Thee. *Ps.* cxix. 164.

1. In the morning, a great while before day. *Mark* i. 35.

2. In the morning watch. *Ps.* lxiii. 6. [vid. also *Ps.* cxxx. 6.]

3. The third hour of the day. *Acts* ii. 15.

4. About the sixth hour. *Acts* x. 9.

5. The hour of prayer, the ninth. *Acts* iii. 1.

---

[1] Transferred from p. 4 of edition of 1675.

3

6. The eventide. *Gen.* xxiv. 63.
7. By night. *Ps.* cxxxiv. 2.
   At midnight. *Ps.* cxix. 62.

2. PLACES OF PRAYER

In all places where I record My Name, I will come to thee, and I will bless thee. *Exod.* xx. 24.

Let[2] Thine eyes be open towards this house night and day, even toward the place of which Thou hast said, My Name shall be there; that Thou mayest hearken unto the prayer which Thy servant shall make towards this place. 1 *Kings* viii. 29.

> Thou that hearest the prayer
> unto Thee shall all flesh come.
> The fierceness of man shall turn to Thy praise,
> and the fierceness of them shalt Thou refrain.
> As for me, I will come into Thy house
> even upon the multitude of Thy mercy,
> and in Thy fear will I worship
> toward Thy Holy Temple.
> Hear the voice of my humble petitions,
> when I cry unto Thee;
> when I hold up my hands
> towards the mercy-seat of Thy Holy Temple.
> We wait for Thy loving-kindness, O God,
> in the midst of Thy Temple.

1. Among the faithful and in the congregation. *Ps.* cxi. 1.
2. Enter into thy closet, and, when thou hast shut thy door, pray to thy Father which is in secret. *Matt.* vi. 6.
3. They went up into an upper room. *Acts* i. 13.

---

[2] Transferred from pp. 5, 6, and 9, of edition 1675.

4. He went up upon the housetop to pray. *Acts* x. 9.
5. They went up together into the Temple. *Acts* iii. 1.
6. We kneeled down on the shore, and prayed. *Acts* xxi. 5.
7. He went forth over the brook Cedron, where was a garden. *John* xviii. 1.
8. Let them rejoice in their beds. *Ps.* cxlix. 5.
9. He departed into a desert place and there prayed. *Mark* i. 35.
10. In every place lifting up holy hands without wrath and doubting. 1 *Tim.* ii. 8.

3. CIRCUMSTANCES OF PRAYER

1. Kneeling, *humiliation.*
   He kneeled down and prayed. *Luke* xxii. 41.
   He went a little further, and fell on His face, and prayed. *Matt.* xxvi. 39.
   My soul is brought low, even unto the dust,
       my belly cleaveth unto the ground.
2. Sinking the head, *shame.*
   Drooping the face. [*Ezr.* ix. 6.]
3. Smiting the breast, [*Luke* xviii. 13.]
       indignation.
4. Shuddering, [*Acts* xvi. 29.] *fear.*
5. Groaning, [*Isai.* lix. 11.] *sorrow.*
   Clasping of hands.
6. Raising of eyes and hands, [*Ps.* xxv. 15; cxliii. 6.] *vehement desire.*
7. Blows, [*Ps.* lxxiii. 14.] *revenge.*

} 2 *Cor.* vii. 11.

II

ORDER OF MATIN PRAYER.

LITANY.

Glory be to Thee, O Lord, glory to Thee.
Glory to Thee who givest me sleep
to recruit my weakness,
and to remit the toils
of this fretful flesh.
To this day and all days,
a perfect, holy, peaceful, healthy, sinless course,
Vouchsafe O Lord.

The Angel of peace, a faithful guide,
guardian of souls and bodies,
to encamp around me,
and ever to prompt what is salutary,
Vouchsafe O Lord.

Pardon and remission
of all sins and of all offences
Vouchsafe O Lord.

To our souls what is good and convenient,
and peace to the world,
Vouchsafe O Lord.

Repentance and strictness
for the residue of our life,
and health and peace to the end,
Vouchsafe O Lord.

Whatever is true, whatever is honest,
whatever just, whatever pure,
whatever lovely, whatever of good report,
if there be any virtue, if any praise,
such thoughts, such deeds,
Vouchsafe O Lord.

A Christian close,
without sin, without shame,
and, should it please Thee, without pain,
and a good answer
at the dreadful and fearful judgment-seat
of Jesus Christ our Lord,
Vouchsafe O Lord.

CONFESSION.

Essence beyond essence, Nature increate,
Framer of the world,
I set Thee, Lord, before my face,
and I lift up my soul unto Thee.
I worship Thee on my knees,
and humble myself under Thy mighty hand.
I stretch forth my hands unto Thee,
my soul gaspeth unto Thee as a thirsty land.
I smite on my breast
and say with the Publican,
God be merciful to me a sinner,
the chief of sinners;
to the sinner above the Publican,
be merciful as to the Publican.
Father of mercies,
I beseech Thy fatherly affection,
despise me not
an unclean worm, a dead dog, a putrid corpse,
despise not Thou the work of Thine own hands,

despise not Thine own image
though branded by sin.
Lord, if Thou wilt, Thou canst make me clean,
Lord, only say the word, and I shall be cleansed.
And Thou, my Saviour Christ,
Christ my Saviour,
Saviour of sinners, of whom I am chief,
despise me not, despise me not, O Lord,
despise not the cost of Thy blood,
who am called by Thy Name;
but look on me with those eyes
with which Thou didst look upon
Magdalene at the feast,
Peter in the hall,
the thief on the wood;—
that with the thief I may entreat Thee humbly,
Remember me, Lord, in Thy kingdom;
that with Peter I may bitterly weep and say:
O that mine eyes were a fountain of tears
that I might weep day and night;
that with Magdalene I may hear Thee say:
Thy sins be forgiven thee,
and with her may love much,
for many sins yea manifold
have been forgiven me.
And Thou, All-holy, Good, and Life-giving Spirit,
despise me not, Thy breath,
despise not Thine own holy things;
but turn Thee again, O Lord, at the last,
and be gracious unto Thy servant.

COMMENDATION.

Blessed art Thou, O Lord,
Our God,
the God of our Fathers;

who turnest the shadow of death into the morning;
and lightenest the face of the earth;
who separatest darkness from the face of the light;
and banishest night and bringest back the day;
who lightenest mine eyes,
that I sleep not in death;
who deliverest me from the terror by night,
from the pestilence that walketh in darkness;
who drivest sleep from mine eyes,
and slumber from mine eyelids;
who makest the outgoings of the morning and evening
to praise Thee;
because I laid me down and slept and rose up again,
for the Lord sustained me;
because I waked and beheld,
and my sleep was sweet unto me.
Blot out as a thick cloud my transgressions,
and as a cloud my sins;
grant me to be a child of light, a child of the day,
to walk soberly, holily, honestly, as in the day,
vouchsafe to keep me this day without sin.
Thou who upholdest the falling and liftest the fallen,
let me not harden my heart in provocation,
or temptation or deceitfulness of any sin.
Moreover, deliver me to-day
from the snare of the hunter
and from the noisome pestilence;
from the arrow that flieth by day,
from the sickness that destroyeth in the noon day.
Defend this day against my evil,
against the evil of this day defend Thou me.
Let not my days be spent in vanity,
nor my years in sorrow.
One day telleth another,
and one night certifieth another.
O let me hear Thy loving-kindness betimes in the

morning,
for in Thee is my trust;
shew Thou me the way that I should walk in,
for I lift up my soul unto Thee.
Deliver me, O Lord, from mine enemies,
for I flee unto Thee.
Teach me to do the thing that pleaseth Thee,
for Thou art my God;
Let Thy loving Spirit lead me forth
into the land of righteousness.
Quicken me, O Lord, for Thy Name's sake,
and for Thy righteousness' sake
bring my soul out of trouble;
remove from me foolish imaginations,
inspire those which are good
and pleasing in Thy sight.
Turn away mine eyes
lest they behold vanity;
let mine eyes look right on,
and let mine eyelids look straight before me.
Hedge up mine ears with thorns
lest they incline to undisciplined words.
Give me early the ear to hear,
and open mine ears to the instruction of Thy oracles.
Set a watch, O Lord, before my mouth,
and keep the door of my lips.
Let my word be seasoned with salt,
that it may minister grace to the hearers.
Let no need be grief unto me
nor offence of heart.
Let me do some work
for which Thou wilt remember me, Lord, for good,
and spare me according to the greatness of Thy mercy.
Into Thine hands I commend
my spirit, soul, and body,
which Thou hast created, redeemed, regenerated,

O Lord, Thou God of truth;
and together with me
all mine and all that belongs to me.
Thou hast vouchsafed them to me,
Lord, in Thy goodness.
Guard us from all evil,
guard our souls,
I beseech Thee, O Lord.
Guard us without falling,
and place us immaculate
in the presence of Thy glory
in that day.
Guard my going out and my coming in
henceforth and for ever.
Prosper, I pray Thee, Thy servant this day,
and grant him mercy
in the sight of those who meet him.
O God, make speed to save me,
O Lord, make haste to help me.
O turn Thee then unto me,
and have mercy upon me;
give Thy strength unto Thy servant,
and help the son of Thine handmaid.
Shew some token upon me for good,
that they who hate me may see it and be ashamed,
because Thou, Lord, hast holpen me
and comforted me.

ORDER OF EVENING PRAYER[1]

MEDITATION.

The day is gone,
and I give Thee thanks, O Lord.
Evening is at hand,
make it bright unto us.
As day has its evening
so also has life;
the even of life is age,
age has overtaken me,
make it bright unto us.
Cast me not away in the time of age;
forsake me not when my strength faileth me.
Even to my old age be Thou He,
and even to hoar hairs carry me;
do Thou make, do Thou bear,
do Thou carry and deliver me.
Abide with me, Lord,
for it is toward evening,
and the day is far spent
of this fretful life.
Let Thy strength be made perfect
in my weakness.

Day is fled and gone,
life too is going,

[1] Page 196, edit. 1675.

this lifeless life.
Night cometh,
and cometh death,
the deathless death.
Near as is the end of day,
so too the end of life.
We then, also remembering it,
beseech of Thee
for the close of our life,
that Thou wouldest direct it in peace,
Christian, acceptable,
sinless, shameless,
and, if it please Thee, painless,
Lord, O Lord,
gathering us together
under the feet of Thine Elect,
when Thou wilt, and as Thou wilt,
only without shame and sins.
Remember we the days of darkness,
for they shall be many,
lest we be cast into outer darkness.
Remember we to outstrip the night
doing some good thing.
Near is judgment;—
a good and acceptable answer
at the dreadful and fearful judgment-seat
of Jesus Christ
vouchsafe to us, O Lord.
By night I lift up my hands in the sanctuary,
and praise the Lord.
The Lord hath granted His loving-kindness
in the day time;
and in the night season did I sing of Him,
and made my prayer unto the God of my life.
As long as I live will I magnify Thee on this manner,
and lift up my hands in Thy Name.

Let my prayer be set forth in Thy sight
as the incense,
and let the lifting up of my hands
be an evening sacrifice.
Blessed art Thou, O Lord, our God,
the God of our fathers,
who hast created the changes of days and nights,
who givest songs in the night,
who hast delivered us from the evil of this day,
who hast not cut off like a weaver my life,
nor from day even to night made an end of me.

CONFESSION.

Lord,
as we add day to day,
so sin to sin.
The just falleth seven times a day;
and I, an exceeding sinner,
seventy times seven;
a wonderful, a horrible thing, O Lord.
But I turn with groans
from my evil ways,
and I return into my heart,
and with all my heart I turn to Thee,
O God of penitents and Saviour of sinners;
and evening by evening I will return
in the innermost marrow of my soul;
and my soul out of the deep
crieth unto Thee.
I have sinned, O Lord, against Thee,
heavily against Thee;
alas, alas, woe is me! for my misery.
I repent, O me! I repent, spare me, O Lord,
I repent, O me, I repent,

help Thou my impenitence.
Be appeased, spare me, O Lord;
be appeased, have mercy on me;
I said, Lord, have mercy upon me,
heal my soul, for I have sinned against Thee.
Have mercy upon me, O Lord,
after Thy great goodness,
according to the multitude of Thy mercies
do away mine offences.
Remit the guilt,
heal the wound,
blot out the stains,
clear away the shame,
rescue from the tyranny,
and make me not a public example.
O bring Thou me out of my trouble,
cleanse Thou me from secret faults,
keep back Thy servant also from presumptuous sins.
My wanderings of mind
and idle talking
lay not to my charge.
Remove the dark and muddy flood
of foul and wicked thoughts.
O Lord,
I have destroyed myself;
whatever I have done amiss, pardon mercifully.
Deal not with us after our sins,
neither reward us after our iniquities.
Look mercifully upon our infirmities;
and for the glory of Thy All-holy Name,
turn from us all those ills and miseries,
which by our sins, and by us through them,
are most righteously and worthily deserved.

COMMENDATION.

To my weariness, O Lord,
vouchsafe Thou rest,
to my exhaustion
renew Thou strength.
Lighten mine eyes that I sleep not in death.
Deliver me from the terror by night,
the pestilence that walketh in darkness.
Supply me with healthy sleep,
and to pass through this night without fear.
O Keeper of Israel,
who neither slumberest nor sleepest,
guard me this night from all evil,
guard my soul, O Lord.
Visit me with the visitation of Thine own,
reveal to me wisdom in the visions of the night.
If not, for I am not worthy, not worthy,
at least, O loving Lord,
let sleep be to me a breathing time
as from toil, so from sin.
Yea, O Lord,
nor let me in my dreams imagine
what may anger Thee,
what may defile me.
Let not my loins be filled with illusions,
yea, let my reins chasten me in the night season,
yet without grievous terror.
Preserve me from the black sleep of sin;
all earthly and evil thoughts
put to sleep within me.
Grant to me light sleep,
rid of all imaginations
fleshly and satanical.
Lord, Thou knowest
how sleepless are mine unseen foes,

and how feeble my wretched flesh,
who madest me;
shelter me with the wing of Thy pity;
awaken me at the fitting time,
the time of prayer;
and give me to seek Thee early,
for Thy glory, and for Thy service.

Here use the form of Intercession, No. 3.

Into Thy hands, O Lord, I commend myself,
my spirit, soul, and body:
Thou didst make, and didst redeem them;
and together with me, all my friends
and all that belongs to me.
Thou hast vouchsafed them to me, Lord,
in Thy goodness.
Guard my lying down and my rising up,
from henceforth and for ever.
Let me remember Thee on my bed,
and search out my spirit;
let me wake up and be present with Thee;
let me lay me down in peace, and take my rest:
for it is Thou, Lord, only
that makest me dwell in safety.

IV

COURSE OF PRAYERS FOR THE WEEK.

THE FIRST DAY.

Introduction.

Through the tender mercies of our God
the day-spring from on high hath visited us.
Glory be to Thee, O Lord, glory to Thee.
Creator of the light,
and Enlightener of the world,—
of the visible light,
the Sun's ray, a flame of fire,
day and night,
evening and morning,—
of the light invisible,
the revelation of God,
writings of the Law,
oracles of Prophets,
music of Psalms,
instruction of Proverbs,
experience of Histories,—
light which never sets.
God is the Lord who hath shewed us light;
bind the sacrifice with cords,
yea even unto the horns of the altar.

O by Thy resurrection raise us up
unto newness of life,
supplying to us frames of repentance.

The God of peace,
who did bring again from the dead
the great Shepherd of the sheep,
through the blood of the everlasting covenant,
our Lord Jesus Christ,
perfect us in every good work,
to do His will,
working in us what is acceptable before Him,
through Jesus Christ,
to whom be glory for ever.

Thou who didst send down on Thy disciples
on this day
Thy Thrice-Holy Spirit,
withdraw not Thou the gift, O Lord, from us,
but renew it in us, day by day,
who ask Thee for it.

1. Confession.

Merciful and pitiful Lord,
Long-suffering and full of pity,
I have sinned, Lord, I have sinned against Thee;
O me, wretched that I am,
I have sinned, Lord, against Thee,
much and grievously,
in attending on vanities and lies.
I conceal nothing:
I make no excuses.
I give Thee glory, O Lord, this day,
I denounce against myself my sins;
Truly I have sinned before the Lord,
and thus and thus have I done,
I have sinned and perverted
that which was right,
and it profited me not.

And what shall I now say?
or with what shall I open my mouth?
What shall I answer, seeing I have done it?
Without plea, without defence, self-condemned, am I.
I have destroyed myself.
Unto Thee, O Lord, belongeth righteousness,
but unto me confusion of face,
because Thou art just in all that is come upon me;
for Thou hast done right,
but I have done wickedly.
And now, Lord, what is my hope?
Truly my hope is even in Thee,
if hope of salvation remain to me,
if Thy loving-kindness cover
the multitude of my iniquities.
O remember, what my substance is,
the work of Thine hands,
the likeness of Thy countenance,
the cost of Thy blood,
a name from Thy Name,
a sheep of Thy pasture,
a son of the covenant,
Despise not Thou the work of Thine own hands.
Hast thou made for nought
Thine own image and likeness?
for nought, if Thou destroy it.
And what profit is there in my blood?
Thine enemies will rejoice;
May they never rejoice, O Lord!
Grant not to them my destruction.
Look upon the face of Thine Anointed,
and in the Blood of Thy covenant,
the propitiation for the sins of the whole world,
Lord, be propitious unto me, a sinner;
even unto me, O Lord, of sinners
chief, chiefest and greatest;

For Thy Name's sake be merciful unto my sin,
for it is great: it exceeds.
For Thy Name's sake, that Name,
beside which, none other under heaven
is given among men,
whereby we must be saved,
the Spirit Himself helping our infirmities,
and making intercession for us,
with plaints unutterable.
For the tender yearnings of the Father,
the bloody wounds of the Son,
the unutterable plaints of the Spirit,
give ear, O Lord, have mercy, O Lord,
O Lord, hearken and do;
defer not, for Thine own sake,
O my God.
For me, I forget not my sins,
they are ever before me;
I remember them in the bitterness of my soul;
I am anxious about them;
I turn away and groan,
I have indignation and revenge
and wrath against myself.
I despise and bruise my own self,
that my penitence, Lord, O Lord,
is not deeper, is not fuller;
help Thou mine impenitence.
And more, and still more,
pierce Thou, rend, crush my heart;
and remit, forgive, pardon
what things are grief to me,
and offence of heart.
Cleanse Thou me from secret faults,
and keep Thy servant also from presumptuous sins.
Magnify Thy mercies towards the wretched sinner;
and in season, Lord, say to me,

Be of good cheer; thy sins are forgiven thee;
My grace is sufficient for thee.
Say unto my soul, I am thy salvation.
Why art thou so heavy, O my soul?
and why art thou so disquieted within thee?
Return unto thy rest, O my soul,
for the Lord hath rewarded thee.
O Lord, rebuke me not in Thine indignation,
neither chasten me in Thy displeasure.
I said, I will confess my sins unto the Lord,
and so Thou forgavest the wickedness of my sin.
Lord, Thou knowest all my desire,
and my groaning is not hid from Thee.
Have mercy upon me, O God,
after Thy great goodness,
according to the multitude of Thy mercies
do away mine offences.
Thou shalt arise, and have mercy on me, O Lord,
for it is time that Thou have mercy upon me,
yea, the time is come.
If Thou, O Lord, shouldest mark iniquities,
O Lord, who shall stand?
Enter not into judgment with Thy servant, O Lord,
for in Thy sight shall no man living be justified.

2. Prayer for Grace.

My hands will I lift up
unto Thy commandments which I have loved.
Open Thou mine eyes that I may see,
incline my heart that I may desire,
order my steps that I may follow,
the way of Thy commandments.
O Lord God, be Thou to me a God,
and beside Thee none else,
none else, nought else with Thee.

Vouchsafe to me, to worship Thee and serve Thee
1. in truth of spirit,
2. in reverence of body,
3. in blessing of lips
4. in private and in public;
5. to pay honour to them that have the rule over me,
by obedience and submission;
to shew affection to my own,
by carefulness and providence;
6. to overcome evil with good;
7. to possess my vessel in sanctification and honour;
8. to have my converse without covetousness,
content with what I have;
9. to speak the truth in love;
10. to be desirous not to lust,
not to lust passionately,
not to go after lusts.

(The hedge of the law, i.e. *precautions.)*

1. To bruise the serpent's head. *Gen.* iii. 15.
2. To remember my latter end. *Deut.* xxvii. 29.
3. To cut off opportunities. 2 *Cor.* xi. 12.
4. To be sober. 1 *Pet.* v. 8.
5. Not to sit idle. *Matt.* xx. 6.
6. To shun the wicked. *Ps.* xxvi. 5.
7. To cleave to the good. *Rom.* xii. 9.
8. To make a covenant with the eyes. *Job* xxxi. 1.
9. To bring my body into subjection. 1 *Cor.* ix. 27.
10. To give myself unto prayer. 1 *Cor.* vii. 5.
11. To betake myself to penitence. 2 *Pet.* iii. 9.
Hedge up my way with thorns,
that I find not the path
for following vanity.
Hold Thou me in with bit and bridle,
lest I fall from Thee.
O Lord compel me to come in to Thee.

3. Profession.

I Believe, O Lord,
in Thee, Father, Word, Spirit, One God;
that by Thy fatherly love and power
all things were created;—
that by Thy goodness and love to man
all things have been begun anew
in Thy Word,—
Who for us men and for our salvation,
was made flesh,
was conceived and born,
suffered and was crucified,
died and was buried,
descended and rose again,
ascended and sat down,
will return and will repay;—
that by the shining-forth and working
of Thy Holy Spirit,
hath been called out of the whole world
a peculiar people into a polity,
in belief of the truth
and sanctity of living:—
that in it we are partakers
of the communion of saints
and forgiveness of sins
in this world,—
that in it we are waiting
for resurrection of the flesh
and life everlasting
in the world to come.—
This most holy faith
which was once delivered to the saints
I believe, O Lord;
help Thou mine unbelief,

and vouchsafe to me
to love the Father for His fatherly love,
to reverence the Almighty for His power,
as a faithful Creator, to commit my soul to Him
in well doing;
vouchsafe to me to partake
from Jesus of salvation,
from Christ of anointing,
from the Only-begotten of adoption;
to worship the Lord
for His conception in faith,
for His birth in humility,
for His sufferings in patience and hatred of sin;
for His cross to crucify beginnings,
for His death to mortify the flesh,
for His burial to bury evil thoughts in good works,
for His descent to meditate upon hell,
for His resurrection upon newness of life,
for His ascension, to mind things above,
for His sitting on high, to mind the good things on
His right,
for His return, to fear His second appearance,
for judgment, to judge myself ere I be judged.
From the Spirit
vouchsafe me the breath of salutary grace.
In the Holy Catholic Church
to have my own calling, and holiness, and portion,
and a fellowship
of her sacred rites, and prayers,
fastings and groans,
vigils, tears, and sufferings,
for assurance of remission of sins,
for hope of resurrection and translation
to eternal life.

4. Intercession.

O Hope of all the ends of the earth,
and of them that remain in the broad sea;
O Thou on whom our fathers hoped,
and Thou didst deliver them;
on whom they waited,
and were not confounded;
O my Hope from my youth,
from my mother's breasts;
on whom I have been cast from the womb,
be Thou my hope
now and evermore,
and my portion in the land of the living;
In Thy nature,
in Thy names, in Thy types,
in word and in deed,
My Hope,
let me not be disappointed of my hope.
O the Hope of all the ends of the earth,
remember Thy whole creation for good,
visit the world in Thy compassion;
O guardian of men,
O loving Lord,
remember all our race.
Thou who hast shut up all in unbelief,
on all have pity, O Lord.
O Thou who didst die and rise again,
to be Lord both of the dead and living,
live we or die we,
Thou art our Lord;
Lord, have pity on living and dead.
O Helper of the helpless,
seasonable aid in affliction,
remember all who are in necessity,
and need Thy succour.

O God of grace and truth,
establish all who stand in truth and grace,
restore all who are sick with heresies and sins.
O wholesome defence of Thine anointed,
remember Thy congregation
which Thou hast purchased and redeemed of old.
O grant to all believers
one heart and one soul.
Thou that walkest amid the golden candlesticks,
remove not our candlestick
out of its place.
Amend what are wanting,
establish what remain,
which Thou art ready to cast away,
which are ready to die.
O Lord of the harvest
send forth labourers, made sufficient by Thee,
into Thy harvest.
O portion of those
who wait in Thy temple,
grant to our Clergy,
rightly to divide the word of truth,
rightly to walk in it;
grant to Thy Christian people
to obey and submit to them.
O King of nations, unto the ends
of the earth;
strengthen all the states
of the inhabited world,
as being Thy ordinance,
though a creation of man.
Scatter the nations that delight in war,
make wars to cease in all the earth.
O Expectation of the isles and their hope,
Lord, save this island,
and all the country in which we sojourn,

from all affliction, peril, and need.
Lord of lords, Ruler of rulers,
remember all rulers
to whom Thou hast given rule in the earth,
and O remember specially
our divinely-guarded king,
and work with him more and more,
and prosper his way in all things.
Speak good things unto his heart,
for Thy Church, and all Thy people,
grant to him profound and perpetual peace,
that in his tranquillity
we may lead a quiet and peaceable life
in all godliness and honesty.
O Thou by whom are ordained the powers that be,
grant to those who are chief in court,
to be chief in virtue and Thy fear;
grant to the Parliament Thy holy wisdom;
to our great men, to do nothing against
but for the truth;
to the courts of law, Thy judgments,
to judge in all things concerning all
without preference, without partiality.
O God of armies,
give a prosperous course and strength
to all the Christian army,
against the enemies of our most holy faith.
Grant to our population
to be subject unto the higher powers,
not only for wrath, but also for conscience-sake.
Grant to farmers and graziers good seasons;
to the fleet and fishers fair weather;
to tradesmen, not to overreach one another;
to mechanics, to pursue their business lawfully,
down to the meanest workman,
down to the poor.

O God, not of us only but of our seed,
bless our children among us,
to advance in wisdom as in stature,
and in favour with Thee and with men.
Thou who wouldest have us provide for our own,
and hatest the unnatural,
remember, Lord, my relations according to the flesh;
grant me to speak peace concerning them,
and to seek their good.
Thou who willest us to make return
to our benefactors,
remember, Lord, for good,
all from whom I have received good;
keep them alive that they may be blessed upon earth,
and deliver them not
into the will of their enemies.
Thou who hast noted
the man who neglects his own, as worse
than an infidel,
remember in Thy good pleasure
all those in my household.
Peace be to my house,
the Son of peace upon all in it.
Thou who wouldest that our righteousness exceed
the righteousness of sinners,
grant me, Lord, to love those who love me,
my own friend, and my father's friend,
and my friend's children,
never to forsake.
Thou who wouldest that we overcome
evil with good,
and pray for those who persecute us,
have pity on mine enemies, Lord,
as on myself;
and lead them together with me
to Thy heavenly kingdom.

Thou who grantest the prayers of Thy servants
one for another,
remember, Lord, for good,
and pity all those
who remember me in their prayers,
or whom I have promised to remember in mine.
Thou who acceptest diligence in every good work,
remember, Lord, as if they prayed to Thee,
those who for any good reason
give not time to prayer.
Arise, and have mercy
on those who are in the last necessity,
for it is time that Thou hast mercy upon them,
yea the time is come.
Have mercy on them, O Lord,
as on me also, when in extremities.
Remember, Lord,
infants, children, the grown, the young,
the middle aged, the old,
hungry, thirsty, naked, sick,
prisoners, foreigners, friendless, unburied,
all in extreme age and weakness,
possessed with devils, and tempted to suicide,
troubled by unclean spirits,
the hopeless, the sick in soul or body,
the weak-hearted,
all in prison and chains, all under
sentence of death;
orphans, widows, foreigners, travellers, voyagers,
women with child, women who give suck,
all in bitter servitude, or mines, or galleys,
or in loneliness.
Thou, Lord, shalt save both man and beast,
how excellent is Thy mercy, O God!
And the children of men shall put their trust
under the shadow of Thy wings.

The Lord bless us, and keep us,
and shew the light of His countenance upon us,
And be merciful unto us,
The Lord lift up His countenance upon us,
And give us peace!
I commend to Thee, O Lord,
my soul, and my body,
my mind, and my thoughts,
my prayers, and my vows,
my senses, and my limbs,
my words, and my works,[1]
my life, and my death;
my brothers, and my sisters,
and their children;
my friends, my benefactors, my well wishers,
those who have a claim on me;
my kindred, and my neighbours,
my country, and all Christendom.
I commend to Thee, Lord,
my impulses, and my startings,
my intentions, and my attempts,
my going out, and my coming in,
my sitting down, and my rising up.

5. Praise.

Up with our hearts;
we lift them to the Lord.
O how very meet, and right, and fitting, and due,
in all, and for all,
at all times, places, manners,
in every season, every spot,
everywhere, always, altogether,
to remember Thee, to worship Thee,

[1] Page 172, edit. 1675.

to confess to Thee, to praise Thee,
to bless Thee, to hymn Thee,
To give thanks to Thee,
Maker, nourisher, guardian, governor,
preserver, worker, perfecter of all,
Lord and Father,
King and God,
fountain of life and immortality,
treasure of everlasting goods.
Whom the heavens hymn,
and the heaven of heavens,
the Angels and all the heavenly powers,
one to other crying continually,—
and we the while, weak and unworthy,
under their feet,—
Holy, Holy, Holy
Lord the God of Hosts;
full is the whole heaven,
and the whole earth,
of the majesty of Thy glory.
Blessed be the glory of the Lord
out of His place,
for His Godhead, His mysteriousness,
His height, His sovereignty, His almightiness,
His eternity, His providence.
The Lord is my strength, my stony rock, and my
defence,
my deliverer, my succour, my buckler,
the horn also of my salvation and my refuge.

THE SECOND DAY.

Introduction.

My voice shalt Thou hear betimes, O Lord,
early in the morning

will I direct my prayer unto Thee,
and will look up.
Blessed art Thou, O Lord,
who didst create the firmament of heaven,
the heavens and the heaven of heavens,
the heavenly powers,
Angels, Archangels,
Cherubim, Seraphim,
waters above the heavens,
mists and exhalations,
for showers, dew, hail, snow as wool,
hoar frost as ashes, ice as morsels,
clouds from the ends of the earth,
lightnings, thunders, winds out of Thy treasures,
storms;
waters beneath the heavens,
for drinking and for bathing.

1. Confession.

I will confess my sins,
and the sins of my fathers,
for I have transgressed and neglected Thee, O Lord,
and walked perversely before Thee.
Set not, O Lord, set not my misdeeds before Thee
nor my life in the light of Thy countenance,
But pardon the iniquity of Thy servant,
according to Thy great mercy;
as Thou hast been merciful to him from a child,
even so now.
I have sinned, what shall I do unto Thee,
O Thou preserver of men?
Why hast Thou set me as a mark against Thee,
so that I am a burden to myself?
O pardon my transgression,
and take away mine iniquity.

Deliver me from going down to the pit,
for Thou hast found a ransom.
Have mercy on me, Son of David,
Lord, help me.
Yea, Lord, even the dogs eat of the crumbs
which fall from their masters' table.
Have patience with me, Lord,
yet I have not wherewith to pay,
I confess to Thee;
forgive me the whole debt, I beseech Thee.
How long wilt Thou forget me, O Lord? for ever?
How long wilt Thou hide Thy face from me?
How long shall I seek counsel in my soul,
and be vexed in my heart day and night?
How long shall mine enemies triumph over me?
Consider and hear me, O Lord my God,
lighten mine eyes that I sleep not in death,
lest mine enemy say: I have prevailed against him,
for if I be cast down, they that trouble me will
rejoice at it;
but my trust is in Thy mercy.

2. Prayer for Grace.

Remove from me

(The Ten Commandments.)

1. all iniquity and profaneness, superstition, and hypocrisy.
2. worship of idols, of persons.
3. rash oath, and curse.
4. neglect or indecency of worship.
5. haughtiness and recklessness.
6. strife and wrath.
7. passion and corruption.
8. indolence and fraud.
9. lying and injuriousness.

10. every evil notion, every impure thought, every base desire, every unseemly thought.

Grant to me,
1. to be religious and pious.
2. to worship and serve.
3. to bless and swear truly.
4. to confess meetly in the congregation.
5. affection and obedience.
6. patience and good temper.
7. purity and soberness.
8. contentedness and goodness.
9. truth and incorruptness.
10. good thoughts, perseverance to the end.

3. Profession.

I believe in God,
1. the Father, Almighty, Maker of heaven and earth.
2. And in Jesus Christ, His Only-Begotten Son, our Lord.
(1.) conceived of the Holy Ghost,
(2.) born of Mary, ever-virgin,
(3.) suffered under Pontius Pilate,
(4.) crucified,
(5.) dead,
(6.) buried.—
(1.) descended into hell,
(2.) risen from the dead,
(3.) ascended into heaven,
(4.) set down on the right hand,
(5.) to return thence,
(6.) to judge both quick and dead.

3. And in the Holy Ghost,

(1.) The Holy Church,
(2.) Catholic,
(3.) communion of saints,
(4.) remission of sins,
(5.) resurrection of flesh,
(6.) life everlasting.

And now, Lord, what is my hope?
Truly my hope is even in Thee;
in Thee, O Lord, have I trusted,
let me never be confounded.

4. Intercession.

Let us pray God,
for the whole creation;
for the supply of seasons,
healthy, fruitful, peaceful;
for the whole race of mankind;
for those who are not Christians;
for the conversion of Atheists, the ungodly;
Gentiles, Turks, and Jews;
for all Christians;
for restoration of all
who languish in errors and sins;
for confirmation of all
who have been granted truth and grace;
for succour and comfort of all
who are dispirited, infirm, distressed, unsettled,
men and women;
for thankfulness and sobriety in all
who are hearty, healthy, prosperous, quiet,
men and women;
For the Catholic Church

its establishment and increase;
for the Eastern,
its deliverance and union;
for the Western,
its adjustment and peace;
for the British,
the supply of what is wanting in it,
the strengthening of what remains in it;
for the episcopate, presbytery, Christian people;
for the states of the inhabited world;
for Christian states,
far off, near at hand;
for our own;
for all in rule;
for our divinely-guarded king,
the queen and the prince;
for those who have place in the court;
for parliament and judicature,
army and police,
commons and their leaders,
farmers, graziers, fishers, merchants,
traders, and mechanics,
down to mean workmen, and the poor;
for the rising generation;
for the good nurture of all the royal family,
of the young ones of the nobility;
for all in universities, in inns of court,
in schools in town or country,
in apprenticeships;
for those who have a claim on me from relationship,
for brothers and sisters,
that God's blessing may be on them,
and on their children;
or from benefits conferred,
that Thy recompence may be on all
who have benefited me,

who have ministered to me in carnal things;
or from trust placed in me,
for all whom I have educated,
all whom I have ordained:
for my college, my parish,
Southwell, St. Paul's, Westminster,
Dioceses of Chichester, Ely, and my present,
clergy, people, helps, governments,
the deanery in the chapel royal,
the almonry,
the colleges committed to me;[1]
or from natural kindness,
for all who love me,
though I know them not;
or from Christian love;
for those who hate me without cause,
some too, even on account of truth and righteousness;
or from neighbourhood,
for all who dwell near me
peaceably and harmlessly;
or from promise,
for all whom I have promised to remember
in my prayers;
or from mutual offices,
for all who remember me in their prayers,
and ask of me the same;
or from stress of engagements,
for all who on sufficient reasons fail to call
upon Thee;
for all who have no intercessor
in their own behalf;
for all who at present are in agony
of extreme necessity or deep affliction;
for all who are attempting any good work

[1] As Visitor.

which will bring glory to the Name of God
or some great good to the Church;
for all who act nobly
either towards things sacred or towards the poor;
for all who have ever been offended by me
either in word or in deed.
God have mercy on me and bless me;
God shew the light of His countenance upon me
and pity me.
God bless me, even our God,
God bless me and receive my prayer;
O direct my life towards Thy commandments,
hallow my soul,
purify my body,
correct my thoughts,
cleanse my desires,
soul and body, mind and spirit,
heart and reins.
Renew me thoroughly, O God,
for, if Thou wilt, Thou canst.

5. Praise.

The Lord, the Lord God,
merciful and pitiful,
long-suffering and full of pity, and true,
keeping pity for thousands,
taking away iniquities and unrighteousnesses and sins;
not clearing the guilty one,
bringing sins of fathers upon children.
I will bless the Lord at all times,
His praise shall ever be in my mouth.
Glory to God in the highest,
and on earth peace,
goodwill towards men.

The Angels,	guardianship;
Archangels,	glory;
Powers,	marvels;
Thrones,	judgment;
Dominions,	beneficence;
Principalities,	government;
Authorities,	against devils;
Cherubim,	knowledge;
Seraphim,	love.

THE THIRD DAY.

Introduction.

O God, Thou art my God,
early will I seek Thee.
Blessed art Thou, O Lord,
who gatheredst the water into the sea,
and broughtest to sight the earth,
and madest to sprout
herb and fruit tree.
There are the depths and the sea as on an heap,
lakes, rivers, springs;
earth, continent, and isles,
mountains, hills, and valleys;
glebe, meadows, glades,
green pasture, corn, and hay;
herbs and flowers
for food, enjoyment, medicine;
fruit trees bearing
wine, oil and spices,
and trees for wood;
and things beneath the earth,
stones, metals, minerals, coal,
blood and fire, and vapour of smoke.

1. Confession.

Who can understand his errors?
Cleanse Thou me from secret faults.
Keep back Thy servant also from presumptuous sins,
lest they have the dominion over me.
For Thy Name's sake,
be merciful unto my sin,
for it is great.
My iniquities have taken such hold upon me
that I am not able to look up,
yea, they are more in number than the hairs of my
head,
and my heart hath failed me.
Be pleased, O Lord, to deliver me,
Make haste, O Lord, to help me.
Magnify Thy mercies upon me,
O Thou who savest them that trust in Thee.
I said, Lord, have mercy upon me,
heal my soul, for I have sinned against Thee;
I have sinned but I am confounded,
and I turn from my evil ways,
and I turn unto mine own heart,
and with my whole heart I turn unto Thee;
and I seek Thy face,
and I beseech Thee, saying,
I have sinned, I have committed iniquity,
I have done unjustly.
I know, O Lord, the plague of my heart,
and lo, I turn to Thee with all my heart,
and with all my strength.
And Thou, O Lord, now from Thy dwelling-place,
and from the glorious throne of Thy kingdom
in heaven
O hear the prayer
and the supplication of Thy servant;

and be propitious towards Thy servant,
and heal his soul.
O God, be merciful to me a sinner,
be merciful to me the chief of sinners.
Father, I have sinned against heaven,
and before Thee,
and am no more worthy to be called Thy son,
make me one of Thy hired servants;
Make me one, or even the last,
or the least among all.
What profit is there in my blood,
when I go down to the pit?
shall the dust give thanks unto Thee?
or shall it declare Thy truth?
Hear, O Lord, and have mercy upon me;
Lord, be Thou my helper;
Turn my heaviness into joy,
my dreamings into earnestness,
my falls into clearings of myself,
my guilt, my offence into indignation,
my sin into fear,
my transgression into vehement desire,
my unrighteousness into strictness,
my pollution into revenge.

2. Prayer for Grace.

Hosanna in the highest.[1]
Remember me, O Lord,
with the favour that Thou bearest unto Thy people,
O visit me with Thy salvation;
that I may see the felicity of Thy chosen,
and rejoice in the gladness of Thy people,
and give thanks with Thine inheritance.

[1] Vide p. 186, edit. 1675.

There is glory which shall be revealed;
for when the Judge cometh
some shall see Thy face cheerful,
and shall be placed on the right,
and shall hear those most welcome words,
"Come, ye blessed."
They shall be caught up in clouds
to meet the Lord;
they shall enter into gladness,
they shall enjoy the sight of Him,
they shall be ever with Him.
These alone, only these are blessed
among the sons of men.
O to me the meanest grant the meanest place
there under their feet;
under the feet of Thine elect,
the meanest among them.
And that this may be,
let me find grace in Thy sight
to have grace,   (*Heb.* xii. 28.)
so as to serve Thee acceptably
with reverence and godly fear.
Let me find that second grace,
not to receive in vain   (2 *Cor.* vi. 1.)
the first grace,
not to come short of it;   (*Heb.* xii. 15.)
yea, not to neglect it,   (1 *Tim.* iv. 14.)
so as to fall from it,   (*Gal.* v. 4.)
but to stir it up,   (2 *Tim.* i. 6.)
so as to increase in it,   (2 *Pet.* iii. 18.)
yea, to abide in it
till the end of my life.
And O, perfect for me what is lacking
of Thy gifts,
of faith,   help Thou mine unbelief,
of hope,   establish my trembling hope,

of love,   kindle its smoking flax.
Shed abroad Thy love in my heart,
so that I may love Thee,
my friend in Thee, my enemy for Thee.
O Thou who givest grace to the humble-minded,
also give me grace to be humble-minded.
O Thou who never failest those who fear Thee,
my Fear and my Hope,
let me fear one thing only,
the fearing aught more than Thee.
As I would that men should do to me
so may I do to them;
not to have thoughts beyond what I should think,
but to have thoughts unto sobriety.
Shine on those who sit in darkness,
and the shadow of death;
guide our feet into the way of peace.
that we may have the same thoughts
one with another,
rightly to divide, rightly to walk,
to edify,
with one accord, with one mouth,
to glorify God;
and if aught otherwise,
to walk in the same rule
as far as we have attained;
to maintain order,
decency and stedfastness.

3. Profession.

Godhead, paternal love, power,
providence:
salvation, anointing, adoption,
lordship;
conception, birth, passion,

cross, death, burial,
descent, resurrection, ascent,
sitting, return, judgment;
Breath and Holiness,
calling from the Universal,
hallowing in the Universal,
communion of saints, and of saintly things,
resurrection,
life eternal.

4. Intercession.

Hosanna on the earth.[2]
Remember, O Lord,
to crown the year with Thy goodness;
for the eyes of all look towards Thee,
and Thou givest their food in due season.
Thou openest Thine hand,
and fillest all things living with plenteousness.
And on us, O Lord, vouchsafe
the blessings of heaven and the dew above,
blessings of fountains and the deep beneath,
courses of sun, conjunctions of moons,
summits of eastern mountains, of the everlasting hills,
fulness of the earth and of produce thereof,
good seasons, wholesome weather,
full crops, plenteous fruits,
health of body, peaceful times,
mild government, kind laws,
wise councils, equal judgments,
loyal obedience, vigorous justice,
fertility in resources, fruitfulness in begetting,
ease in bearing, happiness in offspring,

---

[2] Continuation of the supplication broken by "*Profession*." Vide p. 192, edit. 1675.

careful nurture, sound training,
That our sons may grow up as the young plants,
our daughters as the polished corners of the temple,
that our garners may be full and plenteous
with all manner of store,
that our sheep may bring forth thousands
and ten thousands in our streets:
that there be no decay,
no leading into captivity
and no complaining in our streets.

5. Praise.

Thou, O Lord, art praised in Sion,[3]
and unto Thee shall the vow be performed
in Jerusalem.
Thou art worthy, O Lord our God,
the Holy One,
to receive glory, and honour, and power.
Thou that hearest the prayer,
unto Thee shall all flesh come,
my flesh shall come.
My misdeeds prevail against me,
O be Thou merciful unto our sins;
that I may come and give thanks
with all Thy works,
and bless Thee with Thy holy ones.
O Lord, open Thou my lips,
and my mouth shall shew forth Thy praise.
My soul doth praise the Lord,
for the goodness He hath done
to the whole creation,
and to the whole race of man;
for Thy mercies towards myself,

[3] Vide p. 172, edit. 1675.

soul, body, and estate,
gifts of grace, nature, and fortune;
for all benefits received,
for all successes, now or heretofore,
for any good thing done;
for health, credit, competency,
safety, gentle estate, quiet.
Thou hast not cut off as a weaver my life,
nor from day even to night made an end of me.
He hath vouchsafed me life and breath
until this hour,
from childhood, youth, and hitherto
even unto age.
He holdeth our soul in life
and suffereth not our feet to slip;
rescuing me from perils, sicknesses,
poverty, bondage,
public shame, evil chances;
keeping me from perishing in my sins,
fully waiting my conversion,
leaving in me return into my heart,
remembrance of my latter end,
shame, horror, grief,
for my past sins;
fuller and larger, larger and fuller,
more and still more, O my Lord,
storing me with good hope
of their remission,
through repentance and its works,
in the power of the thrice-holy Keys,
and the mysteries in Thy Church.
Wherefore day by day
for these Thy benefits towards me,
which I remember,—
wherefore also for others very many
which I have let slip

from their number, from my forgetfulness,—
for those which I wished, knew and asked,
and those I asked not, knew not, wished not,—
I confess and give thanks to Thee,
I bless and praise Thee, as is fit, and every day.
And I pray with my whole soul,
and with my whole mind I pray.
Glory be to Thee, O Lord, glory to Thee;
glory to Thee, and glory to Thine All-holy Name,
for all Thy Divine perfections in them;
for Thine incomprehensible and
unimaginable goodness,
and Thy pity towards sinners
and unworthy men,
and towards me of all sinners
far the most unworthy.
Yea, O Lord,
for this, and for the rest,
glory to Thee,
and praise, and blessing, and thanksgiving,
with the voices and concert of voices
of Angels and of men,
of all Thy saints in heaven,
and all Thy creatures in heaven or earth,
and of me, beneath their feet,
unworthy and wretched sinner,
Thy abject creature,
now, in this day and hour,
and every day till my last breath,
and till the end of the world,
and for ages upon ages.

THE FOURTH DAY.

Introduction.

I have thought upon Thee, O Lord,
when I was waking,
for Thou hast been my helper.
Blessed art Thou, O Lord,
who madest the two Lights, Sun and Moon,
greater and lesser,
and the stars
for light, for signs, for seasons,
spring, summer, autumn, winter,
days, weeks, months, years,
to rule over day and night.

1. Confession.

Behold, Thou art angry, for we have sinned.
We are all as an unclean thing
and all our righteousnesses
as filthy rags.
We all do fade as a leaf,
and our iniquities, like the wind,
have taken us away.
But now, O Lord, Thou art our Father,
we are clay, all Thy handiwork.
Be not wroth very sore,
nor remember iniquity for ever;
behold, see, we beseech Thee,
we are all Thy people.
O Lord, though our iniquities testify against us,
do Thou it for Thy Name's sake;
for our backslidings are many,
we have sinned against Thee.
Yet thou, O Lord, art in the midst of us,

and we are called by Thy Name,
leave us not.
O Hope of Israel,
the Saviour thereof in time of trouble,
why shouldest Thou be as a stranger in the land,
and as a wayfaring man that turneth aside
to tarry for a night?
why shouldest Thou be as a man astonished,
as a mighty man that cannot save?
Be merciful to our unrighteousnesses,
and our iniquities remember no more.
Lord, I am carnal,
sold under sin;
there dwelleth in me, that is, in my flesh,
no good thing;
for the good that I would, I do not,
but the evil which I would not, that I do.
I consent unto the law that it is good,
I delight in it after the inner man;
But I see another law in my members,
warring against the law of my mind,
and enslaving me to the law of sin.
Wretched man that I am,
who shall deliver me from the body of this death?
I thank God through Jesus Christ,
that where sin abounded,
grace hath much more abounded.
O Lord, Thy goodness leadeth me to repentance:
O give me sometime repentance
to recover me from the snare of the devil,
who am taken captive by him
at his will.
Sufficient for me the past time of my life
to have done the will of lusts,
walking in lasciviousness, revelling, drunkenness,
and in other excess of profligacy.

O Lamb without blemish and without spot,
who hast redeemed me with Thy precious Blood,
in that very Blood pity me and save me;
in that Blood,
and in that very Name,
besides which is none other under heaven
given among men,
by which we must be saved.
O God, Thou knowest my foolishness,
and my sins are not hid from Thee.
Lord, Thou knowest all my desire,
and my groaning is not hid from Thee.
Let not them that trust in Thee,
O Lord God of hosts,
be ashamed for my cause;
let not those that seek Thee be confounded
through me,
O Lord God of Israel.
Take me out of the mire that I sink not;
O let me be delivered from them that hate me
and out of the deep waters;
Let not the water-flood drown me,
neither let the deep swallow me up,
and let not the pit shut her mouth upon me.

2. Prayer for Grace.

[Defend me from]

	Pride	Amorite.
(against seven	envy.......................................	Hittite.
deadly sins.)	wrath	Perizzite.
	gluttony............................	Girgashite.
	lechery...................................	Hivite.
(covetousness.)	the cares of life	Canaannite.
(sloth.)	lukewarm indifference................	Jebusite.

[Give me]
Humility, pitifulness, patience,
sobriety, purity, contentment, ready zeal.
One thing have I desired of the Lord
which I will require,[1]
that I may dwell in the house of the Lord
all the days of my life,
to behold the fair beauty of the Lord,
and to visit His temple.
Two things have I required of Thee, O Lord,
deny Thou me not before I die;
remove far from me vanity and lies;
give me neither poverty nor riches,
feed me with food convenient for me;
lest I be full and deny Thee
and say, who is the Lord?
or lest I be poor and steal,
and take the Name of my God in vain.
Let me learn to abound,
let me learn to suffer need,
in whatsoever state I am,
therewith to be content.
For nothing earthly, temporal, mortal,
to long nor to wait.
Grant me a happy life
in piety, gravity, purity,
in all things good and fair,
in cheerfulness, in health, in credit,
in competency, in safety, in gentle estate, in quiet;
a happy death,
a deathless happiness.

[1] Vide p. 194, edit. 1675.

3. Profession.

I believe
in the Father, benevolent affection;
in the Almighty, saving power;
in the Creator, providence
for guarding, ruling, perfecting the universe.
In Jesus, salvation,
in Christ, anointing;
in the Only-begotten Son, sonship,
in the Lord, a master's treatment,
in His conception and birth
the cleansing of our unclean conception and birth;
in His sufferings, which we owed,
that we might not pay;
in His cross the curse of the law removed;
in His death the sting of death;
in His burial eternal destruction in the tomb;
in His descent, whither we ought,
that we might not go;
in His resurrection,
as the first fruits of them that sleep;
in His ascent, to prepare a place for us;
in His sitting, to appear and intercede;
in His return, to take unto Him His own;
in His judgment, to render to each
according to his works.
In the Holy Ghost, power from on high,
transforming unto sanctity
from without and invisibly,
yet inwardly and evidently.
In the Church, a body mystical
of the called out of the whole world,
unto intercourse in faith and holiness.
In the communion of Saints, members of this body,
a mutual participation in holy things,

for confidence of remission of sins,
for hope of resurrection, of translation,
to life everlasting.

4. Intercession.

And I have hoped in Thy mercy
from everlasting to everlasting.
How excellent is Thy mercy, O Lord;
If I have hope, it is in Thy mercy,
O let me not be disappointed of my hope.
Moreover we beseech Thee,
remember all, Lord, for good;
have pity upon all, O Sovereign Lord,
be reconciled with us all.
Give peace to the multitudes of Thy people;
scatter offences;
abolish wars;
stop the uprisings of heresies.
Thy peace and love
vouchsafe to us, O God our Saviour,
the Hope of all the ends of the earth.
Remember to crown the year
with Thy goodness;
for the eyes of all wait upon Thee,
and thou givest them their meat in due season.
Thou openest Thy hand,
and fillest all things living with plenteousness.
Remember Thy Holy Church,
from one end of the earth to the other;
and give her peace,
whom Thou hast redeemed with Thy precious blood;
and establish her
unto the end of the world.
Remember those who bear fruit, and act nobly,
in Thy holy Churches,

and who remember the poor and needy;
recompense to them
Thy rich and heavenly gifts;
vouchsafe to them,
for things earthly, heavenly,
for corruptible, incorruptible,
for temporal, eternal.
Remember those who are in virginity,
and purity and ascetic life;
also those who live in honourable marriage,
in Thy reverence and fear.
Remember every Christian soul
in affliction, distress, and trial,
and in need of Thy pity and succour;
also our brethren in captivity, prison, chains,
and bitter bondage;
supplying return to the wandering,
health to the sick,
deliverance to the captives.
Remember religious and faithful kings,
whom Thou hast given to rule
upon the earth;
and especially remember, Lord,
our divinely-guarded king;
strengthen his kingdom,
subdue to him all adversaries,
speak good things to his heart,
for Thy Church, and all Thy people.
Vouchsafe to him deep and undisturbed peace,
that in his serenity
we may lead a quiet and peaceable life
with all godliness and honesty.
Remember, Lord, all power
and authority,
our brethren in the court,
those who are chief in council and judgment,

and all by land and sea
waging Thy wars for us.
Moreover, Lord, remember graciously
our holy Fathers,
the honourable Presbytery, and all the Clergy,
rightly dividing the Word of Truth,
and rightly walking in it.
Remember, Lord, our brethren around us,
and praying with us in this holy hour,
for their zeal and earnestness-sake.
Remember also those who on fair reasons are away,
and pity them and us
in the multitude of Thy pity.
Fill our garners with all manner of store,
preserve our marriages in peace and concord,
nourish our infants,
lead forward our youth.
sustain our aged,
comfort the weak-hearted,
gather together the scattered,
restore the wanderers,
and knit them to Thy Holy Catholic
Apostolic Church.
Set free the troubled
with unclean spirits,
voyage with the voyagers,
travel with the travellers,
stand forth for the widow,
shield the orphan,
rescue the captive,
heal the sick.
Those who are on trial, in mines, in exile, in galleys,
in whatever affliction, necessity, and emergence,
remember, O God;
and all who need Thy great mercy;
and those who love us,

and those who hate;
and those who have desired us unworthy
to make mention of them in our prayers;
and all Thy people remember, O Lord, our God,
and upon all pour out Thy rich pity,
to all performing their requests for salvation;
and those of whom we have not made mention,
through ignorance, forgetfulness, or number
of names,
do Thou Thyself remember, O God,
who knowest the stature and appellation of each,
who knowest every one from his mother's womb.
For Thou art, O Lord, the Succour of the succourless,
the Hope of the hopeless,
The Saviour of the tempest-tost,
the Harbour of the voyager,
the Physician of the sick,
do Thou Thyself become all things to all men.
O Thou who knowest each man and his petition,
each house, and its need,
deliver, O Lord, this city,
and all the country in which we sojourn,
from plague, famine, earthquake, flood,
fire, sword, hostile invasion,
and civil war.
End the schisms of the Churches,
quench the haughty cries of the nations,
and receive us all into Thy kingdom,
acknowledging us as sons of light;
and Thy peace and love
vouchsafe to us, O Lord, our God.
Remember O Lord, our God,
all spirits and all flesh
which we have remembered, and which we have not.
And the close of our life,
Lord, Lord, direct in peace,

Christianly, acceptably, and, should it please Thee,
painlessly,
gathering us together under the feet of Thine elect,
when Thou wilt and how Thou wilt,
only without shame and sins.
The brightness of the Lord our God be upon us,
prosper Thou the work of our hands upon us,
O prosper Thou our handy-work.
Be, Lord,
within me to strengthen me,
without me to guard me,
over me to shelter me,
beneath me to stablish me,
before me to guide me,
after me to forward me,
round about me to secure me.

5. Praise.

Blessed art Thou, Lord, God of Israel,
our Father,
from everlasting to everlasting.
Thine, O Lord,
is the greatness and the power,
the triumph and the victory,
the praise and the strength,
for Thou rulest over all
in heaven and on earth.
At Thy face every king is troubled,
and every nation.
Thine, O Lord, is the kingdom
and the supremacy over all,
and over all rule.
With Thee is wealth, and glory is from
Thy countenance;
Thou rulest over all, O Lord,

the Ruler of all rule;
and in Thine hand is strength and power,
and in Thine hand to give to all things
greatness and strength.
And now, Lord, we confess to Thee,
and we praise Thy glorious Name.

THE FIFTH DAY.

Introduction.

We are satisfied with Thy mercy, O Lord,
in the morning.
Blessed art Thou, O Lord,
who broughtest forth from the water
creeping things of life,
and whales,
and winged fowl.
Be Thou exalted, O God, above the heavens,
and Thy glory above all the earth.
By Thy Ascension, O Lord,
draw us too after Thee,
that we savour of what is above,
not of things on the earth.
By the marvellous mystery
of the Holy Body and precious Blood,
on the evening of this day,
Lord, have mercy.

1. Confession.

Thou who hast said,
"As I live, saith the Lord,
I will not the death of a sinner,
but that the ungodly return from his way
and live;

turn ye, turn ye from your wicked way,
for why will ye die, O house of Israel?"
turn us, O Lord, to Thee,
and so shall we be turned.
Turn us from all our ungodlinesses,
and let them not be to us for punishments.
I have sinned, I have committed iniquity,
I have done wickedly,
from Thy precepts, and Thy judgments.
To Thee, O Lord, righteousness,
and to me confusion of face,
as at this day,
in our despicableness,
wherewith Thou hast despised us.
Lord, to us confusion of face,
and to our rulers
who have sinned against Thee.
Lord, in all things is Thy righteousness,
unto all Thy righteousness;
let then Thine anger and Thy fury be turned away,
and cause Thy face to shine
upon Thy servant.
O my God, incline Thine ear and hear,
open Thine eyes and see my desolation.
O Lord, hear, O Lord forgive,
O Lord hearken and do;
defer not for Thine own sake, O my God,
for Thy servant is called by Thy Name.
In many things we offend all;
Lord, let Thy mercy rejoice against Thy judgment
in my sins.
If I say I have no sin, I deceive myself,
and the truth is not in me;
but I confess my sins many and grievous,
and Thou, O Lord, art faithful and just,
to forgive me my sins when I confess them.

Yea, for this too
I have an Advocate with Thee to Thee,
Thy Only-begotten Son, the Righteous.
May He be the propitiation for my sins,
who is also for the whole world.
Will the Lord cast off for ever?
and will He be no more intreated?
Is His mercy clean gone for ever?
and is His promise come utterly to an end
for evermore?
Hath God forgotten to be gracious?
and will He shut up His loving kindness
in displeasure?
And I said, It is mine own infirmity;
but I will remember the years of the right hand
of the most Highest.

2. Prayer for Grace.

[Give me grace]
to put aside every weight,
and the sin that doth so easily beset us;
all filthiness
and superfluity of naughtiness,
lust of the flesh, of the eyes,
pride of life,
every motion of flesh and spirit
alienated from the will of Thy sanctity:
to be poor in spirit,
that I have a portion in the kingdom of heaven;
to mourn, that I be comforted;
to be meek, that I inherit the earth;
to hunger and thirst for righteousness,
that I be filled;
to be pitiful, that I be pitied;
to be pure in heart, that I see God;

to be a peace-maker that I be called the son of God;
to be prepared for persecutions and revilings
for righteousness' sake,
that my reward be in heaven,—
all this, grant to me, O Lord.

3. Profession.

I, coming to God,
believe that He is,
and that He is a rewarder of them
that diligently seek Him.
I know that my Redeemer liveth,
that He is Christ, the Son of the Living God,
that He is truly the Saviour of the world,
that He came into the world to save sinners,
of whom I am chief.
Through the grace of Jesus Christ
we believe that we shall be saved
like as our fathers.
I know that my skin shall rise up upon the earth,
which undergoeth these things.
I believe to see the goodness of the Lord
in the land of the living.
Our heart shall rejoice in Him,
because we have hoped in His holy Name,
in the Name of the Father,
of the Saviour, Mediator, Intercessor, Redeemer,
of the two-fold Comforter,
under the figures of the Lamb and the Dove.
Let Thy merciful kindness, O Lord, be upon us,
like as we do put our trust in Thee.

4. Intercession.

Let us beseech the Lord in peace,

for the heavenly peace,
and the salvation of our souls;—
for the peace of the whole world;
for the stability of God's holy Churches,
and the union of them all;—
for this holy house,
and those who enter it with faith and reverence;
for our holy Fathers,
the honourable Presbytery, the Diaconate in Christ,
and all, both Clergy and people;—
for this holy retreat, and all the city and country,
and all the faithful who dwell therein;—
for salubrious weather, fruitfulness of earth.
and peaceful times;—
for voyagers, travellers,
those who are in sickness, toil, and captivity,
and for their salvation.
Aid, save, pity, and preserve them,
O God, in Thy grace.
Making mention
of the all-holy, undefiled, and more than blessed
Mary, Mother of God and Ever-Virgin,
with all saints,
let us commend ourselves, and each other,
and all our life,
to Christ our God.
To Thee, O Lord, for it is fitting,
be glory, honour, and worship.
The grace of our Lord, Jesus Christ,
and the love of God,
and the communion of the Holy Ghost,
be with me, and with all of us. Amen.
I commend me and mine, and all that belongs to me,
to Him who is able to keep me without falling,
and to place me immaculate
before the presence of His glory,

to the only wise God and our Saviour;
to whom be glory and greatness,
strength and authority,
both now and for all ages. Amen.

5. Praise.

O Lord, my Lord,
for my being, life, reason,
for nurture, protection, guidance,
for education, civil rights, religion,
for Thy gifts of grace, nature, fortune,
for redemption, regeneration, catechising,
for my call, recall, yea, many calls besides;
for Thy forbearance, long-suffering,
long long-suffering
to me-ward,
many seasons, many years, up to this time;
for all good things received, successes granted me,
good things done;
for the use of things present,
for Thy promise, and my hope
of the enjoyment of good things to come;
for my parents honest and good,
teachers kind,
benefactors never to be forgotten,
religious intimates congenial,
hearers thoughtful,
friends sincere,
domestics faithful,
for all who have advantaged me
by writings, homilies, converse,
prayers, patterns, rebukes, injuries;
for all these, and all others
which I know, which I know not,
open, hidden,

remembered, forgotten,
done when I wished, when I wished not,
I confess to Thee and will confess,
I bless Thee and will bless,
I give thanks to Thee and will give thanks,
all the days of my life.
Who am I, or what is my father's house,
that Thou shouldest look upon a dead dog,
the like of me?
what reward shall I give unto the Lord
for all the benefits which He hath done unto me?
What thanks can I recompense unto God,
for all He hath spared and borne with me until now?
Holy, Holy, Holy,
worthy art Thou,
O Lord and our God, the Holy One,
to receive the glory, and the honour, and the power,
for Thou hast made all things,
and for Thy pleasure they are,
and were created.

THE SIXTH DAY.

Introduction.

Early shall my prayer come before Thee.
Blessed art Thou, O Lord,
who broughtest forth of the earth, wild beasts, cattle,
and all the reptiles,
for food, clothing, help;
and madest man after Thine image, to rule the earth,
and blessedst him.
The fore-counsel, fashioning hand,
breath of life, image of God,
appointment over the works,
charge to the Angels concerning him,

paradise.—
Heart, reins, eyes, ears, tongue, hands, feet,
life, sense, reason, spirit, free will,
memory, conscience,
the revelation of God, writing of the law,
oracles of prophets, music of psalms,
instruction of proverbs, experience of histories,
worship of sacrifices.
Blessed art Thou, O Lord,
for Thy great and precious promise
on this day
concerning the Life-giving Seed,
and for its fulfilment in fulness of the times
on this day.
Blessed art Thou, O Lord,
for the holy Passion
of this day.
O by Thy salutary sufferings
on this day,
save us, O Lord.

1. Confession.

I have withstood Thee, Lord,
but I return to Thee;
for I have fallen by mine iniquity.
But I take with me words,
and I return unto Thee and say,
take away all iniquity and receive us graciously,
so will we render the calves of our lips.
Spare us, Lord, spare,
and give not Thine heritage to reproach,
to Thine enemies.

Lord, Lord, be propitious,
cease, I beseech Thee,

by whom shall Jacob arise?
for he is small.
Repent, O Lord, for this,
and this shall not be.

While observing lying vanities
I forsook my own mercy,
and am cast out of Thy sight.
When my soul fainted within me,
I remembered the Lord;
yet will I look again toward Thy Holy Temple;
Thou hast brought up my life from corruption.

Who is a God like unto Thee,
that pardoneth iniquity
to the remnant of His heritage?
He retaineth not His anger for ever,
because He delighteth in mercy.
Turn again and have compassion upon us, O Lord,
subdue our iniquities,
and cast all our sins into the depths of the sea,
according to Thy truth, and according to Thy mercy.

O Lord, I have heard thy speech and was afraid,
in wrath remember mercy.
Behold me, Lord, clothed in filthy garments;
behold Satan standing at my right hand;
yet, O Lord, by the blood of Thy covenant,
by the fountain opened for sin and for uncleanness,
take away my iniquity,
and cleanse me from my sin.

Save me as a brand
plucked out of the fire.
Father, forgive me, for I knew not,
truly I knew not, what I did

in sinning against Thee.
Lord, remember me
when Thou comest in Thy kingdom.
Lord, lay not mine enemies' sins to their charge,
Lord, lay not my own to mine.
By Thy sweat bloody and clotted,
Thy soul in agony,
Thy head crowned with thorns, bruised with staves,
Thine eyes swimming with tears,
Thine ears full of insults,
Thy mouth moistened with vinegar and gall,
Thy face dishonourably stained with spitting,
Thy neck weighed down with the burden of the cross,
Thy back ploughed with the wheals and gashes
of the scourge,
Thy hands and feet stabbed through,
Thy strong cry, Eli, Eli,
Thy heart pierced with the spear,
the water and blood thence flowing,
Thy body broken,
Thy blood poured out,
Lord, forgive the offence of Thy servant,
and cover all his sins.
Turn away all Thy displeasure,
and turn Thyself from Thy wrathful indignation.
Turn me then, O God our Saviour,
and let Thine anger cease from us.
Wilt Thou be displeased at us for ever,
and stretch out Thy wrath from one generation
to another?
Wilt Thou not turn again and quicken us,
that Thy people may rejoice in Thee?
Shew us Thy mercy, O Lord,
and grant us Thy salvation.

2. Prayer for Grace.

. . . .
the works of the flesh,
adultery, fornication, uncleanness, lasciviousness,
idolatry, witchcraft,
enmities, strifes,
emulations, heats,
quarrels, parties,
heresies, envyings, murders,
drunkennesses, revellings, and such like.
. . . .
the fruits of the Spirit,
love, joy, peace,
long-suffering, gentleness, goodness,
faith, meekness, temperance;
the spirit of wisdom, of understanding,
of counsel, of might,
of knowledge, of godliness,
of fear of the Lord:—
and the gifts of the Spirit,
the word of wisdom, of knowledge,
faith, gifts of healing, working of miracles,
prophecy, discerning of spirits,
kinds of tongues, interpretation of tongues.
May Thy strong hand, O Lord,[1]
be ever my defence;
Thy mercy in Christ
my salvation;
Thy all-veritable word,
my instructor;
the grace of Thy life-bringing Spirit,
my consolation,
all along, and at last.

[1] Vide p. 146, edit. 1675.

The Soul of Christ hallow me,
and the Body strengthen me,
and the Blood ransom me,
and the Water wash me,
and the Bruises heal me,
and the Sweat refresh me,
and the Wound hide me.
The peace of God
which passeth all understanding,
keep my heart and thoughts
in the knowledge and the love of God.

3. Profession.

I believe
that Thou hast created me;
despise not the work of Thine own hands;—
that Thou madest me after Thine image and likeness,
suffer not Thy likeness to be blotted out;—
that Thou hast redeemed me in Thy blood,
suffer not the cost of that redemption to perish;
that Thou hast called me Christian after Thy name,
disdain not Thine own title;
that Thou hast hallowed me in regeneration,
destroy not Thy holy work;—
that Thou hast grafted me into the good olive tree,
the member of a mystical body;
the member of Thy mystical body
cut not off.
O think upon Thy servant as concerning Thy word,
wherein Thou has caused me to put my trust.
My soul hath longed for Thy salvation,
and I have good hope because of Thy word.

4. Intercession.

[I pray]
for the prosperous advance and good condition
of all the Christian army,
against the enemies of our most holy faith;
for our holy fathers,
and all our brotherhood in Christ;
for those who hate and those who love us,
for those who pity and those who minister to us;
for those whom we have promised
to remember in prayer;
for the liberation of captives;
for our fathers and brethren absent;
for those who voyage by sea;
for those who lie in sickness.
Let us pray also for fruitfulness of the earth;
and for every soul of orthodox Christians.
Let us bless pious kings,
orthodox high-priests,
the founders of this holy retreat,
our parents,
and all our forefathers
and our brethren departed.

5. Praise.

Thou who, on man's transgressing Thy command,
and falling,
didst not pass him by, nor leave him, God of goodness;
but didst visit in ways manifold,
as a tender Father,
supplying him with Thy great and precious promise,
concerning the Life-giving Seed,
opening to him the door of faith,
and of repentance unto life,

and in fulness of the times,
sending Thy Christ Himself
to take on Him the seed of Abraham;
and, in the oblation of His life,
to fulfil the Law's obedience;
and, in the sacrifice of His death,
to take off the Law's curse;
and, in His death,
to redeem the world;
and, in His resurrection,
to quicken it:—
O Thou, who doest all things,
whereby to bring again our race to Thee,
that it may be partaker
of Thy divine nature and eternal glory;
who hast borne witness
to the truth of Thy gospel
by many and various wonders,
in the ever-memorable converse of Thy saints,
in their supernatural endurance of torments,
in the overwhelming conversion of all lands
to the obedience of faith,
without might, or persuasion, or compulsion:—
Blessed be Thy Name,
and praised and celebrated,
and magnified, and high exalted,
and glorified, and hallowed;
its record, and its memory,
and every memorial of it,
both now and for evermore.
Worthy art Thou to take the book,
and to open the seals thereof,
for Thou wast slain, and hast redeemed us to God
by Thy blood,
out of every kindred and tongue,
and people, and nation.

Worthy is the Lamb that was slain
to receive the power, and riches, and wisdom,
and strength, and honour, and glory, and blessing.
To Him that sitteth upon the Throne,
and to the Lamb,
be the blessing, and the honour, and the glory,
and the might,
for ever and ever. Amen.
Salvation to our God, which sitteth upon the throne,
and to the Lamb.
Amen: the blessing and the glory and the wisdom,
and the thanksgiving and the honour,
and the power and the strength,
be unto our God,
for ever and ever,
Amen.

THE SEVENTH DAY.

Introduction.

O Lord, be gracious unto us,
we have waited for Thee;
be Thou our arm every morning,
our salvation also in the time of trouble.
Blessed art Thou, O Lord,
who restedst on the seventh day
from all Thy works,
and blessedst and sanctifiedst it:
[concerning the Sabbath,
concerning the Christian rest instead of it,
concerning the burial of Christ,
and the resting from sin,
concerning those who are already gone to rest].

1. Confession.

I am ashamed, and blush, O my God,
to lift up my face to Thee,
for mine iniquities are increased
over my head,
and my trespass is grown up unto the heavens;
since the days of youth
have I been in a great trespass
unto this day;
I cannot stand before Thee because of this.
My sins are more in number than the sand of the sea,
my iniquities are multiplied,
and I not worthy to look up
and see the height of heaven,
from the number of my unrighteousnesses;
and I have no relief,
because I have provoked Thine anger,
and done evil in Thy sight;
not doing Thy will,
not keeping Thy commandments.
And now my heart kneels to Thee,
beseeching Thy goodness.
I have sinned, O Lord, I have sinned,
and I know mine iniquities;
and I ask and beseech,
remit to me, O Lord, remit to me,
and destroy me not in mine iniquities;
nor be Thou angry for ever,
nor reserve evil for me;
nor condemn me
in the lowest parts of the earth.
Because Thou art God, the God of penitents,
and Thou shalt shew in me all Thy loving kindness;
for Thou shalt save me unworthy,
according to Thy much pity,

and I will praise Thee alway.
Lord, if Thou wilt, Thou canst cleanse me;
Lord, only say the word, and I shall be healed.
Lord, save me;
Carest Thou not that we perish?
Say to me, Be of good cheer, thy sins are remitted
to thee.
Jesu, Master, have mercy on me;
Thou Son of David, Jesu, have mercy on me;
Jesu, Son of David, Son of David.
Lord, say to me, Ephphatha.
Lord, I have no man;[1]
Lord, say to me, Be loosed from thine infirmity.
Say unto my soul, I am thy salvation.
Say unto me, My grace is sufficient for thee.
Lord, how long wilt Thou be angry?
shall Thy jealousy burn like fire for ever?
O, remember not our old sins;
but have mercy on us and that soon,
for we are come to great misery;
Help us, O God of our salvation;
for the glory of Thy Name.
O deliver us and be merciful unto our sins,
for Thy Name's sake.

2. Prayer for Grace.

[O Lord, remit]
all my failings, shortcomings, falls,
offences, trespasses, scandals,
transgressions, debts, sins,
faults, ignorances, iniquities,
impieties, unrighteousnesses, pollutions.
The guilt of them,

[1] John v. 7.

be gracious unto,	pardon;
remit,	forgive;
be propitious unto,	spare;
impute not,	charge not, remember not.

The stain,

pass by,	pass over;
disregard,	overlook;
hide,	wash away;
blot out,	cleanse.

The hurt,

remit,	heal,	remedy;
take off,	remove,	away with;
abolish,	annul,	disperse, annihilate;

that they be not found, that they exist not.

Supply

to faith,	virtue;
to virtue,	knowledge;
to knowledge,	continence;
to continence,	patience;
to patience,	godliness;
to godliness,	brotherly love;
to brotherly love,	charity.

That I forget not my cleansing from my former sins,
but give diligence to make my calling
and election sure
through good works.

3. Profession.

I believe in Thee the Father;
Behold then, if Thou a Father and we sons,
as a father pitieth sons,
be Thou of tender mercy towards us, O Lord.
I believe in Thee, the Lord;
behold then, if Thou art Lord and we servants,
our eyes are upon Thee our Lord,
until Thou have mercy upon us.

I believe, that though we be neither sons nor servants,
but dogs only,
yet we have leave to eat of the crumbs
that fall from Thy Table.
I believe that Christ is the Lamb of God;
O Lamb of God that takest away the sins
of the world,
take Thou away mine.
I believe that Jesus Christ came into the world
to save sinners;
Thou who camest to save sinners
save Thou me, of sinners
chief and greatest.
I believe that Christ came to save what was lost;
Thou who camest to save the lost,
never suffer, O Lord, that to be lost which
Thou hast saved.
I believe that the Spirit is the Lord and Giver of life;
Thou who gavest me a living soul,
give me that I receive not my soul in vain.
I believe that the Spirit gives grace
in His sacred things;
give me that I receive not His grace in vain,
nor hope of His sacred things.
I believe that the Spirit intercedes for us
with plaints unutterable;
grant me of His intercession and those plaints
to partake, O Lord.
Our fathers hoped in Thee,
they trusted in Thee, and Thou didst deliver them.
They called upon Thee and were holpen,
they put their trust in Thee, and were not confounded.
As Thou didst our fathers
in the generations of old,
so also deliver us, O Lord,
who trust in Thee.

4. Intercession.

O Heavenly King,
confirm our faithful kings,
stablish the faith,
soften the nations,
pacify the world,
guard well this holy retreat,
and receive us in orthodox faith and repentance,
as a kind and loving Lord.
The power of the Father guide me,
the wisdom of the Son enlighten me,
the working of the Spirit quicken me.
Guard Thou my soul,
stablish my body,
elevate my senses,
direct my converse,
form my habits,
bless my actions,
fulfil my prayers,
inspire holy thoughts,
pardon the past,
correct the present,
prevent the future.

5. Praise.

Now unto Him that is able to do
exceeding abundantly
above all that we ask or think,
according to the power that worketh in us,
to Him be glory
in the Church in Christ
unto all generations
world without end. Amen.
Blessed, and praised, and celebrated,

and magnified, and exalted, and glorified,
and hallowed,
be Thy Name, O Lord,
its record, and its memory,
and every memorial of it;
for the all-honourable senate of the Patriarchs,
the ever-venerable band of the Prophets,
the all-glorious college of the Apostles,
the Evangelists,
the all-illustrious army of the Martyrs,
the Confessors,
the assembly of Doctors,
the Ascetics,
the beauty of Virgins,
for Infants the delight of the world,—

for their faith,	their hope,
their labours,	their truth,
their blood,	their zeal,
their diligence,	their tears,
their purity,	their beauty.

Glory to Thee, O Lord, glory to Thee,
glory to Thee who didst glorify them,
among whom we too glorify Thee.
Great and marvellous are Thy works,
Lord, the God Almighty;
just and true are Thy ways,
O King of Saints.
Who shall not fear Thee, O Lord,
and glorify Thy Name?
for Thou only art holy,
for all the nations shall come and worship
before Thee,
for Thy judgments are made manifest.
Praise our God, all ye His servants,
and ye that fear Him,
both small and great,

Alleluia,
for the Lord God Omnipotent reigneth;
let us be glad and rejoice, and give honour to Him.
Behold the tabernacle of God is with men,
and He will dwell with them;
and they shall be His people,
and God Himself shall be with them,
and shall wipe away all tears from their eyes.
And there shall be no more death;
neither crying, neither pain any more,
for the former things are passed away.

V

ADDITIONAL EXERCISES

DEPRECATION.

O Lord,[1] Thou knowest, and canst, and willest
the good of my soul.
Miserable man am I;
I neither know, nor can, nor, as I ought,
will it.
Thou, O Lord, I beseech Thee,
in Thine ineffable affection,
so order concerning me,
and so dispose,
as Thou knowest to be most pleasing to Thee,
and most good for me,
[Thine is]
goodness, grace;
love, kindness;
benignity, gentleness, consideration;
forbearance, long-suffering;
much pity, great pity;
mercies, multitude of mercies, yearnings of mercies;
kind yearnings, deep yearnings;
in passing over,
in overlooking, in disregarding;
many seasons, many years;
[punishing] unwillingly, not willingly;
not to the full,

---

[1] Vide p. 92, edit. 1675.

not correspondently,
in wrath remembering mercy,
repenting of the evil,
compensating doubly,
ready to pardon,
to be reconciled,
to be appeased.

A LITANY OF DEPRECATION.[2]

Father, the Creator,
Son, the Redeemer,
Spirit, the Regenerator,
destroy me not,
whom Thou hast created, redeemed, regenerated.
Remember not, Lord, my sins,
nor the sins of my forefathers;
neither take vengeance for our sins, theirs, nor mine.
Spare us, Lord, them and me,
spare Thy people,
and, among Thy people, Thy servant,
who is redeemed with Thy precious blood;
and be not angry with us for ever.
Be merciful, be merciful; spare us, Lord,
and be not angry with us for ever.
Be merciful, be merciful; have pity on us, Lord,
and be not angry with us to the full.
Deal not, O Lord,
deal not with me after mine iniquities,
neither recompense me according to my sins;
but after Thy great pity,
deal with me,
and according to the multitude of Thy mercies,
recompense me;

[2] Page 189, edit. 1675.

after that so great pity,
and that multitude of mercies,
as Thou didst to our fathers
in the times of old;—
by all that is dear unto Thee.
From all evil and adversity,
in all time of need;
from this evil and this adversity,
in this time;
raise me, rescue me, save me, O Lord.
Deliver me, O Lord,
and destroy me not.
On the bed of sickness;
in the hour of death;
in the day of judgment,
in that dreadful and fearful day,
rescue me, Lord, and save me;—
from seeing the Judge's face overcast,
from being placed on the left,
from hearing the dreadful word, Depart from Me,
from being bound in chains of darkness,
from being cast into the outer darkness,
from being tormented in the pit of fire and brimstone,
where the smoke of the torments
ascendeth for ever.
Be merciful, be merciful,
spare us, pity us,
O Lord:
and destroy us not for ever,
deliver and save us.
Let it not be, O Lord; and that it be not,
take away from me, O Lord,
hardness of heart,
desperateness after sinning,
blindness of heart,
contempt of Thy threats,

a cauterized conscience,
a reprobate mind,
the sin against the Holy Ghost,
the sin unto death,
the four crying sins;[3]
the six which forerun[4]
the sin against the Holy Ghost.
Deliver me
from all ills and abominations of this world,
from plague, famine, and war;
earthquake, flood, and fire,
the stroke of immoderate rain and drought,
blast and blight;
thunder, lightning and tempest;
epidemic sickness, acute and malignant,
unexpected death;
from ills and difficulties in the Church,
from private interpretation,
from innovation in things sacred,
from heterodox teaching;
from unhealthy enquiries and interminable disputes,
from heresies, schisms, scandals,
public and private,
from making gods of kings,
from flattering of the people,
from the indifference of Saul,
from the scorn of Michal,
from the greediness of Hophni,
from the plunder of Athaliah,
from the priesthood of Micah,
from the brotherhood of Simon and Judas,

[3] Wilful murder, the sin of Sodom, oppressing the poor, defrauding workmen of their wages.
[4] Despair of salvation, presumption of God's mercy, impugning known truth, envy at another's grace, obstinacy in sin, and impenitence.

from the doctrine of men unlearned
and unestablished,
from the pride of novices,
from the people resisting the priest:—
from ills and difficulties in the state,
from anarchy, many rulers, tyranny,
from Asher, Jeroboam, Rehoboam, Gallio, Haman,
the profligacy of Ahithophel,
the foolishness of Zoan,[5]
the statutes of Omri,
the justice of Jezebel,
the overflowings of Belial,[6]
the courage of Peor,
the valley of Achor,
pollution of blood or seed,
incursion of enemies,
a civil war,
bereavement of good governors;
accession of evil and unprincipled governors;
from an intolerable life,
in despondence, sickness, ill-fame,
distress, peril, slavery, restlessness:
from death
in sin, shame, tortures,
desperateness, defilement, violence, treachery;
from death unexpected,
from death eternal.

[5] Isai. xix.
[6] Ps. xviii. 4.

FORMS OF INTERCESSION.

I.[1]

For all creatures,
men,
persons compassed
with infirmity.
Churches
Catholic,
Eastern,
Western,
British.
The Episcopate,
Presbytery,
clergy,
Christian people.
States
of the whole earth,
Christian,
the country.
Those who serve
the soul;
those who serve
the body,
in food,
clothing,
health,
necessaries.
[Those who have a claim
on my prayers,]
in nature,
neighbouring,
our own.
Rulers,
kings,
religious kings,
our own.
councillors,
judges,
nobles,
soldiers,
sailors,
the people,
the rising generation,
schools,
those at court,
in cities,
by benefits,
from trust,
formerly or now,
in friendship,
in love,
in neighbourhood;
from promise,
from mutual offices,
from want of leisure,
from destitution,
from extremity.

---

[1] Vide p. 90, edit. 1675.

2.[2]

Thy whole creation,	the world,
our whole race,	the inhabited earth,
the states of the world,	
the Catholic Church,	the Christian religion,
the separate Churches,	
the separate states,	
our Church,	our country,
our state,	
the orders in each,	
the persons in the orders,	the priesthood,

the person of the king, of the prince,
the City,
the parish in which I was baptized,
All-Hallows, Barking,
My two schools,
my University,
my College,
the parish committed to me, St. Giles's,
the three Churches
of Southwell,
St. Paul's,
Westminster;
the three Dioceses
of Chichester,
Ely,
Winton,
my home,
my kindred,
those who shew me pity,
those who minister to me;
my neighbours,
my friends,
those who have a claim on me.

[2] Vide p. 170, edit. 1675.

3.[3]

The creation,   the race of man,
all in affliction and in prosperity,
          in error,   and in truth,
          in sin,   and in grace;
     the Church Ecumenical,
     Eastern, Western, our own,
          Rulers, Clergy, people.
          States of the earth,
Christian, neighbouring, our own,
     the King, the Queen, the Prince,
               the nobles.
Parliament, Law Courts, army, police.
          The Commons,
     farmers, merchants, artisans,
     down to mean workmen,
               and poor.
Those who have a claim on me,
          from kindred,
          benefaction,
ministration of things temporal,
     charge formerly or now,
          natural kindness,
          Christian love,
          neighbourhood,
     promise on my part,
          their own desire,
     their lack of leisure,
sympathy for their extreme misery;
          any good work,
          any noble action,
     any scandal from me,
having none to pray for them.

[3] Vide p. 206, edit. 1675.

4.[4]

World,	earth inhabited.
Church,	kingdom,
throne,	altar.
Council-chamber,	law courts,
schools,	work-places.
Infants,	boys,
the grown,	youths,
men,	elderly,
aged,	decrepit.
The possessed,	weak-hearted,
sick,	prisoners,
orphans,	widows,
foreigners,	
travellers,	voyagers,
with child,	who give suck,
in bitter bondage,	in desolateness,
overladen.	

MEDITATIONS.

I.

On Christian Duty.

What shall I do that I may inherit eternal life?
    Keep the commandments. *Mark* x. 17.
What shall we do?

---

[4] Vide p. 210, edit. 1675.

Repent and be baptized every one of you.

Acts ii. 37, 38.

What must I do to be saved?

Believe on the Lord Jesus Christ.   *Acts* xvi. 31.

What shall we do then?

(To the multitude.) He who hath two coats, let him impart
to him that hath none.

He that hath meat, let him do likewise.

(To the publicans.) Exact no more than is appointed you.

(To soldiers.) Do violence to no man; neither accuse
any falsely; be content with your wages.

Luke iii. 10–14.

The knowledge and faith
of [God's] justice   [God's] mercy,
[leads] unto

fear,	hope,
abasement,	consolation,
repentance,	thanksgiving,
fasting,	almsgiving,
prayers,	hymns,
patience,	obedience,
a sacrifice.	an oblation.

2.

On the Day of Judgment.

Father Unoriginate, Only-begotten Son,
Life-giving Spirit,
merciful, pitiful, long-suffering,
full of pity, full of kind yearnings,
who lovest the just and pitiest the sinful,
who passest by sins and grantest petitions,
God of penitents,
Saviour of sinners,
I have sinned before Thee, O Lord,

and thus and thus have I done.
Alas, alas! woe, woe.
How was I enticed by my own lust!
How I hated instruction!
Nor felt I fear nor shame
at Thy incomprehensible glory,
Thy awful presence,
Thy fearful power,
Thy exact justice,
Thy winning goodness.
I will call if there be any that will answer me;
to which of the saints shall I turn?
O wretched man that I am,
who shall deliver me from the body of this death?
How fearful is Thy judgment, O Lord!
when the thrones are set
and Angels stand around,
and men are brought in,
the books opened,
the works enquired into,
the thoughts examined,
and the hidden things of darkness.
What judgment shall be upon me?
who shall quench my flame?
who shall lighten my darkness,
if Thou pity me not?
Lord, as Thou art loving,
give me tears,
give me floods, give me to-day.
For then will be the incorruptible Judge,
the horrible judgment-seat,
the answer without excuses,
the inevitable charges,
the shameful punishment,
the endless Gehenna,
the pitiless Angels,

the yawning hell,
the roaring stream of fire,
the unquenchable flame,
the dark prison,
the rayless darkness,
the bed of live coals,
the unwearied worm,
the indissoluble chains,
the bottomless chaos,
the impassable wall,
the inconsolable cry,
none to stand by me,
none to plead for me,
none to snatch me out.
But I repent, Lord, O Lord, I repent,
help Thou mine impenitence,
and more, and still more,
pierce, rend, crush my heart.
Behold, O Lord, that I am
indignant with myself,
for my senseless, profitless,
hurtful, perilous passions;
that I loathe myself,
for these inordinate, unseemly,
deformed, insincere,
shameful, disgraceful
passions,
that my confusion is daily before me,
and the shame of my face hath covered me.
Alas! woe, woe—
O me, how long?
Behold, Lord, that I sentence myself
to punishment everlasting,
yea, and all miseries of this world.
Behold me, Lord, self-condemned;
Behold, Lord, and enter not into judgment

with Thy servant.
And now, Lord,
I humble myself under Thy mighty hand,
I bend to Thee, O Lord, my knees,
I fall on my face to the earth.
Let this cup pass from me!
I stretch forth my hands unto Thee;
I smite my breast, I smite on my thigh.
Out of the deep my soul crieth unto Thee,
as a thirsty land;
and all my bones,
and all that is within me.
Lord, hear my voice.

3.

On Human Frailness.

Have mercy on me, Lord, for I am weak;
remember, Lord, how short my time is;
remember that I am but flesh,
a wind that passeth away, and cometh not again.
My days are as grass, as a flower of the field;
for the wind goeth over me, and I am gone,
and my place shall know me no more.
I am dust and ashes,
earth and grass,
flesh and breath,
corruption and the worm,
a stranger upon the earth,
dwelling in a house of clay,
few and evil my days,
to-day, and not to-morrow,
in the morning, yet not until night,
in a body of sin,
in a world of corruption,

of few days, and full of trouble,
coming up, and cut down like a flower,
and as a shadow, having no stay.
Remember this, O Lord, and suffer, remit;
what profit is there in my blood,
when I go down to the pit?
By the multitude of Thy mercies,
by the riches and excessive redundance
of Thy pity;
by all that is dear to Thee,
all that we should plead,
and before and beyond all things, by Thyself,
by Thyself, O Lord, and by Thy Christ.
Lord, have mercy upon me, the chief of sinners.
O my Lord, let Thy mercy rejoice
against Thy judgment in my sin.
O' Lord, hear, O Lord, forgive,
O Lord, hearken,
O Lord, hearken and do,
do and defer not for Thine own sake,
defer not, O Lord my God.

A PREPARATION
FOR HOLY COMMUNION.

O Lord,
I am not worthy, I am not fit,
that Thou shouldest come under the roof
of my soul;
for it is all desolate and ruined;
nor hast Thou in me fitting place
to lay Thy head.
But, as Thou didst vouchsafe
to lie in the cavern and manger of brute cattle,
as Thou didst not disdain

to be entertained in the house of Simon the leper,
as Thou didst not disdain
that harlot, like me, who was a sinner,
coming to Thee and touching Thee;
as Thou abhorredst not
her polluted and loathsome mouth;
nor the thief upon the cross
confessing Thee:
So me too the ruined, wretched,
and excessive sinner,
deign to receive to the touch and partaking
of the immaculate, supernatural, life-giving,
and saving mysteries
of Thy all-holy Body
and Thy precious Blood.
Listen, O Lord, our God,
from Thy holy habitation,
and from the glorious throne of Thy kingdom,
and come to sanctify us.
O Thou who sittest on high with the Father,
and art present with us here invisibly;
come Thou to sanctify the gifts which lie before Thee,
and those in whose behalf, and by whom,
and the things for which,
they are brought near Thee.
And grant to us communion,
unto faith without shame,
love without dissimulation,
fulfilment of Thy commandments,
alacrity for every spiritual fruit;
hindrance of all adversity,
healing of soul and body;
that we too, with all Saints,
who have been well-pleasing to Thee from the
beginning,
may become partakers

of Thy incorrupt and everlasting goods,
which Thou hast prepared, O Lord, for them that
love Thee;
in whom Thou art glorified
for ever and ever.
Lamb of God,
that takest away the sin of the world,
take away the sin of me,
the utter sinner.

[Unto a pledge of communion. *Acts* ii. 42.
A memorial of the Dispensation. *Eph.* iii. 2.
A showing forth of His death. 1 *Cor.* xi. 26.
A communion of Body and Blood. *Luke* xxii. 19.
A sharing in the Spirit. 1 *Cor.* xii. 13.
Remission of sins. *Matt.* xxvi. 28.
A riddance of things contrary. 1 *Cor.* v. 7.
Rest of conscience. *Matt.* xi. 29.
Blotting out of debts. *Col.* ii. 14.
Cleansing of stains. *Heb.* ix. 14.
Healing of the soul's sicknesses. 1 *Pet.* ii. 24.
Renewing of the covenant. *Psalm* ii. 5.
Food of spiritual life. *John* vi. 27.
Increase of strengthening grace. *Heb.* xiii. 9.
And of winning consolation. *Luke* ii. 25.
Compunction of penitence. 2 *Cor.* vii. 9.
Illumination of mind. *Luke* xxiv. 31.
Exercise of humility. 1 *Peter* v. 5.
Seal of faith. 2 *Cor.* i. 22.
Fulness of wisdom. *Rom.* xi. 33.
Bond of love. *John* xiii. 35.
Call for a collection. 1 *Cor.* xvi. 1.
A means of endurance. 1 *Peter* iv. 1.
Liveliness of thanksgiving. *Psalm* cxvi. 12.
Confidence of prayer. *Ibid.* 13.
Mutual indwelling. *John* vi. 56.
Pledge of the resurrection. *Ibid.* 34.

Acceptable defence in judgment. *Luke* xiv. 18.
Covenant of the inheritance. *Luke* xxii. 20.
Figure of perfection. *John* xvii. 23.]

We then remembering, O sovereign Lord,
in the presence of Thy holy mysteries,
the salutary passion of Thy Christ,
His life-giving cross,
most precious death,
three days' sepulture,
resurrection from the dead,
ascent into heaven,
session at the right hand of Thee, the Father,
His fearful and glorious coming;
we beseech Thee, O Lord,
that we, receiving in the pure testimony
of our conscience,
our portion of Thy sacred things,
may be made one with the holy Body and Blood
of Thy Christ;
and receiving them not unworthily,
we may hold Christ indwelling in our hearts,
and may become a temple
of Thy Holy Spirit.
Yea, O our God,
nor make any of us guilty
of Thy dreadful and heavenly mysteries,
nor infirm in soul or body
from partaking of them unworthily.
But grant us
until our last and closing breath
worthily to receive a hope of Thy holy things,
for sanctification, enlightening, strengthening,
a relief of the weight of my many sins,
a preservative against all satanic working,
a riddance and hindrance of my evil conscience,
a mortification of my passions,

an appropriation of Thy commandments,
an increase of Thy divine grace;
and a securing of Thy kingdom.

***

It is finished and done,
so far as in our power,
Christ our God,
the mystery of Thy dispensation.
For we have held remembrance of Thy death,
we have seen the figure of Thy resurrection,
we have been filled with Thy endless life,
we have enjoyed Thy uncloying dainties,
which graciously vouchsafe all of us,
in the world to come.
Lord, the good God,
pardon every soul,
that purifieth his heart to seek God,
the Lord God of his fathers,
though he be not cleansed
according to the purification of the sanctuary.

MEDITATIONS
AND
DEVOTIONS

DEDICATION

To you,
boys of the Oratory School,
past and present,
this collection of devotional papers
by Cardinal Newman is dedicated.
They are a memento both of
the Cardinal's constant thought of you,
and of his confident assurance that,
after his death,
you would pray for his soul.

PREFATORY NOTICE

The Papers by the late Cardinal Newman contained in this collection were likely, most of them, to have formed part of what he proposed to call a "Year-Book of Devotion" for reading and meditation according to the Seasons and the Feasts of the year. The intention of composing such a book had been in the Cardinal's mind as far back as the early years of his Catholic life, but, though it was never abandoned, various circumstances hindered him from pursuing it, and no portion of this volume was put together with this idea. The book would have varied greatly in the matter of its subjects and in their treatment. For instance, some papers on the Notes of the Church would have formed one subject; of these, excepting some mere preparatory fragments, nothing was written. Again, some sermons would also have formed a part of the readings. A scheme, drawn out by him, of Litanies to run through the whole year shows what he had thought of in that respect, though only the few here printed were put together by him. "The Sayings of the Saints of the Desert" would have been extended over the whole year instead of covering only the few months for which he had prepared them. The "Meditations for Eight Days" were intended to be carried through at least five weeks, and a scheme of them was drawn out for that purpose. The "Dream of Gerontius," if not written expressly for the volume, was to have been added as a November reading, and "Gerontius" was likely not to have stood alone as a poem. Indeed, the book would have become a repository of the Cardinal's thoughts on the various devotional subjects which occupied his mind.

But there are not the materials for such a book. All, then, that has been possible towards carrying out the Cardinal's intention has been to put together such papers as, from what was said by the Cardinal, are considered as likely to have come within the compass of the contemplated volume. It is hoped that this will gratify many of the late Cardinal's friends, some of whom have expressed a strong desire to have some examples of his devotions, or to know the devotions which most attracted him, and which they might make their own. The Meditations on Christian Doctrine would probably have been more numerous, but that the Cardinal destroyed many such writings of his upon the death of his great friend Father St. John, to whose discretion he had intended to commit them. There are here included, therefore, it is believed, nearly all of the Cardinal's devotional papers which are likely to be forthcoming.

That the papers can be presented at all, especially the majority of the Meditations, is owing, it is believed, to the circumstances which accompanied their origin. It was the Cardinal's custom to note down, in the roughest way, any thought that particularly struck him while meditating, that he might reflect upon it during the day or pursue it in the future; and thus he was led on to enlarge such thoughts, and write out the notes and rewrite them carefully (for he always, he said, could meditate best with a pen in his hand). It is chiefly to this custom of the Cardinal's, of keeping the current of holy thoughts within his easy reach, that we owe, it is believed, the preservation of the greater part of this volume.

The headings of the different subjects, and their parts and chapters, have all, with one or two exceptions, been carefully written by their author, but their order evidently had not always been fully determined. It is to

Father Ryder and to Father Eaglesim that this volume is especially indebted: to the former for some important suggestions and curtailments, for the sake of greater clearness; and to the latter for the present order and the supply of the few headings wanted, as well as in other respects.

There were a few friends whose names Cardinal Newman desired to have associated in some way with his own, on account of the special nature of their services to him—services dating, in some cases, from his first years as a Catholic; and now that most of these friends have been removed by death, this book seems to be an especially appropriate place for the purpose. Such was Cardinal Alimonda, late Archbishop of Turin, for services in a time of most serious trouble, very many years ago—services which had been carried on so quietly that the name even of this good friend was unknown to our Cardinal until their elevation at one and the same time to the Sacred College, when an intimacy at once sprang up, and all opportunities were taken by each for maintaining it. Such was Cardinal Place, Archbishop of Rennes, recently deceased, for a number of kindnesses shown to himself, but especially for his many years of care and attention to an ancient friend of the Cardinal's family, Miss Maria Rosina de Giberne, afterwards Sister Maria Pia of the Visitation at Autun, in France—a lady now deceased, who, besides many lesser good offices to the Cardinal, had, when he was in a most extraordinary difficulty arising from a legal trial, rendered him a service which was as signal as it was unique. Three others there are—Cardinal Macchi, with whom a first acquaintance placed him, almost at once, on a footing of fraternal intimacy; Cardinal Capecelatro, the present Archbishop of Capua; and Monsignor Stonor, Archbishop of Trebizond. Cardinal Capecelatro, a member of the Oratory at Naples, had from his early life been unremitting in his

kindness to our Cardinal, though in this case also they
were personally unacquainted until they met in Rome in
1879, when both were there for promotion to honour.
The services of Cardinal Capecelatro were such that
though our Cardinal could not, from modesty, make
mention of them, yet he found an opportunity for acknowledging his sense of them, by dictating from his
death-bed a few words of dedication to his Eminence for
a small volume which in course of time will be
published—the delay of which publication suggests the
mention of his Eminence's name here. Cardinal Newman's own words of Archbishop Stonor, the last time of
speaking of him, will best convey the tribute of gratitude
which the Cardinal, with much warmth and earnestness,
paid him. "All these years that I have been Cardinal," he
said, "Monsignor Stonor has been a friend indeed, for he
has let me make use of him whensoever and for whatsoever I have chosen, and I don't know what I should
have done without him." One name more there is to
mention—and it belongs to America, where though our
Cardinal had so many friends, one was pre-eminently
such—that of Bishop James O'Connor, Bishop of
Omaha, whose unaffected kindness was most grateful to
our Cardinal, lasting as it did through all but the whole of
his Catholic lifetime. For Bishop James O'Connor the
Cardinal had a great affection, remembering always, with
something of gratitude, the modesty and simplicity with
which, as a youth, the future Bishop attached himself to
him and to Father St. John when the three were at
Propaganda together, thus forming a friendship which
distance and years did not lessen, and which later on was
enlivened by personal intercourse when the visits *ad
limina Apostolorum* brought Bishop O'Connor through
England.

This list of names drawn together from countries so
wide apart suggests that this book must not be regarded

as though only for the service of a few friends. It is hoped that the character of the book itself will secure for it a still wider circulation.

WM. P. NEVILLE.

THE ORATORY, BIRMINGHAM:

Easter, 1893

PART I

MEDITATIONS
ON
THE LITANY OF LORETTO
FOR THE
MONTH OF MAY

INTRODUCTORY

(1)

MAY THE MONTH OF PROMISE

May 1

W HY is May chosen as the month in which we exercise a special devotion to the Blessed Virgin?

The first reason is because it is the time when the earth bursts forth into its fresh foliage and its green grass after the stern frost and snow of winter, and the raw atmosphere and the wild wind and rain of the early spring. It is because the blossoms are upon the trees and the flowers are in the gardens. It is because the days have got long, and the sun rises early and sets late. For such gladness and joyousness of external Nature is a fit attendant on our devotion to her who is the Mystical Rose and the House of Gold.

A man may say, "True; but in this climate we have sometimes a bleak, inclement May." This cannot be denied; but still, so much is true that at least it is the month of *promise* and of *hope*. Even though the weather happen to be bad, it is the month that *begins* and heralds in the summer. We know, for all that may be unpleasant in it, that fine weather is coming, sooner or later. "Brightness and beautifulness shall," in the Prophet's words, "appear at the end, and shall not lie: if it make delay, wait for it, for it shall surely come, and shall not be slack."

May then is the month, if not of fulfilment, at least of

promise; and is not this the very aspect in which we most suitably regard the Blessed Virgin, Holy Mary, to whom this month is dedicated?

The Prophet says, "There shall come forth a rod out of the root of Jesse, and a flower shall rise out of his root." Who is the flower but our Blessed Lord? Who is the rod, or beautiful stalk or stem or plant out of which the flower grows, but Mary, Mother of our Lord, Mary, Mother of God?

It was prophesied that God should come upon earth. When the time was now full, how was it announced? It was announced by the Angel coming to Mary. "Hail, full of grace," said Gabriel, "the Lord is with thee; blessed art thou among women." She then was the sure *promise* of the coming Saviour, and therefore May is by a special title her month.

MAY THE MONTH OF JOY

May 2

W HY is May called the month of Mary, and especially dedicated to her? Among other reasons there is this, that of the Church's year, the ecclesiastical year, it is at once the most sacred and the most festive and joyous portion. Who would wish February, March, or April, to be the month of Mary, considering that it is the time of Lent and penance? Who again would choose December, the Advent season—a time of hope, indeed, because Christmas is coming, but a time of fasting too? Christmas itself does not last for a month; and January has indeed the joyful Epiphany, with its Sundays in succession; but these in most years are cut short by the urgent coming of Septuagesima.

May on the contrary belongs to the Easter season, which lasts fifty days, and in that season the whole of May commonly falls, and the first half always. The great Feast of the Ascension of our Lord into heaven is always in May, except once or twice in forty years. Pentecost, called also Whit-Sunday, the Feast of the Holy Ghost, is commonly in May, and the Feasts of the Holy Trinity and Corpus Christi are in May not unfrequently. May, therefore, is the time in which there are such frequent Alleluias, because Christ has risen from the grave, Christ has ascended on high, and God the Holy Ghost has come down to take His place.

Here then we have a reason why May is dedicated to

the Blessed Mary. She is the first of creatures, the most acceptable child of God, the dearest and nearest to Him. It is fitting then that this month should be hers, in which we especially glory and rejoice in His great Providence to us, in our redemption and sanctification in God the Father, God the Son, and God the Holy Ghost.

But Mary is not only the acceptable handmaid of the Lord. She is also Mother of His Son, and the Queen of all Saints, and in this month the Church has placed the feasts of some of the greatest of them, as if to bear her company. First, however, there is the Feast of the Holy Cross, on the 3d of May, when we venerate that Precious Blood in which the Cross was bedewed at the time of our Lord's Passion. The Archangel St. Michael, and three Apostles, have feast-days in this month: St. John, the beloved disciple, St. Philip, and St. James. Seven Popes, two of them especially famous, St. Gregory VII. and St. Pius V.; also two of the greatest Doctors, St. Athanasius and St. Gregory Nazianzen; two holy Virgins especially favoured by God, St. Catherine of Sienna (as her feast is kept in England), and St. Mary Magdalen of Pazzi; and one holy woman most memorable in the annals of the Church, St. Monica, the Mother of St. Augustine. And above all, and nearest to us in this Church, our own holy Patron and Father, St. Philip, occupies, with his Novena and Octave, fifteen out of the whole thirty-one days of the month. These are some of the choicest fruits of God's manifold grace, and they form the court of their glorious Queen.

I

ON THE IMMACULATE CONCEPTION

(1)

MARY IS THE *"VIRGO PURISSIMA,"* THE MOST PURE VIRGIN

May 3

B Y the Immaculate Conception of the Blessed Virgin is meant the great revealed truth that she was conceived in the womb of her mother, St. Anne, without original sin.

Since the fall of Adam all mankind, his descendants, are conceived and born in sin. "Behold," says the inspired writer in the Psalm *Miserere*—"Behold, I was conceived in iniquity, and in sin did my mother conceive me." That sin which belongs to every one of us, and is ours from the first moment of our existence, is the sin of unbelief and disobedience, by which Adam lost Paradise. We, as the children of Adam, are heirs to the consequences of his sin, and have forfeited in him that spiritual robe of grace and holiness which he had given him by his Creator at the time that he was made. In this state of forfeiture and disinheritance we are all of us conceived and born; and the ordinary way by which we are taken out of it is the Sacrament of Baptism.

But Mary *never* was in this state; she was by the eternal decree of God exempted from it. From eternity, God, the Father, Son, and Holy Ghost, decreed to create the race of man, and, foreseeing the fall of Adam, decreed to redeem the whole race by the Son's taking flesh and suffering on the Cross. In that same incomprehensible, eternal instant, in which the Son of God was born of the Father, was also the decree passed of man's redemption through Him. He who was born from Eternity was born by an eternal decree to save us in Time, and to redeem the whole race; and Mary's redemption was determined in that special manner which we call the Immaculate Con-.ception. It was decreed, not that she should be *cleansed* from sin, but that she should, from the first moment of her being, be *preserved* from sin; so that the Evil One never had any part in her. Therefore she was a child of Adam and Eve as if they had never fallen; she did not share with them their sin; she inherited the gifts and graces (and more than those) which Adam and Eve possessed in Paradise. This is her prerogative, and the foundation of all those salutary truths which are revealed to us concerning her. Let us say then with all holy souls, *Virgin most pure, conceived without original sin, Mary, pray for us.*

(2)

MARY IS THE "*VIRGO PRÆDICANDA*," THE VIRGIN WHO IS TO BE PROCLAIMED

May 4

MARY is the *Virgo Prædicanda*, that is, the Virgin who is to be proclaimed, to be heralded, literally, to be *preached*.

We are accustomed to preach abroad that which is wonderful, strange, rare, novel, important. Thus, when our Lord was coming, St. John the Baptist *preached* Him; then, the Apostles went into the wide world, and *preached* Christ. What is the highest, the rarest, the choicest prerogative of Mary? It is that she was without sin. When a woman in the crowd cried out to our Lord, "Blessed is the womb that bare Thee!" He answered, "More blessed are they who hear the word of God and keep it." Those words were fulfilled in Mary. She was filled with grace *in order* to be the Mother of God. But it was a higher gift than her maternity to be thus sanctified and thus pure. Our Lord indeed would not have become her son *unless* He had first sanctified her; but still, the greater blessedness was to have that perfect sanctification. *This* then is why she is the *Virgo Prædicanda*; she is deserving to be preached abroad because she never committed any sin, even the least; because sin had no part in her; because, through the fulness of God's grace, she never thought a thought, or spoke a word, or did an action, which was displeasing, which was not most pleasing, to Almighty God; because in her was displayed the greatest triumph over the enemy of souls. Wherefore, when all seemed lost, in order to show what He could do for us all by dying for us; in order to show what human nature, His work, was capable of becoming; to show how utterly He could bring to naught the utmost efforts, the most concentrated malice of the foe, and reverse all the consequences of the Fall, our Lord began, even before His coming, to do His most wonderful act of redemption, in the person of her who was to be His Mother. By the merit of that Blood which was to be shed, He interposed to hinder her incurring the sin of Adam, before He had made on the Cross atonement for it. And therefore it is that we *preach* her who is the subject of this wonderful grace.

But she was the *Virgo Prædicanda* for another reason. When, why, what things do we preach? We preach what is not known, that it may *become* known. And hence the Apostles are said in Scripture to "preach Christ." To whom? To those who knew Him not—to the heathen world. Not to those who knew Him, but to those who did not know Him. Preaching is a gradual work: first one lesson, then another. Thus were the heathen brought into the Church *gradually*. And in like manner, the preaching of Mary to the children of the Church, and the devotion paid to her by them, has *grown*, grown gradually, with successive ages. Not so much preached about her in *early* times as in *later*. First she was preached as the Virgin of Virgins—then as the Mother of God—then as glorious in her Assumption—then as the Advocate of sinners—then as Immaculate in her Conception. And this last has been the special preaching of the present century; and thus that which was earliest in her own history is the latest in the Church's recognition of her.

(3)

MARY IS THE "MATER ADMIRABILIS," THE WONDERFUL MOTHER

May 5

WHEN Mary, the *Virgo Prædicanda*, the Virgin who is to be proclaimed aloud, is called by the title of *Admirabilis*, it is thereby suggested to us what the *effect* is of the preaching of her as Immaculate in her Conception. The Holy Church proclaims, preaches her, as conceived without original sin; and those who hear, the children of Holy Church, wonder, marvel, are astonished and overcome by the preaching. It is so great a prerogative.

Even created excellence is fearful to think of when it is so high as Mary's. As to the great *Creator*, when Moses desired to see His glory, He Himself says about Himself, "Thou canst not see My face, for man shall not see Me and live;" and St. Paul says, "Our God is a consuming fire." And when St. John, holy as he was, saw only the *Human Nature* of our Lord, as He is in Heaven, "he fell at His feet as dead." And so as regards the appearance of angels. The holy Daniel, when St. Gabriel appeared to him, "fainted away, and lay in a consternation, with his face close to the ground." When this great archangel came to Zacharias, the father of St. John the Baptist, he too "was troubled, and fear fell upon him." But it was otherwise with Mary when the same St. Gabriel came to her. She was overcome indeed, and troubled at his *words*, because, humble as she was in her own opinion of herself, he addressed her as "Full of grace," and "Blessed among women;" but she was able to bear the sight of him.

Hence we learn two things: first, how great a holiness was Mary's, seeing she could endure the presence of an angel, whose brightness smote the holy prophet Daniel even to fainting and almost to death; and secondly, since she is so much holier than that angel, and we so much less holy than Daniel, what great reason we have to call her the *Virgo Admirabilis*, the Wonderful, the Awful Virgin, when we think of her ineffable purity!

There are those who are so thoughtless, so blind, so grovelling as to think that Mary is not as much shocked at wilful sin as her Divine Son is, and that we can make her our friend and advocate, though we go to her without contrition at heart, without even the wish for true repentance and resolution to amend. As if Mary could hate sin less, and love sinners more, than our Lord does! No: she feels a sympathy for those only who wish to *leave* their sins; else, how should she be without sin herself? No: if even to the best of us she is, in the words of Scripture, "fair as the moon, bright as the sun, and *terrible as an army set in array*," what is she to the impenitent sinner?

(4)

MARY IS THE "*DOMUS AUREA*," THE HOUSE OF GOLD

May 6

Why is she called a *House*? And why is she called *Golden*? Gold is the most beautiful, the most valuable, of all metals. Silver, copper, and steel may in their way be made good to the eye, but nothing is so rich, so splendid, as gold. We have few opportunities of seeing it in any quantity; but anyone who has seen a large number of bright gold coins knows how magnificent is the look of gold. Hence it is that in Scripture the Holy City is, by a figure of speech, called Golden. "The City," says St. John, "was pure gold, as it were transparent glass." He means of course to give us a notion of the wondrous beautifulness of heaven, by comparing it with what is the most beautiful of all the substances which we see on earth.

Therefore it is that Mary too is called *golden*; because her graces, her virtues, her innocence, her purity, are of that transcendent brilliancy and dazzling perfection, so costly, so exquisite, that the angels cannot, so to say, keep their eyes off her any more than *we* could help gazing upon any great work of gold.

But observe further, she is a *golden house*, or, I will rather say, a *golden palace*. Let us imagine we saw a whole palace or large church all made of gold, from the foundations to the roof; such, in regard to the number, the variety, the extent of her spiritual excellences, is Mary.

But why called a *house* or palace? And *whose* palace? She is the house and the palace of the Great King, of God Himself. Our Lord, the Co-equal Son of God, once dwelt in her. He was her Guest; nay, more than a guest, for a guest comes into a house as well as leaves it. But our Lord was actually *born in* this holy house. He took His flesh and His blood from this house, from the flesh, from the veins of Mary. Rightly then was she made to be of pure gold, because she was to give of that gold to form the body of the Son of God. She was *golden* in her conception, *golden* in her birth. She went through the fire of her suffering like gold in the furnace, and when she ascended on high, she was, in the words of our hymn,

> Above all the Angels in glory untold.
> Standing next to the King in a vesture of gold.

(5)

MARY IS THE "*MATER AMABILIS*," THE LOVABLE OR DEAR MOTHER

May 7

W HY is she "*Amabilis*" thus specially? It is because she was without sin. Sin is something odious in its very nature, and grace is something bright, beautiful, attractive.

However, it may be said that sinlessness was not enough to make others love her, or to make her dear to others, and that for two reasons: first, because we cannot like anyone that is not like ourselves, and *we* are sinners; and next, because her being holy would not make her pleasant and winning, because holy persons whom we fall in with, are not always agreeable, and we cannot like them, however we may revere them and look up to them.

Now as to the first of these two questions, we may grant that bad men do not, cannot like good men; but our Blessed Virgin Mary is called *Amabilis*, or lovable, as being such to the *children of the Church*, not to those outside of it, who know nothing about her; and no child of Holy Church but has some remains of God's grace in his soul which makes him sufficiently like her, however greatly wanting he may be, to allow of his being able to love her. So we may let this question pass.

But as to the second question, viz., How are we sure that our Lady, when she was on earth, attracted people round her, and made them love her merely because she was holy?—considering that holy people sometimes have not that gift of drawing others to them.

To explain this point we must recollect that there is a vast difference between the state of a soul such as that of the Blessed Virgin, which has *never* sinned, and a soul, however holy, which has *once* had upon it Adam's sin; for, even after baptism and repentance, it suffers necessarily from the spiritual wounds which are the consequence of that sin. Holy men, indeed, never commit *mortal* sin; nay, sometimes have never committed even one mortal sin in the whole course of their lives. But Mary's holiness went beyond this. She never committed even a *venial* sin, and this special privilege is not known to belong to anyone but Mary.

Now, whatever want of amiableness, sweetness, attractiveness, really exists in holy men arises from the *remains* of sin in them, or again from the want of a holiness powerful enough to overcome the defects of nature, whether of soul or body; but, as to Mary, her holiness was such, that if we saw her, and heard her, we should not be able to tell to those who asked us anything about her except simply that she was angelic and heavenly.

Of course her face was most beautiful; but we should not be able to recollect whether it was beautiful or not; we should not recollect any of her features, because it was her beautiful sinless soul, which looked through her eyes, and spoke through her mouth, and was heard in her voice, and compassed her all about; when she was still, or when she walked, whether she smiled, or was sad, her sinless soul, this it was which would draw all those to her who had any grace in them, any remains of grace, any love of holy things. There was a divine music in all she said and did—in her mien, her air, her deportment, that charmed every true heart that came near her. Her innocence, her humility and modesty, her simplicity, sincerity, and truthfulness, her unselfishness, her unaffected interest in everyone who came to her, her purity—it was these qualities which made her so lovable; and were we to see her now, neither our first thought nor our second thought would be, what she could do for us with her Son (though she can do so much), but our first thought would be, "Oh, how beautiful!" and our second thought would be, "Oh, what ugly hateful creatures are we!"

ON THE IMMACULATE CONCEPTION

(5)

MARY IS THE "ROSA MYSTICA," THE MYSTICAL ROSE[1]

May 7

How did Mary become the *Rosa Mystica*, the choice, delicate, perfect flower of God's spiritual creation? It was by being born, nurtured and sheltered in the mystical garden or Paradise of God. Scripture makes use of the figure of a garden, when it would speak of heaven and its blessed inhabitants. A garden is a spot of ground set apart for trees and plants, all good, all various, for things that are sweet to the taste or fragrant in scent, or beautiful to look upon, or useful for nourishment; and accordingly in its spiritual sense it means the home of blessed spirits and holy souls dwelling there together, souls with both the flowers and the fruits upon them, which by the careful husbandry of God they have come to bear, flowers and fruits of grace, flowers more beautiful and more fragrant than those of any garden, fruits more delicious and exquisite than can be matured by earthly husbandman.

All that God has made speaks of its Maker; the mountains speak of His eternity; the sun of His immensity, and the winds of His Almightiness. In like manner flowers and fruits speak of His sanctity, His love, and His provi-

[1] This was written and used in 1874, but the following year it was superseded, and "Sancta Maria" was written and added instead.

126

dence; and such as are flowers and fruits, such must be the place where they are found. That is to say, since they are found in a garden, therefore a garden has also excellences which speak of God, because it is their home. For instance, it would be out of place if we found beautiful flowers on the mountain-crag, or rich fruit in the sandy desert. As then by flowers and fruits are meant, in a mystical sense, the gifts and graces of the Holy Ghost, so by a garden is meant mystically a place of spiritual repose, stillness, peace, refreshment, and delight.

Thus our first parents were placed in "a garden of pleasure" shaded by trees, "fair to behold and pleasant to eat of," with the Tree of Life in the midst, and a river to water the ground. Thus our Lord, speaking from the cross to the penitent robber, calls the blessed place, the heaven to which He was taking him, "paradise," or a garden of pleasure. Therefore St. John, in the Apocalypse, speaks of heaven, the palace of God, as a garden or paradise, in which was the Tree of Life giving forth its fruits every month.

Such was the garden in which the Mystical Rose, the Immaculate Mary, was sheltered and nursed to be the Mother of the All Holy God, from her birth to her espousals to St. Joseph, a term of thirteen years. For three years of it she was in the arms of her holy mother, St. Anne, and then for ten years she lived in the temple of God. In those blessed gardens, as they may be called, she lived by herself, continually visited by the dew of God's grace, and growing up a more and more heavenly flower, till at the end of that period she was meet for the inhabitation in her of the Most Holy. This was the outcome of the Immaculate Conception. Excepting her, the fairest rose in the paradise of God has had upon it blight, and has had the risk of canker-worm and locust. All but Mary; she from the first was perfect in her sweetness and her beautifulness, and at length when the angel Gabriel had to come to her, he found her "full of grace," which had, from her good use of it, accumulated in her from the first moment of her being.

(6)

MARY IS THE "*VIRGO VENERANDA*," THE ALL-WORSHIPFUL VIRGIN

May 8

W E use the word "*Venerable*" generally of what is *old*. That is because only what is old has commonly those qualities which excite reverence or veneration.

It is a great history, a great character, a maturity of virtue, goodness, experience, that excite our reverence, and these commonly cannot belong to the young.

But this is not true when we are considering Saints. A short life with them is a long one. Thus Holy Scripture says, "Venerable age is not that of long time, nor counted by the number of years, but it is the *understanding* of a man that is gray hairs, and a spotless life is old age. The just man, if he be cut short by death, shall be at rest; being made perfect in a short time, he fulfilled a long time."[1]

Nay, there is a heathen writer, who knew nothing of Saints, who lays it down that even to children, to all children, a great reverence should be paid, and that on the ground of their being as yet innocent. And this is a feeling very widely felt and expressed in all countries; so much so that the sight of those who have not sinned (that is, who are not yet old enough to have fallen into mortal sin) has, on the very score of that innocent, smiling youthfulness, often disturbed and turned the plunderer or the assassin in the midst of his guilty doings, filled him with a

[1] Wisdom v.

sudden fear, and brought him, if not to repentance, at least to change of purpose.

And, to pass from the thought of the lowest to the Highest, what shall we say of the Eternal God (if we may safely speak of Him at all) but that He, *because* He is eternal, is ever *young*, without a beginning, and therefore without change, and, in the fulness and perfection of His incomprehensible attributes, now just what He was a million years ago? He is truly called in Scripture the "Ancient of Days," and is therefore infinitely venerable; yet He needs not old age to make him venerable; He has really nothing of those human attendants on venerableness which the sacred writers are obliged figuratively to ascribe to Him, in order to make us feel that profound abasement and reverential awe which we ought to entertain at the thought of Him.

And so of the great Mother of God, as far as a creature can be like the Creator; her ineffable purity and utter freedom from any shadow of sin, her Immaculate Conception, her ever-virginity—these her prerogatives (in spite of her extreme youth at the time when Gabriel came to her) are such as to lead us to exclaim in the prophetic words of Scripture both with awe and with exultation, "Thou art the glory of Jerusalem and the joy of Israel; thou art the honour of our people; therefore hath the hand of the Lord strengthened thee, and therefore art thou blessed forever."

(7)

MARY IS "*SANCTA MARIA*," THE HOLY MARY

May 9

Goᴅ alone can claim the attribute of holiness. Hence we say in the Hymn, "*Tu solus sanctus*," "Thou only art holy." By holiness we mean the absence of whatever sullies, dims, and degrades a rational nature; all that is most opposite and contrary to sin and guilt.

We say that God alone is *holy*, though in truth *all* His high attributes are possessed by Him in that fulness, that it may be truly said that He alone has them. Thus, as to goodness, our Lord said to the young man, "None is good but God alone." He too alone is Power, He alone is Wisdom, He alone is Providence, Love, Mercy, Justice, Truth. This is true; but holiness is singled out as His special prerogative, because it marks more than His other attributes, not only His superiority over all His creatures, but emphatically His separation from them. Hence we read in the Book of Job, "Can man be justified compared with God, or he that is born of a woman appear clean? Behold, even the moon doth not shine, and the stars are not pure, in His sight." "Behold, among His saints none is unchangeable, and the Heavens are not pure in His sight."

This we must receive and understand in the first place; but secondly we know too, that, in His mercy, He has communicated in various measures His great attributes to His rational creatures, and, first of all, as being most necessary, holiness. Thus Adam, from the time of his creation, was gifted, over and above his nature as man, with the grace of God, to unite him to God, and to make him holy. Grace is therefore called holy grace; and, as being holy, it is the connecting principle between God and man. Adam in Paradise might have had knowledge, and skill, and many virtues; but these gifts did not unite him to his Creator. It was holiness that united him, for it is said by St. Paul, "Without holiness no man shall see God."

And so again, when man fell and lost this holy grace, he had various gifts still adhering to him; he might be, in a certain measure, true, merciful, loving, and just; but these virtues did not unite him to God. What he needed was holiness; and therefore the first act of God's goodness to us in the Gospel is to take us out of our *un*holy state by means of the sacrament of Baptism, and by the grace then given us to re-open the communications, so long closed, between the soul and heaven.

We see then the force of our Lady's title, when we call her *"Holy* Mary." When God would prepare a human mother for His Son, this was why He began by giving her an immaculate conception. He began, not by giving her the gift of love, or truthfulness, or gentleness, or devotion, though according to the occasion she had them all. But He began His great work before she was born; before she could think, speak, or act, by making her *holy*, and thereby, while on earth, a citizen of heaven. *"Tota pulchra es, Maria!"* Nothing of the deformity of sin was ever hers. Thus she differs from all saints. There have been great missionaries, confessors, bishops, doctors, pastors. They have done great works, and have taken with them numberless converts or penitents to heaven. They have suffered much, and have a superabundance of merits to show. But Mary in this way resembles her

Divine Son, viz., that, as He, being God, is separate by holiness from all creatures, so she is separate from all Saints and Angels, as being *"full of grace."*

II

ON THE ANNUNCIATION

(1)

MARY IS THE "*REGINA ANGELORUM*," THE QUEEN OF ANGELS

May 10

THIS great title may be fitly connected with the Maternity of Mary, that is, with the coming upon her of the Holy Ghost at Nazareth after the Angel Gabriel's annunciation to her, and with the consequent birth of our Lord at Bethlehem. She, as the Mother of our Lord, comes nearer to Him than any angel; nearer even than the Seraphim who surround Him, and cry continually, "Holy, Holy, Holy."

The two Archangels who have a special office in the Gospel are St. Michael and St. Gabriel—and they both of them are associated in the history of the Incarnation with Mary: St. Gabriel, when the Holy Ghost came down upon her; and St. Michael, when the Divine Child was born.

St. Gabriel hailed her as "Full of grace," and as "Blessed among women," and announced to her that the Holy Ghost would come down upon her, and that she would bear a Son who would be the Son of the Highest.

Of St. Michael's ministry to her, on the birth of that Divine Son, we learn in the Apocalypse, written by the Apostle St. John. We know our Lord came to set up the Kingdom of Heaven among men; and hardly was He born when He was assaulted by the powers of the world who wished to destroy Him. Herod sought to take His life, but he was defeated by St. Joseph's carrying His Mother and Him off into Egypt. But St. John in the Apocalypse tells us that Michael and his angels were the real guardians of Mother and Child, then and on other occasions.

First, St. John saw in vision "a great sign in heaven" (meaning by "heaven" the Church, or Kingdom of God), "a woman clothed with the sun, and with the moon under her feet, and on her head a crown of twelve stars"; and when she was about to be delivered of her Child there appeared "a great red dragon," that is, the evil spirit, ready "to devour her son" when He should be born. The Son was preserved by His own Divine power, but next the evil spirit persecuted her; St. Michael, however, and his angels came to the rescue and prevailed against him.

"There was a great battle," says the sacred writer; "Michael and his Angels fought with the dragon, and the dragon fought and his angels; and that great dragon was cast out, the old serpent, who is called the devil." Now, as then, the Blessed Mother of God has hosts of angels who do her service; and she is their Queen.

(2)

MARY IS THE "*SPECULUM JUSTITIÆ*," THE MIRROR OF JUSTICE

May 11

HERE first we must consider what is meant by *justice*, for the word as used by the Church has not that sense which it bears in ordinary English. By "justice" is not meant the virtue of fairness, equity, uprightness in our dealings; but it is a word denoting all virtues at once, a perfect, virtuous state of soul—righteousness, or moral perfection; so that it answers very nearly to what is meant by *sanctity*. Therefore when our Lady is called the "Mirror of Justice," it is meant to say that she is the Mirror of sanctity, holiness, supernatural goodness.

Next, what is meant by calling her a *mirror*? A mirror is a surface which reflects, as still water, polished steel, or a looking-glass. What did Mary reflect? She reflected our Lord—but *He* is infinite *Sanctity*. She then, as far as a creature could, reflected His Divine sanctity, and therefore she is the *Mirror* of Sanctity, or, as the Litany says, of *Justice*.

Do we ask how she came to reflect His Sanctity?—it was by living with Him. We see every day how like people get to each other who live with those they love. When they live with those whom they don't love, as, for instance, the members of a family who quarrel with each other, then the longer they live together the more unlike each other they become; but when they love each other, as husband and wife, parents and children, brothers with brothers or sisters, friends with friends, then in course of time they get surprisingly like each other. All of us perceive this; we are witnesses to it with our own eyes and ears—in the expression of their features, in their voice, in their walk, in their language, even in their handwriting, they become like each other; and so with regard to their minds, as in their opinions, their tastes, their pursuits. And again doubtless in the state of their souls, which we do not see, whether for good or for bad.

Now, consider that Mary loved her Divine Son with an unutterable love; and consider too she had Him all to herself for thirty years. Do we not see that, as she was full of grace *before* she conceived Him in her womb, she must have had a vast incomprehensible sanctity when she had lived close to God for thirty years?—a sanctity of an angelical order, reflecting back the attributes of God with a fulness and exactness of which no saint upon earth, or hermit, or holy virgin, can even remind us. Truly then she is the *Speculum Justitiæ*, the *Mirror* of Divine *Perfection*.

(3)

MARY IS THE "*SEDES SAPIENTIÆ*," THE SEAT OF WISDOM

May 12

MARY has this title in her Litany, because the Son of God, who is also called in Scripture the Word and Wisdom of God, once dwelt in her, and then, after His birth of her, was carried in her arms and seated in her lap in His first years. Thus, being, as it were, the human throne of Him who reigns in heaven, she is called the *Seat of Wisdom*. In the poet's words:—

> *His throne, thy bosom blest,*
> *O Mother undefiled,*
> *That Throne, if aught beneath the skies,*
> *Beseems the sinless Child.*

But the possession of her Son lasted beyond His infancy—He was under her rule, as St. Luke tells us, and lived with her in her house, till He went forth to preach—that is, for at least a whole thirty years. And this brings us to a reflection about her, cognate to that which was suggested to us yesterday by the title of "Mirror of Justice." For if such close and continued intimacy with her Son created in her a sanctity inconceivably great, must not also the knowledge which she gained during those many years from His conversation of present, past, and future, have been so large, and so profound, and so diversified, and so thorough, that, though she was a poor woman without human advantages, she must in her knowledge of creation, of the universe, and of history, have excelled the greatest of philosophers, and in her theological knowledge the greatest of theologians, and in her prophetic discernment the most favoured of prophets?

What was the grand theme of conversation between her and her Son but the nature, the attributes, the providence, and the works of Almighty God? Would not our Lord be ever glorifying the Father who sent Him? Would He not unfold to her the solemn eternal decrees, and the purposes and will of God? Would He not from time to time enlighten her in all those points of doctrine which have been first discussed and then settled in the Church from the time of the Apostles till now, and all that shall be till the end,—nay, these, and far more than these? All that is obscure, all that is fragmentary in revelation, would, so far as the knowledge is possible to man, be brought out to her in clearness and simplicity by Him who is the Light of the World.

And so of the events which are to come. God spoke to the Prophets: we have His communications to them in Scripture. But He spoke to them in figure and parable. There was one, viz., Moses, to whom He vouchsafed to speak face to face. "If there be among you a prophet of the Lord," God says, "I will appear to him in a vision, and I will speak to him in a dream. But it is not so with my servant Moses. . . . For I will speak to him mouth to mouth, and plainly, and not by riddles and figures doth he see the Lord." This was the great privilege of the inspired Lawgiver of the Jews; but how much was it below that of Mary! Moses had the privilege only now and then, from time to time; but Mary for thirty continuous years saw and heard Him, being all through that time face to face with Him, and being able to ask Him any question which she wished explained, and knowing that the answers she received were from the Eternal God, who neither deceives nor can be deceived.

(4)

MARY IS THE "*JANUA CŒLI*," THE GATE OF HEAVEN

May 13

MARY is called the *Gate* of Heaven, because it was through her that our Lord passed from heaven to earth. The Prophet Ezechiel, prophesying of Mary, says, "the gate shall be closed, it shall not be opened, and no man shall pass through it, since the Lord God of Israel has entered through it—and it shall be closed for the Prince, the Prince Himself shall sit in it."

Now this is fulfilled, not only in our Lord having taken flesh from her, and being her Son, but, moreover, in that she had a place in the economy of Redemption; it is fulfilled in her spirit and will, as well as in her body. Eve had a part in the fall of man, though it was Adam who was our representative, and whose sin made us sinners. It was Eve who began, and tempted Adam. Scripture says: "The woman saw that the tree was good to eat, and fair to the eyes, and delightful to behold; and she took of the fruit thereof, and did eat, and gave to her husband, and he did eat." It was fitting then in God's mercy that, as the woman began the *destruction* of the world, so woman should also begin its *recovery*, and that, as Eve opened the way for the fatal deed of the first Adam, so Mary should open the way for the great achievement of the second Adam, even our Lord Jesus Christ, who came to save the world by dying on the cross for it. Hence Mary is called by the holy Fathers a second and a better Eve, as having taken that first step in the salvation of mankind which Eve took in its ruin.

How, and when, did Mary take part, and the initial part, in the world's restoration? It was when the Angel Gabriel came to her to announce to her the great dignity which was to be her portion. St. Paul bids us "present our bodies to God as a reasonable service." We must not only pray with our lips, and fast, and do outward penance, and be chaste in our bodies; but we must be obedient, and pure in our minds. And so, as regards the Blessed Virgin, it was God's will that she should undertake *willingly* and with *full understanding* to be the Mother of our Lord, and not to be a mere passive instrument whose maternity would have no merit and no reward. The higher our gifts, the heavier our duties. It was no light lot to be so intimately near to the Redeemer of men, as she experienced afterwards when she suffered with him. Therefore, weighing well the Angel's words before giving her answer to them—first she asked whether so great an office would be a forfeiture of that Virginity which she had vowed. When the Angel told her no, then, with the full consent of a full heart, full of God's love to her and her own lowliness, she said, "Behold the handmaid of the Lord; be it done unto me according to thy word." It was by this consent that she became the *Gate of Heaven*.

(5)

MARY IS THE "*MATER CREATORIS*," THE MOTHER OF THE CREATOR

May 14

THIS is a title which, of all others, we should have thought it impossible for any creature to possess. At first sight we might be tempted to say that it throws into confusion our primary ideas of the Creator and the creature, the Eternal and the temporal, the Self-subsisting and the dependent; and yet on further consideration we shall see that we cannot refuse the title to Mary without denying the Divine Incarnation—that is, the great and fundamental truth of revelation, that God became man.

And this was seen from the first age of the Church. Christians were accustomed from the first to call the Blessed Virgin "The Mother of God," because they saw that it was impossible to deny her that title without denying St. John's words, "The Word" (that is, God the Son) "was made flesh."

And in no long time it was found necessary to proclaim this truth by the voice of an Ecumenical Council of the Church. For, in consequence of the dislike which men have of a mystery, the error sprang up that our Lord was not really God, but a man, differing from us in this merely—that God dwelt in Him, as God dwells in all good men, only in a higher measure; as the Holy Spirit dwelt in Angels and Prophets, as in a sort of Temple; or again, as our Lord now dwells in the Tabernacle in church. And then the bishops and faithful people found there was no other way of hindering this false, bad view being taught but by declaring distinctly, and making it a point of faith, that Mary was the Mother, not of man only, but of God. And since that time the title of Mary, as *Mother of God*, has become what is called a dogma, or article of faith, in the Church.

But this leads us to a larger view of the subject. Is this title as given to Mary more wonderful than the doctrine that God, without ceasing to be God, should become man? Is it more mysterious that Mary should be Mother of God, than that *God* should be *man*? Yet the latter, as I have said, is the elementary truth of revelation, witnessed by Prophets, Evangelists, and Apostles all through Scripture. And what can be more consoling and joyful than the wonderful promises which follow from this truth, that Mary is the Mother of God—the great wonder, namely, that we become the brethren of our God; that, if we live well, and die in the grace of God, we shall all of us hereafter be taken up by our Incarnate God to that place where angels dwell; that our bodies shall be raised from the dust, and be taken to Heaven; that we shall be really united to God; that we shall be partakers of the Divine nature; that each of us, soul and body, shall be plunged into the abyss of glory which surrounds the Almighty; that we shall see Him, and share His blessedness, according to the text, "Whosoever shall do the will of My Father that is in Heaven, the same is My brother, and sister, and mother."

(6)

MARY IS THE "*MATER CHRISTI*," THE MOTHER OF CHRIST

May 15

Each of the titles of Mary has its own special meaning and drift, and may be made the subject of a distinct meditation. She is invoked by us as the *Mother of Christ.* What is the force of thus addressing her? It is to bring before us that she it is whom from the first was prophesied of, and associated with the hopes and prayers of all holy men, of all true worshippers of God, of all who "looked for the redemption of Israel" in every age before that redemption came.

Our Lord was called the Christ, or the Messias, by the Jewish prophets and the Jewish people. The two words Christ and Messias mean the same. They mean in English the "Anointed." In the old time there were three great ministries or offices by means of which God spoke to His chosen people, the Israelites, or, as they were afterward called, the Jews, viz., that of Priest, that of King, and that of Prophet. Those who were chosen by God for one or other of these offices were solemnly anointed with oil— oil signifying the grace of God, which was given to them for the due performance of their high duties. But our Lord was all three, a Priest, a Prophet, and a King—a Priest, because He offered Himself as a sacrifice for our sins; a Prophet, because He revealed to us the Holy Law of God; and a King, because He rules over us. Thus He is the one true Christ.

It was in expectation of this great Messias that the chosen people, the Jews, or Israelites, or Hebrews (for these are different names for the same people), looked out from age to age. He was to come to set all things right. And next to this great question which occupied their minds, namely, *When* was He to come, was the question, *Who* was to be His Mother? It had been told them from the first, not that He should come from heaven, but that He should be born of a Woman. At the time of the fall of Adam, God had said that the *seed* of the *Woman* should bruise the Serpent's head. Who, then, was to be that Woman thus significantly pointed out to the fallen race of Adam? At the end of many centuries, it was further revealed to the Jews that the great Messias, or Christ, the seed of the Woman, should be born of their race, and of one particular tribe of the twelve tribes into which that race was divided. From that time every woman of that tribe hoped to have the great privilege of herself being the Mother of the Messias, or Christ; for it stood to reason, since He was so great, the Mother must be great, and good, and blessed too. Hence it was, among other reasons, that they thought so highly of the marriage state, because, not knowing the mystery of the miraculous conception of the Christ when He was actually to come, they thought that the marriage rite was the ordinance necessary for His coming.

Hence it was, if Mary had been as other women, she would have longed for marriage, as opening on her the prospect of bearing the great King. But she was too humble and too pure for such thoughts. She had been inspired to choose that better way of serving God which had not been made known to the Jews—the state of Virginity. She preferred to be His Spouse to being His Mother. Accordingly, when the Angel Gabriel announced to her her high destiny, she shrank from it till she was assured that it would not oblige her to revoke her purpose of a virgin life devoted to her God.

Thus was it that she became the Mother of the Christ, not in that way which pious women for so many ages had expected Him, but, declining the grace of such maternity, she gained it by means of a higher grace. And this is the full meaning of St. Elizabeth's words, when the Blessed Virgin came to visit her, which we use in the Hail Mary: "Blessed art thou among women, and blessed is the fruit of thy womb." And therefore it is that in the Devotion called the "*Crown of Twelve Stars*" we give praise to God the Holy Ghost, through whom she was *both* Virgin *and* Mother.

(7)

MARY IS THE "*MATER SALVATORIS*,"
THE MOTHER OF THE SAVIOUR

May 16

Here again, as in our reflections of yesterday, we must understand what is meant by calling our Lord a Saviour, in order to understand why it is used to form one of the titles given to Mary in her Litany.

The special name by which our Lord was known before His coming was, as we found yesterday, that of Messias, or Christ. Thus He was known to the Jews. But when He actually showed Himself on earth, He was known by three new titles, the Son of God, the Son of Man, and the Saviour; the first expressive of His Divine Nature, the second of His Human, the third of His Personal Office. Thus the Angel who appeared to Mary called Him the Son of God; the angel who appeared to Joseph called Him *Jesus*, which means in English, *Saviour*; and so the Angels, too, called Him a Saviour when they appeared to the shepherds. But He Himself specially calls Himself the Son of Man.

Not Angels only call Him Saviour, but those two greatest of the Apostles, St. Peter and St. Paul, in their first preachings. St. Peter says He is "a Prince and a Saviour," and St. Paul says, "a Saviour, Jesus." And both Angels and Apostles tell us why He is so called—because He has rescued us from the power of the evil spirit, and from the guilt and misery of our sins. Thus the Angel says to Joseph, "Thou shalt call His name Jesus, *for* He shall save His people from their *sins*;" and St. Peter, "God has exalted Him to be Prince and Saviour, to give repentance to Israel, and remission of sins." And He says Himself, "The Son of Man is come to seek and to *save that which is lost.*"

Now let us consider how this affects our thoughts of Mary. To rescue slaves from the power of the Enemy implies a conflict. Our Lord, because He was a Saviour, was a warrior. He could not deliver the captives without a fight, nor without personal suffering. Now, who are they who especially hate wars? A heathen poet answers. "Wars," he says, "are hated by *Mothers*." Mothers are just those who especially suffer in a war. They may glory in the honour gained by their children; but still such glorying does not wipe out one particle of the long pain, the anxiety, the suspense, the desolation, and the anguish which the mother of a soldier feels. So it was with Mary. For thirty years she was blessed with the continual presence of her Son—nay, she had Him in subjection. But the time came when that war called for Him for which He had come upon earth. Certainly He came, not simply to be the Son of Mary, but to be the Saviour of Man, and therefore at length He parted from her. She knew *then* what it was to be the mother of a soldier. He left her side; she saw Him no longer; she tried in vain to get near Him. He had for years lived in her embrace, and after that, at least in her dwelling—but now, in His own words, "The Son of Man had not where to lay His head." And then, when years had run out, she heard of His arrest, His mock trial, and His passion. At last she got near Him— when and where?—on the way to Calvary: and when He had been lifted upon the Cross. And at length she held Him again in her arms: yes—when He was dead. True, He rose from the dead; but still she did not thereby gain Him, for He ascended on high, and she did not at once follow Him. No, she remained on earth many years—in the care, indeed, of His dearest Apostle, St. John. But what was even the holiest of men compared with her own Son, and Him the Son of God? O Holy Mary, Mother of our Saviour, in this meditation we have now suddenly passed from the Joyful Mysteries to the Sorrowful, from Gabriel's Annunciation to thee, to the Seven Dolours. That, then, will be the next series of Meditations which we make about thee.

III

OUR LADY'S DOLOURS

(1)

MARY IS THE "*REGINA MARTYRUM*," THE QUEEN OF MARTYRS[1]

May 17

W HY is she so called?—she who never had any blow, or wound, or other injury to her consecrated person. How can she be exalted over those whose bodies suffered the most ruthless violences and the keenest torments for our Lord's sake? She is, indeed, Queen of all Saints, of those who "walk with Christ in white, for they are worthy;" but how of those "who were slain for the Word of God, and for the testimony which they held?"

To answer this question, it must be recollected that the pains of the soul may be as fierce as those of the body. Bad men who are now in hell, and the elect of God who are in purgatory, are suffering only in their souls, for their bodies are still in the dust; yet how severe is that suffering! And perhaps most people who have lived long can bear witness in their own persons to a sharpness of distress which was like a sword cutting them, to a weight and force of sorrow which seemed to throw them down, though bodily pain there was none.

What an overwhelming horror it must have been for

[1] From this day to the end of the month, being the Novena, and Octave of St. Philip, the Meditations are shorter than the foregoing. — J.H.N.

the Blessed Mary to witness the Passion and the Crucifixion of her Son! Her anguish was, as Holy Simeon
had announced to her, at the time of that Son's Presentation in the Temple, a sword piercing her soul. If our Lord
Himself could not bear the prospect of what was before
Him, and was covered in the thought of it with a bloody
sweat, His soul thus acting upon His body, does not this
show how great mental pain can be? and would it have
been wonderful though Mary's head and heart had given
way as she stood under His Cross?

Thus is she most truly the Queen of *Martyrs*.

(2)

MARY IS THE "*VAS INSIGNE DEVOTIONIS*," THE MOST DEVOUT VIRGIN

May 18

T O be *devout* is to be devoted. We know what is meant by a devoted wife or daughter. It is one whose thoughts centre in the person so deeply loved, so tenderly cherished. She follows him about with her eyes; she is ever seeking some means of serving him; and, if her services are very small in their character, that only shows how intimate they are, and how incessant. And especially if the object of her love be weak, or in pain, or near to die, still more intensely does she live in his life, and know nothing but him.

This intense devotion towards our Lord, forgetting self in love for Him, is instanced in St. Paul, who says, "I know nothing but Jesus Christ and Him crucified." And again, "I live, [yet] now not I, but Christ liveth in me; and [the life] that I now live in the flesh, I live in the faith of the Son of God, who loved me, and delivered Himself for me."[1]

But great as was St. Paul's devotion to our Lord, much greater was that of the Blessed Virgin; because she was His Mother, and because she had Him and all His sufferings actually before her eyes, and because she had the long intimacy of thirty years with Him, and because she

---

[1] "Vivo autem, jam non ego: vivit vero in me Christus. Quod autem nunc vivo in carne: in fide vivo Filii Dei, qui dilexit me, et tradidit semetipsum pro me." (Gal. ii. 20.)

was from her special sanctity so ineffably near to Him in spirit. When, then, He was mocked, bruised, scourged, and nailed to the Cross, she felt as keenly as if every indignity and torture inflicted on Him was struck at herself. She could have cried out in agony at every pang of His.

This is called her *com*passion, or her suffering with her Son, and it arose from this that she was the "Vas insigne *devotionis.*"

(3)

MARY IS THE "*VAS HONORABILE*,"
THE VESSEL OF HONOUR

May 19

S<small>T. PAUL</small> calls elect souls vessels of honour: of honour, because they are elect or chosen: and vessels, because, through the love of God, they are filled with God's heavenly and holy grace. How much more then is Mary a vessel of honour by reason of her having within her, not only the grace of God, but the very Son of God, formed as regards His flesh and blood out of her!

But this title "*honorabile*," as applied to Mary, admits of a further and special meaning. She was a martyr without the rude *dis*honour which accompanied the sufferings of martyrs. The martyrs were seized, haled about, thrust into prison with the vilest criminals, and assailed with the most blasphemous words and foulest speeches which Satan could inspire. Nay, such was the unutterable trial also of the holy women, young ladies, the spouses of Christ, whom the heathen seized, tortured, and put to death. Above all, our Lord Himself, whose sanctity was greater than any created excellence or vessel of grace— even He, as we know well, was buffeted, stripped, scourged, mocked, dragged about, and then stretched, nailed, lifted up on a high cross, to the gaze of a brutal multitude.

But He, who bore the sinner's shame for sinners, spared His Mother, who was sinless, this supreme indignity. Not in the body, but in the soul, she suffered. True, in His Agony she was agonised; in His Passion she suffered a fellow-passion; she was crucified with Him; the spear that pierced His breast pierced through her spirit. Yet there were no visible signs of this intimate martyrdom; she stood up, still, collected, motionless, solitary, under the Cross of her Son, surrounded by Angels, and shrouded in her virginal sanctity from the notice of all who were taking part in His Crucifixion.

(4)

MARY IS THE "*VAS SPIRITUALE*,"
THE SPIRITUAL VESSEL

May 20

To be *spiritual* is to live in the world of spirits—as St. Paul says, "Our conversation is in Heaven." To be *spiritually*-minded is to see by faith all those good and holy beings who actually surround us, though we see them not with our bodily eyes; to see them by faith as vividly as we see the things of earth—the green country, the blue sky, and the brilliant sunshine. Hence it is that, when saintly souls are favoured with heavenly visions, these visions are but the extraordinary continuations and the crown, by a divine intuition, of objects which, by the ordinary operation of grace, are ever before their minds.

These visions consoled and strengthened the Blessed Virgin in all her sorrows. The Angels who were around her understood her, and she understood them, with a directness which is not to be expected in their intercourse with us who have inherited from Adam the taint of sin. Doubtless; but still let us never forget that as she in her sorrows was comforted by Angels, so it is our privilege in the many trials of life to be comforted, in our degree, by the same heavenly messengers of the Most High; nay, by Almighty God Himself, the third Person of the Holy Trinity, who has taken on Himself the office of being our Paraclete, or Present Help.

Let all those who are in trouble take this comfort to themselves, if they are trying to lead a spiritual life. If they call on God, He will answer them. Though they have no earthly friend, they have Him, who, as He felt for His Mother when He was on the Cross, now that He is in His glory feels for the lowest and feeblest of His people.

(5)

MARY IS THE "*CONSOLATRIX AFFLICTORUM*," THE CONSOLER OF THE AFFLICTED

May 21

St. PAUL says that his Lord comforted him in all his tribulations, that he also might be able to comfort them who are in distress, by the encouragement which he received from God. This is the secret of true consolation: those are able to comfort others who, in their own case, have been much tried, and have felt the need of consolation, and have received it. So of our Lord Himself it is said: "In that He Himself hath suffered and been tempted, He is able to succour those also that are tempted."

And this too is why the Blessed Virgin is the comforter of the afflicted. We all know how special a mother's consolation is, and we are allowed to call Mary our Mother from the time that our Lord from the Cross established the relation of mother and son between her and St. John. And she especially can console us because she suffered more than mothers in general. Women, at least delicate women, are commonly shielded from rude experience of the highways of the world; but she, after our Lord's Ascension, was sent out into foreign lands almost as the Apostles were, a sheep among wolves. In spite of all St. John's care of her, which was as great as was St. Joseph's in her younger days, she, more than all the saints of God, was a stranger and a pilgrim upon earth, in proportion to her greater love of Him who *had* been on earth, and had gone away. As, when our Lord was an Infant, she had to flee across the desert to the heathen Egypt, so, when He had ascended on high, she had to go on shipboard to the heathen Ephesus, where she lived and died.

O ye who are in the midst of rude neighbours or scoffing companions, or of wicked acquaintance, or of spiteful enemies, and are helpless, invoke the aid of Mary by the memory of her own sufferings among the heathen Greeks and the heathen Egyptians.

(6)

MARY IS THE "*VIRGO PRUDENTISSIMA,*" THE MOST PRUDENT VIRGIN

May 22

IT may not appear at first sight how the virtue of prudence is connected with the trials and sorrows of our Lady's life; yet there is a point of view from which we are reminded of her prudence by those trials. It must be recollected that she is not only the great instance of the contemplative life, but also of the practical; and the practical life is at once a life of penance and of prudence, if it is to be well discharged. Now Mary was as full of external work and hard service as any Sister of Charity at this day. Of course her duties varied according to the seasons of her life, as a young maiden, as a wife, as a mother, and as a widow; but still her life was full of duties day by day and hour by hour. As a stranger in Egypt, she had duties towards the poor heathen among whom she was thrown. As a dweller in Nazareth, she had her duties towards her kinsfolk and neighbours. She had her duties, though unrecorded, during those years in which our Lord was preaching and proclaiming His Kingdom. After He had left this earth, she had her duties towards the Apostles, and especially towards the Evangelists. She had duties towards the Martyrs, and to the Confessors in prison; to the sick, to the ignorant, and to the poor. Afterwards, she had to seek with St. John another and a heathen country, where her happy death took place. But before that death, how much must she have suffered in her life amid an idolatrous population! Doubtless the Angels screened her eyes from the worst crimes there committed. Still, she was full of duties there—and in consequence she was full of merit. All her acts were perfect, all were the best that could be done. Now, always to be awake, guarded, fervent, so as to be able to act not only without sin, but in the best possible way, in the varying circumstances of each day, denotes a life of untiring mindfulness. But of such a life, Prudence is the presiding virtue. It is, then, through the pains and sorrows of her earthly pilgrimage that we are able to invoke her as the *Virgo prudentissima*.

(7)

MARY IS THE "*TURRIS EBURNEA*," THE IVORY TOWER

May 23

A TOWER is a fabric which rises higher and more conspicuous than other objects in its neighbourhood. Thus, when we say a man "towers" over his fellows, we mean to signify that they look small in comparison of him.

This quality of greatness is instanced in the Blessed Virgin. Though she suffered more keen and intimate anguish at our Lord's Passion and Crucifixion than any of the Apostles by reason of her being His Mother, yet consider how much more noble she was amid her deep distress than they were. When our Lord underwent His agony, they slept for sorrow. They could not wrestle with their deep disappointment and despondency; they could not master it; it confused, numbed, and overcame their senses. And soon after, when St. Peter was asked by bystanders whether he was not one of our Lord's disciples, he denied it.

Nor was he alone in this cowardice. The Apostles, one and all, forsook our Lord and fled, though St. John returned. Nay, still further, they even lost faith in Him, and thought all the great expectations which He had raised in them had ended in a failure. How different this even from the brave conduct of St. Mary Magdalen! and still more from that of the Virgin Mother! It is expressly noted of her that she *stood* by the Cross. She did not grovel in the dust, but *stood upright* to receive the blows, the stabs, which the long Passion of her Son inflicted upon her every moment.

In this magnanimity and generosity in suffering she is, as compared with the Apostles, fitly imaged as a *Tower*. But towers, it may be said, are huge, rough, heavy, obtrusive, graceless structures, for the purposes of war, not of peace; with nothing of the beautifulness, refinement, and finish which are conspicuous in Mary. It is true: therefore she is called the Tower of *Ivory*, to suggest to us, by the brightness, purity, and exquisiteness of that material, how transcendent is the loveliness and the gentleness of the Mother of God.

IV

ON THE ASSUMPTION

(1)

MARY IS THE "*SANCTA DEI GENITRIX*," THE HOLY MOTHER OF GOD

May 24

As soon as we apprehend by faith the great fundamental truth that Mary is the Mother of God, other wonderful truths follow in its train; and one of these is that she was exempt from the ordinary lot of mortals, which is not only to die, but to become earth to earth, ashes to ashes, dust to dust. Die she must, and die she did, as her Divine Son died, for He was man; but various reasons have approved themselves to holy writers, why, although her body was for a while separated from her soul and consigned to the tomb, yet it did not remain there, but was speedily united to her soul again, and raised by our Lord to a new and eternal life of heavenly glory.

And the most obvious reason for so concluding is this—that *other* servants of God have been raised from the grave by the power of God, and it is not to be supposed that our Lord would have granted any such privilege to anyone else without also granting it to His own Mother.

We are told by St. Matthew, that after our Lord's death upon the Cross "the graves were opened, and many bodies of the saints that had slept"—that is, slept the sleep of death, "arose, and coming out of the tombs after His Resurrection, came into the Holy City, and appeared to many." St. Matthew says, "*many* bodies of the Saints"—that is, the holy Prophets, Priests, and Kings of former times—rose again in anticipation of the last day.

Can we suppose that Abraham, or David, or Isaias, or Ezechias, should have been thus favoured, and not God's own Mother? Had she not a claim on the love of her Son to have what any others had? Was she not nearer to Him than the greatest of the Saints before her? And is it conceivable that the law of the grave should admit of relaxation in their case, and not in hers? Therefore we confidently say that our Lord, having preserved her from sin and the consequences of sin by His Passion, lost no time in pouring out the full merits of that Passion upon her body as well as her soul.

(2)

MARY IS THE "*MATER INTEMERATA*," THE SINLESS MOTHER

May 25

ANOTHER consideration which has led devout minds to believe in the Assumption of our Lady into heaven after her death, without waiting for the general resurrection at the last day, is furnished by the doctrine of her Immaculate Conception.

By her Immaculate Conception is meant, that not only did she never commit any sin whatever, even venial, in thought, word, or deed, but further than this, that the guilt of Adam, or what is called original sin, never was her guilt, as it is the guilt attaching to all other descendants of Adam.

By her Assumption is meant that not only her soul, but her body also, was taken up to heaven upon her death, so that there was no long period of her sleeping in the grave, as is the case with others, even great Saints, who wait for the last day for the resurrection of their bodies.

One reason for believing in our Lady's Assumption is that her Divine Son loved her too much to let her body remain in the grave. A second reason—that now before us—is this, that she was not only dear to the Lord as a mother is dear to a son, but also that she was so transcendently holy, so full, so overflowing with grace. Adam and Eve were created upright and sinless, and had a large measure of God's grace bestowed upon them; and, in consequence, their bodies would never have crumbled into dust, had they not sinned; upon which it was said to them, "Dust thou art, and unto dust thou shalt return." If Eve, the beautiful daughter of God, never would have become dust and ashes unless she had sinned, shall we not say that Mary, having never sinned, retained the gift which Eve by sinning lost? What had Mary done to forfeit the privilege given to our first parents in the beginning? Was her comeliness to be turned into corruption, and her fine gold to become dim, without reason assigned? Impossible. Therefore we believe that, though she died for a short hour, as did our Lord Himself, yet, like Him, and by His Almighty power, she was raised again from the grave.

(3)

MARY IS THE "*ROSA MYSTICA*," THE MYSTICAL ROSE

May 26

MARY is the most beautiful flower that ever was seen in the spiritual world. It is by the power of God's grace that from this barren and desolate earth there have ever sprung up at all flowers of holiness and glory. And Mary is the Queen of them. She is the Queen of spiritual flowers; and therefore she is called the *Rose*, for the rose is fitly called of all flowers the most beautiful.

But moreover, she is the *Mystical*, or *hidden* Rose; for mystical means hidden. How is she now "hidden" from us more than are other saints? What means this singular appellation, which we apply to her specially? The answer to this question introduces us to a third reason for believing in the reunion of her sacred body to her soul, and its assumption into heaven soon after her death, instead of its lingering in the grave until the General Resurrection at the last day.

It is this:—if her body was not taken into heaven, where is it? how comes it that it is hidden from us? why do we not hear of her tomb as being here or there? why are not pilgrimages made to it? why are not relics producible of her, as of the saints in general? Is it not even a natural instinct which makes us reverent towards the places where our dead are buried? We bury our great men honourably. St. Peter speaks of the sepulchre of David as known in his day, though he had died many hundred years before. When our Lord's body was taken down from the Cross, He was placed in an honourable tomb. Such too had been the honour already paid to St. John Baptist, his tomb being spoken of by St. Mark as generally known. Christians from the earliest times went from other countries to Jerusalem to see the holy places. And, when the time of persecution was over, they paid still more attention to the bodies of the Saints, as of St. Stephen, St. Mark, St. Barnabas, St. Peter, St. Paul, and other Apostles and Martyrs. These were transported to great cities, and portions of them sent to this place or that. Thus, from the first to this day it has been a great feature and characteristic of the Church to be most tender and reverent towards the bodies of the Saints. Now, if there was anyone who more than all would be preciously taken care of, it would be our Lady. Why then do we hear nothing of the Blessed Virgin's body and its separate relics? Why is she thus the *hidden* Rose? Is it conceivable that they who had been so reverent and careful of the bodies of the Saints and Martyrs should neglect her—her who was the Queen of Martyrs and the Queen of Saints, who was the very Mother of our Lord? It is impossible. Why then is she thus the *hidden* Rose? Plainly because that sacred body is in heaven, not on earth.

(4)

MARY IS THE "*TURRIS DAVIDICA*," THE TOWER OF DAVID

May 27

A TOWER in its simplest idea is a fabric for defence against enemies. David, King of Israel, built for this purpose a notable tower; and as he is a figure or type of our Lord, so is his tower a figure denoting our Lord's Virgin Mother.

She is called the *Tower* of David because she had so signally fulfilled the office of defending her Divine Son from the assaults of His foes. It is customary with those who are not Catholics to fancy that the honours we pay to her interfere with the supreme worship which we pay to Him; that in Catholic teaching she eclipses Him. But this is the very reverse of the truth.

For if Mary's glory is so very great, how cannot His be greater still who is the Lord and God of Mary? He is infinitely above His Mother; and all that grace which filled her is but the overflowings and superfluities of His incomprehensible Sanctity. And history teaches us the same lesson. Look at the Protestant countries which threw off all devotion to her three centuries ago, under the notion that to put her from their thoughts would be exalting the praises of her Son. Has that consequence really followed from their profane conduct towards her? Just the reverse—the countries, Germany, Switzerland, England, which so acted, have in great measure ceased to worship Him, and have given up their belief in His

Divinity; while the Catholic Church, wherever she is to be found, adores Christ as true God and true Man, as firmly as ever she did; and strange indeed would it be, if it ever happened otherwise. Thus Mary is the "Tower of David."

(5)

MARY IS THE "*VIRGO POTENS*," THE POWERFUL VIRGIN

May 28

THIS great universe, which we see by day and by night, or what is called the natural world, is ruled by fixed laws, which the Creator has imposed upon it, and by those wonderful laws is made secure against any substantial injury or loss. One portion of it may conflict with another, and there may be changes in it internally; but, viewed as a whole, it is adapted to stand for ever. Hence the Psalmist says, "He has established the world, which shall not be moved."

Such is the world of nature; but there is another and still more wonderful world. There is a power which avails to alter and subdue this visible world, and to suspend and counteract its laws; that is, the world of Angels and Saints, of Holy Church and her children; and the weapon by which they master its laws is the power of prayer.

By prayer all this may be done, which naturally is impossible. Noe prayed, and God said that there never again should be a flood to drown the race of man. Moses prayed, and ten grievous plagues fell upon the land of Egypt. Josue prayed, and the sun stood still. Samuel prayed, and thunder and rain came in wheat-harvest. Elias prayed, and brought down fire from heaven. Eliseus prayed, and the dead came to life. Ezechias prayed and the vast army of the Assyrians was smitten and perished.

This is why the Blessed Virgin is called *Powerful*—nay, sometimes, *All*-power, because she has, more than anyone else, more than all Angels and Saints, this great, prevailing gift of prayer. No one has access to the Almighty as His Mother has; none has merit such as hers. Her Son will deny her nothing that she asks; and herein lies her power. While she defends the Church, neither height nor depth, neither men nor evil spirits, neither great monarchs, nor craft of man, nor popular violence, can avail to harm us; for human life is short, but Mary reigns above, a Queen for ever.

(6)

MARY IS THE "*AUXILIUM CHRISTIANORUM*," THE HELP OF CHRISTIANS

May 29

OUR glorious Queen, since her Assumption on high, has been the minister of numberless services to the elect people of God upon earth, and to His Holy Church. This title of "Help of Christians" relates to those services of which the Divine Office, while recording and referring to the occasion on which it was given her, recounts five, connecting them more or less with the Rosary.

The first was on the first institution of the Devotion of the Rosary by St. Dominic, when, with the aid of the Blessed Virgin, he succeeded in arresting and overthrowing the formidable heresy of the Albigenses in the South of France.

The second was the great victory gained by the Christian fleet over the powerful Turkish Sultan, in answer to the intercession of Pope St. Pius V., and the prayers of the Associations of the Rosary all over the Christian world; in lasting memory of which wonderful mercy Pope Pius introduced her title "*Auxilium Christianorum*" into her Litany; and Pope Gregory XIII., who followed him, dedicated the first Sunday in October, the day of the victory, to Our Lady of the Rosary.

The third was, in the words of the Divine Office, "the glorious victory won at Vienna, under the guardianship of the Blessed Virgin, over the most savage Sultan of the Turks, who was trampling on the necks of the Christians;

in perpetual memory of which benefit Pope Innocent XI. dedicated the Sunday in the Octave of her Nativity as the feast of her *august Name.*"

The fourth instance of her aid was the victory over the innumerable force of the same Turks in Hungary on the Feast of St. Mary ad Nives, in answer to the solemn supplication of the Confraternities of the Rosary; on occasion of which Popes Clement XI. and Benedict XIII. gave fresh honour and privilege to the Devotion of the Rosary.

And the fifth was her restoration of the Pope's temporal power, at the beginning of this century, after Napoleon the First, Emperor of the French, had taken it from the Holy See; on which occasion Pope Pius VII. set apart May 24, the day of this mercy, as the Feast of the *Help of Christians,* for a perpetual thanksgiving.

(7)

MARY IS THE "*VIRGO FIDELIS*," THE MOST FAITHFUL VIRGIN

May 30

THIS is one of the titles of the Blessed Virgin, which is especially hers from the time of her Assumption and glorious Coronation at the right hand of her Divine Son. How it belongs to her will be plain by considering some of those other instances in which faithfulness is spoken of in Holy Scripture.

The word *faithfulness* means loyalty to a superior, or exactness in fulfilling an engagement. In the latter sense it is applied even to Almighty God Himself, who, in His great love for us, has vouchsafed to limit His own power in action by His word of promise and His covenant with His creatures. He has given His word that, if we will take Him for our portion and put ourselves into His hands, He will guide us through all trials and temptations, and bring us safe to heaven. And to encourage and inspirit us, He reminds us, in various passages of Scripture that He is the *faithful* God, the *faithful* Creator.

And so, His true saints and servants have the special title of "Faithful," as being true to Him as He is to them; as being simply obedient to his will, zealous for His honour, observant of the sacred interests which He has committed to their keeping. Thus Abraham is called the Faithful; Moses is declared to be faithful in all his house; David, on this account, is called the "man after God's own heart"; St. Paul returns thanks that "God accounted him faithful"; and, at the last day, God will say to all those who have well employed their talents, "Well done, good and faithful servant."

Mary, in like manner, is pre-eminently faithful to her Lord and Son. Let no one for an instant suppose that she is not supremely zealous for His honour, or, as those who are not Catholics fancy, that to exalt her is to be unfaithful to Him. Her true servants are still more truly His. Well as she rewards her friends, she would deem him no friend, but a traitor, who preferred her to Him. As He is zealous for her honour, so is she for His. He is the Fount of grace, and all her gifts are from His goodness. O Mary, teach us ever to worship thy Son as the One Creator, and to be devout to thee as the most highly favoured of creatures.

(8)

MARY IS THE "*STELLA MATUTINA*," THE MORNING STAR—AFTER THE DARK NIGHT, BUT ALWAYS HERALDING THE SUN

May 31

W HAT is the nearest approach in the way of symbols, in this world of sight and sense, to represent to us the glories of that higher world which is beyond our bodily perceptions? What are the truest tokens and promises here, poor though they may be, of what one day we hope to see hereafter, as being beautiful and rare? Whatever they may be, surely the Blessed Mother of God may claim them as her own. And so it is; two of them are ascribed to her as her titles, in her Litany—the stars above, and flowers below. She is at once the *Rosa Mystica* and the *Stella Matutina*.

And of these two, both of them well suited to her, the Morning Star becomes her best, and that for three reasons.

First, the rose belongs to this earth, but the star is placed in high heaven. Mary now has no part in this nether world. No change, no violence from fire, water, earth, or air, affects the stars above; and they show themselves, ever bright and marvellous, in all regions of this globe, and to all the tribes of men.

And next, the rose has but a short life; its decay is as sure as it was graceful and fragrant in its noon. But Mary, like the stars, abides for ever, as lustrous now as she was on the day of her Assumption; as pure and perfect, when her Son comes to judgment, as she is now.

Lastly, it is Mary's prerogative to be the *Morning* Star, which heralds in the sun. She does not shine for herself, or from herself, but she is the reflection of her and our Redeemer, and she glorifies Him. When she appears in the darkness, we know that He is close at hand. He is Alpha and Omega, the First and the Last, the Beginning and the End. Behold He comes quickly, and His reward is with Him, to render to everyone according to his works. "Surely I come quickly. Amen. Come, Lord Jesus."

MEMORANDUM

ON THE IMMACULATE CONCEPTION[1]

(1)

1. IT is so difficult for me to enter into the feelings of a person who *understands* the doctrine of the Immaculate Conception, and yet objects to it, that I am diffident about attempting to speak on the subject. I was accused of holding it, in one of the first books I wrote, twenty years ago.[2] On the other hand, this very fact may be an argument against an objector—for why should it not have been difficult to me at that time, if there were a real difficulty in receiving it?

2. Does not the objector consider that *Eve* was created, or born, *without* original sin? Why does not *this* shock him? Would he have been inclined to *worship* Eve in that first estate of hers? Why, then, Mary?

---

[1] This Memorandum is given as written off by the Cardinal for Mr. R. I. Wilberforce, formerly Archdeacon Wilberforce, to aid him in meeting the objections urged by some Protestant friends against the doctrine of the Immaculate Conception. The *italics* are the Cardinal's.

The Memorandum and the Extract which follows are inserted as an endeavour to partially meet the Cardinal's wish that an instruction on the subject of each of the four portions of the Litany should accompany each division; a wish which the Cardinal could not himself fulfil owing to his continued disappointment in regard to the loss of certain notes which he had intended to make use of. It was not till he felt himself too ill to begin writing afresh that he knew the notes would not be forthcoming at all, and he therefore recommended the use of something already written by him to supply the want, mentioning in particular his sermon on the Annunciation. This disappointment also hindered his giving the Meditations his final revision. [W. N.]

[2] *Parochial and Plain Sermons*, vol. ii.

3. Does he not believe that St. John Baptist had the grace of God—*i.e.*, was regenerated, even before his birth? What do we believe of Mary, but that grace was given her at a still earlier period? *All* we say is, that grace was given her from the first moment of her existence.

4. We do not say that she did not owe her salvation to the death of her Son. Just the contrary, we say that she, of all mere children of Adam, is in the truest sense the fruit and the purchase of His Passion. He has done for her more than for anyone else. To others He gives grace and regeneration at a *point* in their earthly existence; to her, from the very beginning.

5. We do not make her *nature* different from others. Though, as St. Austin says, we do not like to name her in the same breath with mention of sin, yet, certainly she *would* have been a frail being, like Eve, *without* the grace of God. A more abundant gift of grace made her what she was from the first. It was not her *nature* which secured her perseverance, but the excess of grace which hindered Nature acting as Nature ever will act. There is no difference in *kind* between her and us, though an inconceivable difference of *degree*. She and we are both simply saved by the grace of Christ.

Thus, sincerely speaking, I really do not see *what* the difficulty is, and should like it set down distinctly in words. I will add that the above statement is no private statement of my own. I never heard of any Catholic who ever had any other view. I never heard of any other put forth by anyone.

(2)

Next, Was it a primitive doctrine? No one can add to revelation. That was given once for all;—but as time goes on, what was given once for all is understood more and more clearly. The greatest Fathers and Saints in this sense have been in error, that, since the matter of which they spoke had not been sifted, and the Church had not spoken, they did not in their *expressions do justice to their own real meaning*. E.g. (1), the Athanasian Creed says that the Son is "immensus" (in the Protestant version, "incomprehensible"). Bishop Bull, though defending the ante-Nicene Fathers, says that it is a marvel that "nearly all of them have the appearance of being *ignorant* of the invisibility and immensity of the Son of God." Do I for a moment think they *were* ignorant? No, but that they spoke *inconsistently*, because they were opposing other errors, and did not observe what they said. When the heretic Arius arose, and they saw the use which was made of their admissions, the Fathers retracted them.

(2) The great Fathers of the fourth century seem, most of them, to consider our Lord in His human nature *ignorant*, and to have grown in knowledge, as St. Luke *seems* to say. This doctrine was *anathematized* by the Church in the next century, when the Monophysites arose.

(3) In like manner, there are Fathers who seem to deny original sin, eternal punishment, &c.

(4) Further, the famous symbol "Consubstantial," as applied to the Son, which is in the Nicene Creed, was *condemned* by a great Council of Antioch, with Saints in it, seventy years before. Why? Because that Council meant something else by the word.

Now, as to the doctrine of the Immaculate Conception, it was *implied* in early times, and never *denied*. In the Middle Ages it *was* denied by St. Thomas and by St. Bernard, but they took the phrase in a different sense from that in which the Church now takes it. They understood it with reference to our Lady's mother, and thought it contradicted the text, "In sin hath my mother conceived me"—whereas *we* do not speak of the Immaculate Conception except as relating to Mary; and the other doctrine (which St. Thomas and St. Bernard did oppose) *is* really heretical.

(3)

As to primitive notion about our Blessed Lady, really, the frequent contrast of Mary with Eve seems very strong indeed. It is found in St. Justin, St. Irenaeus, and Tertullian, three of the earliest Fathers, and in three distinct continents—Gaul, Africa, and Syria. For instance, "the knot formed by Eve's disobedience was untied by the obedience of Mary; that what the Virgin Eve tied through unbelief, that the Virgin Mary unties through faith." Again, "The Virgin Mary becomes the Advocate (Paraclete) of the Virgin Eve, that *as* mankind has been bound to death *through* a Virgin, *through* a Virgin it may be saved, the balance being preserved, a Virgin's disobedience by a Virgin's obedience" (St. Irenaeus, *Haer.* v. 19). Again, "As Eve, becoming disobedient, became *the cause* of death to herself and *to all mankind, so* Mary, too, bearing the predestined Man, and yet a Virgin, being obedient, became the CAUSE OF SALVATION both to herself and to all mankind." Again, "Eve being a Virgin, and incorrupt, bore disobedience and death, but Mary the Virgin, receiving faith and joy, when Gabriel the Angel evangelised her, answered, 'Be it unto me,'" &c. Again, "What Eve failed in believing, Mary by believing *hath* blotted out."

1. Now, can we refuse to see that, according to these Fathers, who are earliest of the early, Mary was a *typical woman* like Eve, that both were endued with special gifts of grace, and that Mary succeeded where Eve failed?

2. Moreover, what light they cast upon St. Alfonso's doctrine, of which a talk is sometimes made, of the two ladders. You see according to these most early Fathers, Mary *undoes* what Eve had done; mankind is *saved through*

a Virgin; the *obedience* of Mary becomes the *cause of salvation to all mankind*. Moreover, the distinct way in which Mary does this is pointed out when she is called by the early Fathers an *Advocate*. The word is used of our Lord and the Holy Ghost—of our Lord, as interceding for us in His own Person; of the Holy Ghost, as interceding in the Saints. This is the *white* way, as our Lord's own special way is the *red* way, viz. of atoning Sacrifice.

3. Further still, what light these passages cast on two texts of Scripture. *Our* reading is, "*She* shall bruise thy head." Now, this fact alone of our reading, "She shall bruise," has some weight, for *why* should not, perhaps, our reading be the right one? But take the comparison of Scripture with Scripture, and see how the whole hangs together as we interpret it. A war between a woman and the serpent is spoken of in Genesis. *Who* is the serpent? Scripture nowhere says till the twelfth chapter of the Apocalypse. There at last, for the first time, the "Serpent" is interpreted to mean the Evil Spirit. Now, *how* is he introduced? Why, by the vision *again* of a Woman, his enemy—and just as, in the first vision in Genesis, the Woman has a "seed," so here a "Child." Can we help saying, then, that the Woman is Mary in the third of Genesis? And if so, and our reading is right, the first prophecy ever given contrasts the Second Woman with the First—Mary with Eve, just as St. Justin, St. Irenaeus, and Tertullian do.

4. Moreover, see the direct bearing of this upon the Immaculate Conception. There was *war* between the woman and the Serpent. This is most emphatically fulfilled if she had nothing to do with sin—for, so far as any one sins, he has an alliance with the Evil One.

(4)

Now I wish it observed *why* I thus adduce the Fathers and Scripture. *Not* to *prove* the doctrine, but to rid it of any such monstrous improbability as would make a person *scruple* to accept it *when* the Church declares it. A Protestant is apt to say: "Oh, I really never, never can accept such a doctrine from the hands of the Church, and I had a thousand thousand times rather determine that the Church spoke falsely, than that so terrible a doctrine was true." Now, my good man, WHY? Do not go off in such a wonderful agitation, like a horse shying at he does not know what. Consider what I have said. Is it, after all, *certainly* irrational? is it *certainly* against Scripture? is it *certainly* against the primitive Fathers? is it *certainly* idolatrous? I cannot help smiling as I put the questions. Rather, may not *something* be said for it from reason, from piety, from antiquity, from the inspired text? You may see no reason at all to believe the voice of the Church; you may not yet have attained to faith in it—but what on earth this doctrine has to do with *shaking* your faith in her, if you have faith, or in sending you to the right-about if you are beginning to think she *may* be from God, is more than my mind can comprehend. Many, many doctrines are far harder than the Immaculate Conception. The doctrine of Original Sin is indefinitely harder. Mary just has *not* this difficulty. It is *no* difficulty to believe that a soul is united to the flesh *without* original sin; the great mystery is that any, that millions on millions, are born with it. Our teaching about Mary has just one difficulty less than our teaching about the state of mankind generally.

I say it distinctly—there may be many excuses at the last day, good and bad, for not being Catholics; *one* I cannot conceive: "O Lord, the doctrine of the Immaculate Conception was so derogatory to Thy grace, so inconsistent with Thy Passion, so at variance with Thy word in Genesis and the Apocalypse, so unlike the teaching of Thy first Saints and Martyrs, as to give me a *right* to reject it at all risks, and Thy Church for teaching it. It is a doctrine as to which my private judgment is fully justified in opposing the Church's judgment. And this is my plea for living and dying a Protestant."

Extract from sermon[1] delivered at Oxford, March 25, 1832

Who can estimate the holiness and perfection of her, who was chosen to be the Mother of Christ? If to him that hath, more is given, and holiness and divine favour go together (and this we are expressly told), what must have been the transcendent purity of her, whom the Creator Spirit condescended to overshadow with His miraculous presence? What must have been her gifts, who was chosen to be the only near earthly relative of the Son of God, the only one whom He was bound by nature to revere and look up to; the one appointed to train and educate Him, to instruct Him day by day, as He grew in wisdom and stature? This contemplation runs to a higher subject, did we dare to follow it; for what, think you, was the sanctified state of that human nature, of which God formed His sinless Son; knowing, as we do, that "that which is born of the flesh is flesh," and that "none can bring a clean thing out of an unclean?". . .

. . . Nothing is so calculated to impress on our minds that Christ is really partaker of our nature, and in all respects man, save sin only, as to associate Him with the thought of her, by whose ministration He became our Brother.

---

[1] Newman's Parochial and Plain Sermons, Serm. xii, vol. ii. published 1835.

NOVENA OF ST. PHILIP

(1)

PHILIP'S HUMILITY[1]

May 17

IF Philip heard of anyone having committed a crime, he would say, "Thank God that I have not done worse."

At confession he would shed abundance of tears, and say, "I have never done a good action."

When a penitent showed that she could not bear the rudeness shown towards him by certain persons who were under great obligations to him, he answered her, "If I were humble, God would not send this to me."

When one of his spiritual children said to him, "Father, I wish to have something of yours for devotion, for I know you are a Saint," he turned to her with a face full of anger, and broke out into these words: "Begone with you! I am a devil, and not a saint."

To another who said to him, "Father, a temptation has come to me to think that you are not what the world takes you for," he made answer: "Be sure of this, that I

---

[1] May, 1875. As far as I can recollect, I think I took the *idea* of these subjects and prayers from the Raccolta Prayers, *before* they were in the Raccolta; else, I should have taken the Raccolta Prayers as they actually stand there.—J. H. N.

Nine Addresses and Prayers in preparation for his Feast. The substance of these Addresses is taken from Bacci's "Life of St. Philip," translated by Father Faber.

187

am a man like my neighbours, and nothing more."

If he heard of any who had a good opinion of him, he used to say, "O poor me! how many poor girls will be greater in Paradise than I shall be!"

He avoided all marks of honour. He could not bear to receive any signs of respect. When people wished to touch his clothes, and knelt as he passed by, he used to say, "Get up! get out of my way!" He did not like people to kiss his hand; though he sometimes let them do so, lest he should hurt their feelings.

He was an enemy to all rivalry and contention. He always took in good part everything that was said to him. He had a particular dislike of affectation, whether in speaking, or in dressing, or in anything else.

He could not bear two-faced persons; as for liars, he could not endure them, and was continually reminding his spiritual children to avoid them as they would a pestilence.

He always asked advice, even on affairs of minor importance. His constant counsel to his penitents was, that they should not trust in themselves, but always take the advice of others, and get as many prayers as they could.

He took great pleasure in being lightly esteemed, nay, even despised.

He had a most pleasant manner of transacting business with others, great sweetness in conversation, and was full of compassion and consideration.

He had always a dislike to speak of himself. The phrases "*I said*," "*I did*," were rarely in his mouth. He exhorted others never to make a display of themselves, especially in those things which tended to their credit, whether in earnest or in joke.

As St. John the Evangelist, when old, was continually saying, "Little children, love one another," so Philip was ever repeating his favourite lesson, "Be humble; think little of yourselves."

He said that if we did a good work, and another took the credit of it to himself, we ought to rejoice and thank God.

He said no one ought to say, "Oh! I shall not fall, I shall not commit sin," for it was a clear sign that he would fall. He was greatly displeased with those who made excuses for themselves, and called such persons "My Lady Eve," because Eve defended herself instead of being humble.

Prayer

PHILIP, my glorious patron, who didst count as dross the praise, and even the good esteem of men, obtain for me also, from my Lord and Saviour, this fair virtue by thy prayers. How haughty are my thoughts, how contemptuous are my words, how ambitious are my works. Gain for me that low esteem of self with which thou wast gifted; obtain for me a knowledge of my own nothingness, that I may rejoice when I am despised, and ever seek to be great only in the eyes of my God and Judge.

(2)

PHILIP'S DEVOTION

May 18

THE inward flame of devotion in Philip was so intense that he sometimes fainted in consequence of it, or was forced to throw himself upon his bed, under the sickness of divine love.

When he was young he sometimes felt this divine fervour so vehemently as to be unable to contain himself, throwing himself as if in agony on the ground and crying out, "No more, Lord, no more."

What St. Paul says of himself seemed to be fulfilled in Philip: "I am filled with consolation—I over-abound with joy."

Yet, though he enjoyed sweetnesses, he used to say that he wished to serve God, not out of interest—that is, because there was pleasure in it—but out of pure love, even though he felt no gratification in loving Him.

When he was a layman, he communicated every morning. When he was old, he had frequent ecstacies during his Mass.

Hence it is customary in pictures of Philip to paint him in red vestments, to record his ardent desire to shed his blood for the love of Christ.

He was so devoted to his Lord and Saviour that he was always pronouncing the name of Jesus with unspeakable sweetness. He had also an extraordinary pleasure in say- ing the Creed, and he was so fond of the "Our Father" that he lingered on each petition in such a way that it seemed as if he never would get through them.

He had such a devotion to the Blessed Sacrament that, when he was ill, he could not sleep till he had communicated.

When he was reading or meditating on the Passion he was seen to turn as pale as ashes, and his eyes filled with tears.

Once when he was ill, they brought him something to drink. He took the glass in his hand, and when he was putting it to his mouth stopped, and began to weep most bitterly. He cried out, "Thou, my Christ, Thou upon the Cross wast thirsty, and they gave Thee nothing but gall and vinegar to drink; and I am in bed, with so many comforts around me, and so many persons to attend to me."

Yet Philip did not make much account of this warmth and acuteness of feeling; for he said that Emotion was not Devotion, that tears were no sign that a man was in the grace of God, neither must we suppose a man holy merely because he weeps when he speaks of religion.

Philip was so devoted to the Blessed Virgin that he had her name continually in his mouth. He had two ejaculations in her honour. One, "Virgin Mary, Mother of God, pray to Jesus for me." The other, simply "Virgin Mother," for he said that in those two words all possible praises of Mary are contained.

He had also a singular devotion to St. Mary Magdalen, on whose vigil he was born, and for the Apostles St. James and St. Philip; also for St. Paul the Apostle, and for St. Thomas of Aquinum, Doctor of the Church.

Prayer

PHILIP, my glorious Patron, gain for me a portion of that gift which thou hadst so abundantly. Alas! thy heart was burning with love; mine is all frozen towards God, and alive only for creatures. I love the world, which can never make me happy; my highest desire is to be well off here below. O my God, when shall I learn to love nothing else but Thee? Gain for me, O Philip, a pure love, a strong love, and an efficacious love, that, loving God here upon earth, I may enjoy the sight of Him, together with thee and all saints, hereafter in heaven.

(3)

PHILIP'S EXERCISE OF PRAYER

May 19

From very boyhood the servant of God gave himself up to prayer, until he acquired such a habit of it, that, wherever he was, his mind was always lifted up to heavenly things.

Sometimes he forgot to eat; sometimes, when he was dressing, he left off, being carried away in his thought to heaven, with his eyes open, yet abstracted from all things around him.

It was easier for Philip to think upon God, than for men of the world to think of the world.

If anyone entered his room suddenly, he would most probably find him so rapt in prayer, that, when spoken to, he did not give the right answer, and had to take a turn or two up and down the room before he fully came to himself.

If he gave way to his habit of prayer in the most trifling degree, he immediately became lost in contemplation.

It was necessary to distract him lest this continual stretch of mind should be prejudicial to his health.

Before transacting business, however trivial, he always prayed; when asked a question, he never answered till he had recollected himself.

He began praying when he went to bed, and as soon as he awoke, and he did not usually sleep more than four, or at the most five hours.

Sometimes, if anyone showed that he had observed

that Philip went to bed late or rose early in order to pray, he would answer, "Paradise is not made for sluggards."

He was more than ordinarily intent on prayer at the more solemn feasts, or at a time of urgent spiritual necessities; above all, in Holy Week.

Those who could not make long meditations he advised to lift up their minds repeatedly to God in ejaculatory prayers, as "Jesus, increase my faith," "Jesus, grant that I may never offend Thee."

Philip introduced family prayer into many of the principal houses of Rome.

When one of his penitents asked him to teach him how to pray, he answered, "Be humble and obedient, and the Holy Ghost will teach you."

He had a special devotion for the Third Person of the Blessed Trinity, and daily poured out before Him most fervent prayers for gifts and graces.

Once, when he was passing the night in prayer in the Catacombs, that great miracle took place of the Divine presence of the Holy Ghost descending upon him under the appearance of a ball of fire, entering into his mouth and lodging in his breast, from which time he had a supernatural palpitation of the heart.

He used to say that when our prayers are in the way of being granted, we must not leave off, but pray as fervently as before.

He especially recommended beginners to meditate on the four last things, and used to say that he who does not in his thoughts and fears go down to hell in his lifetime, runs a great risk of going there when he dies.

When he wished to show the necessity of prayer, he said that a man without prayer was an animal without reason.

Many of his disciples improved greatly in this exercise—not religious only, but secular persons, artisans, merchants, physicians, lawyers, and courtiers—and became such men of prayer as to receive extraordinary favours from God.

Prayer

P HILIP, my holy Patron, teach me by thy example, and gain for me by thy intercessions, to seek my Lord and God at all times and in all places, and to live in His presence and in sacred intercourse with Him. As the children of this world look up to rich men or men in station for the favour which they desire, so may I ever lift up my eyes and hands and heart towards heaven, and betake myself to the Source of all good for those goods which I need. As the children of this world converse with their friends and find their pleasure in them, so may I ever hold communion with Saints and Angels, and with the Blessed Virgin, the Mother of my Lord. Pray with me, O Philip, as thou didst pray with thy penitents here below, and then prayer will become sweet to me, as it did to them.

(4)

PHILIP'S PURITY

May 20

PHILIP well knowing the pleasure which God takes in
cleanness of heart, had no sooner come to years of discretion, and to the power of distinguishing between good
and evil, than he set himself to wage war against the evils
and suggestions of his enemy, and never rested till
he had gained the victory. Thus, notwithstanding he
lived in the world when young, and met with all kinds of
persons, he preserved his virginity spotless in those
dangerous years of his life.

No word was ever heard from his lips which would
offend the most severe modesty, and in his dress, his
carriage, and countenance, he manifested the same
beautiful virtue.

One day, while he was yet a layman, some profligate
persons impudently tempted him to commit sin. When
he saw that flight was impossible, he began to speak to
them of the hideousness of sin and the awful presence of
God. This he did with such manifest distress, such earnestness, and such fervour, that his words pierced their
abandoned hearts as a sword, and not only persuaded
them to give up their horrible thought, but even re-
claimed them from their evil ways.

At another time some bad men, who are accustomed to
think no one better than themselves, invited him on some
pretext into their house, under the belief that he was not
what the world took him to be; and then, having got

possession of him, thrust him into a great temptation. Philip, in this strait, finding the doors locked, knelt down and began to pray to God with such astonishing fervour and heartfelt heavenly eloquence, that the two poor wretches who were in the room did not dare to speak to him, and at last themselves left him and gave him a way to escape.

His virginal purity shone out of his countenance. His eyes were so clear and bright, even to the last years of his life, that no painter ever succeeded in giving the expression of them, and it was not easy for anyone to keep looking on him for any length of time, for he dazzled them like an Angel of Paradise.

Moreover, his body, even in his old age, emitted a fragrance which, even in his decrepit old age, refreshed those who came near him; and many said that they felt devotion infused into them by the mere smell of his hands.

As to the opposite vice. The ill odour of it was not to the Saint a mere figure of speech, but a reality, so that he could detect those whose souls were blackened by it; and he used to say that it was so horrible that nothing in the world could equal it, nothing, in short, but the Evil Spirit himself. Before his penitents began their confession he sometimes said, "O my son, I know your sins already."

Many confessed that they were at once delivered from temptations by his merely laying his hands on their heads. The very mention of his name had a power of shielding from Satan those who were assailed by his fiery darts.

He exhorted men never to trust themselves, whatever experience they might have of themselves, or however long their habits of virtue.

He used to say that humility was the true guard of chastity; and that not to have pity for another in such cases was a forerunner of a speedy fall in ourselves; and

that when he found a man censorious, and secure of
himself, and without fear, he gave him up for lost.

Prayer

PHILIP, my glorious Patron, who didst ever keep un-
sullied the white lily of thy purity, with such jealous care
that the majesty of this fair virtue beamed from thine
eyes, shone in thy hands, and was fragrant in thy breath,
obtain for me that gift from the Holy Ghost, that neither
the words nor the example of sinners may ever make any
impression on my soul. And, since it is by avoiding
occasions of sin, by prayer, by keeping myself employed,
and by the frequent use of the Sacraments that my dread
enemy must be subdued, gain for me the grace to persevere in these necessary observances.

(5)

PHILIP'S TENDERNESS OF HEART

May 21

P HILIP could not endure the very sight of suffering; and though he abhorred riches, he always wished to have money to give in alms.

He could not bear to see children scantily clothed, and did all he could to get new clothes for them.

Oppressed and suffering innocence troubled him especially; when a Roman gentleman was falsely accused of having been the death of a man, and was imprisoned, he went so far as to put his cause before the Pope, and obtained his liberation.

A priest was accused by some powerful persons, and was likely to suffer in consequence. Philip took up his cause with such warmth that he established his innocence before the public.

Another time, hearing of some gipsies who had been unjustly condemned to hard labour, he went to the Pope, and procured their freedom. His love of justice was as great as his tenderness and compassion.

Soon after he became a Priest there was a severe famine in Rome, and six loaves were sent to him as a present. Knowing that there was in the same house a poor foreigner suffering from want of food, he gave them all to him, and had for the first day nothing but olives to eat.

Philip had a special tenderness towards artisans, and those who had a difficulty of selling their goods. There were two watchmakers, skilful artists, but old and burdened with large families. He gave them a large order for watches, and contrived to sell them among his friends.

His zeal and liberality specially shone forth towards poor girls. He provided for them when they had no other means of provision. He found marriage dowries for some of them; to others he gave what was sufficient to gain their admittance into convents.

He was particularly good to prisoners, to whom he sent money several times in the week.

He set no limits to his affection for the shrinking and bashful poor, and was more liberal in his alms towards them.

Poor students were another object of his special compassion; he provided them not only with food and clothing, but also with books for their studies. To aid one of them he sold all his own books.

He felt most keenly any kindness done to him, so that one of his friends said: "You could not make Philip a present without receiving another from him of double value."

He was very tender towards brute animals. Seeing someone put his foot on a lizard, he cried out, "Cruel fellow! what has that poor animal done to you?"

Seeing a butcher wound a dog with one of his knives, he could not contain himself, and had great difficulty in keeping himself cool.

He could not bear the slightest cruelty to be shown to brute animals under any pretext whatever. If a bird came into the room, he would have the window opened that it might not be caught.

Prayer

PHILIP, my glorious Advocate, teach me to look at all I see around me after thy pattern as the creatures of God. Let me never forget that the same God who made me made the whole world, and all men and all animals that are in it. Gain me the grace to love all God's works for God's sake, and all men for the sake of my Lord and Saviour who has redeemed them by the Cross. And especially let me be tender and compassionate and loving towards all Christians, as my brethren in grace. And do thou, who on earth was so tender to all, be especially tender to us, and feel for us, bear with us in all our troubles, and gain for us from God, with whom thou dwellest in beatific light, all the aids necessary for bringing us safely to Him and to thee.

(6)

PHILIP'S CHEERFULNESS

May 22

PHILIP, welcomed those who consulted him with singular benignity, and received them, though strangers,
with as much affection as if he had been a long time
expecting them. When he was called upon to be merry,
he was merry; when he was called upon to feel sympathy
with the distressed, he was equally ready.

Sometimes he left his prayers and went down to sport
and banter with young men, and by this sweetness and
condescension and playful conversation gained their
souls.

He could not bear anyone to be downcast or pensive,
because spirituality is always injured by it; but when he
saw anyone grave and gloomy, he used to say, "Be
merry." He had a particular and marked leaning to
cheerful persons.

At the same time he was a great enemy to anything like
rudeness or foolery; for a buffooning spirit not only does
not advance in religion, but roots out even what is
already there.

One day he restored cheerfulness to Father Francesco
Bernardi, of the Congregation, by simply asking him to
run with him, saying, "Come now, let us have a run
together."

His penitents felt that joy at being in his room that they
used to say, Philip's room is not a room, but an earthly
Paradise.

To others, to merely stand at the door of his room, without going in, was a release from all their troubles. Others recovered their lost peace of mind by simply looking Philip in the face. To dream of him was enough to comfort many. In a word, Philip was a perpetual refreshment to all those who were in perplexity and sadness.

No one ever saw Philip melancholy; those who went to him always found him with a cheerful and smiling countenance, yet mixed with gravity.

When he was ill he did not so much receive as impart consolation. He was never heard to change his voice, as invalids generally do, but spoke in the same sonorous tone as when he was well. Once, when the physicians had given him over, he said, with the Psalmist, *"Paratus sum et non sum turbatus"* ("I am ready, and am not troubled"). He received Extreme Unction four times, but with the same calm and joyous countenance.

Prayer

P HILIP, my glorious Advocate, who didst ever follow the precepts and example of the Apostle St. Paul in rejoicing always in all things, gain for me the grace of perfect resignation to God's will, of indifference to matters of this world, and a constant sight of Heaven; so that I may never be disappointed at the Divine providences, never desponding, never sad, never fretful; that my countenance may always be open and cheerful, and my words kind and pleasant, as becomes those who, in whatever state of life they are, have the greatest of all goods, the favour of God and the prospect of eternal bliss.

(7)

PHILIP'S PATIENCE

May 23

PHILIP was for years and years the butt and laughing-stock of all the hangers-on of the great palaces of the nobility at Rome, who said all the bad of him that came into their heads, because they did not like to see a virtuous and conscientious man.

This sarcastic talk against him lasted for years and years; so that Rome was full of it, and through all the shops and counting-houses the idlers and evil livers did nothing but ridicule Philip.

When they fixed some calumny upon him, he did not take it in the least amiss, but with the greatest calmness contented himself with a simple smile.

Once a gentleman's servant began to abuse him so insolently that a person of consideration, who witnessed the insult, was about to lay hands on him; but, when he saw with what gentleness and cheerfulness Philip took it, he restrained himself, and ever after counted Philip as a saint.

Sometimes his own spiritual children, and even those who lay under the greatest obligations to him, treated him as if he were a rude and foolish person; but he did not show any resentment.

Once, when he was Superior of the Congregation, one of his subjects snatched a letter out of his hand; but the saint took the affront with incomparable meekness, and neither in look, nor word, nor in gesture betrayed the slightest emotion.

Patience had so completely become a habit with him, that he was never seen in a passion. He checked the first movement of resentful feeling; his countenance calmed instantly, and he reassumed his usual modest smile.

Prayer

PHILIP, my holy Advocate, who didst bear persecution and calumny, pain and sickness, with so admirable a patience, gain for me the grace of true fortitude under all the trials of this life. Alas! how do I need patience! I shrink from every small inconvenience; I sicken under every light affliction; I fire up at every trifling contradiction; I fret and am cross at every little suffering of body. Gain for me the grace to enter with hearty good-will into all such crosses as I may receive day by day from my Heavenly Father. Let me imitate thee, as thou didst imitate my Lord and Saviour, that so, as thou hast attained heaven by thy calm endurance of bodily and mental pain, I too may attain the merit of patience, and the reward of life everlasting.

(8)

PHILIP'S CARE FOR THE SALVATION OF SOULS

May 24

W HEN he was a young priest, and had gathered about him a number of spiritual persons, his first wish was to go with them all to preach the gospel to the heathen of India, where St. Francis Xavier was engaged in his wonderful career—and he only gave up the idea in obedience to the holy men whom he consulted.

As to bad Christians at home, such extreme desire had he for their conversion, that even when he was old he took severe disciplines in their behalf, and wept for their sins as if they had been his own.

While a layman, he converted by one sermon thirty dissolute youths.

He was successful, under the grace of God, in bringing back almost an infinite number of sinners to the paths of holiness. Many at the hour of death cried out, "Blessed be the day when first I came to know Father Philip!" Others, "Father Philip draws souls to him as the magnet draws iron."

With a view to the fulfilment of what he considered his special mission, he gave himself up entirely to hearing confessions, exclusive of every other employment. Before sunrise he had generally confessed a good number of penitents in his own room. He went down into the church at daybreak, and never left it till noon, except to say Mass. If no penitents came, he remained near his confessional, reading, saying office, or telling his beads.

If he was at prayer, if at his meals, he at once broke off when his penitents came.

He never intermitted his hearing of confessions for any illness, unless the physician forbade it.

For the same reason he kept his room-door open, so that he was exposed to the view of everyone who passed it.

He had a particular anxiety about boys and young men. He was most anxious to have them always occupied, for he knew that idleness was the parent of every evil. Sometimes he made work for them, when he could not find any.

He let them make what noise they pleased about him, if in so doing he was keeping them from temptation. When a friend remonstrated with him for letting them so interfere with him, he made answer: "So long as they do not sin, they may chop wood upon my back."

He was allowed by the Dominican Fathers to take out their novices for recreation. He used to delight to see them at their holiday meal. He used to say, "Eat, my sons, and do not scruple about it, for it makes me fat to watch you;" and then, when dinner was over, he made them sit in a ring around him, and told them the secrets of their hearts, and gave them good advice, and exhorted them to virtue.

He had a remarkable power of consoling the sick, and of delivering them from the temptations with which the devil assails them.

To his zeal for the conversion of souls, Philip always joined the exercise of corporal acts of mercy. He visited the sick in the hospitals, served them in all their necessities, made their beds, swept the floor round them, and gave them their meals.

Prayer

PHILIP, my holy Patron, who wast so careful for the souls of thy brethren, and especially of thy own people, when on earth, slack not thy care of them now, when thou art in heaven. Be with us, who are thy children and thy clients; and, with thy greater power with God, and with thy more intimate insight into our needs and our dangers, guide us along the path which leads to God and to thee. Be to us a good father; make our priests blameless and beyond reproach or scandal; make our children obedient, our youth prudent and chaste, our heads of families wise and gentle, our old people cheerful and fervent, and build us up, by thy powerful intercessions, in faith, hope, charity, and all virtues.

(9)

PHILIP'S MIRACULOUS GIFTS

May 25

PHILIP'S great and solid virtues were crowned and adorned by the divine Majesty with various and extraordinary favours, which he in vain used every artifice, if possible, to hide.

It was the good-pleasure of God to enable him to penetrate His ineffable mysteries and to know His marvellous providences by means of ecstasies, raptures, and visions, which were of frequent occurrence during the whole of his life.

A friend going one morning to confession to him, on opening the door of his room softly, saw the Saint in the act of prayer, raised upon his feet, his eyes looking to heaven, his hands extended. He stood for a while watching him, and then going close to him spoke to him—but the saint did not perceive him at all. This state of abstraction continued about eight minutes longer; then he came to himself.

He had the consolation of seeing in vision the souls of many, especially of his friends and penitents, go to heaven. Indeed, those who were intimate with him held it for certain, that none of his spiritual children died without his being certified of the state of their souls.

Philip, both by his sanctity and experience, was able to discriminate between true and false visions. He was earnest in warning men against being deluded, which is very easy and probable.

Philip was especially eminent, even among saints, for his gifts of foretelling the future and reading the heart. The examples of these gifts which might be produced would fill volumes. He foretold the deaths of some; he foretold the recovery of others; he foretold the future course of others; he foretold the births of children to those who were childless; he foretold who would be the Popes before their election; he had the gift of seeing things at a distance; and he knew what was going on in the minds of his penitents and others around him.

He knew whether his penitents had said their prayers, and for how long they were praying. Many of them when talking together, if led into any conversation which was dangerous or wrong, would say: "We must stop, for St. Philip will find it out."

Once a woman came to him to confession, when in reality she wished to get an alms. He said to her: "In God's name, good woman, go away; there is no bread for you"—and nothing could induce him to hear her confession.

A man who went to confess to him did not speak, but began to tremble, and when asked, said, "I am ashamed," for he had committed a most grievous sin. Philip said gently: "Do not be afraid; I will tell you what it was"—and, to the penitent's great astonishment, he told him.

Such instances are innumerable. There was not one person intimate with Philip who did not affirm that he knew the secrets of the heart most marvellously.

He was almost equally marvellous in his power of healing and restoring to health. He relieved pain by the touch of his hand and the sign of the Cross. And in the same way he cured diseases instantaneously—at other times by his prayers—at other times he commanded the diseases to depart.

This gift was so well known that sick persons got

possession of his clothes, his shoes, the cuttings of his hair, and God wrought cures by means of them.

Prayer

P HILIP, my holy Patron, the wounds and diseases of my soul are greater than bodily ones, and are beyond thy curing, even with thy supernatural power. I know that my Almighty Lord reserves in His own hands the recovery of the soul from death, and the healing of all its maladies. But thou canst do more for our souls by thy prayers now, my dear Saint, than thou didst for the bodies of those who applied to thee when thou wast upon earth. Pray for me, that the Divine Physician of the soul, Who alone reads my heart thoroughly, may cleanse it thoroughly, and that I and all who are dear to me may be cleansed from all our sins; and, since we must die, one and all, that we may die, as thou didst, in the grace and love of God, and with the assurance, like thee, of eternal life.

LITANY OF ST. PHILIP

Lord, have mercy.
Lord, have mercy.
Christ, have mercy.
Christ, have mercy.
Lord, have mercy.
Lord, have mercy.
Christ, hear us.
Christ, graciously hear us.
God the Father of heaven,
Have mercy on us.
God the Son, Redeemer of the world,
Have mercy on us.
God the Holy Ghost,
Have mercy on us.
Holy Trinity, one God,
Have mercy on us.

Holy Mary,
Pray for us.
Holy Mother of God,
Holy Virgin of Virgins,
St. Philip,
Vessel of the Holy Ghost,
Child of Mary,
Apostle of Rome,
Counsellor of Popes,
Voice of Prophecy,
Man of primitive times,
Winning Saint,

Pray for us.

Hidden hero,
Sweetest of Fathers,
Flower of purity,
Martyr of charity,
Heart of fire,
Discerner of spirits,
Choicest of priests,
Mirror of the divine life,
Pattern of humility,
Example of simplicity,
Light of holy joy,
Image of childhood,
Picture of old age,
Director of souls,
Gentle guide of youth,
Patron of thy own.

Pray for us.

Who didst observe chastity in thy youth,
Who didst seek Rome by divine guidance,
Who didst hide so long in the Catacombs,
Who didst receive the Holy Ghost into thy heart,
Who didst experience such wonderful ecstasies,
Who didst so lovingly serve the little ones,
Who didst wash the feet of pilgrims,
Who didst ardently thirst after martyrdom,
Who didst distribute the daily word of God,
Who didst turn so many hearts to God,
Who didst converse so sweetly with Mary,
Who didst raise the dead,
Who didst set up thy houses in all lands,

Pray for us.

Lamb of God, who takest away the sins of the world,
Spare us, O Lord.
Lamb of God, who takest away the sins of the world,
Graciously hear us, O Lord.
Lamb of God, who takest away the sins of the world,
Have mercy on us.
Christ, hear us.

Christ, graciously hear us.

V. Remember thy Congregation.
R. Which thou hast possessed from the beginning.

Let us pray

O God, who hast exalted blessed Philip, Thy Confessor, in the glory of Thy saints, grant that, as we rejoice in his commemoration, so we may profit by the example of his virtues, through Christ our Lord. Amen.

LITANIÆ DE S. PHILIPPO

Kyrie eleïson.
Christe eleïson.
Kyrie eleïson.
Christe, audi nos.
Christe, exaudi nos.
Pater de cœlis Deus,
Fili, Redemptor mundi, Deus,
Spiritus Sancte, Deus,
Sancta Trinitas, Unus Deus,

Miserere nobis

Sancta Maria,
Sancta Dei Genitrix,
Sancta Virgo Virginum,
Sancte Philippe,
Vas Spiritûs Sancti,
Apostolus Romæ,
Consiliarius Pontificius,
Vox fatidica,
Vir prisci temporis,
Sanctus amabilis,
Heros umbratilis,
Pater suavissimus,
Flos puritatis,
Martyr charitatis,
Cor flammigerum,
Discretor spirituum,
Gemma sacerdotum,
Vitæ divinæ speculum,
Specimen humilitatis,

Ora pro nobis.

Exemplar simplicitatis,
Lux sanctæ lætitiæ,
Imago pueritiæ
Forma senectutis,
Rector animarum,
Piscator fluctuantium,
Manuductor pupillorum,
Patronus tuorum,
Hospes Anglorum,
Qui castitatem adolescens coluisti,
Qui Romam divinitus petiisti,
Qui multos annos in catacumbis delituisti,
Qui ipsum Spiritum in cor recepisti,
Qui mirabiles ecstases sustinuisti,
Qui parvulis amanter serviisti,
Qui peregrinantium pedes lavisti,
Qui martyrium ardentissime sitiisti,
Qui verbum Dei quotidianum distribuisti,
Qui tot corda ad Deum allexisti,
Qui sermones dulces cum Mariâ contulisti,
Qui emortuum ab inferis reduxisti,
Qui domos tuas in omni regione constituisti,

Ora pro nobis.

Ora pro nobis.

Agnus Dei, qui tollis peccata mundi,
Parce nobis, Domine.
Agnus Dei, qui tollis peccata mundi,
Exaudi nos, Domine.
Agnus Dei, qui tollis peccata mundi,
Miserere nobis.
Ora pro nobis, Sancte Philippe,
Ut digni efficiamur promissionibus Christi.

Oremus

Deus, qui beatum Philippum, Confessorem tuum, sanctorum tuorum gloriâ sublimasti, concede propitius, ut cujus commemoratione lætamur, ejus virtutum proficiamus exemplo: per Christum Dominum nostrum. Amen.

PART II

MEDITATIONS ON THE
STATIONS OF THE CROSS[1]

Begin with an Act of Contrition

THE FIRST STATION

Jesus Is Condemned to Death

V. Adoramus te, Christe, et benedicimus tibi.
R. Quia per sanctam Crucem tuam redemisti mundum.

LEAVING the House of Caiphas, and dragged before Pilate and Herod, mocked, beaten, and spit upon, His back torn with scourges, His head crowned with thorns, Jesus, who on the last day will judge the world, is Himself condemned by unjust judges to a death of ignominy and torture.

Jesus is condemned to *death*. His death-warrant is signed, and who signed it but I, when I committed my first mortal sins? My first mortal sins, when I fell away from the state of grace into which Thou didst place me by baptism; these it was that were Thy death-warrant, O Lord. The Innocent suffered for the guilty. Those sins of mine were the voices which cried out, "Let Him be crucified." That willingness and delight of heart with which I committed them was the consent which Pilate gave to this clamorous multitude. And the hardness of heart which followed upon them, my disgust, my de-

[1] Written about 1860; used a second time, 1885.—J. H. N.

spair, my proud impatience, my obstinate resolve to sin on, the love of sin which took possession of me—what were these contrary and impetuous feelings but the blows and the blasphemies with which the fierce soldiers and the populace received Thee, thus carrying out the sentence which Pilate had pronounced?

Pater, Ave, &c.
V. Miserere nostri, Domine.
R. Miserere nostri.
Fidelium animæ, &c.

THE SECOND STATION

Jesus Receives His Cross

V. Adoramus te, Christe, et benedicimus tibi.
R. Quia per sanctam Crucem tuam redemisti mundum.

A STRONG, and therefore heavy Cross, for it is strong enough to bear Him on it when He arrives at Calvary, is placed upon His torn shoulders. He receives it gently and meekly, nay, with gladness of heart, for it is to be the salvation of mankind.

True; but recollect, that heavy Cross is the weight of our sins. As it fell upon His neck and shoulders, it came down with a shock. Alas! what a sudden, heavy weight have I laid upon Thee, O Jesus. And, though in the calm and clear foresight of Thy mind—for Thou seest all things—Thou wast fully prepared for it, yet Thy feeble frame tottered under it when it dropped down upon Thee. Ah! how great a misery is it that I have lifted up my hand against my God. How could I ever fancy He would forgive me! unless He had Himself told us that He underwent His bitter passion in order the He might forgive us. I acknowledge, O Jesus, in the anguish and agony of my heart, that my sins it was that struck Thee on the face, that bruised Thy sacred arms, that tore Thy flesh with iron rods, that nailed Thee to the Cross, and let Thee slowly die upon it.

Pater, Ave. &c.

THE THIRD STATION

Jesus Falls the First Time beneath the Cross

V. Adoramus te, Christe, et benedicimus tibi.
R. Quia per sanctam Crucem tuam redemisti mundum.

JESUS, bowed down under the weight and the length of the unwieldy Cross, which trailed after Him, slowly sets forth on His way, amid the mockeries and insults of the crowd. His agony in the Garden itself was sufficient to exhaust Him; but it was only the first of a multitude of sufferings. He sets off with His whole heart, but His limbs fail Him, and He falls.

Yes, it is as I feared. Jesus, the strong and mighty Lord, has found for the moment our sins stronger than Himself. He falls—yet He bore the load for a while; He tottered, but He bore up and walked onwards. What, then, made Him give way? I say, I repeat, it is an intimation and a memory to thee, O my soul, of thy falling back into mortal sin. I repented of the sins of my youth, and went on well for a time; but at length a new temptation came, when I was off my guard, and I suddenly fell away. Then all my good habits seemed to go at once; they were like a garment which is stripped off, so quickly and utterly did grace depart from me. And at that moment I looked at my Lord, and lo! He had fallen down, and I covered my face with my hands and remained in a state of great confusion.

Pater, Ave, &c.

THE FOURTH STATION

Jesus Meets His Mother

V. Adoramus te, Christe, et benedicimus tibi.
R. Quia per sanctam Crucem tuam redemisti mundum.

JESUS rises, though wounded by His fall, journeys on, with His Cross still on His shoulders. He is bent down; but at one place, looking up, He sees His Mother. For an instant they just see each other, and He goes forward.

Mary would rather have had all His sufferings herself, could that have been, than not have known what they were by ceasing to be near Him. He, too, gained a refreshment, as from some soothing and grateful breath of air, to see her sad smile amid the sights and the noises which were about Him. She had known Him beautiful and glorious, with the freshness of Divine Innocence and peace upon His countenance; *now* she saw Him so changed and deformed that she could scarce have recognised Him, save for the piercing, thrilling, peace-inspiring look He gave her. Still, He was now carrying the load of the world's sins, and, all-holy though He was, He carried the image of them on His very face. He looked like some outcast or outlaw who had frightful guilt upon Him. He had been made sin for us, who knew no sin; not a feature, not a limb, but spoke of guilt, of a curse, of punishment, of agony.

Oh, what a meeting of Son and Mother! Yet there was a mutual comfort, for there was a mutual sympathy. Jesus and Mary—do they forget that Passion-tide through all eternity?

Pater, Ave, &c.

THE FIFTH STATION

Simon of Cyrene Helps Jesus to Carry the Cross

V. Adoramus te, Christe, et benedicimus tibi.
R. Quia per sanctam Crucem tuam redemisti mundum.

At length His strength fails utterly, and He is unable
to proceed. The executioners stand perplexed. What are
they to do? How is He to get to Calvary? Soon they see a
stranger who seems strong and active—Simon of
Cyrene. They seize on him, and compel him to carry the
Cross with Jesus. The sight of the Sufferer pierces the
man's heart. Oh, what a privilege! O happy soul, elect of
God! he takes the part assigned to him with joy.

This came of Mary's intercession. *He* prayed, not for
Himself, except that He might drink the full chalice of
suffering and do His Father's will; but *she* showed herself
a mother by following Him with her prayers, since she
could help Him in no other way. She then sent this
stranger to help Him. It was she who led the soldiers to
see that they might be too fierce with Him. Sweet
Mother, even *do* the like to us. Pray for us ever, Holy
Mother of God, pray for us, whatever be our cross, as we
pass along on our way. Pray for us, and we shall rise
again, though we have fallen. Pray for us when sorrow,
anxiety, or sickness comes upon us. Pray for us when we
are prostrate under the power of temptation, and send
some faithful servant of thine to succour us. And in the

world to come, if found worthy to expiate our sins in the fiery prison, send some good Angel to give us a season of refreshment. Pray for us, Holy Mother of God.

Pater, Ave, &c.

THE SIXTH STATION

Jesus and Veronica

V. Adoramus te, Christe, et benedicimus tibi.
R. Quia per sanctam Crucem tuam redemisti mundum.

As Jesus toils along up the hill, covered with the sweat of death, a woman makes her way through the crowd, and wipes His face with a napkin. In reward of her piety the cloth retains the impression of the Sacred Countenance upon it.

The relief which a Mother's tenderness secured is not yet all she did. Her prayers sent Veronica as well as Simon—Simon to do a man's work, Veronica to do the part of a woman. The devout servant of Jesus did what she could. As Magdalen had poured the ointment at the Feast, so Veronica now offered Him this napkin in His passion. "Ah," she said, "would I could do more! Why have I not the strength of Simon, to take part in the burden of the Cross? But men only can serve the Great High Priest, now that He is celebrating the solemn act of sacrifice." O Jesus! let us one and all minister to Thee according to our places and powers. And as Thou didst accept from Thy followers refreshment in Thy hour of trial, so give to us the support of Thy grace when we are hard pressed by our Foe. I feel I cannot bear up against temptations, weariness, despondency, and sin. I say to myself, what is the good of being religious? I shall fall, O my dear Saviour, I shall certainly fall, unless Thou dost

renew for me my vigour like the eagle's, and breathe life
into me by the soothing application and the touch of the
Holy Sacraments which Thou hast appointed.

Pater, Ave, &c.

THE SEVENTH STATION

Jesus Falls a Second Time

V. Adoramus te, Christe, et benedicimus tibi.
R. Quia per sanctam Crucem tuam redemisti mundum.

T HE pain of His wounds and the loss of blood increasing at every step of His way, again His limbs fail Him, and He falls on the ground.

What has He done to deserve all this? This is the reward received by the long-expected Messias from the Chosen People, the Children of Israel. I know what to answer. He falls because *I* have fallen. I have fallen again. I know well that without Thy grace, O Lord, I could not stand; and I fancied that I had kept closely to Thy Sacraments; yet in spite of my going to Mass and to my duties, I am out of grace again. Why is it but because I have lost my devotional spirit, and have come to Thy holy ordinances in a cold, formal way, without inward affection. I became lukewarm, tepid. I thought the battle of life was over, and became secure. I had no lively faith, no sight of spiritual things. I came to church from habit, and because I thought others would observe it. I ought to be a new creature, I ought to live by faith, hope, and charity; but I thought more of this world than of the world to come— and at last I forgot that I was a servant of God, and followed the broad way that leadeth to destruction, not the narrow way which leadeth to life. And thus I fell from Thee.

Pater, Ave, &c.

THE EIGHTH STATION

Jesus Comforts the Women of Jerusalem

V. Adoramus te, Christe, et benedicimus tibi.
R. Quia per sanctam Crucem tuam redemisti mundum.

AT the sight of the sufferings of Jesus the Holy Women are so pierced with grief that they cry out and bewail Him, careless what happens to them by so doing. Jesus, turning to them, said, "Daughters of Jerusalem, weep not over Me, but weep for yourselves and for your children."

Ah! can it be, O Lord, that *I* shall prove one of those sinful children for whom Thou biddest their mothers to weep. "Weep not for Me," He said, "for I am the Lamb of God, and am making atonement at My own will for the sins of the world. I am suffering now, but I shall triumph; and, when I triumph, those souls, for whom I am dying, will either be my dearest friends or my deadliest enemies." Is it possible? O my Lord, can I grasp the terrible thought that Thou really didst weep for me— weep for me, as Thou didst weep over Jerusalem? Is it possible that *I* am one of the reprobate? possible that I shall lose by Thy passion and death, not gain by it? Oh, withdraw not from me. I am in a very bad way. I have so much evil in me. I have so little of an earnest, brave spirit to set against that evil. O Lord, what will become of me? It is so difficult for me to drive away the Evil Spirit from my heart. Thou alone canst effectually cast him out.

Pater, Ave, &c.

THE NINTH STATION

Again, a Third Time, Jesus Falls

V. Adoramus te, Christe, et benedicimus tibi.
R. Quia per sanctam Crucem tuam redemisti mundum.

Jesus had now reached almost to the top of Calvary;
but, before He had gained the very spot where He was to
be crucifed, again He fell, and is again dragged up and
goaded onwards by the brutal soldiery.

We are told in Holy Scripture of three falls of Satan, the
Evil Spirit. The first was in the beginning; the second,
when the Gospel and the Kingdom of Heaven were
preached to the world; the third will be at the end of all
things. The first is told us by St. John the Evangelist. He
says: "There was a great battle in heaven. Michael and his
Angels fought with the dragon, and the dragon fought,
and his angels. And they prevailed not, neither was their
place found any more in heaven. And that great dragon
was cast out, the old serpent, who is called the devil and
Satan." The second fall, at the time of the Gospel, is
spoken of by our Lord when He says, "I saw Satan, like
lightning, falling from heaven." And the third by the
same St. John: "There came down fire from God out of
heaven, . . . and the devil . . . was cast into the pool of
fire and brimstone."

These three falls—the past, the present, and the future—the Evil Spirit had in mind when he moved Judas
to betray our Lord. This was just his hour. Our Lord,
when He was seized, said to His enemies, "This is your
hour and the power of darkness." Satan knew his time

was short, and thought he might use it to good effect. But little dreaming that he would be acting in behalf of the world's redemption, which our Lord's passion and death were to work out, in revenge, and, as he thought, in triumph, he smote Him once, he smote Him twice, he smote Him thrice, each successive time a heavier blow. The weight of the Cross, the barbarity of the soldiers and the crowd, were but his instruments. O Jesus, the only-begotten Son of God, the Word Incarnate, we praise, adore, and love Thee for Thy ineffable condescension, even to allow Thyself thus for a time to fall into the hands and under the power of the Enemy of God and man, in order thereby to save us from being his servants and companions for eternity.

Or this

This is the worst fall of the three. His strength has for a while utterly failed Him, and it is some time before the barbarous soldiers can bring Him to. Ah! it was His anticipation of what was to happen to me. I get worse and worse. He sees the end from the beginning. He was thinking of me all the time He dragged Himself along, up the Hill of Calvary. He saw that I should fall again in spite of all former warnings and former assistance. He saw that I should become secure and self-confident, and that my enemy would then assail me with some new temptation, to which I never thought I should be exposed. I thought my weakness lay all on one particular side which I knew. I had not a dream that I was not strong on the other. And so Satan came down on my unguarded side, and got the better of me from my self-trust and self-satisfaction. I was wanting in humility. I thought no harm would come on me, I thought I had outlived the danger of sinning; I thought it was an easy thing to get to heaven, and I was not watchful. It was my pride, and so I fell a third time.

Pater, Ave, &c.

THE TENTH STATION

Jesus Is Stripped, and Drenched with Gall

V. Adoramus te, Christe, et benedicimus tibi.
R. Quia per sanctam Crucem tuam redemisti mundum.

At length He has arrived at the place of sacrifice, and they begin to prepare Him for the Cross. His garments are torn from His bleeding body, and He, the Holy of Holiest, stands exposed to the gaze of the coarse and scoffing multitude.

O Thou who in Thy Passion wast stripped of all Thy clothes, and held up to the curiosity and mockery of the rabble, strip me of myself here and now, that in the Last Day I come not to shame before men and Angels. Thou didst endure the shame on Calvary that I might be spared the shame at the Judgment. Thou hadst nothing to be ashamed of personally, and the shame which Thou didst feel was because Thou hadst taken on Thee man's nature. When they took from Thee Thy garments, those innocent limbs of Thine were but objects of humble and loving adoration to the highest Seraphim. They stood around in speechless awe, wondering at Thy beauty, and they trembled at Thy infinite self-abasement. But I, O Lord, how shall I appear if Thou shalt hold me up hereafter to be gazed upon, stripped of that robe of grace which is Thine, and seen in my own personal life and nature? O how hideous I am in myself, even in my best estate. Even when I am cleansed from my mortal sins, what disease and corruption is seen even in my venial sins. How shall I be fit for the society of Angels, how for Thy presence, until Thou burnest this foul leprosy away in the fire of Purgatory?

Pater, Ave, &c.

THE ELEVENTH STATION

Jesus Is Nailed to the Cross

V. Adoramus te, Christe, et benedicimus tibi.
R. Quia per sanctam Crucem tuam redemisti mundum.

THE Cross is laid on the ground, and Jesus stretched upon it, and then, swaying heavily to and fro, it is, after much exertion, jerked into the hole ready to receive it. Or, as others think, it is set upright, and Jesus is raised up and fastened to it. As the savage executioners drive in the huge nails, He offers Himself to the Eternal Father, as a ransom for the world. The blows are struck—the blood gushes forth.

Yes, they set up the Cross on high, and they placed a ladder against it, and, having stripped Him of His garments, made Him mount. With His hands feebly grasping its sides and cross-woods, and His feet slowly, uncertainly, with much effort, with many slips, mounting up, the soldiers propped Him on each side, or He would have fallen. When He reached the projection where His sacred feet were to be, He turned round with sweet modesty and gentleness towards the fierce rabble, stretching out His arms, as if He would embrace them. Then He lovingly placed the backs of His hands close against the transverse beam, waiting for the executioners to come with their sharp nails and heavy hammers to dig into the palms of His hands, and to fasten them securely

to the wood. There He hung, a perplexity to the multitude, a terror to evil spirits, the wonder, the awe, yet the
joy, the adoration of the Holy Angels.

Pater, Ave, &c.

THE TWELFTH STATION

Jesus Dies Upon the Cross

V. Adoramus te, Christe, et benedicimus tibi.
R. Quia per sanctam Crucem tuam redemisti mundum.

JESUS hung for three hours. During this time He prayed for His murderers, promised Paradise to the penitent robber, and committed His Blessed Mother to the guardianship of St. John. Then all was finished, and He bowed His head and gave up His Spirit.

The worst is over. The Holiest is dead and departed. The most tender, the most affectionate, the holiest of the sons of men is gone. Jesus is dead, and with His death my sin shall die. I protest once for all, before men and Angels, that sin shall no more have dominion over me. This Lent I make myself God's own for ever. The salvation of my soul shall be my first concern. With the aid of His grace I will create in me a deep hatred and sorrow for my past sins. I will try hard to detest sin, as much as I have ever loved it. Into God's hands I put myself, not by halves, but unreservedly. I promise Thee, O Lord, with the help of Thy grace, to keep out of the way of temptation, to avoid all occasions of sin, to turn at once from the voice of the Evil One, to be regular in my prayers, so to die to sin that Thou mayest not have died for me on the Cross in vain.

Pater, Ave, &c.

THE THIRTEENTH STATION

Jesus Is Taken from the Cross, and Laid in Mary's Bosom

V. Adoramus te, Christe, et benedicimus tibi.
R. Quia per sanctam Crucem tuam redemisti mundum.

THE multitude have gone home. Calvary is left solitary and still, except that St. John and the holy women are there. Then come Joseph of Arimathea and Nicodemus, and take down from the Cross the body of Jesus, and place it in the arms of Mary.

O Mary, at last thou hast possession of thy Son. Now, when His enemies can do no more, they leave Him in contempt to thee. As His unexpected friends perform their difficult work, thou lookest on with unspeakable thoughts. Thy heart is pierced with the sword of which Simeon spoke. O Mother most sorrowful; yet in thy sorrow there is a still greater joy. The joy in prospect nerved thee to stand by Him as He hung upon the Cross; much more now, without swooning, without trembling, thou dost receive Him to thy arms and on thy lap. Now thou art supremely happy as having Him, though He comes to thee not as He went from thee. He went from thy home, O Mother of God, in the strength and beauty of His manhood, and He comes back to thee dislocated, torn to pieces, mangled, dead. Yet, O Blessed Mary, thou art happier in this hour of woe than on the day of the marriage feast, for then He was leaving thee, and now in the future, as a Risen Saviour, He will be separated from thee no more.

Pater, Ave, &c.

THE FOURTEENTH STATION

Jesus Is Laid in the Tomb

V. Adoramus te, Christe, et benedicimus tibi.
R. Quia per sanctam Crucem tuam redemisti mundum.

Bᴜᴛ for a short three days, for a day and a half—Mary then must give Him up. He is not yet risen. His friends and servants take Him from thee, and place Him in an honourable tomb. They close it safely, till the hour comes for His resurrection.

Lie down and sleep in peace in the calm grave for a little while, dear Lord, and then wake up for an everlasting reign. We, like the faithful women, will watch around Thee, for all our treasure, all our life, is lodged with Thee. And, when our turn comes to die, grant, sweet Lord, that we may sleep calmly too, the sleep of the just. Let us sleep peacefully for the brief interval between death and the general resurrection. Guard us from the enemy; save us from the pit. Let our friends remember us and pray for us, O dear Lord. Let Masses be said for us, so that the pains of Purgatory, so much deserved by us, and therefore so truly welcomed by us, may be over with little delay. Give us seasons of refreshment there; wrap us round with holy dreams and soothing contemplations, while we gather strength to ascend the heavens. And then let our faithful guardian Angels help us up the glorious ladder, reaching from earth to heaven, which Jacob saw in vision. And when we reach the everlasting gates, let them open upon us with the music of Angels; and let St. Peter receive us, and our Lady, the glorious Queen of

Saints, embrace us, and bring us to Thee, and to Thy
Eternal Father, and to Thy Co-equal Spirit, Three Persons, One God, to reign with Them for ever and ever.

Pater, Ave, &c.

Let us Pray

God, Who by the Precious Blood of Thy only-
begotten Son didst sanctify the Standard of the Cross,
grant, we beseech Thee, that we who rejoice in the
glory of the same Holy Cross may at all times and
places rejoice in Thy protection, Through the same
Christ, our Lord.

End with one Pater, Ave, and Gloria, for the
intention of the Sovereign Pontiff.

(Vide the Raccolta.)

SHORT MEDITATIONS ON THE
STATIONS OF THE CROSS

Begin with an Act of Contrition

FIRST STATION

Jesus Condemned to Death

V. Adoramus te, Christe, et benedicimus tibi.
R. Quia per sanctam Crucem tuam redemisti mundum.

THE Holy, Just, and True was judged by sinners, and put to death. Yet, while they judged, they were compelled to acquit Him. Judas, who betrayed Him, said, "I have sinned in that I have betrayed the innocent blood." Pilate, who sentenced Him, said, "I am innocent of the blood of this just person," and threw the guilt upon the Jews. The Centurion who saw Him crucified said, "Indeed this *was* a just man." Thus ever, O Lord, Thou art justified in Thy words, and dost overcome when Thou art judged. And so, much more, at the last day "They shall *look* on Him whom they pierced"; and He who was condemned in weakness shall judge the world in power, and even those who are condemned will confess their judgment is just.

Pater, Ave, &c.
V. Miserere nostri, Domine.
R. Miserere nostri.
Fidelium animæ, &c.

THE SECOND STATION

Jesus Receives His Cross

V. Adoramus te, Christe, et benedicimus tibi.
R. Quia per sanctam Crucem tuam redemisti mundum.

JESUS supports the whole world by His divine power, for He is God; but the weight was less heavy than was the Cross which our sins hewed out for Him. Our sins cost Him this humiliation. He had to take on Him our nature, and to appear among us as a man, and to offer up for us a great sacrifice. He had to pass a life in penance, and to endure His passion and death at the end of it. O Lord God Almighty, who dost bear the weight of the whole world without weariness, who bore the weight of all our sins, though they wearied Thee, as Thou art the Preserver of our bodies by Thy Providence, so be Thou the Saviour of our souls by Thy precious blood.

Pater, Ave, &c.

THE THIRD STATION

Jesus Falls under the Weight of the Cross the First Time

V. Adoramus te, Christe, et benedicimus tibi.
R. Quia per sanctam Crucem tuam redemisti mundum.

SATAN fell from heaven in the beginning; by the just sentence of his Creator he fell, against whom he had rebelled. And when he had succeeded in gaining man to join him in his rebellion, and his Maker came to save him, then his brief hour of triumph came, and he made the most of it. When the Holiest had taken flesh, and was in his power, then in his revenge and malice he determined, as he himself had been struck down by the Almighty arm, to strike in turn a heavy blow at Him who struck him. Therefore it was that Jesus fell down so suddenly. O dear Lord, by this Thy first fall raise us all out of sin, who have so miserably fallen under its power.

Pater, Ave, &c.

THE FOURTH STATION

Jesus Meets His Mother

V. Adoramus te, Christe, et benedicimus tibi.
R. Quia per sanctam Crucem tuam redemisti mundum.

T HERE is no part of the history of Jesus but Mary has her part in it. There are those who profess to be His servants, who think that her work was ended when she bore Him, and after that she had nothing to do but disappear and be forgotten. But we, O Lord, Thy children of the Catholic Church, do not so think of Thy Mother. She brought the tender infant into the Temple, she lifted Him up in her arms when the wise men came to adore Him. She fled with Him to Egypt, she took Him up to Jerusalem when He was twelve years old. He lived with her at Nazareth for thirty years. She was with Him at the marriage-feast. Even when He had left her to preach, she hovered about Him. And now she shows herself as He toils along the Sacred Way with His cross on His shoulders. Sweet Mother, let us ever think of thee when we think of Jesus, and when we pray to Him, ever aid us by thy powerful intercession.

Pater, Ave, &c.

THE FIFTH STATION

Simon of Cyrene Helps Jesus to Carry the Cross

V. Adoramus te, Christe, et benedicimus tibi.
R. Quia per sanctam Crucem tuam redemisti mundum.

JESUS could bear His Cross alone, did He so will; but He permits Simon to help Him, in order to remind us that we must take part in His sufferings, and have a fellowship in His work. His merit is infinite, yet He condescends to let His people add their merit to it. The sanctity of the Blessed Virgin, the blood of the Martyrs, the prayers and penances of the Saints, the good deeds of all the faithful, take part in that work which, nevertheless, is perfect without them. He saves us by His blood, but it is through and with ourselves that He saves us. Dear Lord, teach us to suffer with Thee, make it pleasant to us to suffer for Thy sake, and sanctify all our sufferings by the merits of Thy own.

Pater, Ave, &c.

THE SIXTH STATION

The Face of Jesus Is Wiped by Veronica

V. Adoramus te, Christe, et benedicimus tibi.
R. Quia per sanctam Crucem tuam redemisti mundum.

JESUS let the pious woman carry off an impression of His Sacred Countenance, which was to last to future ages. He did this to remind us all, that His image must ever be impressed on all our hearts. Whoever we are, in whatever part of the earth, in whatever age of the world, Jesus must live in our hearts. We may differ from each other in many things, but in this we must all agree, if we are His true children. We must bear about with us the napkin of St. Veronica; we must ever meditate upon His death and resurrection, we must ever imitate His divine excellence, according to our measure. Lord, let our countenances be ever pleasing in Thy sight, not defiled with sin, but bathed and washed white in Thy precious blood.

Pater, Ave, &c.

THE SEVENTH STATION

Jesus Falls a Second Time

V. Adoramus te, Christe, et benedicimus tibi.
R. Quia per sanctam Crucem tuam redemisti mundum.

SATAN had a second fall, when our Lord came upon earth. By that time he had usurped the dominion of the whole world—and he called himself its king. And he dared to take up the Holy Saviour in his arms, and show Him all kingdoms, and blasphemously promise to give them to Him, His Maker, if He would adore him. Jesus answered, "Begone, Satan!"—and Satan fell down from the high mountain. And Jesus bare witness to it when He said, "I saw Satan, as lightning, falling from heaven." The Evil One remembered this second defeat, and so now he smote down the Innocent Lord a second time, now that he had Him in his power. O dear Lord, teach us to suffer with Thee, and not be afraid of Satan's buffetings, when they come on us from resisting him.

Pater, Ave, &c.

THE EIGHTH STATION

The Women of Jerusalem Mourn for Our Lord

V. Adoramus te, Christe, et benedicimus tibi.
R. Quia per sanctam Crucem tuam redemisti mundum.

Ever since the prophecy of old time, that the Saviour of man was to be born of a woman of the stock of Abraham, the Jewish women had desired to bear Him. Yet, now that He was really come, how different, as the Gospel tells us, was the event from what they had expected. He said to them "that the days were coming when they should say, Blessed are the barren, and the wombs that have not borne, and the breasts which have not given suck." Ah, Lord, we know not what is good for us, and what is bad. We cannot foretell the future, nor do we know, when Thou comest to visit us, in what form Thou wilt come. And therefore we leave it all to Thee. Do Thou Thy good pleasure to us and in us. Let us ever look at Thee, and do Thou look upon us, and give us the grace of Thy bitter Cross and Passion, and console us in Thy own way and at Thy own time.

Pater, Ave, &c.

THE NINTH STATION

Jesus Falls the Third Time

V. Adoramus te, Christe, et benedicimus tibi.
R. Quia per sanctam Crucem tuam redemisti mundum.

SATAN will have a third and final fall at the end of the world, when he will be shut up for good in the everlasting fiery prison. He knew this was to be his end—he has no hope, but despair only. He knew that no suffering which he could at that moment inflict upon the Saviour of men would avail to rescue himself from that inevitable doom. But, in horrible rage and hatred, he determined to insult and torture while he could the great King whose throne is everlasting. Therefore a third time he smote Him down fiercely to the earth. O Jesus, Only-begotten Son of God, the Word Incarnate, we adore with fear and trembling and deep thankfulness Thy awful humiliation, that Thou who art the Highest, should have permitted Thyself, even for one hour, to be the sport and prey of the Evil One.

Pater, Ave, &c.

THE TENTH STATION

Jesus Is Stripped of His Garments

V. Adoramus te, Christe, et benedicimus tibi.
R. Quia per sanctam Crucem tuam redemisti mundum.

JESUS would give up everything of this world, before He left it. He exercised the most perfect poverty. When He left the Holy House of Nazareth, and went out to preach, He had not where to lay His head. He lived on the poorest food, and on what was given to Him by those who loved and served Him. And therefore He chose a death in which not even His clothes were left to Him. He parted with what seemed most necessary, and even a part of Him, by the law of human nature since the fall. Grant us in like manner, O dear Lord, to care nothing for anything on earth, and to bear the loss of all things, and to endure even shame, reproach, contempt, and mockery, rather than that Thou shalt be ashamed of us at the last day.

Pater, Ave, &c.

THE ELEVENTH STATION

Jesus Is Nailed to the Cross

V. Adoramus te, Christe, et benedicimus tibi.
R. Quia per sanctam Crucem tuam redemisti mundum.

JESUS is pierced through each hand and each foot with a sharp nail. His eyes are dimmed with blood, and are closed by the swollen lids and livid brows which the blows of His executioners have caused. His mouth is filled with vinegar and gall. His head is encircled by the sharp thorns. His heart is pierced with the spear. Thus, all His senses are mortified and crucified, that He may make atonement for every kind of human sin. O Jesus, mortify and crucify us with Thee. Let us never sin by hand or foot, by eyes or mouth, or by head or heart. Let all our senses be a sacrifice to Thee; let every member sing Thy praise. Let the sacred blood which flowed from Thy five wounds anoint us with such sanctifying grace that we may die to the world, and live only to Thee.

Pater, Ave, &c.

THE TWELFTH STATION

Jesus Dies Upon the Cross

V. Adoramus te, Christe, et benedicimus tibi.
R. Quia per sanctam Crucem tuam redemisti mundum.

"CONSUMMATUM est." It is completed—it has come to a full end. The mystery of God's love towards us is accomplished. The price is paid, and we are redeemed. The Eternal Father determined not to pardon us without a price, in order to show us especial favour. He condescended to make us valuable to Him. What we buy we put a value on. He might have saved us without a price—by the mere fiat of His will. But to show His love for us He took a price, which, if there was to be a price set upon us at all, if there was any ransom at all to be taken for the guilt of our sins, could be nothing short of the death of His Son in our nature. O my God and Father, Thou hast valued us so much as to pay the highest of all possible prices for our sinful souls—and shall we not love and choose Thee above all things as the one necessary and one only good?

Pater, Ave, &c.

THE THIRTEENTH STATION

Jesus Is Laid in the Arms of His Blessed Mother

V. Adoramus te, Christe, et benedicimus tibi.
R. Quia per sanctam Crucem tuam redemisti mundum.

HE is Thy property now, O Virgin Mother, once again, for He and the world have met and parted. He went out from Thee to do His Father's work—and He has done and suffered it. Satan and bad men have now no longer any claim upon Him—too long has He been in their arms. Satan took Him up aloft to the high mountain; evil men lifted Him up upon the Cross. He has not been in Thy arms, O Mother of God, since He was a child—but now thou hast a claim upon Him, when the world has done its worst. For thou art the all-favoured, all-blessed, all-gracious Mother of the Highest. We rejoice in this great mystery. He has been hidden in thy womb, He has lain in thy bosom, He has been suckled at thy breasts, He has been carried in thy arms—and now that He is dead, He is placed upon thy lap. Virgin Mother of God, pray for us.

Pater, Ave, &c.

THE FOURTEENTH STATION

Jesus Is Laid in the Sepulchre

V. Adoramus te, Christe, et benedicimus tibi.
R. Quia per sanctam Crucem tuam redemisti mundum.

JESUS, when He was nearest to His everlasting triumph, seemed to be farthest from triumphing. When He was nearest upon entering upon His kingdom, and exercising all power in heaven and earth, He was lying dead in a cave of the rock. He was wrapped round in burying-clothes, and confined within a sepulchre of stone, where He was soon to have a glorified spiritual body, which could penetrate all substances, go to and fro quicker than thought, and was about to ascend on high. Make us to trust in thee, O Jesus, that Thou wilt display in us a similar providence. Make us sure, O Lord, that the greater is our distress, the nearer we are to Thee. The more men scorn us, the more Thou dost honour us. The more men insult over us, the higher Thou wilt exalt us. The more they forget us, the more Thou dost keep us in mind. The more they abandon us, the closer Thou wilt bring us to Thyself.

Pater, Ave, &c.

Let us Pray

God, who by the Precious Blood of Thy only-begotten Son didst sanctify the standard of the Cross, grant, we beseech Thee, that we who rejoice in the glory of the same Holy Cross may at all times and places rejoice in Thy protection, through the same Christ, our Lord.

End with one Pater, Ave, and Gloria, for the intention of the Sovereign Pontiff.

(Vide the Raccolta.)

TWELVE MEDITATIONS AND
INTERCESSIONS FOR GOOD FRIDAY[1]

(1)

JESUS THE LAMB OF GOD

BEHOLD the Lamb of God, behold Him who taketh
away the sins of the world. So spoke St. John Baptist,
when he saw our Lord coming to him. And in so speaking, he did but appeal to that title under which our Lord
was known from the beginning. Just Abel showed forth
his faith in Him by offering of the firstlings of his flock.
Abraham, in place of his son Isaac whom God spared,
offered the like for a sacrifice. The Israelites were en-
joined to sacrifice once a year, at Easter time, a lamb—
one lamb for each family, a lamb without blemish—to be
eaten whole, all but the blood, which was sprinkled, as
their protection, about their house doors. The Prophet
Isaias speaks of our Lord under the same image: "He shall
be led as a sheep to the slaughter, and shall be dumb as a
lamb before his shearers" (liii. 7); and all this because "He
was wounded for our iniquities, He was bruised for our
sins; . . . by His bruises we are healed" (liii. 5). And in
like manner the Holy Evangelist St. John, in the visions
of the Apocalypse, thus speaks of Him: "I saw, . . .

[1] *Add two more Prayers—for Catholic Schools and for the Dead, and leave
out the Introductions of Prefaces, and you will have fourteen Devotions for the
Via Crucis.—J. H. N.*

The Prayer for Catholic Schools has not yet been found. For the
Prayer for the Dead *vide* p. 282.—W. N.

(Apoc. v. 6), and behold a lamb standing as it were slain;" and then he saw all the blessed "fall down before the Lamb," . . . (verses 8, 9), and they sung a new canticle saying, "Thou wast slain, and hast redeemed us to God in Thy blood, out of every tribe and tongue and people and nation" (verse 9). . . . "Worthy is the Lamb that was slain, to receive power, and divinity, and wisdom, and strength, and honour, and glory, and benediction" (verse 12).

This is Jesus Christ, who when darkness, sin, guilt and misery had overspread the earth, came down from Heaven, took our nature upon Him, and shed His precious blood upon the Cross for all men.

Let us pray for all pagan nations, that they may be converted.

O Lord Jesus Christ, O King of the whole world, O Hope and Expectation of all nations, O Thou who hast bought all men for Thy own at the price of Thy most precious blood, look down in pity upon all races who are spread over the wide earth, and impart to them the knowledge of Thy truth. Remember, O Lord, Thy own most bitter sufferings of soul and body in Thy betrayal, Thy passion and Thy crucifixion, and have mercy upon their souls. Behold, O Lord, but a portion of mankind has heard of Thy Name— but a portion even professes to adore Thee—and yet thousands upon thousands in the East and the West, in the North and the South, hour after hour, as each hour comes, are dropping away from this life into eternity. Remember, O my dear Lord, and lay it to heart, that to the dishonour of Thy name, and to the triumph of Thine enemies, fresh victims are choking up the infernal pit, and are taking up their dwelling there for ever. Listen to the intercessions of Thy Saints, let Thy Mother plead with Thee, let not the prayers of Holy Church Thy Spouse be offered up in vain. Impute not to the poor heathen their many sins, but visit the earth

quickly and give all men to know, to believe, and to serve
Thee, in whom is our salvation, life and resurrection,
who with the Father, etc.

(2)

JESUS THE SON OF DAVID

OUR Lord asked the Pharisees, saying, "What think ye of Christ? Whose son is He? They say unto Him, The Son of David." For so the Prophet Isaias had foretold; "there shall come forth a rod out of the root of Jesse," Jesse was the father of David, the King of the Jews—and by "rod" or plant is meant the Blessed Virgin; "there shall come forth a rod out of the root of Jesse, and a flower shall rise up out of his root" (Isaias xi.1); by the flower of the plant is meant our Lord the son of the Blessed Mary. "And the Spirit of the Lord shall rest upon Him" (verse 2); this the Holy Ghost did at His Baptism. And Jeremias says: "Behold the days come, and I will raise up to David a just Branch, and a King shall reign, and shall be wise, and shall execute judgment and justice in the earth. In those days Juda shall be saved . . . and this is the name that they shall call Him—the Lord our Just One" (Jeremias xxiii. 5–6). Hence the Jews when disputing whether our Lord were the Christ, said, "Doth not the Scripture say, that Christ cometh out of the seed of David?" (John vii. 42).

It was the glory of the Jews that the promised Saviour, the Christ, the Sacrifice and Propitiation of the whole human race, the Almighty Liberator, was to be of their race and country—yet, dreadful to say, when He came, they rejected Him, they put Him to death. "He came unto His own, and His own received Him not" (John i. 11). And as they rejected Him, He rejected them. They put Him to death, and He gave them up to their enemies, who burned up their city Jerusalem, cast them out of their country, and they have been a wandering people ever since.

Let us pray for the Jewish nation, that they may turn to their Lord and God whom they have crucified.

O seed of Abraham, O Son of David, O Adonai and leader of the house of Israel, who didst appear to Moses in the burning bush, and didst on Mount Sinai deliver to him Thy Law; O Key of David, and sceptre of the house of Israel, who openest and no one shutteth, who shuttest and no one openeth; visit not, O dear Lord, the sins of the fathers upon the children, continue not Thy wrath for ever, but spare this poor nation, which was once so high in Thy sight, and now hath fallen so low. O remember not those old Priests and Scribes, the Pharisees and Sadducees, remember not Annas and Caiphas, Judas, and the insane multitude who cried out "Crucify Him." In wrath remember mercy. Forgive their obstinacy and forgive their impenitence—forgive their blindness to things spiritual, and their avowed love of this world and its enjoyments. Touch their hearts and give them true faith and repentance. Have mercy, O Jesus, on Thy own brethren—have mercy on the countrymen of Thy Mother, of St. Joseph, of Thy Apostles, of St. Paul, of Thy great Saints Abraham, Moses, Samuel, David. O Lord, hear: O Lord, be appeased: O Lord, hearken and do (Dan. ix. 19): delay not for Thine own sake, O my God, for Thy Name was once named upon the city Jerusalem and Thy people.

(3)

JESUS THE LORD OF GRACE

W HEN our Lord rejected His own countrymen, the
Jews, who had rejected Him, He chose other nations
instead of them. Thus the Holy Evangelist, after saying,
"He came unto His own, and His own received Him
not" (John i. 11–13), adds, "But as many as received
Him, to them He gave power to be made the sons of
God, to them that believe in His name: who are born, not
of blood, nor of the will of the flesh, nor of the will of
man, but of God." That is, so that men believed in Him,
whatever was their race or country, He made them His
sons and gave them the gifts of grace and the promise of
heaven. He had warned the Jews of this, before their time
of grace was over. "I say unto you," He said, "that the
kingdom of God shall be taken from you, and shall be
given to a nation bringing forth the fruits thereof" (Matt.
xxi. 43). And hence St. Paul, His great Apostle, when he
found the Jews would not listen to Him, when they "gain-
said and blasphemed," shook his garments (Acts xviii. 6)
and said, "Your blood be upon your own heads;
I am clean; from henceforth I will go unto the Gentiles."
And if God cast off His own people, the Jews, so, much
more, will He cast off any other people who cast off Him.
Hence the same St. Paul says, "If some of the branches
(Rom. xi. 17–21) (that is, the Jews) be broken (off), and
thou (that is, a man of some other nation) art ingrafted in
them (instead), and art made partaker of the root and of
the fatness of the olive tree; boast not. . . . Because of
unbelief they were broken off; but thou standest by faith;

be not high-minded, but fear. For, if God hath not spared the natural branches, *fear* lest He spare not thee." This misery has happened to this country, to our own England; God chose it and blessed it for near a thousand years; it rebelled, lost faith, and He cast it off out of His Church.

Let us pray for the recovery of our own country England to the faith and the Church of Christ.

O Sapientia, O Wisdom who hast issued out of the mouth of the Highest, and reachest in Thy Providence from the beginning to the end of all things, and disposest all things in sweetness and in strength, it was by Thy unmerited grace, we acknowledge it, O Lord, that this country of ours was so many centuries ago brought into the true fold, and gifted with the knowledge of Thy Truth and the grace of Thy Sacraments. Alas! how things have changed since then! The people was small then and of little account; now it stands highest among the nations of the earth. Then it was obscure and poor—now it has amazing wealth and pre-eminent power; but then it was great in Thy sight, and now on the contrary it is little, for it has lost Thee. O my God, what doth it profit, though we gain the whole world and lose our own souls? or what exchange shall we give for our souls? Wilt Thou forget, O Lord, what by Thy grace we once were, before we turned from Thee? Wilt Thou not listen to all our Saints and Martyrs who are now reigning with Thee and are ever interceding for us? O, look not upon our haughtiness and pride; look not upon our contempt of truths invisible; look not upon our impurity; but look upon Thy own merits; look upon the wounds in Thy hands; look upon Thy past mercies towards us; and, in spite of our wilfulness, subdue our hearts to Thee, O Saviour of men, and renew Thy work in the midst of the years, in the midst of the years re-establish Thou it.

(4)

JESUS THE AUTHOR AND FINISHER OF FAITH

ST. PAUL tells us to "look on Jesus, the Author and Finisher of faith." Faith is the first step towards salvation, and without it we have no hope. For St. Paul says, "Without faith it is impossible to please God." It is a divine light; by it we are brought out of darkness into sunshine; by it, instead of groping, we are able to see our way towards heaven. Moreover, it is a great *gift*, which comes from above, and which we cannot obtain except from Him who is the object of it. He, our Lord Jesus Himself, and He alone, gives us the grace to believe in Him. Hence the Holy Apostle calls Him the author of our faith—and He finishes and perfects it also—from first to last it is altogether from Him. Therefore it was that our Lord said, "If thou canst believe, all things are possible to him that believeth" (Mark ix. 22–23). And hence the poor man to whom He spoke, who believed indeed already, but still feebly, made answer—"crying out with tears, I *do* believe, Lord; help Thou my unbelief." Hence, too, on another occasion, the Apostles said to our Lord, "Increase our faith" (Luke xvii. 5). And St. Paul draws out fully the whole matter when he reminds his converts, "And you (hath He raised), when you were dead in your offences and sins, wherein in time past you walked, according to the course of this world, . . . in which we all conversed in time past, . . . and were by nature children of wrath, even as the rest; but God (who is rich in mercy), for His exceeding charity wherewith He loved us, even when we were dead in sins hath quickened us

together in Christ. . . . By grace you are saved through
faith, and that not of yourself, for it is the gift of God"
(Ephesians ii. 1–8).

*Let us pray for all the scorners, scoffers, and unbelievers, all false
teachers and opposers of the truth, who are to be found in this land.*

O Lord Jesus Christ, upon the Cross Thou didst say:
"Father, forgive them, for they know not what they do."
And this surely, O my God, is the condition of vast
multitudes among us now; they know not what they
might have known, or they have forgotten what once
they knew. They deny that there is a God, but they know
not what they are doing. They laugh at the joys of heaven
and the pains of hell, but they know not what they are
doing. They renounce all faith in Thee, the Saviour of
man, they despise Thy Word and Sacraments, they revile
and slander Thy Holy Church and her Priests, but they
know not what they are doing. They mislead the wandering, they frighten the weak, they corrupt the young,
but they know not what they do. Others, again, have a
wish to be religious, but mistake error for truth—they go
after fancies of their own, and they seduce others and
keep them from Thee. They know not what they are
doing, but Thou canst make them know. O Lord, we
urge Thee by Thy own dear words, "Lord and Father,
forgive them, for they know not what they do." Teach
them now, open their eyes here, before the future comes;
give them faith in what they must see hereafter, if they
will not believe in it here. Give them full and saving faith
here; destroy their dreadful delusions, and give them to
drink of that living water, which whoso hath shall not
thirst again.

(5)

JESUS THE LORD OF ARMIES

AMONG the visions which the beloved disciple St.
John was given to see, and which he has recorded in his
Apocalypse, one was that of our Lord as the commander
and leader of the hosts of the Saints in their warfare with
the world. "I saw," he says, "and behold a white horse,
and He that sat on him had a bow, and there was a crown
given Him; and He went forth conquering that He might
conquer" (Apoc. vi. 2). And again, "I saw heaven opened,
and behold a white horse, and He that sat upon him was
called Faithful and True, and with justice doth He judge
and fight" (Apoc. xix. 11). . . . "And he was clothed
with a garment, sprinkled with blood, and His Name is
called, *The Word of God*. And the armies that are in
heaven followed Him on white horses, clothed in fine
linen, white and clean" (verse 13). Such is the Captain of
the Lord's Host, and such are His soldiers. He and they
ride on white horses, which means, that their cause is
innocent, and upright and pure. Warriors of this world
wage *unjust* wars, but our Almighty Leader fights for a
heavenly cause and with heavenly weapons—and in like
manner His soldiers fight the good fight of faith; they
fight against their and their Master's three great enemies,
the World, the Flesh, and the Devil. He is covered with
blood, but it is His own blood, which He shed for our
redemption. And His followers are red with blood, but
still again it is His blood, for it is written "they have
washed their robes, and have made them white in the
blood of the Lamb" (Apoc. vii. 14). And again He and
they are certain of victory because it is said "He went

forth conquering that He might conquer" (Apoc. vi. 2). So let us say with the Psalmist "Gird Thy sword upon Thy thigh, O Thou most mighty. . . . Because of truth and meekness and justice Thy right hand shall conduct Thee wonderfully" (Psalm xliv. 4–5).

Let us pray for the whole Church Militant here upon earth.

O Lion of the Tribe of Judah, the root of David, who fightest the good fight, and hast called on all men to join Thee, give Thy courage and strength to all Thy soldiers over the whole earth, who are fighting under the standard of Thy Cross. Give grace to every one in his own place to fight Thy battle well. Be with Thy missionaries in pagan lands, put right words into their mouths, prosper their labours, and sustain them under their sufferings with Thy consolations, and carry them on, even through torment and blood (if it be necessary), to their reward in heaven. Give the grace of wisdom to those in high station, that they may neither yield to fear, nor be seduced by flattery. Make them prudent as serpents, and simple as doves. Give Thy blessing to all preachers and teachers, that they may speak Thy words and persuade their hearers to love Thee. Be with all faithful servants of Thine, whether in low station or in high, who mix in the world; instruct them how to speak and how to act every hour of the day, so as to preserve their own souls from evil and to do good to their companions and associates. Teach us, one and all, to live in thy presence and to see Thee, our Great Leader and Thy Cross—and thus to fight valiantly and to overcome, that at the last we may sit down with Thee in Thy Throne, as Thou also hast overcome and art set down with Thy Father in His Throne.

(6)

JESUS THE ONLY BEGOTTEN SON

JESUS is the only Son of the only Father—as it is said in
the Creed, "I believe in one God, the Father Almighty,"
and then "and in Jesus Christ, His only Son our Lord."
And so He Himself says in the Gospel, "As the Father
hath life in Himself, so He hath given to the Son also to
have life in Himself" (John v. 26). And He said to the
man whom He cured of blindness, "Dost thou believe in
the Son of God? It is He that talketh with thee" (John ix.
35–37). And St. John the Evangelist says, "The Word
was made flesh and dwelt among us, and we saw His
glory, the glory as it were of the only begotten of the
Father" (John i. 14). And St. John Baptist says, "The
Father loveth the Son and He hath given all things into
His hand. He that believeth in the Son, hath life everlasting" (John iii. 35, 36). And St. Paul says, "There is one
body and one Spirit—as ye are called in one hope of your
calling. One Lord, one faith, one baptism, One God and
Father of all" (Eph. iv. 4–6).

Thus Almighty God has set up *all* things in unity—and
therefore His Holy Church in a special way, as the Creed
again says, "One Holy Catholic and Apostolic Church."
It is His wise and gracious will that His followers should
not follow their own way, and form many bodies, but
one. This was the meaning of the mystery of His garment
at the time of His crucifixion, which "was without seam,
woven from the top throughout" (John xix. 23). And
therefore was it that the soldiers were not allowed to

break His sacred limbs, for like the Jewish Easter Lamb
not a bone of Him was to be broken.

Let us pray for the unity of the Church and
the reconciliation and peace of all Christians.

O Lord Jesus Christ, who, when Thou wast about to
suffer, didst pray for Thy disciples to the end of time that
they might all be one, as Thou art in the Father, and the
Father in Thee, look down in pity on the manifold
divisions among those who profess Thy faith, and heal
the many wounds which the pride of man and the craft of
Satan have inflicted upon Thy people. Break down the
walls of separation which divide one party and denomi-
nation of Christians from another. Look with compassion on the souls who have been born in one or other of
these various communions which not Thou, but man
hath made. Set free the prisoners from these unauthorised
forms of worship, and bring them all into that one
communion which thou didst set up in the beginning, the
One Holy Catholic and Apostolic Church. Teach all men
that the see of St. Peter, the Holy Church of Rome, is the
foundation, centre, and instrument of unity. Open their
hearts to the long-forgotten truth that our Holy Father,
the Pope, is thy Vicar and Representative; and that in
obeying Him in matters of religion, they are obeying
Thee, so that as there is but one holy company in heaven
above, so likewise there may be but one communion,
confessing and glorifying Thy holy Name here below.

(7)

JESUS THE ETERNAL KING

OUR Lord was called Jesus, when He took flesh of the Blessed Virgin. The Angel Gabriel said to her, "Behold, thou shalt bring forth a Son, and thou shalt call His Name Jesus." But, though He then gained a new name, He had existed from eternity; He never was not—He never had a beginning—and His true name, therefore, is the Eternal King. He ever reigned with His Father and the Holy Ghost, three Persons, one God. And hence, shortly before His crucifixion, He said, "Glorify Thou Me, O Father, with Thyself, with the glory which I had, before the world was, with Thee" (John xvii. 5). He Who was the Eternal King in heaven, came to be King, and Lord, and Lawgiver, and Judge upon earth. Hence the prophet Isaias says, foretelling His coming, *A child* is born to us, and a Son is given to us, and the government is upon His shoulder; and His Name shall be called Wonderful, Counsellor, God the Mighty, the Father of the world to come, the Prince of Peace" (Isaias ix. 6). And when He left the world, He left His power behind Him, and divided it among His followers. He gave one portion of His power to one, another to another. He gave the fulness of His power to St. Peter, and to his successors, who, in consequence, are His vicars and representatives—so that, as the Father sent the Son, so the Son has sent St. Peter. But not only St. Peter and the other Apostles, but all bishops and prelates in Holy Church, all pastors of souls, all Christian kings have power from Him, and stand to us in His place.

Let us pray for our Holy Father the Pope,
and all Rulers in the Church.

O Emmanuel, God with us, who art the Light that enlighteneth all men, who from the time when Thou camest upon earth, hast never left it to itself, who, after teaching Thy Apostles, gave them to teach others to succeed them, and didst especially leave St. Peter and his successors, Bishops of Rome, to take Thy place towards us, and to guide and rule us in Thy stead age after age, till the end come; Thou hast sent grievous trials for many years upon the Holy See of Rome. We believe and confess, O Lord, without any hesitation at all, that Thou hast promised a continuous duration to Thy Church while the world lasts—and we confess before Thee, that we are in no doubt or trouble whatever, we have not a shadow of misgiving as to the permanence and the spiritual well-being either of Thy Church itself or of its rulers. Nor do we know what is best for Thy Church, and for the interests of the Catholic faith, and for the Pope, or the bishops throughout the world at this time. We leave the event entirely to Thee; we do so without any anxiety, knowing that everything must turn to the prosperity of Thy ransomed possession, even though things may look threatening for a season. Only we earnestly entreat that Thou wouldest give Thy own servant and representative, the Pope Leo, true wisdom and courage, and fortitude, and the consolations of Thy grace in this life, and a glorious immortal crown in the life to come.

(8)

JESUS THE BEGINNING OF THE NEW CREATION.

OUR Lord Jesus Christ is said by His Almighty power to have begun a new creation, and to be Himself the first fruit and work of it. Mankind were lost in sin, and were thereby, not only not heirs of heaven, but the slaves of the Evil one. Therefore He who made Adam in the beginning resolved in His mercy to make a new Adam, and by a further ineffable condescension determined that that new Adam should be Himself. And therefore, by His holy Prophet Isaias, He announced before He came, "Behold I create new heavens and a new earth" (Isaias lxv. 17). On the other hand St. Paul calls Him "The image of the invisible God, the first-born of every creature" (Col. i. 15). And St. John calls Him "the Amen, the faithful and true witness, who is the beginning of the creation of God" (Apoc. iii. 14). The Creator came as if He were a creature, because He took upon Him a created nature—and as, at the first, Eve was formed out of the side of Adam, so now, when He hung on the cross, though not a bone of Him was broken, his side was pierced, and out of it came the grace, represented by the blood and the water, out of which His bride and spouse, His Holy Church, was made. And thus all the sanctity of all portions of that Holy Church is derived from Him as a beginning; and He feeds us with His Divine Flesh in the Holy Eucharist, in order to spread within us, in the hearts of all of us, the blessed leaven of the New Creation. All the wisdom of the Doctors, and the courage and endurance of the Martyrs, and the purity of Virgins, and the zeal of Preachers, and the humility and mortification of religious men, is from Him, as the beginning of the new and heavenly creation of God.

Let us pray for all ranks and conditions of men
in Thy Holy Church.

O Lord, who art called the Branch, the Orient, the Splendour of the eternal light, and the Sun of Justice, who art that Tree, of whom Thy beloved disciple speaks as the Tree of life, bearing twelve fruits, and its leaves for the healing of the nations, give Thy grace and blessing on all those various states and conditions in Thy Holy Church, which have sprung from Thee and live in Thy Life. Give to all Bishops the gifts of knowledge, discernment, prudence, and love. Give to all priests to be humble, tender, and pure; give to all pastors of Thy flock to be zealous, vigilant, and unworldly; give to all religious bodies to act up to their rule, to be simple and without guile, and to set their hearts upon invisible things and them only. Grant to fathers of families to recollect that they will have hereafter to give account of the souls of their children; grant to all husbands to be tender and true; to all wives to be obedient and patient; grant to all children to be docile; to all young people to be chaste; to all the aged to be fervent in spirit; to all who are engaged in business, to be honest and unselfish; and to all of us the necessary graces of faith, hope, charity, and contrition.

(9)

JESUS THE LOVER OF SOULS

THE inspired writer says, "Thou hast mercy upon all, because Thou canst do all things, and overlookest the sins of men for the sake of repentance. For Thou lovest all things that are, and hatest none of the things which Thou hast made. . . . And how could anything endure, if Thou wouldst not? or be preserved, if not called by Thee? But Thou sparest all, because they are Thine, O Lord, who lovest souls" (Wisdom xi. 24–27). This is what brought Him from Heaven, and gave Him the Name of Jesus— for the Angel said to St. Joseph about Mary, "She shall bring forth a Son, and thou shalt call His Name Jesus; for He shall save His people from their sins" (Matt. i. 21). It was His great love for souls and compassion for sinners which drew Him from Heaven. Why did He consent to veil His glory in mortal flesh, except that He desired so much to save those who had gone astray and lost all hope of salvation." Hence He says Himself, "The Son of Man is come to seek and to save that which was lost" (Matt. xvii. 11, Luke xix. 10). Rather than that we should perish, He did all that even omnipotence could do consistently with its holy Attributes, for He gave Himself. And He loves each of us so much that He has died for each one as fully and absolutely as if there were no one else for Him to die for. He is our best friend, our True Father, the only real Lover of our souls—He takes all means to make us love Him in return, and He refuses us nothing if we do.

Let us pray for the conversion of all sinners.

O Lord, "who didst give Thyself for us, that Thou mightest redeem us from all iniquity, and mightest cleanse to Thyself a people acceptable, a pursuer of good works," look upon Thy baptized, look on the multitude of those who once were Thine and have gone from Thee. Ah, for how short a time do they keep Thy grace in their hearts, how soon do they fall off from Thee, with what difficulty do they return; and even, though they repent and come to penance, yet how soon, in the words of Scripture, doth the dog return to his vomit, and the sow that was washed to her wallowing in the mire. O my God, save us all from the seven deadly sins, and rescue those who have been made captive by them. Convert all sinners—bring judgments down upon them, if there is no other way of reclaiming them. Touch the hearts of all proud men, wrathful, revengeful men; of the obstinate, of the self-relying, of the envious, of the slanderer, of the hater of goodness and truth; of the slothful and torpid; of all gluttons and drunkards; of the covetous and unmerciful; of all licentious talkers; of all who indulge in impure thoughts, words, or deeds. Make them understand that they are going straight to hell, and save them from themselves and from Satan.

(10)

JESUS OUR GUIDE AND GUARDIAN

T HERE are men who think that God is so great that He disdains to look down upon *us*, our doings and our fortunes. But He who did not find it beneath His Majesty to make us, does not think it beneath Him to observe and to visit us. He says Himself in the Gospel: "Are not five sparrows sold for two farthings? and not one of them is forgotten before God. Yea, the very hairs of your head are all numbered. Fear not, therefore: you are of more value than many sparrows." He determined from all eternity that He would create us. He settled our whole fortune—and, if He did not absolutely decree to bring us to heaven, it is because we have free will, and by the very constitution of our nature He has put it in part out of His own power, for we must do *our* part, if to heaven we attain. But He has done every thing short of this. He died for us all upon the Cross, that, if it were possible to save us, we might be saved. And He calls upon us lovingly, begging us to accept the benefit of His meritorious and most Precious Blood. And those who trust Him He takes under His special protection. He marks out their whole life for them; He appoints all that happens to them; He guides them in such way as to secure their salvation; He gives them just so much of health, of wealth, of friends, as is best for them; He afflicts them only when it is for their good; He is never angry with them. He measures out just that number of years which is good for them; and He appoints the hour of their death in such a way as to secure their perseverance up to it.

Let us pray for ourselves and for all our needs.

O my Lord and Saviour, in Thy arms I am safe; keep me and I have nothing to fear; give me up and I have nothing to hope for. I know not what will come upon me before I die. I know nothing about the future, but I rely upon Thee. I pray Thee to give me what is good for me; I pray Thee to take from me whatever may imperil my salvation; I pray Thee not to make me rich, I pray Thee not to make me very poor; but I leave it all to Thee, because Thou knowest and I do not. If Thou bringest pain or sorrow on me, give me grace to bear it well— keep me from fretfulness and selfishness. If Thou givest me health and strength and success in this world, keep me ever on my guard lest these great gifts carry me away from Thee. O Thou who didst die on the Cross for me, even for me, sinner as I am, give me to know Thee, to believe on Thee, to love Thee, to serve Thee; ever to aim at setting forth Thy glory; to live to and for Thee; to set a good example to all around me; give me to die just at that time and in that way which is most for Thy glory, and best for my salvation.

(11)

JESUS SON OF MARY

W HEN our Lord came upon earth, He might have created a fresh body for Himself out of nothing—or He might have formed a body for Himself out of the earth, as He formed Adam. But He preferred to be born, as other men are born, of a human mother. Why did He do so? He did so to put honour on all those earthly relations and connections which are ours by nature; and to teach us that, though He has begun a new creation, He does not wish us to cast off the old creation, as far as it is not sinful. Hence it is our duty to love and honour our parents, to be affectionate to our brothers, sisters, friends, husbands, wives, not only not less, but even more, than it was man's duty before our Lord came on earth. As we become better Christians, more consistent and zealous servants of Jesus, we shall become only more and more anxious for the good of all around us—our kindred, our friends, our acquaintances, our neighbours, our superiors, our inferiors, our masters, our employers. And this we shall do from the recollection how our Lord loved His Mother. He loves her still in heaven with a special love. He refuses her nothing. We then on earth must feel a tender solicitude for all our relations, all our friends, all whom we know or have dealings with. And moreover, we must love not only those who love us, but those who hate us or injure us, that we may imitate Him, who not only was loving to His Mother, but even suffered Judas, the traitor, to kiss Him, and prayed for His murderers on the cross.

*Let us pray God for our relations, friends,
well wishers, and enemies, living and dead.*

O Jesus, son of Mary, whom Mary followed to the
Cross when Thy disciples fled, and who didst bear her
tenderly in mind in the midst of Thy sufferings, even in
Thy last words, who didst commit her to Thy best
beloved disciple, saying to her, "Woman, behold thy
son," and to him, "Behold thy Mother," we, after Thy
pattern, would pray for all who are near and dear to us,
and we beg Thy grace to do so continually. We beg Thee
to bring them all into the light of Thy truth, or to keep
them in Thy truth if they already know it, and to keep
them in a state of grace, and to give them the gift of
perseverance. We thus pray for our parents, for our
fathers and our mothers, for our children, for every one
of them, for our brothers and sisters, for every one of our
brothers, for every one of our sisters, for our cousins and
all our kindred, for our friends, and our father's friends,
for all our old friends, for our dear and intimate friends,
for our teachers, for our pupils, for our masters and
employers, for our servants or subordinates, for our
associates and work-fellows, for our neighbours, for our
superiors and rulers; for those who wish us well, for
those who wish us ill; for our enemies; for our rivals; for
our injurers and for our slanderers. And not only for the
living, but for the dead, who have died in the grace of
God, that He may shorten their time of expiation, and
admit them into His presence above.

(12)

JESUS OUR DAILY SACRIFICE

Our Lord not only offered Himself as a Sacrifice on the Cross, but He makes Himself a perpetual, a daily sacrifice, to the end of time. In the Holy Mass that One Sacrifice on the Cross once offered is renewed, continued, applied to our benefit. He seems to say, My Cross was raised up 1800 years ago, and only for a few hours— and very few of my servants were present there—but I intend to bring millions into my Church. For their sakes then I will perpetuate my Sacrifice, that each of them may be as though they had severally been present on Calvary. I will offer Myself up day by day to the Father, that every one of my followers may have the opportunity to offer his petitions to Him, sanctified and recommended by the all-meritorious virtue of my Passion. Thus I will be a Priest for ever, after the order of Melchisedech—My priests shall stand at the Altar—but not they, but I rather, will offer. I will not let them offer mere bread and wine, but I myself will be present upon the Altar instead, and I will offer up myself invisibly, while they perform the outward rite. And thus the Lamb that was slain once for all, though He is ascended on high, ever remains a victim from His miraculous presence in Holy Mass under the figure and appearance of mere earthly and visible symbols.

Let us pray for all who day by day have calls upon us.

My Lord Jesus Christ, Thou hast given me this great gift, that I am allowed, not only to pray for myself, but to intercede for others in Thy Holy Mass. Therefore, O Lord, I pray Thee to give all grace and blessing upon this town and every inhabitant of it—upon the Catholic Church in it, for our Bishop, and his clergy, and for all Catholic places of worship and their congregations. I pray Thee to bless and prosper all the good works and efforts of all priests, religious, and pious Catholics—I pray for all the sick, all the suffering, all the poor, all the oppressed—I pray for all prisoners—I pray for all evil doers. I pray for all ranks in the community—I pray for the Queen and Royal Family—for the Houses of Parliament—for the judges and magistrates—for all our soldiers—for all who defend us in ships—I pray for all who are in peril and danger. I pray for all who have benefited me, befriended me, or aided me. I pray for all who have asked my prayers—I pray for all whom I have forgotten. Bring us all after the troubles of this life into the haven of peace, and reunite us all together for ever, O my dear Lord, in Thy glorious heavenly kingdom.[1]

[1] Vide footnote, p. 257.

PRAYER FOR THE FAITHFUL DEPARTED

O GOD of the Spirits of all flesh, O Jesu, Lover of souls, we recommend unto Thee the souls of all those Thy servants, who have departed with the sign of faith and sleep the sleep of peace. We beseech Thee, O Lord and Saviour, that, as in Thy mercy to them Thou becamest man, so now Thou wouldest hasten the time, and admit them to Thy presence above. Remember, O Lord, that they are Thy creatures, not made by strange gods, but by Thee, the only Living and True God; for there is no other God but Thou, and none that can equal Thy works. Let their souls rejoice in Thy light, and impute not to them their former iniquities, which they committed through the violence of passion, or the corrupt habits of their fallen nature. For, although they have sinned, yet they always firmly believed in the Father, Son, and Holy Ghost; and before they died, they reconciled themselves to Thee by true contrition and the Sacraments of Thy Church.

O Gracious Lord, we beseech Thee, remember not against them the sins of their youth and their ignorances; but according to Thy great mercy, be mindful of them in Thy heavenly glory. May the heavens be opened to them, and the Angels rejoice with them. May the Archangel St. Michael conduct them to Thee. May Thy holy Angels come forth to meet them, and carry them to the city of the heavenly Jerusalem. May St. Peter, to whom Thou gavest the keys of the kingdom of heaven, receive them. May St. Paul, the vessel of election, stand by them. May St. John, the beloved disciple, who had the revelation of the secrets of heaven, intercede for them. May all the Holy Apostles, who received from Thee the power of binding and loosing, pray for them. May all the Saints and elect of God, who in this world suffered torments for Thy Name, befriend them; that, being freed from the prison beneath, they may be admitted into the glories of that kingdom, where with the Father and the Holy Ghost Thou livest and reignest one God, world without end.

Come to their assistance, all ye Saints of God; gain for them deliverance from their place of punishment; meet them, all ye Angels; receive these holy souls, and present them before the Lord. Eternal rest give to them, O Lord. And may perpetual light shine on them.

May they rest in peace. Amen.[1]

---

[1] The Prayer for Catholic Schools has not yet been found. Vide footnote on p. 257.—W. N.

MEDITATIONS FOR EIGHT DAYS

Sunday

OUR LORD

1. P<small>LACE</small> yourself in the presence of God, kneeling with your hands clasped.

2. Read slowly and devoutly

Apocalypse, chap. i, verses 10–18.

"I was," &c. *down to* "of death and of hell."

3. Bring all you have read before you at once, as if you saw our Lord.

4. Then say to Him whatever comes into your mind to say; for instance:—

> "His eyes were as a flame of fire," and "His countenance shone as the sun shineth in his strength."

> (1) O my God, the day will come when I shall see that countenance and those eyes, when my soul returns to Him to be judged.

> (2) Those eyes are so *piercing*: they see through me; nothing is hid from them. Thou countest every hair of my head; Thou knowest every breath I breathe; Thou seest every morsel of food I take.

> (3) Those eyes are so *pure*. They are so clear that I can look into their depths, as into some transparent well of water, though I cannot see the bottom; for Thou art infinite.

Being a portion of an attempt to teach a young invalid to meditate.

(4) Those eyes are so *loving*; so gentle, so sweet; they seem to say, "Come to Me."

5. *Conclusion.* O Lord, make me love Thee, make me love Thee.

Monday

GUARDIAN ANGEL

1. PLACE yourself in the presence of God, kneeling with your hands clasped.

2. Read slowly and devoutly

Psalm xc. (as it is found in Compline)

3. Bring all you have read before you, as if you saw the Angels protecting you, especially your Guardian Angel.

4. Then say to God whatever is suggested to you; for instance:—

"He hath given His Angels charge over thee, to keep thee in all thy ways. In their hands they shall bear thee up, lest thou dash thy foot against a stone."

(1) O my God, I will go forward in Thy way, for my Guardian goes with me. I am very blind; I know not what is before me. I know not what will happen to me in life. I do not know whether I shall live long, or die young. But this I know, that in health and sickness, in joy and sorrow, in youth and age, Thou wilt be with me.

(2) O my sweet Guardian, how beautiful thou art. I wish I could see thee. And thou art as pure and holy as thou art beautiful, and thy breath inspires chaste thoughts. And as gentle and kind as thou art pure.

5. *Conclusion.*—God of Angels, have mercy on me. Queen of Angels, pray for me.

Tuesday

ST. JOSEPH

1. PLACE yourself in the presence of God, kneeling with your hands clasped.

2. Read slowly and devoutly

Psalm xiv.

3. Bring all you have read before you at once, as if you saw our Lord.

4. Then say to Him whatever comes into your mind to say; for instance:—

(1) Joseph was pure and innocent in a way unlike any other man who ever lived, our Lord excepted. His soul was as white as snow. He had nothing whatever within his heart to make him ashamed, and he would have found it most difficult to find matter for confession. O Joseph, make me so blameless and irreproachable that I should not care though friends saw into my heart as perfectly as Jesus and Mary saw into thine. O gain me the grace of holy simplicity and affectionateness, so that I may love thee, Mary, and, above all, Jesus, as thou didst love Jesus and Mary.

(2) Joseph was as humble as he was sinless. He never thought of himself, but always of the Infant Saviour, whom he carried in his arms. O holy Joseph, make me like thee in purity, simplicity, innocence and devotion.

5. *Conclusion.*—Jesus, mercy! Mary, Joseph, pray for me.

Wednesday

ALL SAINTS

1. PLACE yourself in the presence of God, kneeling with hands clasped.

2. Read slowly and devoutly

Apocalypse, chap. vii. verses 9–17.

3. Bring all this before you as in a picture.

4. Then say to Him whatever comes into your mind to say; for instance:—

"They are before the throne of God, and serve Him day and night in His Temple." "They shall not hunger nor thirst any more;" "The Lamb shall lead them to the fountains of living waters."

(1) My dear Lord and Saviour, shall I ever see Thee in heaven? This world is very beautiful, very attractive, and there are many things and persons whom I love in it. But Thou art the most beautiful and best of all. Make me acknowledge this with my heart, as well as by faith and in my reason.

(2) My Lord, I know nothing here below lasts; nothing here below satisfies. Pleasures come and go; I quench my thirst and am thirsty again. But the saints in heaven are always gazing on Thee, and drinking in eternal blessedness from Thy dear and gracious and most awful and most glorious countenance.

5. *Conclusion.*—May my lot be with the saints.

Thursday

THE PARACLETE

1. PLACE yourself in the presence of God, kneeling with hands clasped.

2. Read slowly and devoutly

Psalm ciii. verses 29–36.

3. Try to imagine the secret power of God dispensing blessing and grace every moment all over the earth.

4. Then say what is suggested by that thought; for instance:—

(1) How mysterious is my sovereign Lord and God! He is doing things innumerable always everywhere; yet one does not interfere with another. He hears everything which is said everywhere, yet He never confuses one thing with another. He sustains everything day and night, yet He is not wearied. He is at once most occupied, yet ever in repose. He is sovereign and supreme, yet He ministers, like a servant, to the whole creation.

(2) He is thus mysterious in His works—much more mysterious is He in His nature. God the Holy Ghost is the one God—but so is God the Father, so is God the Son. How is it that God is at once perfectly one, and perfectly three? I cannot tell—no wit of man can tell, no angel can tell it fully—for He is incomprehensible.

(3) O my Lord, God the Holy Ghost, I adore Thee, because Thou art so mysterious, so incomprehensible. Unless Thou wert incomprehensible,

Thou wouldst not be God. For how can the Infinite be other than incomprehensible to me?

5. *Conclusion.*—Holy angels, who see God's face, teach me to have faith in Him.

Friday

JESUS

1. PLACE yourself in the presence of God, kneeling with hands clasped.

2. Read slowly and devoutly

St. Luke xxii. verses 40 *to* 46
(*as it occurs in the Passion on Holy Wednesday*).

3. Bring what you have read before you, as a picture.

4. Then say to Him whatever comes into your mind to say; for instance:—

(1) What is it that bows down the Almighty Son of God? What is it that so terrifies and overwhelms my dear Saviour? What is it that thus convulses Him from head to foot? See how He trembles! He falls on his knees as under a tremendous load! His flesh quivers, and at length out of its pores comes a dew. It is red, and it trickles down Him, and falls heavily on the ground. It is His precious blood, and this is His agony.

(2) Alas! I know well enough what was the cause of it. He came on earth to undergo it, and to destroy it by undergoing it. It is the weight of sin. The sins of every child of Adam, of the whole race, were all then heaped into one mass, higher than the mountains, and placed upon His head. The burden would have crushed anyone else, even the highest Archangel, even the Blessed Mother of God. One human heart alone could undergo it, the heart of the Divine Son; yet see how His soul and body agonised with it,

though it was the soul and body of God Incarnate.

(3) My most dear Saviour, give me some little tenderness to grieve for Thee suffering for me.

5. *Conclusion.*—My dear Mother Mary, thou wert sinless, teach me to grieve with Thee.

Saturday

MARY

1. PLACE yourself in the presence of God, kneeling with your hands clasped.

2. Read slowly and devoutly

Isaias xxxv. (as on Ember Saturday Mass in Advent)

3. Think of Mary as robed in white, like the lily.

4. And say:—

(1) Thou, Mary, art the Virgin of Vrigins. To have a virgin soul is to love nothing on earth in comparison of God, or except for His sake. That soul is virginal which is ever looking for its Beloved who is in heaven, and which sees Him in whatever is lovely upon earth, loving earthly friends very dearly, but in their proper place, as His gifts, and His representatives, but loving Jesus alone with sovereign affection, and bearing to lose all, so that she may keep Him.

(2) O Mary, I wish I could see how you used to behave towards father and mother, especially towards St. Anne; and then how you behaved towards the priests of the temple; and then towards St. Joseph; and towards St. Elizabeth, and St. John Baptist; and afterwards towards the Apostles, especially towards St. John. I should see how sweet and lovely you were to every one of them; but still your heart was with Jesus only. And they would all feel and understand this, however kind you were to them.

5. *Conclusion.*—O Mary, when will you gain for me some little of this celestial purity, this true whiteness of soul, that I may fix my heart on my true love?

Sunday

OUR LORD

1. PLACE yourself in the presence of God, kneeling with your hands clasped.

2. Read slowly and devoutly

The Apocalypse as last Sunday.

3. Bring all you have read before you at once, as if you saw our Lord.

4. Then say, "His head and hairs were white like white wool, and as snow."

(1) Thy hair is white, O Jesus, because Thou art the Ancient of days, as the Prophet Daniel speaks. From everlasting to everlasting Thou art God. Thou didst come indeed to us as a little child—Thou didst hang upon the Cross at an age of life before as yet grey hairs come—but, O my dear Lord, there was always something mysterious about Thee, so that men were not quite sure of Thy age. The Pharisees talked of Thee as near fifty. For Thou hadst lived millions upon millions of years, and Thy face awfully showed it. And even when Thou wast a child, Thy hair shone so bright that people said, "It is snow."

(2) O my Lord, Thou art ever old, and ever young. Thou hast all perfection, and old age in Thee is ten thousand times more beautiful than the most beautiful youth. Thy white hair is an ornament, not a sign of decay. It is as dazzling as the sun, as white as the light, and as glorious as gold.

5. *Conclusion.*—Jesus, may I ever love Thee, not with human eyes, but with the eyes of the Spirit, which sees not as man sees.

LITANIES

(I)

From Quinguagesima down to end of Second Week in Lent

LITANY OF PENANCE

LORD, have mercy.
Lord, have mercy.
Christ, have mercy.
Christ, have mercy.
Lord, have mercy.
Lord, have mercy.
Christ, hear us.
Christ, graciously hear us.

God the Father of Heaven,
God the Son, Redeemer of the world,
God the Holy Ghost,
Holy Trinity, one God,
Incarnate Lord,
Lover of souls,
Saviour of sinners,

Have mercy on us.

Being the finished portion of a Scheme of Litanies for the whole year.
All these Litanies, except the Litany of St. Philip, are founded upon the Litanies to be met with in the ordinary Catholic Prayer books. None of them are Indulgenced, and none authorised for the use in public. The Litany of St. Philip was composed by Cardinal Newman about 1851, and altered by him from time to time till printed in 1856.—W. N.

Who didst come to seek those that were lost,
Who didst fast for them forty days and nights,
By Thy tenderness towards Adam when he fell,
By Thy faithfulness to Noe in the ark,
By Thy remembrance of Lot in the midst of sinners,
By Thy mercy on the Israelites in the desert,
By Thy forgiveness of David after his confession,
By Thy patience with wicked Achab on his humiliation,
By Thy restoration of the penitent Manasses,
By Thy long suffering towards the Ninevites, when
they went in sackcloth and ashes,
By Thy blessing on the Maccabees, who fasted before the battle,
By Thy choice of John to go before Thee as the
preacher of penance,
By Thy testimony to the Publican, who hung his
head and smote his breast,
By Thy welcome given to the returning Prodigal,
By Thy gentleness with the woman of Samaria,
By Thy condescension towards Zacchæus, persuading him to restitution,
By Thy pity upon the woman taken in adultery,
By Thy love of Magdalen, who loved much,
By Thy converting look, at which Peter wept,
By Thy gracious words to the thief upon the cross,

Have mercy on us.

We sinners,
Beseech Thee, hear us.
That we may judge ourselves, and so escape Thy
judgment,
That we may bring forth worthy fruits of penance,
That sin may not reign in our mortal bodies,
That we may work out our salvation with fear and
trembling,
Son of God,

We beseech Thee, hear us.

Lamb of God, who takest away the sins of the world,
Spare us, O Lord.
Lamb of God, who takest away the sins of the world,
Graciously hear us, O Lord.
Lamb of God, who takest away the sins of the world,
Have mercy on us.
Christ, hear us.
Christ, graciously hear us.

O Lord, hear our prayer.
And let our cry come unto Thee.

Let us Pray.

Grant, we beseech Thee, O Lord, to Thy faithful, pardon and peace, that they may be cleansed from all their offences, and also serve Thee with a quiet mind, through Christ our Lord.—*Amen.*

(2)

From Third Sunday in Lent, to Passion Sunday, exclusive

LITANY OF THE PASSION

Lord, have mercy.
Lord, have mercy.
Christ, have mercy.
Christ, have mercy.
Lord, have mercy.
Lord, have mercy.
Christ, hear us.
Christ, graciously hear us.

God the Father of Heaven,
God the Son, Redeemer of the world,
God the Holy Ghost,
Holy Trinity, one God,

Jesus, the Eternal Wisdom,
The Word made flesh,
Hated by the world,
Sold for thirty pieces of silver,
Sweating blood in Thy agony,
Betrayed by Judas,
Forsaken by Thy disciples,
Struck upon the cheek,
Accused by false witnesses,
Spit upon in the face,
Denied by Peter,
Mocked by Herod,

Have mercy on us.

Scourged by Pilate,
Rejected for Barabbas,
Loaded with the cross,
Crowned with thorns,
Stripped of Thy garments,
Nailed to the tree,
Reviled by the Jews,
Scoffed at by the malefactor,
Wounded in the side,
Shedding Thy last drop of blood,
Forsaken by Thy Father,
Dying for our sins,
Taken down from the cross,
Laid in the sepulchre,
Rising gloriously,
Ascending into Heaven,
Sending down the Paraclete,
Jesus our Sacrifice,
Jesus our Mediator,
Jesus our Judge,

Have mercy on us.

Be merciful.
Spare us, O Lord.
Be merciful.
Graciously hear us, O Lord.

From all sin,
From all evil,
From anger and hatred,
From malice and revenge,
From unbelief and hardness of heart,
From blasphemy and sacrilege,
From hypocrisy and covetousness,
From blindness of the understanding,
From contempt of Thy warnings,
From relapse after Thy judgments,

Lord Jesus, deliver us.

From danger of soul and body,
From everlasting death,

We sinners, *Beseech Thee, hear us.*

That Thou wouldest spare us,
That Thou wouldest pardon us,
That Thou wouldest defend Thy Church,
That Thou wouldest bless Thy own,
That Thou wouldest convert Thy foes,
That Thou wouldest spread the truth,
That Thou wouldest destroy error,
That Thou wouldest break to pieces false gods,
That Thou wouldest increase Thy elect,
That Thou wouldest let loose the holy souls in
    prison,
That Thou wouldest unite us to Thy Saints above,

We beseech Thee, hear us.

Lamb of God, who takest away the sins of the world,
Spare us, O Lord.
Lamb of God, who takest away the sins of the world,
Graciously hear us, O Lord.
Lamb of God, who takest away the sins of the world,
Have mercy on us.
Christ, hear us.
Christ, graciously hear us.
Lord, have mercy.
Christ, have mercy.
Lord, have mercy.

We adore Thee, O Christ, and we bless Thee,
Because through Thy Holy Cross Thou didst redeem the world.

Let us Pray.

    O God, who for the redemption of the world wast
pleased to be born; to be circumcised; to be rejected; to be

betrayed; to be bound with thongs; to be led to the slaughter; to be shamefully gazed at; to be falsely accused; to be scourged and torn; to be spit upon, and crowned with thorns; to be mocked and reviled; to be buffeted and struck with rods; to be stripped; to be nailed to the cross; to be hoisted up thereon; to be reckoned among thieves; to have gall and vinegar to drink; to be pierced with a lance: through Thy most holy passion, which we, Thy sinful servants, call to mind, and by Thy holy cross and gracious death, deliver us from the pains of hell, and lead us whither Thou didst lead the thief who was crucified with Thee, who with the Father and the Holy Ghost livest and reignest, God, world without end.—*Amen.*

(3)

For Passion Tide

LITANY OF THE SEVEN DOLOURS
OF THE BLESSED VIRGIN MARY

LORD, have mercy.
Lord, have mercy.
Christ, have mercy.
Christ, have mercy.
Lord, have mercy.
Lord, have mercy.
Christ, hear us.
Christ, graciously hear us.

God the Father of Heaven,
God the Son, Redeemer of the world,
God the Holy Ghost,
Holy Trinity, one God,

Have mercy on us.

Mother of sorrows,
Mother, whose soul was pierced by the sword,
Mother, who didst flee with Jesus into Egypt,
Mother, who didst seek Him sorrowing for three days,
Mother, who didst see Him scourged, and crowned with thorns,
Mother, who didst stand by Him whilst He hung upon the cross,
Mother, who didst receive Him into thine arms when He was dead,

Pray for us.

Mother, who didst see Him buried in the tomb,

O Mary, Queen of Martyrs,
O Mary, comfort of the sorrowful,
O Mary, help of the weak,
O Mary, strength of the fearful,
O Mary, light of the desponding,
O Mary, nursing-mother of the sick,
O Mary, refuge of sinners,

Pray for us.

Through the bitter passion of thy Son,
Through the piercing anguish of thy heart,
Through thy heavy weight of woe,
Through thy sadness and desolation,
Through thy maternal pity,
Through thy perfect resignation,
Through thy meritorious prayers,

From immoderate sadness,
From a cowardly spirit,
From an impatient temper,
From fretfulness and discontent,
From sullenness and gloom,
From despair and unbelief,
From final impenitence,

Save us by thy prayers.

We sinners,
Beseech thee, hear us.
Preserve us from sudden death,
Teach us how to die,
Succour us in our last agony,
Guard us from the enemy,
Bring us to a happy end,
Gain for us the gift of perseverance,
Aid us before the judgment seat,

We beseech thee, hear us.

Mother of God,
Mother, most sorrowful,
Mother, most desolate,

Lamb of God, who takest away the sins of the world,
Spare us, O Lord.
Lamb of God, who takest away the sins of the world,
Graciously hear us, O Lord.
Lamb of God, who takest away the sins of the world,
Have mercy on us.
Christ, hear us.
Christ, graciously hear us.
Lord, have mercy.
Christ, have mercy.
Lord, have mercy.

Succour us, O Blessed Virgin Mary,
In every time, and in every place.

Let us Pray.

O Lord Jesus Christ, God and man, grant, we beseech Thee, that Thy dear Mother Mary, whose soul the sword pierced in the hour of Thy passion, may intercede for us, now, and in the hour of our death, through Thine own merits, O Saviour of the world, who with the Father and the Holy Ghost livest and reignest, God, world without end.—*Amen.*

(4)

From Easter Day to May 1st

LITANY OF THE RESURRECTION

LORD, have mercy.
Lord, have mercy.
Christ, have mercy.
Christ, have mercy.
Lord, have mercy.
Lord, have mercy.
Christ, hear us.
Christ, graciously hear us.

God the Father of Heaven,
God the Son, Redeemer of the world,
God the Holy Ghost,
Holy Trinity, one God,

Jesus, Redeemer of mankind,
Jesus, Conqueror of sin and Satan,
Jesus, triumphant over Death,
Jesus, the Holy and the Just,
Jesus, the Resurrection and the Life,
Jesus, the Giver of grace,
Jesus, the Judge of the world,
Who didst lay down Thy life for Thy sheep,
Who didst rise again the third day,
Who didst manifest Thyself to Thy chosen,
Visiting Thy blessed Mother,
Appearing to Magdalen while she wept,

Have mercy on us.

Sending Thy angels to the holy women,
Comforting the Eleven,
Saying to them, Peace,
Breathing on them the Holy Ghost,
Confirming the faith of Thomas,
Committing Thy flock to Peter,
Speaking of the Kingdom of God,

Have mercy on us.

We sinners, *Beseech Thee, hear us,*
That we may walk in newness of life,
That we may advance in the knowledge of Thee,
That we may grow in grace,
That we may ever have the bread of life,
That we may persevere unto the end,
That we may have confidence before Thee at Thy
    coming,
That we may behold Thy face with joy,
That we may be placed at Thy right hand in the
    judgment,
That we may have our lot with the saints,

We beseech Thee, hear us.

Lamb of God, who takest away the sins of the world,
Spare us, O Lord.
Lamb of God, who takest away the sins of the world,
Graciously hear us, O Lord.
Lamb of God, who takest away the sins of the world,
Have mercy on us.
Christ, hear us.
Christ, graciously hear us.
Lord, have mercy.
Christ, have mercy.
Lord, have mercy.

Christ is risen, Alleluia.
He is risen indeed, and hath appeared unto Simon, Alleluia.

Let us Pray.

O God, who by Thy only begotten Son hast overcome death, and opened on us the way to eternal life, vouchsafe, we beseech Thee, so to confirm us by Thy grace, that we may in all things walk after the manner of those who have been redeemed from their sins, through the same Jesus Christ our Lord.—*Amen.*

(5)

From August 1 to August 15.

LITANY OF THE IMMACULATE HEART OF MARY

LORD, have mercy.
Lord, have mercy.
Christ, have mercy.
Christ, have mercy.
Lord, have mercy.
Lord, have mercy.
Christ, hear us.
Christ, graciously hear us.

God the Father of Heaven,
God the Son, Redeemer of the world,
God the Holy Ghost,
Holy Trinity, one God,

Have mercy on us.

Heart of Mary,
Heart, after God's own Heart,
Heart, in union with the Heart of Jesus,
Heart, the vessel of the Holy Ghost,
Heart of Mary, shrine of the Trinity,
Heart of Mary, home of the Word,
Heart of Mary, immaculate in thy creation,
Heart of Mary, flooded with grace,
Heart of Mary, blessed of all hearts,
Heart of Mary, Throne of glory,
Heart of Mary, Abyss of humbleness,

Pray for us.

Heart of Mary, Victim of love,
Heart of Mary, nailed to the Cross,
Heart of Mary, comfort of the sad,
Heart of Mary, refuge of the sinner,
Heart of Mary, hope of the dying,
Heart of Mary, seat of mercy,

Pray for us.

Lamb of God, who takest away the sins of the world,
Spare us, O Lord.
Lamb of God, who takest away the sins of the world,
Graciously hear us, O Lord.
Lamb of God, who takest away the sins of the world,
Have mercy on us.
Christ, hear us.
Christ, graciously hear us.
Lord, have mercy.
Christ, have mercy.
Lord, have mercy.

V. Immaculate Mary, meek and humble of heart.
R. *Conform our hearts to the heart of Jesus.*

Let us Pray.

O most merciful God, who for the salvation of sinners
and the refuge of the wretched, hast made the Immaculate Heart of Mary most like in tenderness and pity to the
Heart of Jesus, grant that we, who now commemorate
her most sweet and loving heart, may by her merits and
intercession, ever live in the fellowship of the Hearts of
both Mother and Son, through the same Christ our
Lord.—*Amen.*

(6)

From August 15 to August 31

LITANY OF THE HOLY NAME OF MARY

LORD, have mercy.
Lord, have mercy.
Christ, have mercy.
Christ, have mercy.
Lord, have mercy.
Lord, have mercy.
Christ, hear us.
Christ, graciously hear us.
Son of Mary, hear us.
Son of Mary, graciously hear us.

Heavenly Father, who hast Mary for Thy daughter,
Eternal Son, who hast Mary for Thy mother,
Holy Spirit, who hast Mary for Thy spouse,
Glorious Trinity, who hast Mary for Thy handmaid, *Have mercy on us.*

Mary, Mother of the Living God,
Mary, Daughter of the Light Unapproachable,
Mary, our light,
Mary, our sister,
Mary, stem of Jesse,
Mary, offspring of kings,
Mary, best work of God,
Mary, immaculate,
Mary, all fair,
Mary, Virgin Mother, *Pray for us.*

Mary, suffering with Jesus,
Mary, pierced with a sword,
Mary, bereft of consolation,
Mary, standing by the Cross,
Mary, ocean of bitterness,
Mary, rejoicing in God's will,
Mary, our Lady,
Mary, our Queen,
Mary, bright as the sun,
Mary, fair as the moon,
Mary, crowned with twelve stars,
Mary, seated on the right hand of Jesus,
Mary, our sweetness,
Mary, our hope,
Mary, glory of Jerusalem,
Mary, joy of Israel,
Mary, honour of our people,

Pray for us.

Lamb of God, who takest away the sins of the world,
Spare us, O Lord.
Lamb of God, who takest away the sins of the world,
Graciously hear us, O Lord.
Lamb of God, who takest away the sins of the world,
Have mercy on us.
V. Hail Mary, full of grace, the Lord is with thee.
R. Blessed art Thou among women.

Let us Pray.

O Almighty God, who seest how earnestly we desire to place ourselves under the shadow of the name of Mary, vouchsafe, we beseech Thee, that as often as we invoke her in our need, we may receive grace and pardon from Thy holy heaven, through Christ our Lord.— *Amen.*

"ANIMA CHRISTI"[1]

(Translated)

SOUL of Christ, be my sanctification;
Body of Christ, be my salvation;
Blood of Christ, fill all my veins;
Water of Christ's side, wash out my stains;
Passion of Christ, my comfort be;
O good Jesu, listen to me;
In thy wounds I fain would hide,
Ne'er to be parted from Thy side;
Guard me, should the foe assail me;
Call me when my life shall fail me;
Bid me come to Thee above,
With Thy saints to sing Thy love,
World without end. Amen.

[1] *Translated about 1854.*

THE HEART OF MARY

HOLY the womb that bare Him,
Holy the breasts that fed,
But holier still the royal heart
   That in His passion bled.

A SHORT SERVICE
FOR ROSARY SUNDAY

Hymn–Litany in the "Crown of Jesus," p. 410.
Hymn. Then

IN Jesus Christ is the fulness of the Godhead with all its infinite sanctity. In Mary is reflected the sanctity of Jesus, as by His grace it could be found in a creature.

Mary, as the pattern both of maidenhood and maternity, has exalted woman's state and nature, and made the Christian virgin and the Christian mother understand the sacredness of their duties in the sight of God.

Her very image is as a book in which we may read at a glance the mystery of the Incarnation, and the mercy of the Redemption; and withal her own gracious perfections also, who was made by her Divine Son the very type of humility, gentleness, fortitude, purity, patience, love.

What Christian mother can look upon her image and not be moved to pray for gentleness, watchfulness, and obedience like Mary's? What Christian maiden can look upon her without praying for the gifts of simplicity, modesty, purity, recollection, gentleness such as hers?

Who can repeat her very name without finding in it a music which goes to the heart, and brings before him thoughts of God and Jesus Christ, and heaven above, and fills him with the desire of those graces by which heaven is gained?

Hail then, great Mother of God, Queen of Saints, Royal Lady clothed with the sun and crowned with the stars of heaven, whom all generations have called and shall call blessed. We will take our part in praising thee in our own time and place with all the redeemed of our Lord, and will exalt thee in the full assembly of the saints and glorify thee in the Heavenly Jerusalem.

Three Hail Mary's.
Prayers in the "Crown of Jesus," p. 508.[1]
Hymn.

[1] The *Crown of Jesus* was a sodality prayerbook.

AVE MARIS STELLA

HAIL, STAR OF THE SEA

Truly art thou a star, O Mary! Our Lord indeed Himself, Jesus Christ, He is the truest and chiefest Star, the bright and morning Star, as St. John calls Him; that Star which was foretold from the beginning as destined to rise out of Israel, and which was displayed in figure by the star which appeared to the wise men in the East. But if the wise and learned and they who teach men in justice shall shine as stars for ever and ever; if the angels of the Churches are called stars in the Hand of Christ; if He honoured the apostles even in the days of their flesh by a title, calling them lights of the world; if even those angels who fell from heaven are called by the beloved disciple stars; if lastly all the saints in bliss are called stars, in that they are like stars differing from stars in glory; therefore most assuredly, without any derogation from the honour of our Lord, is Mary His mother called the Star of the Sea, and the more so because even on her head she wears a crown of twelve stars. Jesus is the Light of the world, illuminating every man who cometh into it, opening our eyes with the gift of faith, making souls luminous by His Almighty grace; and Mary is the Star, shining with the light of Jesus, fair as the moon, and special[1] as the sun, the star of the heavens, which it is good to look upon, the star of the sea, which is welcome to the tempest-tossed, at

[1] The Cardinal's MS. has "special" as being translation of the Latin "electa."

whose smile the evil spirit flies, the passions are hushed, and peace is poured upon the soul.

Hail then, Star of the Sea, we joy in the recollection of thee. Pray for us ever at the throne of Grace; plead our cause, pray with us, present our prayers to thy Son and Lord—now and in the hour of death, Mary be thou our help.

A TRIDUO TO ST. JOSEPH

First Day

CONSIDER THE GLORIOUS TITLES OF ST. JOSEPH.

He was the true and worthy Spouse of Mary, supplying in a visible manner the place of Mary's Invisible Spouse, the Holy Ghost. He was a virgin, and his virginity was the faithful mirror of the virginity of Mary. He was the Cherub, placed to guard the new terrestrial Paradise from the intrusion of every foe.

V. Blessed be the name of Joseph.

R. Henceforth and forever. Amen.

Let us Pray.

God, who in Thine ineffable Providence didst vouchsafe to choose Blessed Joseph to be the husband of Thy most holy Mother, grant, we beseech Thee, that we may be made worthy to receive him for our intercessor in heaven, whom on earth we venerate as our holy Protector: who livest and reignest world without end. Amen. (*Vide "The Raccolta."*)

Second Day

CONSIDER THE GLORIOUS TITLES OF ST. JOSEPH.

His was the title of father of the Son of God, because he was the Spouse of Mary, ever Virgin. He was our Lord's father, because Jesus ever yielded to him the obedience of a son. He was our Lord's father, because to him were entrusted, and by him were faithfully fulfilled, the duties of a father, in protecting Him, giving Him a home, sustaining and rearing Him, and providing Him with a trade.

V. Blessed be the name of Joseph.

R. Henceforth and for ever. Amen.

Let us Pray.

God, who in Thine ineffable Providence didst vouchsafe, &c.

Third Day

CONSIDER THE GLORIOUS TITLES OF ST. JOSEPH.

HE is Holy Joseph, because according to the opinion of a great number of doctors, he, as well as St. John Baptist, was sanctified even before he was born. He is Holy Joseph, because his office, of being spouse and protector of Mary, specially demanded sanctity. He is Holy Joseph, because no other Saint but he lived in such and so long intimacy and familiarity with the source of all holiness, Jesus, God incarnate, and Mary, the holiest of creatures.

V. Blessed be the name of Joseph.
R. Henceforth and for ever. Amen.

Let us Pray.

God, who in Thine ineffable Providence didst vouchsafe, &c.

FOUR PRAYERS TO ST. PHILIP

PRAYER I

O MY dear and holy Patron, Philip, I put myself into thy hands, and for the love of Jesus, for that love's sake which chose thee and made thee a saint, I implore thee to pray for me, that, as He has brought thee to heaven, so in due time He may take me to heaven too.

Thou hast had experience of the trials and troubles of this life; thou knowest well what it is to bear the assaults of the devil, the mockery of the world, and the temptations of flesh and blood. Thou knowest how weak is human nature, and how treacherous the human heart, and thou art so full of sympathy and compassion, that, amidst all thy present ineffable glory and blessedness, thou canst, I know, give a thought to me.

Think of me then, my dear St. Philip, be sure to think of me, even though I am at times so unmindful of thee. Gain for me all things necessary for my perseverance in the grace of God, and my eternal salvation. Gain for me, by thy powerful intercession, the strength to fight a good fight, to witness boldly for God and religion in the midst of sinners, to be brave when Satan would frighten or

Being part of an unfinished Novena to St. Philip.
These four Prayers to St. Philip form "Part of a Novena to St. Philip," which ends abruptly at the end of the fourth day's prayer, to which for the sake of uniformity the Invocations at the conclusion have been added. [W. N.]

force me to what is wrong, to overcome myself, to do my whole duty, and thus to be acquitted in the judgment.

Vessel of the Holy Ghost, Apostle of Rome, Saint of primitive times, pray for me.

PRAYER II

O MY dear and holy Patron, Philip, I put myself into thy hands, and for the love of Jesus, for that love's sake, which chose thee and made thee a saint, I implore thee to pray for me, that, as He has brought thee to heaven, so in due time He may take me to heaven also.

And I ask of thee especially to gain for me a true devotion such as thou hadst to the Holy Ghost, the Third Person in the Ever-blessed Trinity; that, as He at Pentecost so miraculously filled thy heart with his grace, I too may in my measure have the gifts necessary for my salvation.

Therefore I ask thee to gain for me those His seven great gifts, to dispose and excite my heart towards faith and virtue.

Beg for me the gift of Wisdom, that I may prefer heaven to earth, and know truth from falsehood:

The gift of Understanding, by which I may have imprinted upon my mind the mysteries of His Word:

The gift of Counsel, that I may see my way in all perplexities:

The gift of Fortitude, that with bravery and stubbornness I may battle with my foe:

The gift of Knowledge, to enable me to direct all my doings with a pure intention to the glory of God:

The gift of Religion, to make me devout and conscientious:

And the gift of Holy Fear, to make me feel awe, reverence and sobriety amid all my spiritual blessings.

Sweetest Father, Flower of Purity, Martyr of Charity, pray for me.

PRAYER III

O MY dear and holy Patron, Philip, I put myself into thy hands, and for the love of Jesus, for that love's sake which chose and made thee a saint, I implore thee to pray for me, that, as He has brought thee to heaven, so in due time He may take me to heaven also.

And I beg of thee to gain for me a true devotion to the Holy Ghost, by means of that grace which He Himself, the Third Person of the glorious Trinity, bestows. Gain for me a portion of that overflowing devotion which thou hadst towards Him when thou wast on earth; for that, O my dear father, was one of thy special distinctions from other saints, that, though they all adored supremely and solely the Holy Ghost as their one God, yet thou, like Pope St. Gregory, the Apostle of England, didst adore Him not only in the unity of the Godhead, but also as proceeding from the Father and the Son, the gift of the Most High and the Giver of life.

Gain for me, O holy Philip, such a measure of thy devotion towards Him, that, as He did deign to come into thy heart miraculously and set it on fire with love, He may reward us too with some special and corresponding gift of grace. O Philip, let us not be the cold sons of so fervent a Father. It will be a great reproach to thee, if thou dost not make us in some measure like thyself. Gain for us the grace of prayer and meditation, power to command our thoughts and keep from distractions, and the gift of conversing with God without being wearied.

Heart of fire, Light of holy joy, Victim of love, pray for me.

PRAYER IV

O MY dear and holy Patron, Philip, I put myself into thy hands, and for the love of Jesus, for that love's sake which chose thee and made thee a saint, I implore thee to pray for me, that, as He has brought thee to heaven, so in due time He may take me to heaven also.

Thou art my glorious protector, and, after Jesus, Mary, and Joseph, canst do most for me in life and death. In thy labours thou didst follow thy Lord and Saviour, and in thy hidden life and hidden virtues, in thy purity, humility, and fervour, art nearest to Mary and Joseph of all saints. I have long dedicated myself to thee, but I have done nothing worthy of thee, and I am ashamed to call myself thine, because thou hast a right to have followers of great innocence, great honesty of purpose, and great resolution, and these virtues I have not.

Thou, Philip, hast no anxiety about thyself, for thou art already in heaven, therefore thou canst afford to have a care for me. Watch over me, keep me from lagging behind, gain for me the grace necessary to keep me up to my duty, so that I may make progress in all virtues, in the three theological virtues of faith, hope, and charity; in the four cardinal virtues of prudence, fortitude, justice, temperance; moreover in humility, in chastity, in liberality, in meekness, and in truthfulness.

Director of souls, Patron of thine own, who didst turn so many hearts to God, pray for me.

A SHORT ROAD TO PERFECTION

September 27, 1856

IT is the saying of holy men that, if we wish to be perfect, we have nothing more to do than to perform the ordinary duties of the day well. A short road to perfection—short, not because easy, but because pertinent and intelligible. There are no short ways to perfection, but there are sure ones.

I think this is an instruction which may be of great practical use to persons like ourselves. It is easy to have vague ideas what perfection is, which serve well enough to talk about, when we do not intend to aim at it; but as soon as a person really desires and sets about seeking it himself, he is dissatisfied with anything but what is tangible and clear, and constitutes some sort of direction towards the practice of it.

We must bear in mind what is meant by perfection. It does not mean any extraordinary service, anything out of the way, or especially heroic—not all have the opportunity of heroic acts, of sufferings—but it means what the word perfection ordinarily means. By perfect we mean that which has no flaw in it, that which is complete, that which is consistent, that which is sound—we mean the opposite to imperfect. As we know well what *im*perfection in religious service means, we know by the contrast what is meant by perfection.

He, then, is perfect who does the work of the day perfectly, and we need not go beyond this to seek for perfection. You need not go out of the *round* of the day.

I insist on this because I think it will simplify our views, and fix our exertions on a definite aim. If you ask me what you are to do in order to be perfect, I say, first—Do not lie in bed beyond the due time of rising; give your first thoughts to God; make a good visit to the Blessed Sacrament; say the Angelus devoutly; eat and drink to God's glory; say the Rosary well; be recollected; keep out bad thoughts; make your evening meditation well; examine yourself daily; go to bed in good time, and you are already perfect.

PRAYER FOR THE LIGHT OF TRUTH

I should like an enquirer to say continually:

O MY God, I confess that *Thou canst* enlighten my darkness. I confess that Thou *alone* canst. I *wish* my darkness to be enlightened. I do not know whether Thou wilt: but that Thou canst and that I wish, are sufficient reasons for me to *ask*, what Thou at least hast not forbidden my asking. I hereby promise that by Thy grace which I am asking, I will embrace whatever I at length feel certain is the truth, if ever I come to be certain. And by Thy grace I will guard against all self-deceit which may lead me to take what nature would have, rather than what reason approves.

PRAYER FOR A HAPPY DEATH

OH, my Lord and Saviour, support me in that hour in the strong arms of Thy Sacraments, and by the fresh fragrance of Thy consolations. Let the absolving words be said over me, and the holy oil sign and seal me, and Thy own Body be my food, and Thy Blood my sprinkling; and let my sweet Mother, Mary, breathe on me, and my Angel whisper peace to me, and my glorious Saints . . . smile upon me; that in them all, and through them all, I may receive the gift of perseverance, and die, as I desire to live, in Thy faith, in Thy Church, in Thy service, and in Thy love. Amen.

PART III

MEDITATIONS
ON
CHRISTIAN DOCTRINE

A SHORT VISIT TO
THE BLESSED SACRAMENT
BEFORE MEDITATION

In the Name of the Father, and of the Son,
and of the Holy Ghost. Amen.

I place myself in the presence of Him, in whose Incarnate Presence I am before I place myself there.

I adore Thee, O my Saviour, present here as God and man, in soul and body, in true flesh and blood.

I acknowledge and confess that I kneel before that Sacred Humanity, which was conceived in Mary's womb, and lay in Mary's bosom; which grew up to man's estate, and by the Sea of Galilee called the Twelve, wrought miracles, and spoke words of wisdom and peace; which in due season hung on the cross, lay in the tomb, rose from the dead, and now reigns in heaven.

I praise, and bless, and give myself wholly to Him, who is the true Bread of my soul, and my everlasting joy.

Sunday

O Sapientia, quæ ex ore Altissimi prodiisti, attingens à fine usque ad finem, fortiter suaviterque disponens omnia: Veni ad docendum nos viam prudentiæ.

Monday

O Adonai, et Dux domus Israel, qui Moysi in igne flammae rubi apparuisti, et ei in Sina legem dedisti: Veni ad redimendum nos in brachio extento.

Tuesday

O Radix Jesse, qui stas in signum populorum, super

March 1, 1855.

quem continebunt reges os suum, quem Gentes depreca-
buntur: Veni ad liberandum nos, jam noli tardare.

Wednesday

O Clavis David, et Sceptrum domus Israel, qui aperis
et nemo claudit, claudis et nemo aperit: Veni, et educ
vinctum de domo carceris, sedentem in tenebris et umbrâ
mortis.

Thursday

O Oriens, Splendor lucis æternæ, et sol justitiae: Veni
et illumina sedentes in tenebris et umbrâ mortis.

Friday

O Rex Géntium, et desideratus earum, lapisque angu-
laris, qui facis utraque unum: Veni et salva hominem,
quem de limo formasti.

Saturday

O Emmanuel, Rex et Legifer noster, Expectatio gen-
tium, et Salvador earum: Veni ad salvandum nos, Domine Deus noster.

The Latin Antiphons are taken from the Breviary in Advent.

I

HOPE IN GOD—CREATOR

(I)

March 6, 1848

1. GOD has created all things for good; all things for their greatest good; everything for its own good. What is the good of one is not the good of another; what makes one man happy would make another unhappy. God has determined, unless I interfere with His plan, that I should reach that which will be my greatest happiness. He looks on me individually, He calls me by my name, He knows what I can do, what I can best be, what is my greatest happiness, and He means to give it me.

2. God knows what is my greatest happiness, but I do not. There is no rule about what is happy and good; what suits one would not suit another. And the ways by which perfection is reached vary very much; the medicines necessary for our souls are very different from each other. Thus God leads us by strange ways; we know He wills our happiness, but we neither know what our happiness is, nor the way. We are blind; left to ourselves we should take the wrong way; we must leave it to Him.

3. Let us put ourselves into His hands, and not be startled though He leads us by a strange way, a *mirabilis via*, as the Church speaks. Let us be sure He will lead us right, that He will bring us to that which is, not indeed what *we* think best, nor what is best for another, but what is best for us.

Colloquy. O, my God, I will put myself without reserve into Thy hands. Wealth or woe, joy or sorrow,
friends or bereavement, honour or humilation, good
report or ill report, comfort or discomfort, Thy presence
or the hiding of Thy countenance, all is good if it comes
from Thee. Thou art wisdom and Thou art love—what
can I desire more? Thou hast led me in Thy counsel, and
with glory hast Thou received me. What have I in
heaven, and apart from Thee what want I upon earth?
My flesh and my heart faileth: but God is the God of my
heart, and my portion for ever.

(2)

March 7

1. God was all-complete, all-blessed in Himself; but it
was His will to create a world for His glory. He is
Almighty, and might have done all things Himself, but it
has been His will to bring about His purposes by the
beings He has created. We are all created to His
glory—we are created to do His will. I am created to do
something or to be something for which no one else is
created; I have a place in God's counsels, in God's world,
which no one else has; whether I be rich or poor, despised
or esteemed by man, God knows me and calls me by my
name.

2. God has created me to do Him some definite service;
He has committed some work to me which He has not
committed to another. I have my mission—I never may
know it in this life, but I shall be told it in the next.
Somehow I am necessary for His purposes, as necessary
in my place as an Archangel in his—if, indeed, I fail, He
can raise another, as He could make the stones children of
Abraham. Yet I have a part in this great work; I am a link
in a chain, a bond of connexion between persons. He has

not created me for naught. I shall do good, I shall do His work; I shall be an angel of peace, a preacher of truth in my own place, while not intending it, if I do but keep His commandments and serve Him in my calling.

3. Therefore I will trust Him. Whatever, wherever I am, I can never be thrown away. If I am in sickness, my sickness may serve Him; in perplexity, my perplexity may serve Him; if I am in sorrow, my sorrow may serve Him. My sickness, or perplexity, or sorrow may be necessary causes of some great end, which is quite beyond us. He does nothing in vain; He may prolong my life, He may shorten it; He knows what He is about. He may take away my friends, He may throw me among strangers, He may make me feel desolate, make my spirits sink, hide the future from me—still He knows what He is about.

O Adonai, O Ruler of Israel, Thou that guidest Joseph like a flock, O Emmanuel, O Sapientia, I give myself to Thee. I trust Thee wholly. Thou art wiser than I—more loving to me than I myself. Deign to fulfil Thy high purposes in me whatever they be—work in and through me. I am born to serve Thee, to be Thine, to be Thy instrument. Let me be Thy blind instrument. I ask not to see—I ask not to know—I ask simply to be used.

(3)

1. What mind of man can imagine the love which the Eternal Father bears towards the Only Begotten Son? It has been from everlasting,—and it is infinite; so great is it that divines call the Holy Ghost by the name of that love, as if to express its infinitude and perfection. Yet reflect, O my soul, and bow down before the awful mystery, that, as the Father loves the Son, so doth the Son love thee, if thou art one of His elect; for He says expressly, "As the Father hath loved Me, I also have loved you. Abide in

My love." What mystery in the whole circle of revealed truths is greater than this?

2. The love which the Son bears to thee, a creature, is like that which the Father bears to the uncreated Son. O wonderful mystery! *This*, then, is the history of what else is so strange: that He should have taken my flesh and died for me. The former mystery anticipates the latter; that latter does but fulfil the former. Did He not love me so inexpressibly, He would not have suffered for me. I understand now why He died for me, because He loved me as a father loves his son—not as a human father merely, but as the Eternal Father the Eternal Son. I see now the meaning of that else inexplicable humiliation: He preferred to regain me rather than to create new worlds.

3. How constant is He in His affection! He has loved us from the time of Adam. He has said from the beginning, "I will never leave thee nor forsake thee." He did not forsake us in our sin. He did not forsake me. He found me out and regained me. He made a point of it—He resolved to restore me, in spite of myself, to that blessedness which I was so obstinately set against. And now what does He ask of me, but that, as He has loved me with an everlasting love, so I should love Him in such poor measures as I can show.

O mystery of mysteries, that the ineffable love of Father to Son should be the love of the Son to us! Why was it, O Lord? What good thing didst Thou see in me a sinner? Why wast Thou set on me? "What is man, that Thou art mindful of him, and the son of man that Thou visitest him?" This poor flesh of mine, this weak sinful soul, which has no life except in Thy grace, Thou didst set Thy love upon it. Complete Thy work, O Lord, and as Thou hast loved me from the beginning, so make me to love Thee unto the end.

II

HOPE IN GOD—REDEEMER

(I)

THE MENTAL SUFFERINGS OF OUR LORD

August 18, 1855

1. AFTER all His discourses were consummated (Matt. xxvi. 1), fully finished and brought to an end, then He said, The Son of man will be betrayed to crucifixion. As an army puts itself in battle array, as sailors, before an action, clear the decks, as dying men make their will and then turn to God, so though our Lord could never cease to speak good words, did He sum up and complete His teaching, and then commence His passion. Then He removed by His own act the prohibition which kept Satan from Him, and opened the door to the agitations of His human heart, as a soldier, who is to suffer death, may drop his handkerchief himself. At once Satan came on and seized upon his brief hour.

2. An evil temper of murmuring and criticism is spread among the disciples. One was the source of it, but it seems to have been spread. The thought of His death was before Him, and He was thinking of it and His burial after it. A woman came and anointed His sacred head. The action spread a soothing tender feeling over His pure soul. It was a mute token of sympathy, and the whole house was filled with it. It was rudely broken by the harsh voice of the traitor now for the first time giving

utterance to his secret heartlessness and malice. *Ut quid perditio hæc?* "To what purpose is this waste?"—the unjust steward with his impious economy making up for his own private thefts by grudging honour to his Master. Thus in the midst of the sweet calm harmony of that feast at Bethany, there comes a jar and discord; all is wrong: sour discontent and distrust are spreading, for the devil is abroad.

3. Judas, having once shown what he was, lost no time in carrying out his malice. He went to the Chief Priests and bargained with them to betray his Lord for a price. Our Lord saw all that took place within him; He saw Satan knocking at his heart, and admitted there and made an honoured and beloved guest and an intimate. He saw him go to the Priests and heard the conversation between them. He had seen it by His foreknowledge all the time he had been about Him, and when He chose him. What we know feebly as to be, affects us far more vividly and very differently when it actually takes place. Our Lord had at length felt, and suffered Himself to feel, the cruelty of the ingratitude of which He was the sport and victim. He had treated Judas as one of His most familiar friends. He had shown marks of the closest intimacy; He had made him the purse-keeper of Himself and His followers. He had given him the power of working miracles. He had admitted him to a knowledge of the mysteries of the kingdom of heaven. He had sent him out to preach and made him one of His own special representatives, so that the Master was judged of by the conduct of His servant. A heathen, when smitten by a friend, said, "Et tu Brutë!" What desolation is in the sense of ingratitude! God who is met with ingratitude daily cannot from His Nature feel it. He took a human heart, that He might feel it in its fulness. And now, O my God, though in heaven, dost Thou not feel my ingratitude towards Thee?

March 10

4. I see the figure of a man, whether young or old I cannot tell. He may be fifty or he may be thirty. Sometimes He looks one, sometimes the other. There is something inexpressible about His face which I cannot solve. Perhaps, as He bears *all* burdens, He bears that of old age too. But so it is; His face is at once most venerable, yet most childlike, most calm, most sweet, most modest, beaming with sanctity and with loving kindness. His eyes rivet me and move my heart. His breath is all fragrant, and transports me out of myself. Oh, I will look upon that face forever, and will not cease.

5. And I see suddenly some one come to Him, and raise his hand and sharply strike Him on that heavenly face. It is a hard hand, the hand of a rude man, and perhaps has iron upon it. It could not be so sudden as to take Him by surprise who knows all things past and future, and He shows no sign of resentment, remaining calm and grave as before; but the expression of His face is marred; a great wheal arises, and in a little time that all-gracious Face is hid from me by the effects of this indignity, as if a cloud came over It.

6. A hand was lifted up against the Face of Christ. Whose hand was that? My conscience tells me: "thou art the man." I trust it is not so with me now. But, O my soul, contemplate the awful fact. *Fancy* Christ before thee, and *fancy* thyself lifting up thy hand and striking Him! Thou wilt say, "It is impossible: I could not do so." Yes, thou hast done so. When thou didst sin wilfully, then thou hast done so. He is beyond pain now: still thou hast struck Him, and had it been in the days of His flesh, He would have felt pain. Turn back in memory, and recollect the time, the day, the hour, when by wilful mortal sin, by scoffing at sacred things, or by profaneness, or by dark hatred of this thy Brother, or by acts of

impurity, or by deliberate rejection of God's voice, or in any other devilish way known to thee, thou hast struck The All-holy One.

O injured Lord, what can I say? I am very guilty concerning Thee, my Brother; and I shall sink in sullen despair if Thou dost not raise me. I cannot look on Thee; I shrink from Thee; I throw my arms round my face; I crouch to the earth. Satan will pull me down if Thou take not pity. It is terrible to turn to Thee; but oh turn Thou me, and so shall I be turned. It is a purgatory to endure the sight of Thee, the sight of myself—I most vile, Thou most holy. Yet make me look once more on Thee whom I have so incomprehensibly affronted, for Thy countenance is my only life, my only hope and health lies in looking on Thee whom I have pierced. So I put myself before Thee; I look on Thee again; I endure the pain in order to the purification.

O my God, how can I look Thee in the face when I think of my ingratitude, so deeply seated, so habitual, so immovable—or rather so awfully increasing! Thou loadest me day by day with Thy favours, and feedest me with Thyself, as Thou didst Judas, yet I not only do not profit thereby, but I do not even make any acknowledgment at the time. Lord, how long? when shall I be free from this real, this fatal captivity? He who made Judas his prey, has got foothold of me in my old age, and I cannot get loose. It is the same day after day. When wilt Thou give me a still greater grace than Thou hast given, the grace to profit by the graces which Thou givest? When wilt Thou give me Thy effectual grace which alone can give life and vigour to this effete, miserable, dying soul of mine? My God, I know not in what sense I can pain Thee in Thy glorified state; but I know that every fresh sin, every fresh ingratitude I now commit, was among the blows and stripes which once fell on Thee in Thy passion. O let me have as little share in those Thy past sufferings as possible. Day by day goes, and I find I have been more and more, by the new sins of each day, the cause of them. I know that at best I have a real share *in solido* of them all, but still it is shocking to find myself having a greater and greater share. Let others wound Thee—let not me. Let not me have to think that Thou wouldest have had this or that pang of soul or body the less, except for me. O my God, I am so fast in prison that I cannot get out. O Mary, pray for me. O Philip, pray for me, though I do not deserve Thy pity.

(2)

OUR LORD REFUSES SYMPATHY

1. SYMPATHY may be called an eternal law, for it is signified or rather transcendentally and archetypically fulfilled in the ineffable mutual love of the Divine Trinity. God, though infinitely One, has ever been Three. He ever has rejoiced in His Son and His Spirit, and they in Him—and thus through all eternity He has existed, not solitary, though alone, having in this incomprehensible multiplication of Himself and reiteration of His Person, such infinitely perfect bliss, that nothing He has created can add aught to it. The devil only is barren and lonely, shut up in himself—and his servants also.

2. When, for our sakes, the Son came on earth and took our flesh, yet He would not live without the sympathy of others. For thirty years He lived with Mary and Joseph and thus formed a shadow of the Heavenly Trinity on earth. O the perfection of that sympathy which existed between the three! Not a look of one, but the other two understood, as expressed, better than if expressed in a thousand words—nay more than understood, accepted, echoed, corroborated. It was like three instruments absolutely in tune which all vibrate when one vibrates, and

vibrate either one and the same note, or in perfect harmony.

3. The first weakening of that unison was when Joseph died. It was no jar in the sound, for to the last moment of his life, he was one with them, and the sympathy between the three only became more intense, and more sweet, while it was brought into new circumstances and had a wider range in the months of his declining, his sickness, and death. Then it was like an air ranging through a number of notes performed perfectly and exactly in time and tune by all three. But it ended in a lower note than before, and when Joseph went, a weaker one. Not that Joseph, though so saintly, added much in volume of sound to the other two, but sympathy, by its very meaning, implies number, and, on his death, one, out of three harps, was unstrung and silent.

4. O what a moment of sympathy between the three, the moment before Joseph died—they supporting and hanging over him, he looking at them and reposing in them with undivided, unreserved, supreme, devotion, for he was in the arms of God and the Mother of God. As a flame shoots up and expires, so was the ecstasy of that last moment ineffable, for each knew and thought of the reverse which was to follow on the snapping of that bond. One moment, very different, of joy, not of sorrow, was equal to it in intensity of feeling, that of the birth of Jesus. The birth of Jesus, the death of Joseph, moments of unutterable sweetness, unparalleled in the history of mankind. St. Joseph went to limbo, to wait his time, out of God's Presence. Jesus had to preach, suffer, and die; Mary to witness His sufferings, and, even after He had risen again, to go on living without Him amid the changes of life and the heartlessness of the heathen.

5. The birth of Jesus, the death of Joseph, those moments of transcendentally pure, and perfect and living sympathy, between the three members of this earthly

Trinity, were its beginning and its end. The death of Joseph, which broke it up, was the breaking up of more than itself. It was but the beginning of that change which was coming over Son and Mother. Going on now for thirty years, each of them had been preserved from the world, and had lived for each other. Now He had to go out to preach and suffer, and, as the foremost and most inevitable of His trials, and one which from first to last He voluntarily undertook, even when not imperative, He deprived Himself of the enjoyment of that intercommunion of hearts—of His heart with the heart of Mary—which had been His from the time He took man's nature, and which He had possessed in an archetypal and transcendent manner with His Father and His Spirit from all eternity.

O my soul, thou art allowed to contemplate this union of the three, and to share thyself its sympathy, by faith though not by sight. My God, I believe and know that then a communion of heavenly things was opened on earth which has never been suspended. It is my duty and my bliss to enter into it myself. It is my duty and my bliss to be in tune with that most touching music which then began to sound. Give me that grace which alone can make me hear and understand it, that it may thrill through me. Let the breathings of my soul be with Jesus, Mary, and Joseph. Let me live in obscurity, out of the world and the world's thought, with them. Let me look to them in sorrow and in joy, and live and die in their sweet sympathy.

6. The *last* day of the earthly intercourse between Jesus and Mary was at the marriage feast at Cana. Yet even then there was something taken from that blissful intimacy, for they no longer lived simply for each other, but showed themselves in public, and began to take their place in the dispensation which was opening. He manifested forth His glory by His first miracle; and hers also,

by making her intercession the medium of it. He honoured her still more, by breaking through the appointed order of things for her sake, and though His time of miracles was not come, anticipating it at her instance. While He wrought His miracle, however, He took leave of her in the words "Woman, what is between thee and Me?" Thus He parted with her absolutely, though He parted with a blessing. It was leaving Paradise feeble and alone.

7. For in truth it was fitting that He who was to be the true High Priest, should thus, while He exercised His office for the whole race of man, be free from all human ties, and sympathies of the flesh. And one reason for His long abode at Nazareth with His Mother may have been to show, that, as He gave up His Father's and His own glory on high, to become man, so He gave up the innocent and pure joys of His earthly home, in order that He might be a Priest. So, in the old time, Melchisedech is described as without father or mother. So the Levites showed themselves truly worthy of the sacerdotal office and were made the sacerdotal tribe, because they steeled themselves against natural affection, said to father or mother, "I know you not," and raised the sword against their own kindred, when the honour of the Lord of armies demanded the sacrifice. In like manner our Lord said to Mary, "What is between Me and thee?" It was the setting apart of the sacrifice, the first ritual step of the Great Act which was to be solemnly performed for the salvation of the world. "What is between Me and thee, O woman?" is the offertory before the oblation of the Host. O my dear Lord, Thou who hast given up Thy mother for me, give me grace cheerfully to give up all my earthly friends and relations for Thee.

8. The Great High Priest said to His kindred, "I know you not." Then, as He did so, we may believe that the most tender heart of Jesus looked back upon His whole

time since His birth, and called before Him those former days of His infancy and childhood, when He had been with others from whom He had long been parted. Time was when St. Elizabeth and the Holy Baptist had formed part of the Holy Family. St. Elizabeth, like St. Joseph, had been removed by death, and was waiting His coming to break that bond which detained both her and St. Joseph from heaven. St. John had been cut off from his home and mankind, and the sympathies of earth, long since—and had now begun to preach the coming Saviour, and was waiting and expecting His manifestation.

Give me grace, O Jesus, to live in sight of that blessed company. Let my life be spent in the presence of Thee and Thy dearest friends. Though I see them not, let not what I do see seduce me to give my heart elsewhere. Because Thou hast blessed me so much and given to me friends, let me not depend or rely or throw myself in any way upon them, but in Thee be my life, and my conversation and daily walk among those with whom Thou didst surround Thyself on earth, and dost now delight Thyself in heaven. Be my soul with Thee, and, because with Thee, with Mary and Joseph and Elizabeth and John.

9. Nor did He, as time went on, give up Mary and Joseph only. There still remained to Him invisible attendants and friends, and He had their sympathy, but them He at length gave up also. From the time of His birth we may suppose He held communion with the spirits of the Old Fathers, who had prepared His coming and prophesied of it. On one occasion He was seen all through the night, conversing with Moses and Elias, and that conversation was about His Passion. What a field of thought is thus opened to us, of which we know how little. When He passed whole nights in prayer, it was greater refreshment to soul and body than sleep. Who could support and (so to say) re-invigorate the Divine

Lord better than that "*laudabilis numerus*" of Prophets of which He was the fulfilment and antitype? Then He might talk with Abraham who saw His day, or Moses who spoke to Him; or with His especial types, David and Jeremias; or with those who spoke most of Him, as Isaias and Daniel. And here was a fund of great sympathy. When He came up to Jerusalem to suffer, He might be met in spirit by all the holy priests, who had offered sacrifices in shadow of Him; just as now the priest recalls in Mass the sacrifices of Abel, Abraham, and Melchisedech, and the fiery gift which purged the lips of Isaias, as well as holding communion with the Apostles and Martyrs.

10. Let us linger for a while with Mary—before we follow the steps of her Son, our Lord. There was an occasion when He refused leave to one who would bid his own home farewell, before he followed Him; and such was, as it seems, almost His own way with His Mother; but will He be displeased, if we one instant stop with her, though our meditation lies with Him? O Mary, we are devout to thy seven woes—but was not this, though not one of those seven, one of the greatest, and included those that followed, from thy knowledge of them beforehand? How didst thou bear that first separation from Him? How did the first days pass when thou wast desolate? where didst thou hide thyself? where didst thou pass the long three years and more, while He was on His ministry? Once—at the beginning of it—thou didst attempt to get near Him, and then we hear nothing of thee, till we find thee standing at His cross. And then, after that great joy of seeing Him again, and the permanent consolation, never to be lost, that with Him all suffering and humiliation was over, and that never had she to weep for Him again, still she was separated from him for many years, while she lived in the flesh, surrounded by the wicked world, and in the misery of His absence.

11. The blessed Mary, among her other sorrows, suffered the loss of her Son, after He had lived under the same roof with her for thirty years. When He was no more than twelve, He gave her a token of what was to be, and said, "I must be about my Father's business;" and when the time came, and He began His miracles, He said to her, "What is to Me and to thee?"—What is common to us two?—and soon He left her. Once she tried to see Him, but in vain, and could not reach Him for the crowd, and He made no effort to receive her, nor said a kind word; and then at the last, once more she tried, and she reached him in time, to see Him hanging on the cross and dying. He was only forty days on earth after His resurrection, and then He left her in old age to finish her life without Him. Compare her thirty happy years, and her time of desolation.

12. I see her in her forlorn home, while her Son and Lord was going up and down the land without a place to lay His head, suffering both because she was so desolate and He was so exposed. How dreary passed the day; and then came reports that He was in some peril or distress. She heard, perhaps, He had been led into the wilderness to be tempted. She would have shared all His sufferings, but was not permitted. Once there was a profane report which was believed by many, that He was beside Himself, and His friends and kindred went out to get possession of Him. She went out too to see Him, and tried to reach Him. She could not for the crowd. A message came to Him to that effect, but He made no effort to receive her, nor said a kind word. She went back to her home disappointed, without the sight of Him. And so she remained, perhaps in company with those who did not believe in Him.

13. I see her too after His ascension. This, too, is a time of bereavement, but still of consolation. It was still a twilight time, but not a time of grief. The Lord was

absent, but He was not on earth, He was not in suffering. Death had no power over Him. And He came to her day by day in the Blessed Sacrifice. I see the Blessed Mary at Mass, and St. John celebrating. She is waiting for the moment of her Son's Presence: now she converses with Him in the sacred rite; and what shall I say now? She receives Him, to whom once she gave birth.

O Holy Mother, stand by me now at Mass time, when Christ comes to me, as thou didst minister to Thy infant Lord—as Thou didst hang upon His words when He grew up, as Thou wast found under His cross. Stand by me, Holy Mother, that I may gain somewhat of thy purity, thy innocence, thy faith, and He may be the one object of my love and my adoration, as He was of thine.

14. There were others who more directly ministered to Him, and of whom we are told more—the Holy Angels. It was the voice of the Archangel that announced to the prophet His coming which consigned the Eternal to the womb of Mary. Angels hymned His nativity and all the Angels of God worshipped at his crib. An Angel sent Him into Egypt and brought Him back. Angels ministered to Him after His temptation. Angels wrought His miracles, when He did not will to exert His Almighty fiat. But He bade them go at length, as He had bidden His Mother go. One remained at His agony. Afterwards He said, "Think ye not I could pray to My Father, and He would send me myriads of Angels?"—implying that in fact His guards had been withdrawn. The Church prays Him, on His ascension, "King of Glory, Lord of Angels, leave us not orphans." He, the Lord of Angels, was at this time despoiled of them.

15. He took other human friends, when He had given up His Mother—the twelve Apostles—as if He desired that in which He might sympathise. He chose them, as He says, to be, "not servants but friends." He made them His confidants. He told them things which He did not tell

others. It was His will to favour, nay, to indulge them, as a father behaves towards a favourite child. He made them more blessed than kings and prophets and wise men, from the things He told them. He called them "His little ones," and preferred them for His gifts to the wise and prudent. He exulted, while He praised them, that they had continued with Him in His temptations, and as if in gratitude He announced that they should sit upon twelve thrones judging the twelve tribes of Israel. He rejoiced in their sympathy when His solemn trial was approaching. He assembled them about Him at the last supper, as if they were to support Him in it. "With desire," He says, "have I desired to eat this Pasch with you, before I suffer." Thus there was an interchange of good offices, and an intimate sympathy between them. But it was His adorable will that they too should leave Him, that He should be left to Himself. One betrayed, another denied Him, the rest ran away from Him, and left Him in the hands of His enemies. Even after He had risen, none would believe in it. Thus he trod the winepress alone.

16. He who was Almighty, and All-blessed, and who flooded His own soul with the full glory of the vision of His Divine Nature, would still subject that soul to all the infirmities which naturally belonged to it; and, as He suffered it to rejoice in the sympathy, and to be desolate under the absence, of human friends, so, when it pleased Him, He could, and did, deprive it of the light of the presence of God. This was the last and crowning misery that He put upon it. He had in the course of His ministry fled from man to God; he had appealed to Him; He had taken refuge from the rude ingratitude of the race whom He was saving in divine communion. He retired of nights to pray. He said, "the Father loveth the Son, and shews to Him all things that He doth Himself." He returned thanks to Him for hiding His mysteries from the wise to reveal them to the little ones. But now He deprived

Himself of this elementary consolation, by which He lived, and that, not in part only, but in its fulness. He said, when His passion began, "My soul is sorrowful even unto death;" and at the last, "My God, why hast Thou forsaken Me?" Thus He was stripped of all things.

My God and Saviour, who wast thus deprived of the light of consolation, whose soul was dark, whose affections were left to thirst without the true object of them, and all this for man, take not from *me* the light of Thy countenance, lest I shrivel from the loss of it and perish in my infirmity. Who can sustain the loss of the Sun of the soul but Thou? Who can walk without light, or labour without the pure air, but Thy great Saints? As for me, alas, I shall turn to the creature for my comfort, if Thou wilt not give me Thyself. I shall not mourn, I shall not hunger or thirst after justice, but I shall look about for whatever is at hand, and feed on offal, or stay my appetite with husks, ashes, or chaff, which if they poison me not, at least nourish not. O my God, leave me not in that dry state in which I am; give me the comfort of Thy grace. How can I have any tenderness or sweetness, unless I have Thee to look upon? how can I continue in prayer, as is my duty doubly, since I belong to the Oratory, unless Thou encourage me and make it pleasant to me? It is hardly that an old man keeps any warmth in him; it is slowly that he recovers what is lost. Yet, O my God, St. Philip is my father—and he seems never in his life to have been desolate. Thou didst give him trials, but didst thou ever take from him the light of Thy countenance! O Philip, wilt thou not gain for me some tithe of thy own peace and joy, thy cheerfulness, thy gentleness, and thy self-denying charity? I am in all things the most opposite to thee, yet I represent thee.

(3)

THE BODILY SUFFERINGS OF OUR LORD

April 19, Wednesday in Holy Week

1. His bodily pains were greater than those of any martyr, because He willed them to be greater. All pain of body depends, as to be felt at all, so to be felt in this or that degree, on the nature of the living mind which dwells in that body. Vegetables have no feeling because they have no living mind or spirit within them. Brute animals feel more or less according to the intelligence within them. Man feels more than any brute, because he has a soul; Christ's soul felt more than that of any other man, because His soul was exalted by personal union with the Word of God. Christ felt bodily pain more keenly than any other man, as much as man feels pain more keenly than any other animal.

2. It is a relief to pain to have the thoughts drawn another way. Thus, soldiers in battle often do not know when they are wounded. Again, persons in raging fevers seem to suffer a great deal; then afterwards they can but recollect general discomfort and restlessness. And so excitement and enthusiasm are great alleviations of bodily pain; thus savages die at the stake amid torments singing songs; it is a sort of mental drunkenness. And so again, an instantaneous pain is comparatively bearable; it is the continuance of pain which is so heavy, and if we had no memory of the pain we suffered last minute, and also suffer in the present, we should find pain easy to bear; but what makes the second pang grievous is because there has been a first pang; and what makes the third more grievous is that there has been a first and second; the pain seems to grow because it is prolonged. Now Christ suffered, not as in a delirium or in excitement, or

in inadvertency, but He looked pain in the face! He offered His whole mind to it, and received it, as it were, directly into His bosom, and suffered all He suffered with a full consciousness of suffering.

3. Christ would not drink the drugged cup which was offered to Him to cloud His mind. He willed to have the full sense of pain. His soul was so intently fixed on His suffering as not to be distracted from it; and it was so active, and recollected the past and anticipated the future, and the whole passion was, as it were, concentrated on each moment of it, and all that He had suffered and all that He was to suffer lent its aid to increase what He was suffering. Yet withal His soul was so calm and sober and unexcited as to be passive, and thus to receive the full burden of the pain on it, without the power of throwing it off Him. Moreover, the sense of conscious innocence, and the knowledge that His sufferings would come to an end, might have supported Him; but He repressed the comfort and turned away His thoughts from these alleviations that He might suffer absolutely and perfectly.

O my God and Saviour, who went through such sufferings for me with such lively consciousness, such precision, such recollection, and such fortitude, enable me, by Thy help, if I am brought into the power of this terrible trial, bodily pain, enable me to bear it with some portion of Thy calmness. Obtain for me this grace, O Virgin Mother, who didst see thy Son suffer and didst suffer with Him; that I, when I suffer, may associate my sufferings with His and with thine, and that through His passion, and thy merits and those of all Saints, they may be a satisfaction for my sins and procure for me eternal life.

Maundy Thursday

4. Our Lord's sufferings were so great, because His soul was in suffering. What shows this is that His soul

began to suffer before His bodily passion, as we see in the agony in the garden. The first anguish which came upon His body was not from without—it was not from the scourges, the thorns, or the nails, but from His soul. His soul was in such agony that He called it death: "My soul is sorrowful even unto death." The anguish was such that it, as it were, burst open His whole body. It was a pang affecting His heart; as in the deluge the floods of the great deep were broken up and the windows of heaven were open. The blood, rushing from his tormented heart, forced its way on every side, formed for itself a thousand new channels, filled all the pores, and at length stood forth upon His skin in thick drops, which fell heavily on the ground.

5. He remained in this living death from the time of His agony in the garden; and as His first agony was from His soul, so was His last. As the scourge and the cross did not begin His sufferings, so they did not close them. It was the agony of His soul, not of His body, which caused His death. His persecutors were surprised to hear that He was dead. How, then, did He die? That agonised, tormented heart, which at the beginning so awfully relieved itself in the rush of blood and the bursting of His pores, at length broke. It broke and He died. It would have broken *at once*, had He not kept it from breaking. At length the moment came. He gave the word and His heart broke.

6. O tormented heart, it was love, and sorrow, and fear, which broke Thee. It was the sight of human sin, it was the sense of it, the feeling of it laid on Thee; it was zeal for the glory of God, horror at seeing sin so near Thee, a sickening, stifling feeling at its pollution, the deep shame and disgust and abhorrence and revolt which it inspired, keen pity for the souls whom it has drawn headlong into hell—all these feelings together Thou didst allow to rush upon Thee. Thou didst submit Thyself to their powers, and they were Thy death. That strong

heart, that all-noble, all-generous, all-tender, all-pure heart was slain by sin.

O most tender and gentle Lord Jesus, when will my heart have a portion of Thy perfections? When will my hard and stony heart, my proud heart, my unbelieving, my impure heart, my narrow selfish heart, be melted and conformed to Thine? O teach me so to contemplate Thee that I may become like Thee, and to love Thee sincerely and simply as Thou hast loved me.

(4)

IT IS CONSUMMATED

April 22

1. I᠎T is over now, O Lord, as with Thy sufferings, so with our humiliations. We have followed Thee from Thy fasting in the wilderness till Thy death on the Cross. For forty days we have professed to do penance. The time has been long and it has been short; but whether long or short, it is now over. It is over, and we feel a pleasure that it is over; it is a relief and a release. We thank Thee that it is over. We thank Thee for the time of sorrow, but we thank Thee more as we look forward to the time of festival. Pardon our shortcomings in Lent and reward us in Easter.

2. We have, indeed, done very little for Thee, O Lord. We recollect well our listlessness and weariness; our indisposition to mortify ourselves when we had no plea of health to stand in the way; our indisposition to pray and to meditate—our disorder of mind—our discontent, our peevishness. Yet some of us, perhaps, have done something for Thee. Look on us as a whole, O Lord, look on us as a community, and let what some have done well plead for us all.

3. O Lord, the end is come. We are conscious of our languor and lukewarmness; we do not deserve to rejoice in Easter, yet we cannot help doing so. We feel more of pleasure, we rejoice in Thee more than our past humiliation warrants us in doing; yet may that very joy be its own warrant. O be indulgent to us, for the merits of Thy own all-powerful Passion, and for the merits of Thy Saints. Accept us as Thy little flock, in the day of small things, in a fallen country, in an age when faith and love are scarce. Pity us and spare us and give us peace.

O my own Saviour, now in the tomb but soon to arise, Thou hast paid the price; it is done—*consummatum est*—it is secured. O fulfil Thy resurrection in us, and as Thou hast purchased us, claim us, take possession of us, make us Thine.

III

GOD AND THE SOUL

(1)

GOD THE BLESSEDNESS OF THE SOUL

1. To possess Thee, O Lover of Souls, is happiness,
and the only happiness of the immortal soul! To enjoy the
sight of Thee is the only happiness of eternity. At present
I might amuse and sustain myself with the vanities of
sense and time, but they will not last for ever. We shall be
stripped of them when we pass out of this world. All
shadows will one day be gone. And what shall I do then?
There will be nothing left to me but the Almighty God. If
I cannot take pleasure in the thought of Him, there is no
one else then to take pleasure in; God and my soul will be
the only two beings left in the whole world, as far as I am
concerned. He will be all in all, whether I wish it or no.
What a strait I shall then be in if I do not love Him, and
there is then nothing else to love! if I feel averse to Him,
and He is then ever looking upon me!

2. Ah, my dear Lord, how can I bear to say that Thou
wilt be all in all, whether I wish it or no? Should I not
wish it with my whole heart? What can give me happiness but Thou? If I had all the resources of time and sense
about me, just as I have now, should I not in course of
ages, nay of years, weary of them? Did this world last for
ever, would it be able ever to supply my soul with food?
Is there any earthly thing which I do not weary of at
length even now? Do old men love what young men
love? Is there not constant change? I am sure then, my

God, that the time would come, though it might be long in coming, when I should have exhausted all the enjoyment which the world could give. Thou alone, my dear Lord, art the food for eternity, and Thou alone. Thou only canst satisfy the soul of man. Eternity would be misery without Thee, even though Thou didst not inflict punishment. To see Thee, to gaze on Thee, to contemplate Thee, this alone is inexhaustible. Thou indeed art unchangeable, yet in Thee there are always more glorious depths and more varied attributes to search into; we shall ever be beginning as if we had never gazed upon Thee. In Thy presence are torrents of delight, which whoso tastes will never let go. This is my true portion, O my Lord, here and hereafter!

3. My God, how far am I from acting according to what I know so well! I confess it, my heart goes after shadows. I love anything better than communion with Thee. I am ever eager to get away from Thee. Often I find it difficult even to say my prayers. There is hardly any amusement I would not rather take up than set myself to think of Thee. Give me grace, O my Father, to be utterly ashamed of my own reluctance! Rouse me from sloth and coldness, and make me desire Thee with my whole heart. Teach me to love meditation, sacred reading, and prayer. Teach me to love that which must engage my mind for all eternity.

(2)

JESUS CHRISTUS HERI ET HODIE:
IPSE ET IN SÆCULA

Jesus Christ yesterday and to-day, and the same for ever.

1. ALL things change here below. I say it, O Lord; I believe it; and I shall feel it more and more the longer I

live. Before Thy eyes, most awful Lord, the whole future
of my life lies bare. Thou knowest exactly what will
befall me every year and every day till my last hour. And,
though I know not what Thou seest concerning me, so
much I know, viz. that Thou dost read in my life perpetual change. Not a year will leave me as it found me,
either within or without. I never shall remain any time in
one state. How many things are sure to happen to me,
unexpected, sudden, hard to bear! I know them not. I
know not how long I have to live. I am hurried on,
whether I will it or no, through continual change. O my
God, what can I trust in? There is nothing I dare trust in;
nay, did I trust in anything of earth, I believe for that very
reason it would be taken away from me. I know Thou
wouldest take it away, if Thou hadst love for me.

2. Everything short of Thee, O Lord, is changeable,
but Thou endurest. Thou art ever one and the same. Ever
the true God of man, and unchangeably so. Thou art the
rarest, most precious, the sole good; and withal Thou art
the most lasting. The creature changes, the Creator
never. Then only the creature stops changing, when it
rests on Thee. On Thee the Angels look and are at peace;
that is why they have perfect bliss. They never can lose
their blessedness, for they never can lose Thee. They
have no anxiety, no misgivings—because they love the
Creator; not any being of time and sense, but "Jesus
Christ, the same yesterday and to-day, who is also for
ever."

3. My Lord, my Only God, "*Deus meus et omnia,*" let
me never go after vanities. "*Vanitas vanitatum et omnia
vanitas.*" All is vanity and shadow here below. Let me not
give my heart to anything here. Let nothing allure me
from Thee; O keep me wholly and entirely. Keep thou
this most frail heart and this most weak head in Thy
Divine keeping. Draw me to Thee morning, noon, and
night for consolation. Be Thou my own bright Light, to

which I look, for guidance and for peace. Let me love
Thee, O my Lord Jesus, with a pure affection and a
fervent affection! Let me love Thee with the fervour, only
greater, with which men of this earth love beings of this
earth. Let me have that tenderness and constancy in
loving Thee, which is so much praised among men,
when the object is of the earth. Let me find and feel Thee
to be my only joy, my only refuge, my only strength,
my only comfort, my only hope, my only fear, my only
love.

(3)

AN ACT OF LOVE

1. My Lord, I believe, and know, and feel, that Thou
art the Supreme Good. And, in saying so, I mean, not
only supreme Goodness and Benevolence, but that Thou
art the sovereign and transcendent Beautifulness. I believe that, beautiful as is Thy creation, it is mere dust and
ashes, and of no account, compared with Thee, who art
the infinitely more beautiful Creator. I know well, that
therefore it is that the Angels and Saints have such perfect
bliss, because they see Thee. To see even the glimpse of
Thy true glory, even in this world throws holy men into
an ecstasy. And I feel the truth of all this, in my own
degree, because Thou hast mercifully taken our nature
upon Thee, and hast come to me as man. "*Et vidimus
gloriam ejus, gloriam quasi Unigeniti a Patre*"—"and we saw
His glory, the glory as it were of the only begotten of the
Father." The more, O my dear Lord, I meditate on Thy
words, works, actions, and sufferings in the Gospel, the
more wonderfully glorious and beautiful I see Thee to be.

2. And therefore, O my dear Lord, since I perceive
Thee to be so beautiful, I love Thee, and desire to love
Thee more and more. Since Thou art the One Goodness,

Beautifulness, Gloriousness, in the whole world of being, and there is nothing like Thee, but Thou art infinitely more glorious and good than even the most beautiful of creatures, therefore I love Thee with a singular love, a one, only, sovereign love. Everything, O my Lord, shall be dull and dim to me, after looking at Thee. There is nothing on earth, not even what is most naturally dear to me, that I can love in comparison of Thee. And I would lose everything whatever rather than lose Thee. For Thou, O my Lord, art my supreme and only Lord and love.

3. My God, Thou knowest infinitely better than I, how little I love Thee. I should not love Thee at all, except for Thy grace. It is Thy grace which has opened the eyes of my mind, and enabled them to see Thy glory. It is Thy grace which has touched my heart, and brought upon it the influence of what is so wonderfully beautiful and fair. How can I help loving Thee, O my Lord, except by some dreadful perversion, which hinders me from looking at Thee? O my God, whatever is nearer to me than Thou, things of this earth, and things more naturally pleasing to me, will be sure to interrupt the sight of Thee, unless Thy grace interfere. Keep Thou my eyes, my ears, my heart, from any such miserable tyranny. Break my bonds— raise my heart. Keep my whole being fixed on Thee. Let me never lose sight of Thee; and, while I gaze on Thee, let my love of Thee grow more and more every day.

IV

SIN

(I)

AGAINST THEE ONLY HAVE I SINNED

1. THOU, O Lord, after living a whole eternity in ineffable bliss, because Thou art the one and sole Perfection, at length didst begin to create spirits to be with Thee and to share Thy blessedness according to their degree; and the return they made Thee was at once to rebel against Thee. First a great part of the Angels, then mankind, have risen up against Thee, and served others, not Thee. Why didst Thou create us, but to make us happy? Couldest Thou be made more happy by creating us? and how could we be happy but in obeying Thee? Yet we determined not to be happy as Thou wouldest have us happy, but to find out a happiness of our own; and so we left Thee. O my God, what a return is it that we—that I—make Thee when we sin! what dreadful unthankfulness is it! and what will be my punishment for refusing to be happy, and for preferring hell to heaven! I know what the punishment will be; Thou wilt say, "Let him have it all his own way. He wishes to perish; let him perish. He despises the graces I give him; they shall turn to a curse."

2. Thou, O my God, hast a claim on me, and I am wholly Thine! Thou art the Almighty Creator, and I am Thy workmanship. I am the work of Thy Hands, and Thou art my owner. As well might the axe or the hammer exalt itself against its framer, as I against Thee.

Thou owest me nothing; I have no rights in respect to Thee, I have only duties. I depend on Thee for life, and health, and every blessing every moment. I have no more power of exercising will as to my life than axe or hammer. I depend on Thee far more entirely than anything here depends on its owner and master. The son does not depend on the father for the continuance of life—the matter out of which the axe is made existed first—but I depend wholly on Thee—if Thou withdraw Thy breath from me for a moment, I die. I am wholly and entirely Thy property and Thy work, and my one duty is to serve Thee.

3. O my God, I confess that before now I have utterly forgotten this, and that I am continually forgetting it! I have acted many a time as if I were my own master, and turned from Thee rebelliously. I have acted according to my own pleasure, not according to Thine. And so far have I hardened myself, as not to feel as I ought how evil this is. I do not understand how dreadful sin is—and I do not hate it, and fear it, as I ought. I have no horror of it, or loathing. I do not turn from it with indignation, as being an insult to Thee, but I trifle with it, and, even if I do not commit great sins, I have no great reluctance to do small ones. O my God, what a great and awful difference is there between what I am and what I ought to be!

(2)

AGAINST THEE ONLY HAVE I SINNED

1. My God, I dare not offend any earthly superior; I am afraid—for I know I shall get into trouble—yet I dare offend Thee. I know, O Lord, that, according to the greatness of the person offended against, the greater is the offence. Yet I do not fear to offend Thee, whom to offend is to offend the infinite God. O my dear Lord, how

should I myself feel, what should I say of myself, if I were to strike some revered superior on earth? if I were violently to deal a blow upon some one as revered as a father, or a priest; if I were to strike them on the face? I cannot bear even to think of such a thing—yet what is this compared with lifting up my hand against Thee? and what is sin but this? To sin is to insult Thee in the grossest of all conceivable ways. This then, O my soul! is what the sinfulness of sin consists in. It is lifting up my hand against my Infinite Benefactor, against my Almighty Creator, Preserver and Judge—against Him in whom all majesty and glory and beauty and reverence and sanctity centre; against the one only God.

2. O my God, I am utterly confounded to think of the state in which I lie! What will become of me if Thou art severe? What is my life, O my dear and merciful Lord, but a series of offences, little or great, against Thee! O what great sins I have committed against Thee before now—and how continually in lesser matters I am sinning! My God, what will become of me? What will be my position hereafter if I am left to myself! What can I do but come humbly to Him whom I have so heavily affronted and insulted, and beg Him to forgive the debt which lies against me? O my Lord Jesus, whose love for me has been so great as to bring Thee down from heaven to save me, teach me, dear Lord, my sin—teach me its heinousness—teach me truly to repent of it— and pardon it in Thy great mercy!

3. I beg Thee, O my dear Saviour, to recover me! Thy grace alone can do it. I cannot save myself. I cannot recover my lost ground. I cannot turn to Thee, I cannot please Thee, or save my soul without Thee. I shall go from bad to worse, I shall fall from Thee entirely, I shall quite harden myself against my neglect of duty, if I rely on my own strength. I shall make myself my centre instead of making Thee. I shall worship some idol of my

own framing instead of Thee, the only true God and my
Maker, unless Thou hinder it by Thy grace. O my dear
Lord, hear me! I have lived long enough in this unde-
cided, wavering, unsatisfactory state. I wish to be Thy
good servant. I wish to sin no more. Be gracious to me,
and enable me to be what I know I ought to be.

(3)

THE EFFECTS OF SIN

1. MY Lord, Thou art the infinitely merciful God.
Thou lovest all things that Thou hast created. Thou art
the lover of·souls. How then is it, O Lord, that I am in a
world so miserable as this is? Can this be the world which
Thou hast created, so full of pain and suffering? Who
among the sons of Adam lives without suffering from his
birth to his death? How many bad sicknesses and diseases
are there! how many frightful accidents! how many great
anxieties! how are men brought down and broken by
grief, distress, the tumult of passions, and continual fear!
What dreadful plagues are there ever on the earth: war,
famine, and pestilence! Why is this, O my God? Why is
this, O my soul? Dwell upon it, and ask thyself, Why is
this? Has God changed His nature? yet how evil has the
earth become!

2. O my God, I know full well why all these evils are.
Thou hast not changed Thy nature, but man has ruined
his own. We have sinned, O Lord, and therefore is this
change. All these evils which I see and in which I partake
are the fruit of sin. They would not have been, had we
not sinned. They are but the first instalment of the
punishment of sin. They are an imperfect and dim image
of what sin is. Sin is infinitely worse than famine, than
war, than pestilence. Take the most hideous of diseases,
under which the body wastes away and corrupts, the

blood is infected; the head, the heart, the lungs, every organ disordered, the nerves unstrung and shattered; pain in every limb, thirst, restlessness, delirium—all is nothing compared with that dreadful sickness of the soul which we call sin. They all are the effects of it, they all are shadows of it, but nothing more. That cause itself is something different in kind, is of a malignity far other and greater than all these things. O my God, teach me this! Give me to understand the enormity of that evil under which I labour and know it not. Teach me what sin is.

3. All these dreadful pains of body and soul are the fruits of sin, but they are nothing to its punishment in the world to come. The keenest and fiercest of bodily pains is nothing to the fire of hell; the most dire horror or anxiety is nothing to the never-dying worm of conscience; the greatest bereavement, loss of substance, desertion of friends, and forlorn desolation is nothing compared to the loss of God's countenance. Eternal punishment is the only true measure of the guilt of sin. My God, teach me this. Open my eyes and heart, I earnestly pray Thee, and make me understand how awful a body of death I bear about me. And, not only teach me about it, but in Thy mercy and by Thy grace remove it.

(4)

THE EVIL OF SIN

1. My God, I know that Thou didst create the whole universe very good; and if this was true of the material world which we see, much more true is it of the world of rational beings. The innumerable stars which fill the firmament, and the very elements out of which the earth is made, all are carried through their courses and their operations in perfect concord; but much higher was the concord which reigned in heaven when the Angels were

first created. At that first moment of their existence the main orders of the Angels were in the most excellent harmony, and beautiful to contemplate; and the creation of man was expected next, to continue that harmony in the instance of a different kind of being. Then it was that suddenly was discovered a flaw or a rent in one point of this most delicate and exquisite web—and it extended and unravelled the web, till a third part of it was spoilt; and then again a similar flaw was found in human kind, and it extended over the whole race. This dreadful evil, destroying so large a portion of all God's works, is sin.

2. My God, such is sin in Thy judgment; what is it in the judgment of the world? A very small evil or none at all. In the judgment of the Creator it is that which has marred His spiritual work; it is a greater evil than though the stars got loose, and ran wild in heaven, and chaos came again. But man, who is the guilty one, calls it by soft names. He explains it away. The world laughs at it, and is indulgent to it; and, as to its deserving eternal punishment, it rises up indignant at the idea, and rather than admit it, would deny the God who has said it does. The world thinks sin the same sort of imperfection as an impropriety, or want of taste or infirmity. O my soul, consider carefully the great difference between the views of sin taken by Almighty God and the world! Which of the two views do you mean to believe?

3. O my soul, which of the two wilt thou believe—the word of God or the word of man? Is God right or is the creature right? Is sin the greatest of all possible evils or the least? My Lord and Saviour, I have no hesitation which to believe. Thou art true, and every man a liar. I will believe Thee, above the whole world. My God, imprint on my heart the infamous deformity of sin. Teach me to abhor it as a pestilence—as a fierce flame destroying on every side; as my death. Let me take up arms against it, and devote myself to fight under Thy banner in overcoming it.

(5)

THE HEINOUSNESS OF SIN

1. MY Lord, I know well that Thou art all perfect, and needest nothing. Yet I know that Thou hast taken upon Thyself the nature of man, and, not only so, but in that nature didst come upon earth, and suffer all manner of evil, and didst die. This is a history which has hung the heavens with sackcloth, and taken from this earth, beautiful as it is, its light and glory. Thou didst come, O my dear Lord, and Thou didst suffer in no ordinary way, but unheard of and extreme torments! The all-blessed Lord suffered the worst and most various of pains. This is the corner truth of the Gospel: it is the one foundation, Jesus Christ and He crucified. I know it, O Lord, I believe it, and I put it steadily before me.

2. Why is this strange anomaly in the face of nature? Does God do things for naught? No, my soul, it is sin; it is thy sin, which has brought the Everlasting down upon earth to suffer. Hence I learn how great an evil sin is. The death of the Infinite is its sole measure. All that slow distress of body and mind which He endured, from the time He shed blood at Gethsemani down to His death, all that pain came from sin. What sort of evil is that, which had to be so encountered by such a sacrifice, and to be reversed at such a price! Here then I understand best how horrible a thing sin is. It is horrible; because through it have come upon men all those evils whatever they are, with which the earth abounds. It is more horrible, in that it has nailed the Son of God to the accursed tree.

3. My dear Lord and Saviour, how can I make light of that which has had such consequences! Henceforth I will, through Thy grace, have deeper views of sin than before. Fools make jest of sin, but I will view things in their true light. My suffering Lord, I have made Thee suffer. Thou

art most beautiful in Thy eternal nature, O my Lord;
Thou art most beautiful in Thy sufferings! Thy adorable
attributes are not dimmed, but increased to us as we gaze
on Thy humiliation. Thou art more beautiful to us than
before. But still I will never forget that it was man's sin,
my sin, which made that humiliation necessary. *Amor
meus crucifixus est*—"my Love is crucified," but by none
other than me. I have crucified Thee, my sin has crucified
Thee. O my Saviour, what a dreadful thought—but I
cannot undo it; all I can do is to hate that which made
Thee suffer. Shall I not do that at least? Shall I not love
my Lord just so much as to hate that which is so great an
enemy of His, and break off all terms with it? Shall I not
put off sin altogether? By Thy great love of me, teach me
and enable me to do this, O Lord. Give me a deep,
rooted, intense hatred of sin.

(6)

THE BONDAGE OF SIN

1. THOU, O my Lord and God, Thou alone art strong,
Thou alone art holy! Thou art the *Sanctus Deus, Sanctus
fortis*—"Holy God, holy and strong!" Thou art the sanctity and the strength of all things. No created nature has
any stay or subsistence in itself, but crumbles and melts
away, if Thou art not with it, to sustain it. My God,
Thou art the strength of the Angels, of the Saints in
glory—of holy men on earth. No being has any sanctity
or any strength apart from Thee. My God, I wish to
adore Thee as such. I wish with all my heart to understand and to confess this great truth, that not only Thou
art Almighty, but that there is no might at all, or power,
or strength, anywhere but in Thee.

2. My God, if Thou art the strength of all spirits, O
how pre-eminently art Thou my strength! O how true it
is, so that nothing is more so, that I have no strength but

in Thee! I feel intimately, O my God, that, whenever I am left to myself, I go wrong. As sure as a stone falls down to the earth if it be let go, so surely my heart and spirit fall down hopelessly if they are let go by Thee. Thou must uphold me by Thy right hand, or I cannot stand. How strange it is, but how true, that all my natural tendencies are towards sloth, towards excess, towards neglect of religion, towards neglect of prayer, towards love of the world, not towards love of Thee, or love of sanctity, or love of self-governance. I approve and praise what I do not do. My heart runs after vanities, and I tend to death, I tend to corruption and dissolution, apart from Thee, *Deus immortalis*.

3. My God, I have had experience enough what a dreadful bondage sin is. If Thou art away, I find I cannot keep myself, however I wish it—and am in the hands of my own self-will, pride, sensuality, and selfishness. And they prevail with me more and more every day, till they are irresistible. In time the old Adam within me gets so strong, that I become a mere slave. I confess things to be wrong which nevertheless I do. I bitterly lament over my bondage, but I cannot undo it. O what a tyranny is sin! It is a heavy weight which cripples me—and what will be the end of it? By Thy all-precious merits, by Thy Almighty power, I intreat Thee, O my Lord, to give me life and sanctity and strength! *Deus sanctus*, give me holiness; *Deus fortis*, give me strength; *Deus immortalis*, give me perseverance. *Sanctus Deus, Sanctus fortis, Sanctus immortalis, miserere nobis*.

(7)

EVERY SIN HAS ITS PUNISHMENT

1. THOU art the all-seeing, all-knowing God. Thy eyes, O Lord, are in every place. Thou art a real spectator of everything which takes place anywhere. Thou art ever

with me. Thou art present and conscious of all I think, say, or do. *Tu Deus qui vidisti me*—"Thou, God, who hast seen me." Every deed or act, however slight; every word, however quick and casual; every thought of my heart, however secret, however momentary, however forgotten, Thou seest, O Lord, Thou seest and Thou notest down. Thou hast a book; Thou enterest in it every day of my life. I forget; Thou dost not forget. There is stored up the history of all my past years, and so it will be till I die—the leaves will be filled and turned over—and the book at length finished. *Quo ibo a Spiritu Tuo*—"whither shall I go from Thy Spirit?" I am in Thy hands, O Lord, absolutely.

2. My God, how often do I act wrongly, how seldom rightly! how dreary on the whole are the acts of any one day! All my sins, offences, and negligences, not of one day only, but of all days, are in Thy book. And every sin, offence, negligence, has a separate definite punishment. That list of penalties increases, silently but surely, every day. As the spendthrift is overwhelmed by a continually greater weight of debt, so am I exposed continually to a greater and greater score of punishments catalogued against me. I *forget* the sins of my childhood, my boyhood, my adolescence, my youth. They are all noted down in that book. *There* is a complete history of all my life; and it will one day be brought up against me. Nothing is lost, all is remembered. O my soul, what hast thou to go through! What an examination that will be, and what a result! I shall have put upon me the punishment of ten thousand sins—I shall for this purpose be sent to Purgatory—how long will it last? when shall I ever get out? Not till I have paid the last farthing. When will this possibly be?

3. O my dear Lord, have mercy upon me! I trust Thou hast forgiven me my sins—but the punishment remains. In the midst of Thy love for me, and recognising me as

Thine own, Thou wilt consign me to Purgatory. There I shall go through my sins once more, in their punishment. There I shall suffer, but here is the time for a thorough repentance. Here is the time of good works, of obtaining indulgences, of wiping out the debt in every possible way. Thy saints, though to the eyes of man without sin, really had a vast account—and they settled it by continual trials here. I have neither their merit nor their sufferings. I cannot tell whether I can make such acts of love as will gain me an indulgence of my sins. The prospect before me is dark—I can only rely on Thy infinite compassion. O my dear Lord, who hast in so many ways shown Thy mercy towards me, pity me here! Be merciful in the midst of justice.

V

THE POWER OF THE CROSS

1. O MY God, who could have imagined, by any light of nature, that it was one of Thy attributes to lower Thyself, and to work out Thy purposes by Thy own humiliation and suffering? Thou hadst lived from eternity in ineffable blessedness. My God, I might have understood as much as this, viz. that, when Thou didst begin to create and surround Thyself with a world of creatures, that these attributes would show themselves in Thee which before had no exercise. Thou couldest not show Thy power when there was nothing whatever to exercise it. Then too, Thou didst begin to show thy wonderful and tender providence, Thy faithfulness, Thy solicitous care for those whom Thou hadst created. But who could have fancied that Thy creation of the universe implied and involved in it Thy humiliation? O my great God, Thou hast humbled Thyself, Thou hast stooped to take our flesh and blood, and hast been lifted up upon the tree! I praise and glorify Thee tenfold the more, because Thou hast shown Thy power by means of Thy suffering, than hadst Thou carried on Thy work without it. It is worthy of Thy infinitude thus to surpass and transcend all our thoughts.

2. O my Lord Jesu, I believe, and by Thy grace will ever believe and hold, and I know that it is true, and will be true to the end of the world, that nothing great is done without suffering, without humiliation, and that all things are possible by means of it. I believe, O my God, that poverty is better than riches, pain better than plea-

sure, obscurity and contempt than name, and ignominy and reproach than honour. My Lord, I do not ask Thee to bring these trials on me, for I know not if I could face them; but at least, O Lord, whether I be in prosperity or adversity, I will believe that it is as I have said. I will never have faith in riches, rank, power, or reputation. I will never set my heart on worldly success or on worldly advantages. I will never wish for what men call the prizes of life. I will ever, with Thy grace, make much of those who are despised or neglected, honour the poor, revere the suffering, and admire and venerate Thy saints and confessors, and take my part with them in spite of the world.

3. And lastly, O my dear Lord, though I am so very weak that I am not fit to ask Thee for suffering as a gift, and have not strength to do so, at least I will beg of Thee grace to meet suffering well, when Thou in Thy love and wisdom dost bring it upon me. Let me bear pain, reproach, disappointment, slander, anxiety, suspense, as Thou wouldest have me, O my Jesu, and as Thou by Thy own suffering hast taught me, when it comes. And I promise too, with Thy grace, that I will never set myself up, never seek pre-eminence, never court any great thing of the world, never prefer myself to others. I wish to bear insult meekly, and to return good for evil. I wish to humble myself in all things, and to be silent when I am ill-used, and to be patient when sorrow or pain is prolonged, and all for the love of Thee, and Thy Cross, knowing that in this way I shall gain the promise both of this life and of the next.

VI

THE RESURRECTION

(I)

THE TEMPLES OF THE HOLY GHOST

1. I ADORE Thee, O Eternal Word, for Thy gracious condescension, in not only taking a created nature, a created spirit or soul, but a material body. The Most High decreed that for ever and ever He would subject Himself to a created prison. He who from eternity was nothing but infinite incomprehensible Spirit, beyond all laws but those of His own transcendent Greatness, willed that for the eternity to come He should be united, in the most intimate of unions, with that which was under the conditions of a creature. Thy omnipotence, O Lord, ever protects itself—but nothing short of that omnipotence could enable Thee so to condescend without a loss of power. Thy Body has part in Thy power, rather than Thou hast part in its weakness. For this reason, my God, it was, that Thou couldst not but rise again, if Thou wast to die—because Thy Body, once taken by Thee, never was or could be separated from Thee, even in the grave. It was Thy Body even then, it could see no corruption; it could not remain under the power of death, for Thou hadst already wonderfully made it Thine, and whatever was Thine must last in its perfection for ever. I adore Thy Most Holy Body, O my dear Jesus, the instrument of our redemption!

2. I look at Thee, my Lord Jesus, and think of Thy

Most Holy Body, and I keep it before me as the pledge of my own resurrection. Though I die, as die I certainly shall, nevertheless I shall not for ever die, for I shall rise again. My Lord, the heathen who knew Thee not, thought the body to be of a miserable and contemptible nature—they thought it the seat, the cause, the excuse of all moral evil. When their thoughts soared highest, and they thought of a future life, they considered that the destruction of the body was the condition of that higher existence. That the body was really part of themselves and that its restoration could be a privilege, was beyond their utmost imagination. And indeed, what mind of man, O Lord, could ever have fancied without Thy revelation that what, according to our experience, is so vile, so degraded, so animal, so sinful, which is our fellowship with the brutes, which is full of corruption and becomes dust and ashes, was in its very nature capable of so high a destiny! that it could become celestial and immortal, without ceasing to be a body! And who but Thou, who art omnipotent, could have made it so! No wonder then, that the wise men of the world, who did not believe in Thee, scoffed at the Resurrection. But I, by Thy grace, will ever keep before me how differently I have been taught by Thee. O best and first and truest of Teachers! O Thou who art the Truth, I know, and believe with my whole heart, that this very flesh of mine will rise again. I know, base and odious as it is at present, that it will one day, if I be worthy, be raised incorruptible and altogether beautiful and glorious. This I know; this, by Thy grace, I will ever keep before me.

3. O my God, teach me so to live, as one who does believe the great dignity, the great sanctity of that material frame in which Thou hast lodged me. And therefore, O my dear Saviour! do I come so often and so earnestly to be partaker of Thy Body and Blood, that by means of Thy own ineffable holiness I may be made holy. O my

Lord Jesus, I know what is written, that our bodies are the temples of the Holy Ghost. Should I not venerate that which Thou dost miraculously feed, and which Thy Co-equal Spirit inhabits! O my God, who wast nailed to the Cross, *confige timore tuo carnes meas*—"pierce Thou my flesh with Thy fear;" crucify my soul and body in all that is sinful in them, and make me pure as Thou art pure.

(2)

GOD ALONE

Thomas says to Him, "My Lord and my God."

1. I ADORE Thee, O my God, with Thomas; and if I have, like him, sinned through unbelief, I adore Thee the more. I adore Thee as the One Adorable, I adore Thee as more glorious in Thy humiliation, when men despised Thee, than when Angels worshipped Thee. *Deus meus et omnia*—"My God and my all." To have Thee is to have everything I can have. O my Eternal Father, give me Thyself. I dared not have made so bold a request, it would have been presumption, unless Thou hadst encouraged me. Thou hast put it into my mouth, Thou hast clothed Thyself in my nature, Thou hast become my Brother, Thou hast died as other men die, only in far greater bitterness, that, instead of my eyeing Thee fearfully from afar, I might confidently draw near to Thee. Thou dost speak to me as Thou didst speak to Thomas, and dost beckon me to take hold of Thee. My God and my all, what could I say more than this, if I spoke to all eternity! I am full and abound and overflow, when I have Thee; but without Thee I am nothing—I wither away, I dissolve and perish. My Lord and my God, my God and my all, give me Thyself and nothing else.

2. Thomas came and touched Thy sacred wounds. O

will the day ever come when I shall be allowed actually and visibly to kiss them? What a day will that be when I am thoroughly cleansed from all impurity and sin, and am fit to draw near to my Incarnate God in His palace of light above! what a morning, when having done with all penal suffering, I see Thee for the first time with these very eyes of mine, I see Thy countenance, gaze upon Thy eyes and gracious lips without quailing, and then kneel down with joy to kiss Thy feet, and am welcomed into Thy arms. O my only true Lover, the only Lover of my soul, Thee will I love now, that I may love Thee then. What a day, a long day without ending, the day of eternity, when I shall be so unlike what I am *now*, when I feel in myself a body of death, and am perplexed and distracted with ten thousand thoughts, any one of which would keep me from heaven. O my Lord, what a day when I shall have done once for all with all sins, venial as well as mortal, and shall stand perfect and acceptable in Thy sight, able to bear Thy presence, nothing shrinking from Thy eye, not shrinking from the pure scrutiny of Angels and Archangels, when I stand in the midst and they around me!

3. O my God, though I am not fit to see or touch Thee yet, still I will ever come within Thy reach, and desire that which is not yet given me in its fulness. O my Saviour, Thou shalt be my sole God!—I will have no Lord but Thee. I will break to pieces all idols in my heart which rival Thee. I will have nothing but Jesus and Him crucified. It shall be my life to pray to Thee, to offer myself to Thee, to keep Thee before me, to worship Thee in Thy holy Sacrifice, and to surrender myself to Thee in Holy Communion.

(3)

THE FORBEARANCE OF JESUS

Videte manus meas, etc. Habetis aliquid quod manducetur?
See my hands, etc. Have you here anything to eat?

1. I ADORE Thee, O my Lord, for Thy wonderful patience and Thy compassionate tenderhearted condescension. Thy disciples, in spite of all Thy teaching and miracles, disbelieved Thee when they saw Thee die, and fled. Nor did they take courage afterwards, nor think of Thy promise of rising again on the third day. They did not believe Magdalen, nor the other women, who said they had seen Thee alive again. Yet Thou didst appear to them—Thou didst show them Thy wounds—Thou didst let them touch Thee—Thou didst eat before them, and give them Thy peace. O Jesu, is any obstinacy too great for Thy love? does any number of falls and relapses vanquish the faithfulness and endurance of Thy compassion? Thou dost forgive not only seven times, but to seventy times seven. Many waters cannot quench a love like Thine. And such Thou art all over the earth, even to the end—forgiving, sparing, forbearing, waiting, though sinners are ever provoking Thee; pitying and taking into account their ignorance, visiting all men, all Thine enemies, with the gentle pleadings of Thy grace, day after day, year after year, up to the hour of their death—for He knoweth whereof we are made; He knoweth we are but dust.

2. My God, what hast Thou done for me! Men say of Thee, O my only Good, that Thy judgments are severe, and Thy punishments excessive. All I can say is, that I have not found them so in my own case. Let others speak for themselves, and Thou wilt meet and overcome them to their own confusion in the day of reckoning. With

them I have nothing to do—*Thou* wilt settle with them—but for me the only experience that *I* have is Thy dealings with myself, and here I bear witness, as I know so entirely and feel so intimately, that to me Thou hast been nothing but forbearance and mercy. O how Thou dost forget that I have ever rebelled against Thee! Again and again dost Thou help me. I fall, yet Thou dost not cast me off. In spite of all my sins, Thou dost still love me, prosper me, comfort me, surround me with blessings, sustain me, and further me. I grieve Thy good grace, yet Thou dost give more. I insult Thee, yet Thou never dost take offence, but art as kind as if I had nothing to explain, to repent of, to amend—as if I were Thy best, most faithful, most steady and loyal friend. Nay, alas! I am even led to presume upon Thy love, it is so like easiness and indulgence, though I ought to fear Thee. I confess it, O my true Saviour, every day is but a fresh memorial of Thy unwearied, unconquerable love!

3. O my God, suffer me still—bear with me in spite of my waywardness, perverseness, and ingratitude! I improve very slowly, but really I am moving on to heaven, or at least I wish to move. I am putting Thee before me, vile sinner as I am, and I am really thinking in earnest of saving my soul. Give me time to collect my thoughts, and make one good effort. I protest I will put off this languor and lukewarmness—I will shake myself from this sullenness and despondency and gloom—I will rouse myself, and be cheerful, and walk in Thy light. I will have no hope or joy but Thee. Only give me Thy grace—meet me with Thy grace, I will through Thy grace do what I can—and Thou shalt perfect it for me. Then I shall have happy days in Thy presence, and in the sight and adoration of Thy five Sacred Wounds.

VII

GOD WITH US

(I)

THE FAMILIARITY OF JESUS

1. THE Holy Baptist was separated from the world. He was a Nazarite. He went out from the world, and placed himself over against it, and spoke to it from his vantage ground, and called it to repentance. Then went out all Jerusalem to him into the desert, and he confronted it face to face. But in his teaching he spoke of One who should come to them and speak to them in a far different way. He should not separate Himself from them, He should not display Himself as some higher being, but as their brother, as of their flesh and of their bones, as one among many brethren, as one of the multitude and amidst them; nay, He was among them already. "*Medius vestrum stetit, quem vos nescitis*"—"there hath stood in the midst of you, whom you know not." That greater one called Himself the Son of man—He was content to be taken as ordinary in all respects, though He was the Highest. St. John and the other Evangelists, though so different in the character of their accounts of Him, agree most strikingly here. The Baptist says, "There is in the midst of you One whom you know not." Next we read of his pointing Jesus out privately, not to crowds, but to one or two of his own religious followers; then of their seeking Jesus and being allowed to follow Him home. At length Jesus begins to disclose Himself and to manifest His glory in miracles;

384

GOD WITH US

but where? At a marriage feast, where there was often excess, as the architriclinus implies. And how? in adding to the wine, the instrument of such excess, when it occurred. He was at that marriage feast not as a teacher, but as a guest, and (so to speak) in a social way, for He was with His Mother. Now compare this with what He says in St. Matthew's Gospel of Himself: "John came neither eating nor drinking—The Son of man came eating and drinking, and they say: Behold a man that is a glutton and wine-drinker." John might be hated, but he was respected; Jesus was despised. See also Mark i. 22, 27, 37, iii. 21, for the astonishment and rudeness of all about Him. The objection occurs *at once*, ii. 16. What a marked feature it must have been of our Lord's character and mission, since two Evangelists, so independent in their narrations, record it! The prophet had said the same (Isai. liii. "He shall," &c.).

2. This was, O dear Lord, because Thou so lovest this human nature which Thou hast created. Thou didst not love us merely as Thy creatures, the work of Thy hands, but as men. Thou lovest all, for Thou hast created all; but Thou lovest man more than all. How is it, Lord, that this should be? What is there in man, above others? *Quid est homo, quod memor es ejus? yet, nusquam Angelos apprehendit*— "What is man, that Thou art mindful of him?" . . . "nowhere doth he take hold of the angels." Who can sound the depth of Thy counsels and decrees? Thou hast loved man more than Thou hast loved the Angels: and therefore, as Thou didst not take on Thee an angelic nature when Thou didst manifest Thyself for our salvation, so too Thou wouldest not come in any shape or capacity or office which was above the course of ordinary human life—not as a Nazarene, not as a Levitical priest, not as a monk, not as a hermit, but in the fulness and exactness of that human nature which so much Thou lovest. Thou camest not only a perfect man, but as

proper man; not formed anew out of earth, not with the spiritual body which Thou now hast, but in that very flesh which had fallen in Adam, and with all our infirmities, all our feelings and sympathies, sin expected.

3. O Jesu, it became Thee, the great God, thus abundantly and largely to do Thy work, for which the Father sent Thee. Thou didst not do it by halves—and, while that magnificence of Sacrifice is Thy glory as God, it is our consolation and aid as sinners. O dearest Lord, Thou art more fully man than the holy Baptist, than St. John, Apostle and Evangelist, than Thy own sweet Mother. As in Divine knowledge of me Thou art beyond them all, so also in experience and personal knowledge of my nature. Thou art my elder brother. How can I fear, how should I not repose my whole heart on one so gentle, so tender, so familiar, so unpretending, so modest, so natural, so humble? Thou art now, though in heaven, just the same as Thou wast on earth: the mighty God, yet the little child—the all-holy, yet the all-sensitive, all-human.

(2)

JESUS THE HIDDEN GOD

Noli incredulus esse, sed fidelis.
Be not faithless, but believing.

1. I ADORE Thee, O my God, who art so awful, because Thou art hidden and unseen! I adore Thee, and I desire to live by faith in what I do not see; and considering what I am, a disinherited outcast, I think it has indeed gone well with me that I am allowed, O my unseen Lord and Saviour, to worship Thee anyhow. O my God, I know that it is sin that has separated between Thee and me. I know it is sin that has brought on me the penalty of ignorance. Adam, before he fell, was visited by Angels.

Thy Saints, too, who keep close to Thee, see visions, and in many ways are brought into sensible perception of Thy presence. But to a sinner such as I am, what is left but to possess Thee without seeing Thee? Ah, should I not rejoice at having that most extreme mercy and favour of possessing Thee at all? It is sin that has reduced me to live by faith, as I must at best, and should I not rejoice in such a life, O Lord my God? I see and know, O my good Jesus, that the only way in which I can possibly approach Thee in this world is the way of faith, faith in what Thou hast told me, and I thankfully follow this only way which Thou hast given me.

2. O my God, Thou dost over-abound in mercy! To live by faith is my necessity, from my present state of being and from my sin; but Thou hast pronounced a blessing on it. Thou hast said that I am more blessed if I believe on Thee, than if I saw Thee. Give me to share that blessedness, give it to me in its fulness. Enable me to believe as if I saw; let me have Thee always before me as if Thou wert always bodily and sensibly present. Let me ever hold communion with Thee, my hidden, but my living God. Thou art in my innermost heart. Thou art the life of my life. Every breath I breathe, every thought of my mind, every good desire of my heart, is from the presence within me of the unseen God. By nature and by grace Thou art in me. I see Thee not in the material world except dimly, but I recognise Thy voice in my own intimate consciousness. I turn round and say Rabboni. O be ever thus with me; and if I am tempted to leave *Thee*, do not Thou, O my God, leave *me!*

3. O my dear Saviour, would that I had any right to ask to be allowed to make reparation to Thee for all the unbelief of the world, and all the insults offered to Thy Name, Thy Word, Thy Church, and the Sacrament of Thy Love! But, alas, I have a long score of unbelief and ingratitude of my own to atone for. Thou art in the

Sacrifice of the Mass, Thou art in the Tabernacle, verily
and indeed, in flesh and blood; and the world not only
disbelieves, but mocks at this gracious truth. Thou didst
warn us long ago by Thyself and by Thy Apostles that
Thou wouldest hide Thyself from the world. The prophecy is fulfilled more than ever now; but *I* know what the
world knows not. O accept my homage, my praise,
my adoration!—let me at least not be found wanting. I
cannot help the sins of others—but one at least of those
whom Thou hast redeemed shall turn round and with a
loud voice glorify God. The more men scoff, the more
will I believe in Thee, the good God, the good Jesus, the
hidden Lord of life, who hast done me nothing else but
good from the very first moment that I began to live.

(3)

JESUS THE LIGHT OF THE SOUL

Mane nobiscum, Domine, quoniam advesperascit.
Stay with us, because it is towards evening.

1. I ADORE Thee, O my God, as the true and only Light!
From Eternity to Eternity, before any creature was,
when Thou wast alone, alone but not solitary, for Thou
hast ever been Three in One, Thou wast the Infinite
Light. There was none to see Thee but Thyself. The
Father saw that Light in the Son, and the Son in the
Father. Such as Thou wast in the beginning, such Thou
art now. Most separate from all creatures in this Thy
uncreated Brightness. Most glorious, most beautiful.
Thy attributes are so many separate and resplendent
colours, each as perfect in its own purity and grace as if it
were the sole and highest perfection. Nothing created is
more than the very shadow of Thee. Bright as are the
Angels, they are poor and most unworthy shadows of

Thee. They pale and look dim and gather blackness before Thee. They are so feeble beside Thee, that they are unable to gaze upon Thee. The highest Seraphim veil their eyes, by deed as well as by word proclaiming Thy unutterable glory. For me, I cannot even look upon the sun, and what is this but a base material emblem of Thee? How should I endure to look even on an Angel? and how could I look upon Thee and live? If I were placed in the illumination of Thy countenance, I should shrink up like the grass. O most gracious God, who shall approach Thee, being so glorious, yet how can I keep from Thee?

2. How can I keep from Thee? For Thou, who art the Light of Angels, art the only Light of my soul. Thou enlightenest every man that cometh into this world. I am utterly dark, as dark as hell, without Thee. I droop and shrink when Thou art away. I revive only in proportion as Thou dawnest upon me. Thou comest and goest at Thy will. O my God, I cannot keep Thee! I can only beg of Thee to stay. "Mane nobiscum, Domine, quoniam advesperascit." Remain till morning, and then go not without giving me a blessing. Remain with me till death in this dark valley, when the darkness will end. Remain, O Light of my soul, *jam advesperascit!* The gloom, which is not Thine, falls over me. I am nothing. I have little command of myself. I cannot do what I would. I am disconsolate and sad. I want something, I know not what. It is Thou that I want, though I so little understand this. I say it and take it on faith; I partially understand it, but very poorly. Shine on me, O *Ignis semper ardens et nunquam deficiens!*—"O fire ever burning and never failing"—and I shall begin, through and in Thy Light, to see Light, and to recognise Thee truly, as the Source of Light. *Mane nobiscum;* stay, sweet Jesus, stay for ever. In this decay of nature, give more grace.

3. Stay with me, and then I shall begin to shine as Thou shinest: so to shine as to be a light to others. The light, O

Jesus, will be all from Thee. None of it will be mine. No merit to me. It will be Thou who shinest through me upon others. O let me thus praise Thee, in the way which Thou dost love best, by shining on all those around me. Give light to them as well as to me; light them with me, through me. Teach me to show forth Thy praise, Thy truth, Thy will. Make me preach Thee without preaching—not by words, but by my example and by the catching force, the sympathetic influence, of what I do—by my visible resemblance to Thy saints, and the evident fulness of the love which my heart bears to Thee.

VIII

GOD ALL-SUFFICIENT

Ostende nobis Patrem et sufficit nobis. . . .
Philippe, qui videt Me, videt et Patrem.

Show us the Father, and it is enough for us. . . .
Philip, he that seeth Me, seeth the Father also.

1. THE Son is in the Father and the Father in the Son. O
adorable mystery which has been from eternity! I adore
Thee, O my incomprehensible Creator, before whom I
am an atom, a being of yesterday or an hour ago! Go back
a few years and I simply did not exist; I was not in being,
and things went on without me: but Thou art from
eternity; and nothing whatever for one moment could go
on without Thee. And from eternity too Thou hast
possessed Thy Nature; Thou hast been—this awful glorious mystery—the Son in the Father and the Father in the
Son. Whether we be in existence, or whether we be not,
Thou art one and the same always, the Son sufficient for
the Father, the Father for the Son—and all other things,
in themselves, but vanity. All things once were not, all
things might not be, but it would be enough for the
Father that He had begotten His co-equal consubstantial
Son, and for the Son that He was embraced in the Bosom
of the Eternal Father. O adorable mystery! Human reason has not conducted me to it, but I believe. I believe,
because Thou hast spoken, O Lord. I joyfully accept Thy
word about Thyself. Thou must know what Thou art—
and who else? Not I surely, dust and ashes, except so far

as Thou tellest me. I take then Thy own witness, O my Creator! and I believe firmly, I repeat after Thee, what I do not understand, because I wish to live a life of faith; and I prefer faith in Thee to trust in myself.

2. O my great God, from eternity Thou wast sufficient for Thyself! The Father was sufficient for the Son, and the Son for the Father; art Thou not then sufficient for me, a poor creature, Thou so great, I so little! I have a double all-sufficiency in the Father and the Son. I will take then St. Philip's word and say, Show us the Father, and it *suffices* us. It suffices us, for then are we full to overflowing, when we have Thee. O mighty God, strengthen me with Thy strength, console me with Thy everlasting peace, soothe me with the beauty of Thy countenance; enlighten me with Thy uncreated brightness; purify me with the fragrance of Thy ineffable holiness. Bathe me in Thyself, and give me to drink, as far as mortal man may ask, of the rivers of grace which flow from the Father and the Son, the grace of Thy consubstantial, co-eternal Love.

3. O my God, let me never forget this truth—that not only art Thou my Life, but my only Life! Thou art the Way, the Truth, and the Life. Thou art my Life, and the Life of all who live. All men, all I know, all I meet, all I see and hear of, live not unless they live by Thee. They live in Thee, or else they live not at all. No one can be saved out of Thee. Let me never forget this in the business of the day. O give me a true love of souls, of those souls for whom Thou didst die. Teach me to pray for their conversion, to do my part towards effecting it. However able they are, however amiable, however high and distinguished, they cannot be saved unless they have Thee. O my all-sufficient Lord, Thou only sufficest! Thy blood is sufficient for the whole world. As Thou art sufficient for me, so Thou art sufficient for the entire race

of Adam. O my Lord Jesus, let Thy Cross be more than sufficient for them, let it be effectual! Let it be effectual for me more than all, lest I "have all and abound," yet bring no fruit to perfection.

IX

GOD ALONE UNCHANGEABLE

Quo ego vado, non potes Me modo sequi, sequeris autem postea.

Whither I go, thou canst not follow Me now, but thou shalt follow hereafter.

1. THOU alone, O my God, art what Thou ever hast been! Man changes. Thou art unchangeable; nay, even as man Thou hast ever been unchangeable, for Jesus is yesterday and to-day Himself, and for ever. Thy word endureth in heaven and earth. Thy decrees are fixed; Thy gifts are without repentance. Thy Nature, Thy Attributes, are ever the same. There ever was Father, ever Son, ever Holy Ghost. I adore Thee in the peace and serenity of Thy unchangeableness. I adore Thee in that imperturbable heaven, which is Thyself. Thou wast perfect from the first; nothing couldest Thou gain, and nothing mightest Thou lose. There was nothing that could touch Thee, because there was nothing but what Thou didst create and couldst destroy. Again, I adore Thee in this Thy infinite stability, which is the centre and stay of all created things.

2. Man on the contrary is ever changing. Not a day passes but I am nearer the grave. Whatever be my age, whatever the number of my years, I am ever narrowing the interval between time and eternity. I am ever changing in myself. Youth is not like age; and I am continually changing, as I pass along out of youth towards the end of life. O my God, I am crumbling away, as I go on! I am

already dissolving into my first elements. My soul indeed cannot die, for Thou hast made it immortal; but my bodily frame is continually resolving into that dust out of which it was taken. All below heaven changes: spring, summer, autumn, each has its turn. The fortunes of the world change; what was high, lies low; what was low rises high. Riches take wings and flee away; bereavements happen. Friends become enemies, and enemies friends. Our wishes, aims, and plans change. There is nothing stable but Thou, O my God! And Thou art the centre and life of all who change, who trust Thee as their Father, who look to Thee, and who are content to put themselves into Thy hands.

3. I know, O my God, I must change, if I am to see Thy face! I must undergo the change of death. Body and soul must die to this world. My real self, my soul, must change by a true regeneration. None but the holy can see Thee. Like Peter, I cannot have a blessing now, which I shall have afterwards. "Thou canst not follow me now, but thou shalt follow hereafter." Oh, support me, as I proceed in this great, awful, happy change, with the grace of Thy unchangeableness. My unchangeableness here below is perseverance in changing. Let me day by day be moulded upon Thee, and be changed from glory to glory, by ever looking towards Thee, and ever leaning on Thy arm. I know, O Lord, I must go through trial, temptation, and much conflict, if I am to come to Thee. I know not what lies before me, but I know as much as this. I know, too, that if Thou art not with me, my change will be for the worse, not for the better. Whatever fortune I have, be I rich or poor, healthy or sick, with friends or without, all will turn to evil if I am not sustained by the Unchangeable; all will turn to good if I have Jesus with me, yesterday and to-day the same, and for ever.

X

GOD IS LOVE

Jesus saith to him, Lovest thou Me more than these?

1. THOU askest us to love Thee, O my God, and Thou art Thyself Love. There was one attribute of Thine which Thou didst exercise from eternity, and that was Love. We hear of no exercise of Thy power whilst Thou wast alone, nor of Thy justice before there were creatures on their trial; nor of Thy wisdom before the acts and works of Thy Providence; but from eternity Thou didst love, for Thou art not only One but Three. The Father loved from eternity His only begotten Son, and the Son returned to Him an equal love. And the Holy Ghost is that love in substance, wherewith the Father and the Son love one another. This, O Lord, is Thine ineffable and special blessedness. It is love. I adore Thee, O my infinite Love!

2. And when Thou hadst created us, then Thou didst but love more, if that were possible. Thou didst love not only Thy own Co-equal Self in the multiplied Personality of the Godhead, but Thou didst love Thy creatures also. Thou wast love to us, as well as Love in Thyself. Thou wast love to man, more than to any other creatures. It was love that brought Thee from heaven, and subjected Thee to the laws of a created nature. It was love alone which was able to conquer Thee, the Highest—and bring Thee low. Thou didst die through Thine infinite love of sinners. And it is love, which keeps Thee here still, even now that Thou hast ascended on high, in a small tabernacle, and under cheap and common outward forms. O

Amor meus, if Thou wert not infinite Love, wouldest Thou remain here, one hour, imprisoned and exposed to slight, indignity, and insult? O my God, I do not know what infinity means—but one thing I see, that Thou art loving to a depth and height far beyond any measurement of mine.

3. And now Thou biddest me love Thee in turn, for Thou hast loved me. Thou wooest me to love Thee specially, above others. Thou dost say, "Lovest thou Me more than these?" O my God, how shameful that such a question need be put to me! yet, after all, do I really love Thee more than the run of men? The run of men do not really love Thee at all, but put Thee out of their thoughts. They feel it unpleasant to them to think of Thee; they have no sort of heart for Thee, yet Thou hast need to ask me whether I love Thee even a little. Why should I not love Thee much, how can I help loving Thee much, whom Thou hast brought so near to Thyself, whom Thou hast so wonderfully chosen out of the world to be Thy own special servant and son? Have I not cause to love Thee abundantly more than others, though all ought to love Thee? I do not know what Thou hast done for others personally, though Thou hast died for all—but I know what Thou hast done specially for me. Thou hast done that for me, O my love, which ought to make me love Thee with all my powers.

XI

THE SANCTITY OF GOD

1. THOU art holy, O Lord, in that Thou art infinitely separate from everything but Thyself, and incommunicable. I adore Thee. O Lord, in this Thy proper sanctity and everlasting purity, for that all Thy blessedness comes from within, and nothing touches Thee from without. I adore Thee as infinitely blessed, yet having all Thy blessedness in Thyself. I adore Thee in that perfect and most holy knowledge of Thyself, in which we conceive the generation of the Word. I adore Thee in that infinite and most pure love of Thyself, a love of Thy Son, and Thy Son's love for Thee, in which we conceive the procession of the Holy Ghost. I adore Thee in that blessedness which Thou didst possess in Thyself from all eternity. My God, I do not understand these heavenly things. I use words which I cannot master; but I believe, O God, that to be true, which I thus feebly express in human language.

2. My God, I adore Thee, as holy without, as well as holy within. I adore Thee as holy in all Thy works as well as in Thy own nature. No creature can approach Thy incommunicable sanctity, but Thou dost approach, and touch, and compass, and possess, all creatures; and nothing lives but in Thee, and nothing hast Thou created but what is good. I adore Thee, as having made everything good after its kind. I adore Thee, as having infused Thy preserving and sustaining power into all things, while Thou didst create them, so that they continue to live, though Thou dost not touch them, and do not crumble back into nothing. I adore Thee, as having put

real power into them, so that they are able to act, although from Thee and with Thee and yet of themselves. I adore Thee as having given power to will what is right, and Thy holy grace to Thy rational creatures. I adore Thee as having created man upright, and having bountifully given him an integrity of nature, and having filled him with Thy free grace, so that he was like an Angel upon earth; and I adore Thee still more, for having given him Thy grace over again in still more copious measure, and with far more lasting fruits, through Thy Eternal Son incarnate. In all Thy works Thou art holy, O my God, and I adore Thee in them all.

3. Holy art Thou in all Thy works, O Lord, and, if there is sin in the world it is not from Thee—it is from an enemy, it is from me and mine. To me, to man, be the shame, for we might will what is right, and we will what is evil. What a gulf is there between Thee and me, O my Creator—not only as to nature but as to will! Thy will is ever holy; how, O Lord, shall I ever dare approach Thee? What have I to do with Thee? Yet I must approach Thee; Thou wilt call me to Thee when I die, and judge me. Woe is me, for I am a man of unclean lips, and dwell in the midst of a people of unclean lips! Thy Cross, O Lord, shows the distance that is between Thee and me, while it takes it away. It shows both my great sinfulness and Thy utter abhorrence of sin. Impart to me, my dear Lord, the doctrine of the Cross in its fulness, that it may not only teach me my alienation from Thee, but convey to me the virtue of Thy reconciliation.

XII

THE FORTY DAYS' TEACHING

(I)

THE KINGDOM OF GOD

1. O MY Lord Jesus, how wonderful were those conversations which Thou didst hold from time to time with Thy disciples after Thy resurrection. When Thou wentest with two of them to Emmaus, Thou didst explain all the prophecies which related to Thyself. And Thou didst commit to the Apostles the Sacraments in fulness, and the truths which it was Thy will to reveal, and the principles and maxims by which Thy Church was to be maintained and governed. And thus Thou didst prepare them against the day of Pentecost (as the risen bodies were put into shape for the Spirit in the Prophet's vision), when life and illumination was to be infused into them. I will think over all Thou didst say to them with a true and simple faith. The "kingdom of God" was Thy sacred subject. Let me never for an instant forget that Thou hast established on earth a kingdom of Thy own, that the Church is Thy work, Thy establishment, Thy instrument; that we are under Thy rule, Thy laws and Thy eye—that when the Church speaks Thou dost speak. Let not familiarity with this wonderful truth lead me to be insensible to it—let not the weakness of Thy human representatives lead me to forget that it is Thou who dost speak and act through them. It was just when Thou wast going away, that then Thou didst leave this kingdom of Thine to take

Thy place on to the end of the world, to speak for Thee, as Thy visible form, when Thy Personal Presence, sensible to man, was departing. I will in true loving faith bring Thee before me, teaching all the truths and laws of this kingdom to Thy Apostles, and I will adore Thee, while in my thoughts I gaze upon Thee and listen to Thy words.

2. Come, O my dear Lord, and teach me in like manner. I need it not, and do not ask it, as far as this, that the word of truth which in the beginning was given to the Apostles by Thee, has been handed down from age to age, and has already been taught to me, and Thy Infallible Church is the warrant of it. But I need Thee to teach me day by day, according to each day's opportunities and needs. I need Thee to give me that true Divine instinct about revealed matters that, knowing one part, I may be able to anticipate or to approve of others. I need that understanding of the truths about Thyself which may prepare me for all Thy other truths—or at least may save me from conjecturing wrongly about them or commenting falsely upon them. I need the mind of the Spirit, which is the mind of the holy Fathers, and of the Church by which I may not only say what they say on definite points, but think what they think; in all I need to be saved from an originality of thought, which is not true if it leads away from Thee. Give me the gift of discriminating between true and false in all discourse of mind.

3. And, for that end, give me, O my Lord, that purity of conscience which alone can receive, which alone can improve Thy inspirations. My ears are dull, so that I cannot hear Thy voice. My eyes are dim, so that I cannot see Thy tokens. Thou alone canst quicken my hearing, and purge my sight, and cleanse and renew my heart. Teach me, like Mary, to sit at Thy feet, and to hear Thy word. Give me that true wisdom, which seeks Thy will by prayer and meditation, by direct intercourse with

Thee, more than by reading and reasoning. Give me the discernment to know Thy voice from the voice of strangers, and to rest upon it and to seek it in the first place, as something external to myself; and answer me through my own mind, if I worship and rely on Thee as above and beyond it.

(2)

RESIGNATION TO GOD'S WILL

Quid ad te? Tu me sequere.
What is it to thee? Follow thou Me.

1. O MY God, Thou and Thou alone art all-wise and all-knowing! Thou knowest, Thou hast determined everything which will happen to us from first to last. Thou hast ordered things in the wisest way, and Thou knowest what will be my lot year by year till I die. Thou knowest how long I have to live. Thou knowest how I shall die. Thou hast precisely ordained everything, sin excepted. Every event of my life is the best for me that could be, for it comes from Thee. Thou dost bring me on year by year, by Thy wonderful Providence, from youth to age, with the most perfect wisdom, and with the most perfect love.

2. My Lord, who camest into this world to do Thy Father's will, not Thine own, give me a most absolute and simple submission to the will of Father and Son. I believe, O my Saviour, that Thou knowest just what is best for me. I believe that Thou lovest me better than I love myself, that Thou art all-wise in Thy Providence, and all-powerful in Thy protection. I am as ignorant as Peter was what is to happen to me in time to come; but I resign myself entirely to my ignorance, and thank Thee with all my heart that Thou hast taken me out of my own keeping, and, instead of putting such a serious charge

upon me, hast bidden me put myself into Thy hands. I
can ask nothing better than this, to be Thy care, not my
own. I protest, O my Lord, that, through Thy grace, I
will follow Thee whithersoever Thou goest, and will not
lead the way. I will wait on Thee for Thy guidance, and,
on obtaining it, I will act upon it in simplicity and
without fear. And I promise that I will not be impatient,
if at any time I am kept by Thee in darkness and perplexity; nor will I ever complain or fret if I come into any
misfortune or anxiety.

3. I know, O Lord, Thou wilt do Thy part towards
me, as I, through Thy grace, desire to do my part
towards Thee. I know well Thou never canst forsake
those who seek Thee, or canst disappoint those who trust
Thee. Yet I know too, the more I pray for Thy protection, the more surely and fully I shall have it. And
therefore now I cry out to Thee, and intreat Thee, first
that Thou wouldest keep me from myself, and from
following any will but Thine. Next I beg of Thee, that in
Thy infinite compassion, Thou wouldest temper Thy
will to me, that it may not be severe, but indulgent to
me. Visit me not, O my loving Lord—if it be not wrong
so to pray—visit me not with those trying visitations
which saints alone can bear! Pity my weakness, and lead
me heavenwards in a safe and tranquil course. Still I leave
all in Thy hands, my dear Saviour—I bargain for
nothing—only, if Thou shalt bring heavier trials on me,
give me more grace—flood me with the fulness of Thy
strength and consolation, that they may work in me not
death, but life and salvation.

(3)

OUR LORD'S PARTING WITH HIS APOSTLES

1. I ADORE Thee, O my God! together with Thy Apostles, during the forty days in which Thou didst visit them after Thy resurrection. So blessed was the time, so calm, so undisturbed from without, that it was good to be there with Thee, and when it was over, they could hardly believe that it was more than begun. How quickly must that first *Tempus Paschale* have flown! and they perhaps hardly knew when it was to end. At least, they did not like to anticipate its ending, but were engrossed with the joy of the present moment. O what a time of consolation! What a contrast to what had lately taken place! It was their happy time on earth—the foretaste of heaven; not noticed, not interfered with, by man. They passed it in wonder, in musing, in adoration, rejoicing in Thy light, O my risen God!

2. But Thou, O my dear Lord, didst know better than they! They hoped and desired, perhaps fancied, that that resting time, that *refrigerium*, never would end till it was superseded by something better; but Thou didst know, in Thy eternal wisdom, that, in order to arrive at what was higher than any blessing which they were then enjoying, it was fitting, it was necessary, that they should sustain conflict and suffering. Thou knewest well, that unless Thou hadst departed, the Paraclete could not have come to them; and therefore Thou didst go, that they might gain more by Thy sorrowful absence than by Thy sensible visitations. I adore Thee, O Father, for sending the Son and the Holy Ghost! I adore Thee, O Son, and Thee, O Holy Ghost, for vouchsafing to be sent to us!

3. O my God, let me never forget that seasons of consolation are refreshments here, and nothing more; not our abiding state. They will not remain with us except in

heaven. Here they are only intended to prepare us for doing and suffering. I pray Thee, O my God, to give them to me from time to time. Shed over me the sweetness of Thy Presence, lest I faint by the way; lest I find religious service wearisome, through my exceeding infirmity, and give over prayer and meditation; lest I go about my daily work in a dry spirit, or am tempted to take pleasure in it for its own sake, and not for Thee. Give me Thy Divine consolations from time to time; but let me not rest in them. Let me use them for the purpose for which Thou givest them. Let me not think it grievous, let me not be downcast, if they go. Let them carry me forward to the thought and the desire of heaven.

(4)

GOD'S WAYS NOT OUR WAYS

Quia hæc locutus sum vobis, tristitia implevit cor vestrum. Sed ego veritatem dico vobis. Expedit vobis.

Because I have spoken these things to you, sorrow hath filled your heart. But I tell you the truth: it is expedient for you.

1. O MY Saviour, I adore Thee for Thy infinite wisdom, which sees what we do not see, and orderest all things in its own most perfect way. When Thou didst say to the Apostles that Thou wast going away, they cried out, as if Thou hadst, if it may be so said, broken faith with them. They seemed to say to Thee, "O Jesu, did we not leave all things for Thee? Did we not give up home and family, father and wife, friends and neighbours, our habits, our accustomed way of living, that we might join Thee? Did we not divorce ourselves from the world, or rather die to it, that we might be eternally united and live to Thee? And now Thou sayest that Thou art leaving us.

Is this reasonable? is this just? is this faithfulness to Thy promise? Did we bargain for this? O Lord Jesus, we adore Thee, but we are confounded, and we know not what to say!''

2. Yet let God be true, and every man a liar. Let the Divine Word triumph in our minds over every argument and persuasion of sensible appearances. Let faith rule us and not sight. Thou art justified, O Lord, when Thou art arraigned, and dost gain the cause when Thou art judged. For Thou didst know that the true way of possessing Thee was to lose Thee. Thou didst know that what man stands most of all in need of, and in the first place, is not an outward guide, though that he needs too, but an inward, intimate, invisible aid. Thou didst intend to heal him thoroughly, not slightly; not merely to reform the surface, but to remove and destroy the heart and root of all his ills. Thou then didst purpose to visit his soul, and Thou didst depart in body, that Thou mightest come again to him in spirit. Thou didst not stay with Thy Apostles therefore, as in the days of Thy flesh, but Thou didst come to them and abide with them for ever, with a much more immediate and true communion in the power of the Paraclete.

3. O my God, in Thy sight, I confess and bewail my extreme weakness, in distrusting, if not Thee, at least Thy own servants and representatives, when things do not turn out as I would have them, or expected! Thou hast given me St. Philip, that great creation of Thy grace, for my master and patron—and I have committed myself to him—and he has done very great things for me, and has in many ways fulfilled towards me all that I can fairly reckon he had promised. But, because in some things he has disappointed me, and delayed, I have got impatient; and have served him, though without conscious disloy-alty, yet with peevishness and coldness. O my dear Lord, give me a generous faith in Thee and in Thy servants!

XIII

THE ASCENSION

(I)

HE ASCENDED

1. My Lord, I follow Thee up to heaven; as Thou goest up, my heart and mind go with Thee. Never was triumph like this. Thou didst appear a babe in human flesh at Bethlehem. That flesh, taken from the Blessed Virgin, was not before Thou didst form it into a body; it was a new work of Thy hands. And Thy soul was new altogether, created by Thy Omnipotence, at the moment when Thou didst enter into her sacred breast. That pure soul and body, taken as a garment for Thyself, began on earth, and never had been elsewhere. This is the triumph. Earth rises to heaven. I see Thee going up. I see that Form which hung upon the Cross, those scarred hands and feet, that pierced side; they are mounting up to heaven. And the Angels are full of jubilee; the myriads of blessed spirits, which people the glorious expanse, part like the waters to let Thee pass. And the living pavement of God's palaces is cleft in twain, and the Cherubim with flaming swords, who form the rampart of heaven against fallen man, give way and open out, that Thou mayest enter, and Thy saints after Thee. O memorable day!

2. O memorable day! The Apostles feel it to be so, now that it is come, though they felt so differently before it came. When it was coming they dreaded it. They could not think but it would be a great bereavement; but now,

as we read, they returned to Jerusalem "with great joy." O what a time of triumph! They understood it now. They understood how weak it had been in them to grudge their Lord and Master, the glorious Captain of their salvation, the Champion and First fruits of the human family, this crown of His great work. It was the triumph of redeemed man. It is the completion of his redemption. It was the last act, making the whole sure, for now man is actually in heaven. He has entered into possession of his inheritance. The sinful race has now one of its own children there, its own flesh and blood, in the person of the Eternal Son. O what a wonderful marriage between heaven and earth! It began in sorrow; but now the long travail of that mysterious wedding day is over; the marriage feast is begun; marriage and birth have gone together; man is new born when Emmanuel enters heaven.

3. O Emmanuel, O God in our flesh! we too hope, by Thy grace, to follow Thee. We will cling to the skirts of Thy garments, as Thou goest up; for without Thee we cannot ascend. O Emmanuel, what a day of joy when we shall enter heaven! O inexpressible ecstasy, after all trouble! There is none strong but Thou. *Tenuisti manum dexteram meam: et in voluntate tua deduxisti me, et cum gloria suscepisti me. Quid enim mihi est in caelo, et a Te quid volui super terram? Defecit caro mea et cor meum; Deus cordis mei, et pars mea Deus in æternum.*—"Thou hast held me by my right hand; and by Thy will Thou hast conducted me, and with Thy glory Thou hast received me. For what have I in heaven? And besides Thee what do I desire upon earth? For Thee my flesh and my heart hath fainted away: Thou art the God of my heart, and the God that is my portion for ever."

(2)

ASCENDIT IN CŒLUM

He ascended into Heaven

1. My Lord is gone up into heaven. I adore Thee, Son of Mary, Jesu Emmanuel, my God and my Saviour. I am allowed to adore Thee, my Saviour and my own Brother, for Thou art God. I follow Thee in my thoughts, O Thou First fruits of our race, as I hope one day by Thy grace to follow Thee in my person. To go to heaven is to go to God. God is there and God alone: for perfect bliss is there and nothing else, and none can be blessed who is not bathed and hidden and absorbed in the glory of the Divine Nature. All holy creatures are but the vestment of the Highest, which He has put on for ever, and which is bright with His uncreated light. There are many things on earth, and each is its own centre, but one Name alone is named above. It is God alone. This is that true supernatural life; and if I would live a supernatural life on earth, and attain to the supernatural eternal life which is in heaven, I have one thing to do, viz. to live on the thought of God here. Teach me this, O God; give me Thy supernatural grace to practise it; to have my reason, affections, intentions, aims, all penetrated and possessed by the love of Thee, plunged and drowned in the one Vision of Thee.

2. There is but one Name and one Thought above: there are many thoughts below. This is the earthly life, which leads to death, viz. to follow the numberless objects and aims and toils and amusements which men pursue on earth. Even the good that is here below does not lead to heaven; it is spoilt in the handselling; it perishes in the using; it has no stay, no integrity, no consistency. It runs off into evil before it has well ceased,

before it has well begun to be good. It is at best vanity, when it is nothing worse. It has in it commonly the seeds of real sin. My God, I acknowledge all this. My Lord Jesu, I confess and know that Thou only art the True, the Beautiful, and the Good. Thou alone canst make me bright and glorious, and canst lead me up after Thee. Thou art the way, the truth, and the life, and none but Thou. Earth will never lead me to heaven. Thou alone art the Way; Thou alone.

3. My God, shall I for one moment doubt where my path lies? Shall I not at once take Thee for my portion? To whom should I go? Thou hast the words of Eternal Life. Thou camest down for the very purpose of doing that which no one here below could do for me. None but He who is in heaven can bring me to heaven. What strength have I to scale the high mountain? Though I served the world ever so well, though I did my duty in it (as men speak), what could the world do for me, however hard it tried? Though I filled my station well, did good to my fellows, had a fair name or a wide reputation, though I did great deeds and was celebrated, though I had the praise of history, how would all this bring me to heaven? I choose Thee then for my One Portion, because Thou livest and diest not. I cast away all idols. I give myself to *Thee*. I pray Thee to teach me, guide me, enable me, and receive me to Thee.

(3)

OUR ADVOCATE ABOVE

1. I ADORE Thee, O my Lord, as is most fitting, for Thou art gone to heaven to take my part there, and defend my interests. I have one to plead for me with the Lord of all. On earth we try to put ourselves under the protection of powerful men when we have any important

business on hand; we know the value of their influence, and we make much of any promise they make us. Thou art omnipotent, and Thou dost exert Thy omnipotence for me. There are millions of men in the world: Thou didst die for them all; but Thou livest for Thy people, whom Thou hast chosen out of the world. And still more marvellously dost Thou live for Thy predestinate. Thou hast engraven them upon the palms of Thy hands; their names are ever before Thee. Thou countest the full roll of them; Thou knowest them by heart: Thou orderest the crown of the world for them; and, when their number shall be completed, the world shall end.

2. For me, Thou hast chosen me for present grace— and thus Thou hast put me in the way for future glory. I know perfectly well that, whatever be Thy secret counsels about me, it will be simply, entirely, most really my own fault if I am not written in Thy book. I cannot understand Thee: I can understand myself enough to know and be sure of this. Thou hast put me on such especial vantage ground that the prize is almost in my hand. If I am at present in the society of Angels or Saints, it is hard if I cannot make interest with them that the fellowship begun between them and me should endure. Men of the world know how to turn such opportunities to account in their own matters. If Thou hast given me Mary for my Mother, who, O my God! is Thine, cannot I now establish, as it were, a family interest in her, so that she will not cast me off at the last? If I have the right to pray and the gift of impetration, may I not thereby secure that perseverance to the end, which I cannot merit, and which is the sign and assurance of my predestination? I have in my hands all the means of that which I have not, and may infallibly obtain, even though I cannot certainly secure it.

3. O my Lord, I sink down almost in despair, in utter remorse certainly and disgust at myself, that I so utterly

neglect these means which Thou hast put into my hands, content to let things take their course, as if grace would infallibly lead to glory without my own trouble in the matter. What shall I say to Thee, O my Saviour! except that I am in the chains of habit, feeble, helpless, stunted, growthless, and as if I were meant to walk through life, as the inferior creatures, with my face down to the earth, on hands and feet, or crawling on, instead of having an erect posture and a heavenward face? O give me what I need—contrition for all those infinitely numerous venial sins, negligences, slovenliness, which are the surest foreboding that I am not of Thy predestinate. Who can save me from myself but Thou?

(4)

OUR ADVOCATE ABOVE

1. I CANNOT penetrate Thy secret decrees, O Lord! I know Thou didst die for all men really; but since thou hast not effectually willed the salvation of all, and since Thou mightest have done so, it is certain that Thou doest for one what Thou dost not do for another. I cannot tell what has been Thy everlasting purpose about myself, but, if I go by all the signs which Thou hast lavished upon me, I may hope that I am one of those whose names are written in Thy book. But this I know and feel most entirely, what I believe in the case of all men, but know and feel in my own case, that, if I do not attain to that crown which I see and which is within my reach, it is entirely my own fault. Thou hast surrounded me from childhood with Thy mercies; Thou hast taken as much pains with me as if I was of importance to Thee, and my loss of heaven would be Thy loss of me. Thou hast led me on by ten thousand merciful providences; Thou hast brought me near to Thee in the most intimate of ways;

Thou hast brought me into Thy house and chamber; Thou hast fed me with Thyself. Dost Thou not love me? really, truly, substantially, efficaciously love me, without any limitation of the word? I know it. I have an utter conviction of it. Thou art ever waiting to do me benefits, to pour upon me blessings. Thou art ever waiting for me to ask Thee to be merciful to me.

2. Yes, my Lord, Thou dost desire that I should ask Thee; Thou art ever listening for my voice. There is nothing I cannot get from Thee. Oh I confess my heinous neglect of this great privilege. I am very guilty. I have trifled with the highest of gifts, the power to move Omnipotence. How slack am I in praying to Thee for my own needs! how little have I thought of the needs of others! How little have I brought before Thee the needs of the world—of Thy Church! How little I have asked for graces in detail! and for aid in daily wants! How little have I interceded for individuals! How little have I ac-companied actions and undertakings, in themselves good, with prayer for Thy guidance and blessing!

3. O my Lord Jesu, I will use the time. It will be too late to pray, when life is over. There is no prayer in the grave—there is no meriting in Purgatory. Low as I am in Thy all holy sight, I am strong in Thee, strong through Thy Immaculate Mother, through Thy Saints: and thus I can do much for the Church, for the world, for all I love. O let not the blood of souls be on my head! O let me not walk my own way without thinking of Thee. Let me bring everything before Thee, asking Thy leave for ev-erything I purpose, Thy blessing on everything I do. I will not move without Thee. I will ever lift up my heart to Thee. I will never forget that Thou art my Advocate at the Throne of the Highest. As the dial speaks of the sun, so will I be ruled by Thee above, if Thou wilt take me and rule me. Be it so, my Lord Jesus. I give myself wholly to Thee.

XIV

THE PARACLETE

(I)

THE PARACLETE, THE LIFE OF ALL THINGS

1. I ADORE Thee, my Lord and God, the Eternal Paraclete, co-equal with the Father and the Son. I adore Thee
as the Life of all that live. Through Thee the whole
material Universe hangs together and consists, remains in
its place, and moves internally in the order and reciproc-
ity of its several parts. Through Thee the earth was
brought into its present state, and was matured through
its six days to be a habitation for man. Through Thee, all
trees, herbs, fruits, thrive and are perfected. Through
Thee, spring comes after winter and renews all things.
That wonderful and beautiful, that irresistible burst into
life again, in spite of all obstacles, that awful triumph of
nature, is but Thy glorious Presence. Through Thee the
many tribes of brute animals live day by day, drawing in
their breath from Thee. Thou art the life of the whole
creation, O Eternal Paraclete—and if of this animal and
material framework, how much more of the world of
spirits! Through Thee, Almighty Lord, the angels and
saints sing Thee praises in heaven. Through Thee our
own dead souls are quickened to serve Thee. From Thee
is every good thought and desire, every good purpose,
every good effort, every good success. It is by Thee that
sinners are turned into saints. It is by Thee the Church is
refreshed and strengthened, and champions start forth,

and martyrs are carried on to their crown. Through Thee new religious orders, new devotions in the Church come into being; new countries are added to the faith, new manifestations and illustrations are given to the ancient Apostolic creed. I praise and adore Thee, my Sovereign Lord God, the Holy Ghost.

2. I adore Thee, O dread Lord, for what Thou hast done for my soul. I acknowledge and feel, not only as a matter of faith but of experience, that I cannot have one good thought or do one good act without Thee. I know, that if I attempt anything good in my own strength, I shall to a certainty fail. I have bitter experience of this. My God, I am only safe when Thou dost breathe upon me. If Thou withdraw Thy breath, forthwith my three mortal enemies rush on me and overcome me. I am as weak as water, I am utterly impotent without Thee. The minute Thou dost cease to act in me, I begin to languish, to gasp, and to faint away. Of my good desires, whatever they may be, of my good aims, aspirations, attempts, successes, habits, practices, Thou art the sole cause and present continual source. I have nothing but what I have received, and I protest now in Thy presence, O Sovereign Paraclete, that I have nothing to glory in, and everything to be humbled at.

3. O my dear Lord, how merciful Thou hast been to me. When I was young, Thou didst put into my heart a special devotion to Thee. Thou hast taken me up in my youth, and in my age Thou wilt not forsake me. Not for my merit, but from Thy free and bountiful love Thou didst put good resolutions into me when I was young, and didst turn me to Thee. Thou wilt never forsake me. I do earnestly trust so—never certainly without fearful provocation on my part. Yet I trust and pray, that Thou wilt keep me from that provocation. O keep me from the provocation of lukewarmness and sloth. O my dear Lord, lead me forward from strength to strength, gently,

sweetly, tenderly, lovingly, powerfully, effectually, remembering my fretfulness and feebleness, till Thou bringest me into Thy heaven.

(2)

THE PARACLETE, THE LIFE OF THE CHURCH

1. I ADORE Thee, O my Lord, the Third Person of the All-Blessed Trinity, that Thou hast set up in this world of sin a great light upon a hill. Thou hast founded the Church, Thou hast established and maintained it. Thou fillest it continually with Thy gifts, that men may see, and draw near, and take, and live. Thou hast in this way brought down heaven upon earth. For Thou hast set up a great company which Angels visit by that ladder which the Patriarch saw in vision. Thou hast by Thy Presence restored the communion between God above and man below. Thou hast given him that light of grace which is one with and the commencement of the light of glory. I adore and praise Thee for Thy infinite mercy towards us, O my Lord and God.

2. I adore Thee, O Almighty Lord, the Paraclete, because Thou in Thy infinite compassion hast brought me into this Church, the work of Thy supernatural power. I had no claim on Thee for so wonderful a favour over anyone else in the whole world. There were many men far better than I by nature, gifted with more pleasing natural gifts, and less stained with sin. Yet Thou, in Thy inscrutable love for me, hast chosen me and brought me into Thy fold. Thou hast a reason for everything Thou dost. I know there must have been an all-wise reason, as we speak in human language, for Thy choosing me and not another—but I know that that reason was something external to myself. I did nothing towards it—I did everything against it. I did everything to thwart Thy pur-

THE PARACLETE 417

pose. And thus I owe all to Thy grace. I should have lived and died in darkness and sin; I should have become worse and worse the longer I lived; I should have got more to hate and abjure Thee, O Source of my bliss; I should have got yearly more fit for hell, and at length I should have gone there, but for Thy incomprehensible love to me. O my God, that overpowering love took me captive. Was any boyhood so impious as some years of mine! Did I not in fact dare Thee to do Thy worst? Ah, how I struggled to get free from Thee; but Thou art stronger than I and hast prevailed. I have not a word to say, but to bow down in awe before the depths of Thy love.

3. And then, in course of time, slowly but infallibly did Thy grace bring me on into Thy Church. Now then give me this further grace, Lord, to use all this grace well, and to turn it to my salvation. Teach me, make me, to come to the fountains of mercy continually with an awakened, eager mind, and with lively devotion. Give me a love of Thy Sacraments and Ordinances. Teach me to value as I ought, to prize as the inestimable pearl, that pardon which again and again Thou givest me, and the great and heavenly gift of the Presence of Him whose Spirit Thou art, upon the Altar. Without Thee I can do nothing, and Thou art there where Thy Church is and Thy Sacraments. Give me grace to rest in them for ever, till they are lost in the glory of Thy manifestation in the world to come.

(3)

THE PARACLETE, THE LIFE OF MY SOUL

1. My God, I adore Thee for taking on Thee the charge of sinners; of those, who not only cannot profit Thee, but who continually grieve and profane Thee. Thou hast taken on Thyself the office of a minister, and that for those who did not ask for it. I adore Thee for Thy

418   MEDITATIONS AND DEVOTIONS

incomprehensible condescension in ministering to me. I know and feel, O my God, that Thou mightest have left me, as I wished to be left, to go my own way, to go straight forward in my wilfulness and self-trust to hell. Thou mightest have left me in that enmity to Thee which is in itself death. I should at length have died the second death, and should have had no one to blame for it but myself. But Thou, O Eternal Father, hast been kinder to me than I am to myself. Thou hast given me, Thou hast poured out upon me Thy grace, and thus I live.

2. My God, I adore Thee, O Eternal Paraclete, the light and the life of my soul. Thou mightest have been content with merely giving me good suggestions, inspiring grace and helping from without. Thou mightest thus have led me on, cleansing me with Thy inward virtue, when I changed my state from this world to the next. But in Thine infinite compassion Thou hast from the first entered into my soul, and taken possession of it. Thou hast made it Thy Temple. Thou dwellest in me by Thy grace in an ineffable way, uniting me to Thyself and the whole company of angels and saints. Nay, as some have held, Thou art present in me, not only by Thy grace, but by Thy eternal substance, as if, though I did not lose my own individuality, yet in some sense I was even here absorbed in God. Nay—as though Thou hadst taken possession of my very body, this earthly, fleshly, wretched tabernacle—even my body is Thy Temple. O astonishing, awful truth! I believe it, I know it, O my God!

3. O my God, can I sin when Thou art so intimately with me? Can I forget who is with me, who is in me? Can I expel a Divine Inhabitant by that which He abhors more than anything else, which is the one thing in the whole world which is offensive to Him, the only thing which is not His? Would not this be a kind of sin against the Holy Ghost? My God, I have a double security against sinning; first the dread of such a profanation of all Thou art to me

in Thy very Presence; and next because I do trust that that Presence will preserve me from sin. My God, Thou wilt go from me, if I sin; and I shall be left to my own miserable self. God forbid! I will use what Thou hast given me; I will call on Thee when tried and tempted. I will guard against the sloth and carelessness into which I am continually falling. Through Thee I will never forsake Thee.

(4)

THE PARACLETE, THE FOUNT OF LOVE

1. My God, I adore Thee, as the Third Person of the Ever-Blessed Trinity, under the name and designation of Love. Thou art that Living Love, wherewith the Father and the Son love each other. And Thou art the Author of supernatural love in our hearts—"Fons vivus, ignis, charitas." As a fire Thou didst come down from heaven on the day of Pentecost; and as a fire Thou burnest away the dross of sin and vanity in the heart and dost light up the pure flame of devotion and affection. It is Thou who unitest heaven and earth by showing to us the glory and beauty of the Divine Nature, and making us love what is in Itself so winning and transporting. I adore Thee, O uncreate and everlasting Fire, by which our souls live, by which alone they are made fit for heaven.

2. My God, the Paraclete, I acknowledge Thee as the Giver of that great gift, by which alone we are saved, supernatural love. Man is by nature blind and hard-hearted in all spiritual matters; how is he to reach heaven? It is by the flame of Thy grace, which consumes him in order to new-make him, and so to fit him to enjoy what without Thee he would have no taste for. It is Thou, O Almighty Paraclete, who hast been and art the strength, the vigour and endurance, of the martyr in the midst of

his torments. Thou art the stay of the confessor in his
long, tedious, and humiliating toils. Thou art the fire, by
which the preacher wins souls, without thought of himself, in his missionary labours. By Thee we wake up from
the death of sin, to exchange the idolatry of the creature
for the pure love of the Creator. By Thee we make acts of
faith, hope, charity, and contrition. By Thee we live in
the atmosphere of earth, proof against its infection. By
Thee we are able to consecrate ourselves to the sacred
ministry, and fulfil our awful engagements to it. By the
fire which Thou didst kindle within us, we pray, and
meditate, and do penance. As well could our bodies live,
if the sun were extinguished, as our souls, if Thou art
away.

3. My most Holy Lord and Sanctifier, whatever there
is of good in me is Thine. Without Thee, I should but get
worse and worse as years went on, and should tend to be
a devil. If I differ at all from the world, it is because Thou
hast chosen me out of the world, and hast lit up the love
of God in my heart. If I differ from Thy Saints, it is
because I do not ask earnestly enough for Thy grace, and
for enough of it, and because I do not diligently improve
what Thou hast given me. Increase in me this grace of
love, in spite of all my unworthiness. It is more precious
than anything else in the world. I accept it in place of all
the world can give me. O give it to me! It is my life.

XV

THE HOLY SACRIFICE

(I)

THE MASS

1. I ADORE Thee, O my Lord God, with the most profound awe for thy passion and crucifixion, in sacrifice for our sins. Thou didst suffer incommunicable sufferings in Thy sinless soul. Thou wast exposed in Thy innocent body to ignominious torments, to mingled pain and shame. Thou wast stripped and fiercely scourged, Thy sacred body vibrating under the heavy flail as trees under the blast. Thou wast, when thus mangled, hung up upon the Cross, naked, a spectacle for all to see Thee quivering and dying. What does all this imply, O Mighty God! What a depth is here which we cannot fathom! My God, I know well, Thou couldst have saved us at Thy word, without Thyself suffering; but Thou didst choose to purchase us at the price of Thy Blood. I look on Thee, the Victim lifted up on Calvary, and I know and protest that that death of Thine was an expiation for the sins of the whole world. I believe and know, that Thou alone couldst have offered a meritorious atonement; for it was Thy Divine Nature which gave Thy sufferings worth. Rather then than I should perish according to my deserts, Thou wast nailed to the Tree and didst die.

2. Such a sacrifice was not to be forgotten. It was not to be—it could not be—a mere event in the world's history, which was to be done and over, and was to pass away

except in its obscure, unrecognised effects. If that great
deed was what we believe it to be, what we know it is, it
must remain present, though past; it must be a standing
fact for all times. Our own careful reflection upon it tells
us this; and therefore, when we are told that Thou, O
Lord, though Thou hast ascended to glory, hast renewed
and perpetuated Thy sacrifice to the end of all things, not
only is the news most touching and joyful, as testifying
to so tender a Lord and Saviour, but it carries with it the
full assent and sympathy of our reason. Though we
neither could, nor would have dared, anticipate so wonderful a doctrine, yet we adore its very suitableness to
Thy perfections, as well as its infinite compassionateness
for us, now that we are told of it. Yes, my Lord, though
Thou hast left the world, Thou art daily offered up in the
Mass; and, though Thou canst not suffer pain and death,
Thou dost still subject Thyself to indignity and restraint
to carry out to the full Thy mercies towards us. Thou
dost humble Thyself daily; for, being infinite, Thou
couldst not end Thy humiliation while they existed for
whom Thou didst submit to it. So Thou remainest a
Priest for ever.

3. My Lord, I offer Thee myself in turn as a sacrifice of
thanksgiving. Thou hast died for me, and I in turn make
myself over to Thee. I am not my own. Thou hast
bought me; I will by my own act and deed complete the
purchase. My wish is to be separated from everything of
this world; to cleanse myself simply from sin; to put
away from me even what is innocent, if used for its own
sake, and not for Thine. I put away reputation and
honour, and influence, and power, for my praise and
strength shall be in Thee. Enable me to carry out what I
profess.

(2)

HOLY COMMUNION

1. MY God, who can be inhabited by Thee, except the pure and holy? Sinners may come to Thee, but to whom shouldst Thou come except to the sanctified? My God, I adore Thee as the Holiest; and, when Thou didst come upon earth, Thou didst prepare a holy habitation for Thyself in the most chaste womb of the Blessed Virgin. Thou didst make a dwelling place special for Thyself. She did not receive Thee without first being prepared for Thee; for from the moment that she was at all, she was filled with Thy grace, so that she never knew sin. And so she went on increasing in grace and merit year after year, till the time came, when Thou didst send down the Archangel to signify to her Thy presence within her. So holy must be the dwelling place of the Highest. I adore and glorify Thee, O Lord my God, for Thy great holiness.

2. O my God, holiness becometh Thy House, and yet Thou dost make Thy abode in my breast. My Lord, my Saviour, to me Thou comest, hidden under the semblance of earthly things, yet in that very flesh and blood which Thou didst take from Mary. Thou, who didst first inhabit Mary's breast, dost come to me. My God, Thou seest me; I cannot see myself. Were I ever so good a judge about myself, ever so unbiassed, and with ever so correct a rule of judging, still, from my very nature, I cannot look at myself, and view myself truly and wholly. But Thou, as Thou comest to me, contemplatest me. When I say, *Domine, non sum dignus*—"Lord, I am not worthy"— Thou whom I am addressing, alone understandest in their fulness the words which I use. Thou seest how unworthy so great a sinner is to receive the One Holy God, whom the Seraphim adore with trembling. Thou

seest, not only the stains and scars of past sins, but the mutilations, the deep cavities, the chronic disorders which they have left in my soul. Thou seest the innumerable living sins, though they be not mortal, living in their power and presence, their guilt, and their penalties, which clothe me. Thou seest all my bad habits, all my mean principles, all wayward lawless thoughts, my multitude of infirmities and miseries, yet Thou comest. Thou seest most perfectly how little I really feel what I am now saying, yet Thou comest. O my God, left to myself should I not perish under the awful splendour and the consuming fire of Thy Majesty. Enable me to bear Thee, lest I have to say with Peter, "Depart from me, for I am a sinful man, O Lord!"

3. My God, enable me to bear Thee, for Thou alone canst. Cleanse my heart and mind from all that is past. Wipe out clean all my recollections of evil. Rid me from all languor, sickliness, irritability, feebleness of soul. Give me a true perception of things unseen, and make me truly, practically, and in the details of life, prefer Thee to anything on earth, and the future world to the present. Give me courage, a true instinct determining between right and wrong, humility in all things, and a tender longing love of Thee.

(3)

THE FOOD OF THE SOUL

Sitivit in Te anima mea

For Thee my soul hath thirsted

1. IN Thee, O Lord, all things live, and Thou dost give them their food. *Oculi omnium in Te sperant*—"the eyes of all hope in Thee." To the beasts of the field Thou givest

meat and drink. They live on day by day, because Thou dost give them day by day to live. And, if Thou givest not, they feel their misery at once. Nature witnesses to this great truth, for they are visited at once with great agony, and they cry out and wildly wander about, seeking what they need. But, as to us Thy children, Thou feedest us with another food. Thou knowest, O my God, who madest us, that nothing can satisfy us but Thyself, and therefore Thou hast caused Thy own self to be meat and drink to us. O most adorable mystery! O most stupendous of mercies! Thou most Glorious, and Beautiful, and Strong, and Sweet, Thou didst know well that nothing else would support our immortal natures, our frail hearts, but Thyself; and so Thou didst take a human flesh and blood, that they, as being the flesh and blood of God, might be our life.

2. O what an awful thought! Thou dealest otherwise with others, but, as to me, the flesh and blood of God is my sole life. I shall perish without it; yet shall I not perish with it and by it? How can I raise myself to such an act as to feed upon God? O my God, I am in a strait—shall I go forward, or shall I go back? I will go forward: I will go to meet Thee. I will open my mouth, and receive Thy gift. I do so with great awe and fear, but what else can I do? to whom should I go but to Thee? Who can save me but Thou? Who can cleanse me but Thou? Who can make me overcome myself but Thou? Who can raise my body from the grave but Thou? Therefore I come to Thee in all these my necessities, in fear, but in faith.

3. My God, Thou art my life; if I leave Thee, I cannot but thirst. Lost spirits thirst in hell, because they have not God. They thirst, though they fain would have it otherwise, from the necessity of their original nature. But I, my God, wish to thirst for Thee with a better thirst. I wish to be clad in that new nature, which so longs for Thee from loving Thee, as to overcome in me the fear of

coming to Thee. I come to Thee, O Lord, not only because I am unhappy without Thee, not only because I feel I need Thee, but because Thy grace draws me on to seek Thee for Thy own sake, because Thou art so glorious and beautiful. I come in great fear, but in greater love. O may I never lose, as years pass away, and the heart shuts up, and all things are a burden, let me never lose this youthful, eager, elastic love of Thee. Make Thy grace supply the failure of nature. Do the more for me, the less I can do for myself. The more I refuse to open my heart to Thee, so much the fuller and stronger be Thy supernatural visitings, and the more urgent and efficacious Thy presence in me.

XVI

THE SACRED HEART

1. O SACRED Heart of Jesus, I adore Thee in the oneness of the Personality of the Second Person of the Holy Trinity. Whatever belongs to the Person of Jesus, belongs therefore to God, and is to be worshipped with that one and the same worship which we pay to Jesus. He did not take on Him His human nature, as something distinct and separate from Himself, but as simply, absolutely, eternally His, so as to be included by us in the very thought of Him. I worship Thee, O Heart of Jesus, as being Jesus Himself, as being that Eternal Word in human nature which He took wholly and lives in wholly, and therefore in Thee. Thou art the Heart of the Most High made man. In worshipping Thee, I worship my Incarnate God, Emmanuel. I worship Thee, as bearing a part in that Passion which is my life, for Thou didst burst and break, through agony, in the garden of Gethsemani, and Thy precious contents trickled out, through the veins and pores of the skin, upon the earth. And again, Thou hadst been drained all but dry upon the Cross; and then, after death, Thou wast pierced by the lance, and gavest out the small remains of that inestimable treasure, which is our redemption.

2. My God, my Saviour, I adore Thy Sacred Heart, for that heart is the seat and source of all Thy tenderest human affections for us sinners. It is the instrument and organ of Thy love. It did beat for us. It yearned over us. It ached for us, and for our salvation. It was on fire through zeal, that the glory of God might be manifested

in and by us. It is the channel through which has come to us all Thy overflowing human affection, all Thy Divine Charity towards us. All Thy incomprehensible compassion for us, as God and Man, as our Creator and our Redeemer and Judge, has come to us, and comes, in one inseparably mingled stream, through that Sacred Heart. O most Sacred symbol and Sacrament of Love, divine and human, in its fulness, Thou didst save me by Thy divine strength, and Thy human affection, and then at length by that wonder-working blood, wherewith Thou didst overflow.

3. O most Sacred, most loving Heart of Jesus, Thou art concealed in the Holy Eucharist, and Thou beatest for us still. Now as then Thou sayest, *Desiderio desideravi*— "With desire I have desired." I worship Thee then with all my best love and awe, with my fervent affection, with my most subdued, most resolved will. O my God, when Thou dost condescend to suffer me to receive Thee, to eat and drink Thee, and Thou for a while takest up Thy abode within me, O make my heart beat with Thy Heart. Purify it of all that is earthly, all that is proud and sensual, all that is hard and cruel, of all perversity, of all disorder, of all deadness. So fill it with Thee, that neither the events of the day nor the circumstances of the time may have power to ruffle it, but that in Thy love and Thy fear it may have peace.

XVII

THE INFINITE PERFECTION OF GOD

Ex ipso, et per ipsum, et in ipso sunt omnia

1. *Ex ipso.* I adore Thee, O my God, as the origin and source of all that is in the world. Once nothing was in being but Thou. It was so for a whole eternity. Thou alone hast had no beginning. Thou hast ever been in being without beginning. Thou hast necessarily been a whole eternity by Thyself, having in Thee all perfections stored up in Thyself, by Thyself; a world of worlds; an infinite abyss of all that is great and wonderful, beautiful and holy; a treasury of infinite attributes, all in one; infinitely one while thus infinitely various. My God, the thought simply exceeds a created nature, much more mine. I cannot attain to it; I can but use the words, and say "I believe," without comprehending. But this I can do. I can adore Thee, O my great and good God, as the one source of all perfection, and that I do, and with Thy grace will do always.

2. *Per ipsum.* And when other beings began to be, they lived through Thee. They did not begin of themselves. They did not come into existence except by Thy determinate will, by Thy eternal counsel, by Thy sole operation. They are wholly from Thee. From eternity, in the deep ocean of Thy blessedness, Thou didst predestinate everything which in its hour took place. Not a substance, ever so insignificant, but is Thy design and Thy work. Much more, not a soul comes into being, but by Thy direct appointment and act. Thou seest, Thou hast seen

from all eternity, every individual of Thy creatures. Thou hast seen me, O my God, from all eternity. Thou seest distinctly, and ever hast seen, whether I am to be saved or to be lost. Thou seest my history through all ages in heaven or in hell. O awful thought! My God, enable me to bear it, lest the thought of Thee confound me utterly; and lead me forward to salvation.

3. *In ipso.* And I believe and know, moreover, that all things live in Thee. Whatever there is of being, of life, of excellence, of enjoyment, of happiness, in the whole creation, is, in its substance, simply and absolutely Thine. It is by dipping into the ocean of Thy infinite perfections that all beings have whatever they have of good. All the beautifulness and majesty of the visible world is a shadow or a glimpse of Thee, or the manifestation or operation in a created medium of one or other of Thy attributes. All that is wonderful in the way of talent or genius is but an unworthy reflexion of the faintest gleam of the Eternal Mind. Whatever we do well, is not only by Thy help, but is after all scarcely an imitation of that sanctity which is in fulness in Thee. O my God, shall I one day see Thee? what sight can compare to that great sight! Shall I see the source of that grace which enlightens me, strengthens me, and consoles me? As I came from Thee, as I am made through Thee, as I live in Thee, so, O my God, may I at last return to Thee, and be with Thee for ever and ever.

XVIII

THE INFINITE KNOWLEDGE OF GOD

*Omnia nuda et aperta sunt oculis ejus; non est ulla creatura
invisibilis in conspectu ejus*

*All things are naked and open to his eyes; neither is there any
creature invisible in his sight*

1. My God, I adore Thee, as beholding all things.
Thou knowest in a way altogether different and higher
than any knowledge which can belong to creatures. We
know by means of sight and thought; there are few things
we know in any other way; but how unlike this knowledge, not only in extent, but in its nature and its charac-
teristics, is Thy knowledge! The Angels know many
things, but their knowledge compared to Thine is mere
ignorance. The human soul, which Thou didst take into
Thyself when Thou didst become man, was filled from
the first with all the knowledge possible to human nature:
but even that was nothing but a drop compared to the
abyss of that knowledge, and its keen luminousness,
which is Thine as God.

2. My God, could it be otherwise? for from the first
and from everlasting Thou wast by Thyself; and Thy
blessedness consisted in knowing and contemplating
Thyself, the Father in the Son and Spirit, and the Son and
Spirit severally in each other and in the Father, thus
infinitely comprehending the infinite. If Thou didst
know Thy infinite self thus perfectly, Thou didst know
that which was greater and more than anything else could

be. All that the whole universe contains, put together, is after all but finite. It is finite, though it be illimitable! it is finite, though it be so multiform; it is finite, though it be so marvellously skilful, beautiful, and magnificent; but Thou art the infinite God, and, knowing Thyself, much more dost Thou know the whole universe, however vast, however intricate and various, and all that is in it.

3. My great God, Thou knowest all that is in the universe, because Thou Thyself didst make it. It is the very work of Thy hands. Thou art Omniscient, because Thou art omni-creative. Thou knowest each part, however minute, as perfectly as Thou knowest the whole. Thou knowest mind as perfectly as Thou knowest matter. Thou knowest the thoughts and purposes of every soul as perfectly as if there were no other soul in the whole of Thy creation. Thou knowest me through and through; all my present, past, and future are before Thee as one whole. Thou seest all those delicate and evanescent motions of my thought which altogether escape myself. Thou canst trace every act, whether deed or thought, to its origin, and canst follow it into its whole growth, to its origin, and canst follow it into its whole growth and consequences. Thou knowest how it will be with me at the end; Thou hast before Thee that hour when I shall come to Thee to be judged. How awful is the prospect of finding myself in the presence of my Judge! Yet, O Lord, I would not that Thou shouldst not know me. It is my greatest stay to know that Thou readest my heart. O give me more of that open-hearted sincerity which I have desired. Keep me ever from being afraid of Thy eye, from the inward consciousness that I am not honestly trying to please Thee. Teach me to love Thee more, and then I shall be at peace, without any fear of Thee at all.

THE PROVIDENCE OF GOD

1. I ADORE Thee, my God, as having laid down the ends and the means of all things which Thou hast created. Thou hast created everything for some end of its own, and Thou dost direct it to that end. The end, which Thou didst in the beginning appoint for man, is Thy worship and service, and his own happiness in paying it; a blessed eternity of soul and body with Thee for ever. Thou hast provided for this, and that in the case of every man. As Thy hand and eye are upon the brute creation, so are they upon us. Thou sustainest everything in life and action for its own end. Not a reptile, not an insect, but Thou seest and makest to live, while its time lasts. Not a sinner, not an idolater, not a blasphemer, not an atheist lives, but by Thee, and in order that he may repent. Thou art careful and tender to each of the beings that Thou hast created, as if it were the only one in the whole world. For Thou canst see every one of them at once, and Thou lovest every one in this mortal life, and pursuest every one by itself, with all the fulness of Thy attributes, as if Thou wast waiting on it and ministering to it for its own sake. My God, I love to contemplate Thee, I love to adore Thee, thus the wonderful worker of all things every day in every place.

2. All Thy acts of providence are acts of love. If Thou sendest evil upon us, it is in love. All the evils of the physical world are intended for the good of Thy creatures, or are the unavoidable attendants on that good. And Thou turnest that evil into good. Thou visitest men

with evil to bring them to repentance, to increase their virtue, to gain for them greater good hereafter. Nothing is done in vain, but has its gracious end. Thou dost punish, yet in wrath Thou dost remember mercy. Even Thy justice when it overtakes the impenitent sinner, who had exhausted Thy loving providences towards him, is mercy to others, as saving them from his contamination, or granting them a warning. I acknowledge with a full and firm faith, O Lord, the wisdom and goodness of Thy Providence, even in Thy inscrutable judgments and Thy incomprehensible decrees.

3. O my God, my whole life has been a course of mercies and blessings shewn to one who has been most unworthy of them. I require no faith, for I have had long experience, as to Thy providence towards me. Year after year Thou hast carried me on—removed dangers from my path—recovered me, recruited me, refreshed me, borne with me, directed me, sustained me. O forsake me not when my strength faileth me. And Thou never wilt forsake me. I may securely repose upon Thee. Sinner as I am, nevertheless, while I am true to Thee, Thou wilt still and to the end, be superabundantly true to me. I may rest upon Thy arm; I may go to sleep in Thy bosom. Only give me, and increase in me, that true loyalty to Thee, which is the bond of the covenant between Thee and me, and the pledge in my own heart and conscience that Thou, the Supreme God, wilt not forsake me, the most miserable of Thy children.

XX

GOD IS ALL IN ALL

Unus deus et Pater omnium, qui est super omnes,
et per omnia, et in omnibus nobis

One God and Father of all, who is above all,
and through all, and in us all

1. GOD alone is in heaven; God is all in all. Eternal
Lord, I acknowledge this truth, and I adore Thee in this
sovereign and most glorious mystery. There is One God,
and He fills heaven; and all blessed creatures, though they
ever remain in their individuality, are, as the very means
of their blessedness, absorbed, and (as it were) drowned
in the fulness of Him who is *super omnes, et per omnia, et in*
omnibus. If ever, through Thy grace, I attain to see Thee
in heaven, I shall see nothing else but Thee, because I
shall see all whom I see in Thee, and seeing them I shall
see Thee. As I cannot see things here below without
light, and to see them is to see the rays which come from
them, so in that Eternal City *claritas Dei illuminavit eam, et*
lucerna ejus est Agnus—the glory of God hath enlightened
it, and the Lamb is the lamp thereof. My God, I adore
Thee now (at least I will do so to the best of my powers)
as the One Sole True Life and Light of the soul, as I shall
know and see Thee to be hereafter, if by Thy grace I
attain to heaven.

2. Eternal, Incomprehensible God, I believe, and confess, and adore Thee, as being infinitely more wonderful,
resourceful, and immense, than this universe which I see.

435

I look into the depths of space, in which the stars are scattered about, and I understand that I should be millions upon millions of years in creeping along from one end of it to the other, if a bridge were thrown across it. I consider the overpowering variety, richness, intricacy of Thy work; the elements, principles, laws, results which go to make it up. I try to recount the multitudes of kinds of knowledge, of sciences, and of arts of which it can be made the subject. And, I know, I should be ages upon ages in learning everything that is to be learned about this world, supposing me to have the power of learning it at all. And new sciences would come to light, at present unsuspected, as fast as I had mastered the old, and the conclusions of today would be nothing more than starting points of to-morrow. And I see moreover, and the more I examined it, the more I should understand, the marvellous beauty of these works of Thy hands. And so, I might begin again, after this material universe, and find a new world of knowledge, higher and more wonderful, in Thy intellectual creations, Thy angels and other spirits, and men. But all, all that is in these worlds, high and low, are but an atom compared with the grandeur, the height and depth, the glory, on which Thy saints are gazing in their contemplation of Thee. It is the occupation of eternity, ever new, inexhaustible, ineffably ecstatic, the stay and the blessedness of existence, thus to drink in and be dissolved in Thee.

3. My God, it was Thy supreme blessedness in the eternity past, as it is Thy blessedness in all eternities, to know Thyself, as Thou alone canst know Thee. It was by seeing Thyself in Thy Co-equal Son and Thy Co-eternal Spirit, and in Their seeing Thee, that Father, Son, and Holy Ghost, Three Persons, One God, was infinitely blessed. O my God, what am I that Thou shouldst make my blessedness to consist in that which is Thy own! That

Thou shouldst grant me to have not only the sight of
Thee, but to share in Thy very own joy! O prepare me
for it, teach me to thirst for it.

XXI

GOD THE INCOMMUNICABLE
PERFECTION

1. ALMIGHTY God, Thou art the One Infinite Fulness.
From eternity Thou art the One and only absolute and
most all-sufficient seat and proper abode of all conceivable best attributes, and of all, which are many more,
which cannot be conceived. I hold this as a matter of
reason, though my imagination starts from it. I hold it
firmly and absolutely, though it is the most difficult of all
mysteries. I hold it from the actual experience of Thy
blessings and mercies towards me, the evidences of Thy
awful Being and attributes, brought home continually to
my reason, beyond the power of doubting or disputing. I
hold it from that long and intimate familiarity with it, so
that it is part of my rational nature to hold it; because I am
so constituted and made up upon the idea of it, as a
keystone, that not to hold it would be to break my mind
to pieces. I hold it from that intimate perception of it in
my conscience, as a fact present to me, that I feel it as easy
to deny my own personality as the personality of God,
and have lost my grounds for believing that I exist
myself, if I deny existence to Him. I hold it because I
could not bear to be without Thee, O my Lord and Life,
because I look for blessings beyond thought by being
with Thee. I hold it from the terror of being left in this
wild world without stay or protection. I hold it from
humble love to Thee, from delight in Thy glory and
exaltation, from my desire that Thou shouldst be great
and the only great one. I hold it for Thy sake, and because
I love to think of Thee as so glorious, perfect, and

438

beautiful. There is one God, and none other but He.

2. Since, O Eternal God, Thou art so incommunicably great, so one, so perfect in that oneness, surely one would say, Thou ever must be most distant from Thy creatures, didst Thou create any;—separated from them by Thy eternal ancientness on their beginning to be, and separated by Thy transcendency of excellence and Thy absolute contrariety to them. What couldst Thou give them out of Thyself, which would suit their nature, so different from Thine? What good of Thine could be their good, or do them good, except in some poor external way? If Thou couldst be the happiness of man, then might man in turn, or some gift from him, be the happiness of the bird of prey or the wild beast, the cattle of his pasture, or the myriads of minute creatures which we can scarcely see. Man is not so far above them, as Thou above him. For what is every creature in Thy sight, O Lord, but a vanity and a breath, a smoke which stays not, but flits by and passes away, a poor thing which only vanishes so much the sooner, because Thou lookest on it, and it is set in the illumination of Thy countenance? Is not this, O Lord, the perplexity of reason? From the Perfect comes the Perfect; yet Thou canst not make a second God, from the nature of the case; and therefore either canst not create at all, or of necessity must create what is infinitely unlike, and therefore, in a sense, unworthy of the Creator.

3. What communion then can there be between Thee and me? O my God! what am I but a parcel of dead bones, a feeble, tottering, miserable being, compared with Thee. I am Thy work, and Thou didst create me pure from sin, but how canst Thou look upon me in my best estate of nature, with complacency? how canst Thou see in me any image of Thyself, the Creator? How is this, my Lord? Thou didst pronounce Thy work very good, and didst make man in Thy image. Yet there is an infinite gulf between Thee and me, O my God.

XXII

GOD COMMUNICATED TO US

1. THOU hast, O Lord, an incommunicable perfection, but still that Omnipotence by which Thou didst create, is sufficient also to the work of communicating Thyself to the spirits which Thou hast created. Thy Almighty Life is not for our destruction, but for our living. Thou remainest ever one and the same in Thyself, but there goes from Thee continually a power and virtue, which by its contact is our strength and good. I do not know how this can be; my reason does not satisfy me here; but in nature I see intimations, and by faith I have full assurance of the truth of this mystery. By Thee we cross the gulf that lies between Thee and us. The Living God is lifegiving. Thou art the Fount and Centre, as well as the Seat, of all good. The traces of Thy glory, as the many-coloured rays of the sun, are scattered over the whole face of nature, without diminution of Thy perfections, or violation of Thy transcendent and unapproachable Essence. How it can be, I know not; but so it is. And thus, remaining one and sole and infinitely removed from all things, still Thou art the fulness of all things, in Thee they consist, of Thee they partake, and into Thee, retaining their own individuality, they are absorbed. And thus, while we droop and decay in our own nature, we live by Thy breath; and Thy grace enables us to endure Thy presence.

2. Make me then like Thyself, O my God, since, in spite of myself, such Thou canst make me, such I can be made. Look on me, O my Creator, pity the work of Thy hands, *ne peream in infirmitate meâ*—"that I perish not in

440

my infirmity." Take me out of my natural imbecility, since that is possible for me, which is so necessary. Thou hast shewn it to be possible in the face of the whole world by the most overwhelming proof, by taking our created nature on Thyself, and exalting it in Thee. Give me in my own self the benefit of this wondrous truth, now it has been so publicly ascertained and guaranteed. Let me have in my own person, what in Jesus Thou hast given to my nature. Let me be partaker of that Divine Nature in all the riches of Its attributes, which in fulness of substance and in personal presence became the Son of Mary. Give me that life, suitable to my own need, which is stored up for us all in Him who is the Life of men. Teach me and enable me to live the life of Saints and Angels. Take me out of the languor, the irritability, the sensitiveness, the incapability, the anarchy, in which my soul lies, and fill it with Thy fulness. Breathe on me, that the dead bones may live. Breathe on me with that Breath which infuses energy and kindles fervour. In asking for fervour, I ask for all that I can need, and all that Thou canst give; for it is the crown of all gifts and all virtues. It cannot really and fully be, except where all are at present. It is the beauty and the glory, as it is also the continual safeguard and purifier of them all. In asking for fervour, I am asking for effectual strength, consistency, and perseverance; I am asking for deadness to every human motive, and simplicity of intention to please Thee: I am asking for faith, hope, and charity in their most heavenly exercise. In asking for fervour I am asking to be rid of the fear of man, and the desire of his praise; I am asking for the gift of prayer, because it will be so sweet; I am asking for that loyal perception of duty, which follows on yearning affection; I am asking for sanctity, peace, and joy all at once. In asking for fervour, I am asking for the brightness of the Cherubim and the fire of the Seraphim, and the whiteness of all Saints. In asking for fervour, I am asking for that which, while it implies all gifts, is that in which I signally fail. Nothing would be a trouble to me, nothing a difficulty, had I but fervour of soul.

3. Lord, in asking for fervour, I am asking for Thyself, for nothing short of Thee, O my God, who hast given Thyself wholly to us. Enter my heart substantially and personally, and fill it with fervour by filling it with Thee. Thou alone canst fill the soul of man, and Thou hast promised to do so. Thou art the living Flame, and ever burnest with love of man: enter into me and set me on fire after Thy pattern and likeness.

XXIII.

GOD THE SOLE STAY FOR ETERNITY

1. MY God I believe and know and adore Thee as infinite in the multiplicity and depth of Thy attributes. I adore Thee as containing in Thee an abundance of all that can delight and satisfy the soul. I know, on the contrary, and from sad experience I am too sure, that whatever is created, whatever is earthly, pleases but for the time, and then palls and is a weariness. I believe that there is nothing at all here below, which I should not at length get sick of. I believe, that, though I had all the means of happiness which this life could give, yet in time I should tire of living, feeling everything trite and dull and un-profitable. I believe, that, were it my lot to live the long antediluvian life, and to live it without Thee, I should be utterly, inconceivably, wretched at the end of it. I think I should be tempted to destroy myself for very weariness and disgust. I think I should at last lose my reason and go mad, if my life here was prolonged long enough. I should feel it like solitary confinement, for I should find myself shut up in myself without companion, if I could not converse with Thee, my God. Thou only, O my Infinite Lord, art ever new, though Thou art the ancient of days—the last as well as the first.

2. Thou, O my God, art ever new, though Thou art the most ancient—Thou alone art the food for eternity. I am to live forever, not for a time—and I have no power over my being; I cannot destroy myself, even though I were so wicked as to wish to do so. I must live on, with intellect and consciousness for ever, in spite of myself.

Without Thee eternity would be another name for eternal misery. In Thee alone have I that which can stay me up for ever: Thou alone art the food of my soul. Thou alone art inexhaustible, and ever offerest to me something new to know, something new to love. At the end of millions of years I shall know Thee so little, that I shall seem to myself only beginning. At the end of millions of years I shall find in Thee the same, or rather, greater sweetness than at first, and shall seem then only to be beginning to enjoy Thee: and so on for eternity I shall ever be a little child beginning to be taught the rudiments of Thy infinite Divine nature. For Thou art Thyself the seat and centre, of all good, and the only substance in this universe of shadows, and the heaven in which blessed spirits live and rejoice.

3. My God, I take Thee for my portion. From mere prudence I turn from the world to Thee; I give up the world for Thee. I renounce that which promises for Him who performs. To whom else should I go? I desire to find and feed on Thee here; I desire to feed on Thee, Jesu, my Lord, who art risen, who hast gone up on high, who yet remainest with Thy people on earth. I look up to Thee; I look for the Living Bread which is in heaven, which comes down from heaven. Give me ever of this Bread. Destroy this life, which will soon perish—even though Thou dost not destroy it, and fill me with that supernatural life, which will never die.

CONCLUSION

WRITTEN IN PROSPECT OF DEATH

March 13th, 1864, Passion Sunday, 7 o'clock a.m.

I WRITE in the direct view of death as in prospect. No one in the house, I suppose, suspects anything of the kind. Nor anyone anywhere, unless it be the medical men.

I write at once—because, on my own feelings of mind and body, it is as if nothing at all were the matter with me, just now; but because I do not know how long this perfect possession of my sensible and available health and strength may last.

I die in the faith of the One Holy Catholic Apostolic Church. I trust I shall die prepared and protected by her Sacraments, which our Lord Jesus Christ has committed to her, and in that communion of Saints which He inaugurated when He ascended on high, and which will have no end. I hope to die in that Church which our Lord founded on Peter, and which will continue till His second coming.

I commit my soul and body to the Most Holy Trinity, and to the merits and grace of our Lord Jesus, God Incarnate, to the intercession and compassion of our dear Mother Mary; to St. Joseph; and St. Philip Neri, my father, the father of an unworthy son; to St. John the Evangelist; St. John the Baptist; St. Henry; St. Athanasius, and St. Gregory Nazianzen; to St. Chrysostom, and St. Ambrose.

Also to St. Peter, St. Gregory I., and St. Leo. Also to the great Apostle, St. Paul.

Also to my tender Guardian Angel, and to all Angels, and to all Saints.

And I pray to God to bring us all together again in heaven, under the feet of the Saints. And, after the pattern of Him, who seeks so diligently for those who are astray, I would ask Him especially to have mercy on those who are external to the True Fold, and to bring them into it before they die.

J.H.N.

WRITTEN IN PROSPECT OF DEATH

July 23, 1876

I WISH, with all my heart, to be buried in Father Ambrose St. John's grave—and I give this as my last, my imperative will. [This I confirm and insist on, and command. Feb. 13, 1881.]

If a tablet is put up in the cloister, such as the three there already, I should like the following, if good Latinity, and if there is no other objection: *e.g.*, it must not be if persons to whom I should defer thought it sceptical. [J.H.N., Feb.13, 1881.]

JOANNES HENRICUS NEWMAN

EX UMBRIS ET IMAGINIBUS

IN VERITATEM

DIE——A.S. 18

Requiescat in pace

My only difficulty is St. Paul, Heb. x. I, where he assigns 'umbra' to the Law—but surely, though we have in many respects an εἰκών of the Truth, there is a good deal of σκία still, as in the doctrine of the Holy Trinity.

Cardinal Newman was born Feb. 21, 1801, received into the Catholic Church, October 9, 1845, created Cardinal, May 12, 1879, and died late in the evening of Aug. 11, 1890.

VERSES ON
VARIOUS OCCASIONS

"cui pauca relicti
Jugera ruris erant; nec fertilis illa juvencis
Nec pecori opportuna seges, nec commoda Baccho,
Hic rarum tamen in dumis olus, albaque circum
Lilia, verbanasque premens, vescumque papaver,
Regum æquabat opes animis."

DEDICATION
TO EDWARD BADELEY, ESQ.

My dear Badeley,

I have not been without apprehension lest in dedicating to you a number of poetical compositions, I should hardly be making a suitable offering to a member of a grave profession, which is especially employed in rubbing off the gloss with which imagination and sentiment invest matters of every-day life, and in reducing statements of fact to their legitimate dimensions. And, besides this, misgivings have not unnaturally come over me on the previous question; viz., whether, after all, the contents of the volume are sufficient importance to make it an acceptable offering to any friend whatever.

And I must frankly confess, as to the latter difficulty, that certainly it never would have occurred to me thus formally to bring together under one title effusions which I have ever considered ephemeral, had I not lately found from publications of the day, what I never suspected before, that there are critics, and they strangers to me, who think well both of some of my compositions and of my power of composing. It is this commendation, bestowed on me to my surprise as well as to my gratification, which has encouraged me just now to republish what I have from time to time written; and if, in doing so, I shall be found, as is not unlikely, to have formed a volume of unequal merit, my excuse must be, that I despair of discovering any standard by which to discriminate aright between one poetical attempt and another. Accordingly, I am thrown, from the nature of the case, whether I will or no, upon my own judgment, which, biassed by the associations of memory and by personal feelings, and measuring perhaps, by the pleasure of verse-making, the worth of the verse, is disposed either to preserve them all, or to put them all aside.

Here another contrast presents itself between the poetical art and the science of law. Your profession has its definitive authorities, its prescriptions, its precedents, and its principles, by which to determine the claim of its authors on public attention; but what philosopher will undertake to rule matters of taste, or to bring under one idea or method works so different from each other as those of Homer, Aeschylus, and Pindar; of Terence, Ovid, Juvenal, and Martial? What court is sitting, and what code is received, for the satisfactory determination of the poetical pretensions of writers of the day? Whence can we hope to gain a verdict upon them, except from the unscientific tribunals of Public Opinion and of Time? In Poetry, as in Metaphysics, a book is of necessity a venture.

And now, coming to the suitableness of my offering, I know well, my dear Badeley, how little you will be disposed to criticize what comes to you from me, whatever be its intrinsic value. Less still in this case, considering that a chief portion of the volume grew out of that Religious Movement which you yourself, as well as I, so faithfully followed from first to last. And least of all, when I tell you that I wish it to be the poor expression, long-delayed, of my gratitude, never intermitted, for the great services which you rendered to me years ago, by your legal skill and affectionate zeal, in a serious matter in which I found myself in collision with the law of the land. Those services I have ever desired in some public, however inadequate, way to record; and now, as time hurries on and opportunities are few, I am forced to ask you to let me acknowledge my debt to you as I can, since I cannot as I would.

We are now, both of us, in the decline of life: may that warm attachment which has lasted between us inviolate for so many years, be continued, by the mercy of God, to the end of our earthly course, and beyond it!

I am, my dear Badeley,

Affectionately yours,

J. H. N.

The Oratory.
December 21, 1867.

I.

SOLITUDE.

THERE is in stillness oft a magic power
To calm the breast, when struggling passions lower;
Touch'd by its influence, in the soul arise
Diviner feelings, kindred with the skies.
By this the Arab's kindling thoughts expand,
When circling skies inclose the desert sand;
For this the hermit seeks the thickest grove,
To catch th' inspiring glow of heavenly love.
It is not solely in the freedom given
To purify and fix the heart on heaven;
There is a Spirit singing aye in air,
That lifts us high above all mortal care.
No mortal measure swells that mystic sound,
No mortal minstrel breathes such tones around,—
The Angels' hymn,—the sovereign harmony
That guides the rolling orbs along the sky,—
And hence perchance the tales of saints who view'd
And heard Angelic choirs in solitude.
By most unheard,—because the earthly din
Of toil or mirth has charms their ears to win.
Alas for man! he knows not of the bliss,
The heaven that brightens such a life as this.

Oxford.
Michaelmas Term, 1818.

II.

MY BIRTHDAY.

1.

LET the sun summon all his beams to hold
  Bright pageant in his court, the cloud-paved sky
Earth trim her fields and leaf her copses cold;
  Till the dull month with summer-splendours vie.
  It is my Birthday;—and I fain would try,
Albeit in rude, in heartfelt strains to praise
  My God, for He hath shielded wondrously
From harm and envious error all my ways,
And purged my misty sight, and fixed on heaven
        my gaze.

2.

Not in that mood, in which the insensate crowd
  Of wealthy folly hail their natal day,—
With riot throng, and feast, and greetings loud,
  Chasing all thoughts of God and heaven away.
  Poor insect! feebly daring, madly gay,
What! joy because the fulness of the year
  Marks thee for greedy death a riper prey?
Is not the silence of the grave too near?
Viewest thou the end with glee, meet scene for
        harrowing fear?

3.

Go then, infatuate! where the festive hall,
  The curious board, the oblivious wine invite;
Speed with obsequious haste at Pleasure's call,
  And with thy revels scare the far-spent night.
  Joy thee, that clearer dawn upon thy sight
The gates of death;—and pride thee in thy sum
  Of guilty years, and thy increasing white
Of locks; in age untimely frolicksome,
Make much of thy brief span, few years are yet to come!

4.

Yet wiser such, than he whom blank despair
  And fostered grief's ungainful toil enslave;
Lodged in whose furrowed brow thrives fretful care,
  Sour graft of blighted hope; who, when the wave
  Of evil rushes, yields,—yet claims to rave
At his own deed, as the stern will of heaven.
  In sooth against his Maker idly brave,
Whom e'en the creature-world has tossed and
    driven,
Cursing the life he mars, "a boon so kindly given."[1]

5.

He dreams of mischief; and that brainborn ill
  Man's open face bears in his jealous view.
Fain would he fly his doom; that doom is still
  His own black thoughts, and they must aye pursue.
  Too proud for merriment, or the pure dew
Soft glistening on the sympathising cheek;
  As some dark, lonely, evil-natured yew,

[1] "Is life a boon so kindly given," &c., vide *Childe Harold*, Canto ii.

Whose poisonous fruit—so fabling poets speak—
Beneath the moon's pale gleam the midnight hag
    doth seek.

6.

No! give to me, Great Lord, the constant soul,
   Nor fooled by pleasure nor enslaved by care;
Each rebel-passion (for Thou canst) control,
   And make me know the tempter's every snare.
   What, though alone my sober hours I wear,
No friend in view, and sadness o'er my mind
   Throws her dark veil?—Thou but accord this prayer,
And I will bless Thee for my birth, and find
That stillness breathes sweet tones, and solitude is kind.

7.

Each coming year, O grant it to refine
   All purer motions of this anxious breast;
Kindle the steadfast flame of love divine,
   And comfort me with holier thoughts possest;
   Till this worn body slowly sink to rest,
This feeble spirit to the sky aspire,—
   As some long-prisoned dove toward her nest—
There to receive the gracious full-toned lyre,
Bowed low before the Throne 'mid the bright
    seraph choir.

Oxford.
February 21, 1819.[2]

[2] The diction of these Verses has been altered in some places at a later date.

III.

PARAPHRASE

OF ISAIAH, CHAP. LXIV.

O THAT Thou wouldest rend the breadth of sky,
    That veils Thy presence from the sons of men!
O that, as erst Thou camest from on high
    Sudden in strength, Thou so would'st come again!
Track'd out by judgments was Thy fiery path,
Ocean and mountain withering in Thy wrath!

Then would Thy name—the Just, the Merciful—
    Strange dubious attributes to human mind,
Appal Thy foes; and, kings, who spurn Thy rule,
    Then, then would quake to hopeless doom consign'd.
See, the stout bows, and totters the secure,
While pleasure's bondsman hides his head impure!

Come down! for then shall from its seven bright springs
    To him who thirsts the draught of life be given;
Eye hath not seen, ear hath not heard the things
    Which He hath purposed for the heirs of heaven,—
A God of love, guiding with gracious ray
Each meek rejoicing pilgrim on his way.

Yea, though we err, and Thine averted face
    Rebukes the folly in Thine Israel done,
Will not that hour of chastisement give place
    To beams, the pledge of an eternal sun?
Yes! for His counsels to the end endure;
We shall be saved, our rest abideth sure.

Lord, Lord! our sins . . . our sins . . . unclean are we,
  Gross and corrupt; our seeming-virtuous deeds
Are but abominate; all, dead to Thee,
  Shrivel, like leaves when summer's green recedes;
While, like the autumn blast, our lusts arise,
And sweep their prey where the fell serpent lies.

None, there is none to plead with God in prayer
  Bracing his laggart spirit to the work
Of intercession; conscience-sprung despair,
  Sin-loving still, doth in each bosom lurk.
Guilt calls Thee to avenge;—Thy risen ire
Sears like a brand, we gaze and we expire.

But now, O Lord, our Father! we are Thine,
  Design and fashion; senseless while we lay,
Thou, as the potter, with a Hand Divine,
  Didst mould Thy vessels of the sluggish clay.
Mark not our guilt, Thy word of wrath recall,
Lo, we are Thine by price, Thy people all!

Alas for Zion! 'tis a waste;—the fair,
  The holy place in flames;—where once our sires
Kindled the sacrifice of praise and prayer,
  Far other brightness gleams from Gentile fires.
Low lies our pride;—and wilt Thou self-deny
Thy rescuing arm unvex'd amid thine Israel's cry?

Brighton.
September, 1821.

IV.

TO F. W. N.

A BIRTHDAY OFFERING.

DEAR Frank, this morn has usher'd in
　　The manhood of thy days;
A boy no more, thou must begin
　　To choose thy future ways;
To brace thy arm, and nerve thy heart,
For maintenance of a noble part.

And thou a voucher fair hast given,
　　Of what thou wilt achieve,
Ere age has dimmed thy sun-lit heaven,
　　In weary life's chill eve;
Should Sovereign Wisdom in its grace
Vouchsafe to thee so long a race.

My brother, we are link'd with chain
　　That time shall ne'er destroy;
Together we have been in pain,
　　Together now in joy;
For duly I to share may claim
The present brightness of thy name,

My brother, 'tis no recent tie
　　Which binds our fates in one,
E'en from our tender infancy
　　The twisted thread was spun;—

VERSES ON VARIOUS OCCASIONS

Her deed, who stored in her fond mind
Our forms, by sacred love enshrined.

In her affection all had share,
    All six, she loved them all;
Yet on her early-chosen Pair
    Did her full favour fall;[1]
And we became her dearest theme.
Her waking thought, her nightly dream.

Ah! brother, shall we e'er forget
    Her love, her care, her zeal?
We cannot pay the countless debt,
    But we must ever feel;
For through her earnestness were shed
Prayer-purchased blessings on our head.

Though in the end of days she stood,
    And pain and weakness came,
Her force of thought was unsubdued,
    Her fire of love the same;
And e'en when memory fail'd its part,
We still kept lodgment in her heart,

And when her Maker from the thrall
    Of flesh her spirit freed,
No suffering companied the call,
    —In mercy 'twas decreed,—
One moment here, the next she trod
The viewless mansion of her God.

Now then at length she is at rest,
    And, after many a woe,

---

[1] Of course the allusion is not to the author's mother; a mother has
no favourites.

Rejoices in that Saviour blest
   Who was her hope below;
Kept till the day when He shall own
His saints before His Father's throne,

So it is left for us to prove
   Her prayers were not in vain;
And that God's grace-according love
   Has come as gentle rain,
Which, falling in the vernal hour,
Tints the young leaf, perfumes the flower.

Dear Frank, we both are summon'd now
   As champions of the Lord;—
Enroll'd am I, and shortly thou
   Must buckle on thy sword;
A high employ, nor lightly given,
To serve as messengers of heaven!

Deep in my heart that gift I hide;
   I change it not away
For patriot-warrior's hour of pride,
   Or statesman's tranquil sway;
For poet's fire, or pleader's skill
To pierce the soul and tame the will.

O! may we follow undismay'd
   Where'er our God shall call!
And may His Spirit's present aid
   Uphold us lest we fall!
Till in the end of days we stand,
As victors in a deathless land.

Chiswick.
June 27, 1826.

V.

NATURE AND ART.

FOR AN ALBUM.

"MAN goeth forth"[1] with reckless trust
    Upon his wealth of mind,
As if in self a thing of dust
    Creative skill might find;
He schemes and toils; stone, wood, and ore
Subject or weapon of his power.

By arch and spire, by tower-girt heights,
    He would his boast fulfil;
By marble births, and mimic lights,—
    Yet lacks one secret still;
Where is the master-hand shall give
To breathe, to move, to speak, to live?

O take away this shade of might,
    The puny toil of man,
And let great Nature in my sight
    Unroll her gorgeous plan;
I cannot bear those sullen walls,
Those eyeless towers, those tongueless halls.

Art's labour'd toys of highest name
    Are nerveless, cold, and dumb;
And man is fitted but to frame

---

[1] Psalm civ. [ciii.] 23

A coffin or a tomb;
Well suits, when sense has pass'd away,
Such lifeless work the lifeless clay.

Here let me sit where wooded hills
    Skirt yon far-reaching plain;
While cattle bank its winding rills,
    And suns embrown its grain;
Such prospect is to me right dear,
For freedom, health, and joy are here.

There is a spirit ranging through
    The earth, the stream, the air;
Ten thousand shapes, garbs ever new,
    That busy One doth wear;
In colour, scent, and taste, and sound
The energy of Life is found.

The leaves are rustling in the breeze,
    The bird renews her song;
From field to brook, o'er heath, o'er trees
    The sunbeam glides along;
The insect, happy in its hour,
Floats softly by, or sips the flower.

Now dewy rain descends, and now
    Brisk showers the welkin shroud;
I care not, though with angry brow
    Frowns the red thunder-cloud;
Let hail-storm pelt, and lightning harm,
'Tis Nature's work, and has its charm.

Ah! lovely Nature! others dwell
    Full favour'd in thy court;
I of thy smiles but hear them tell,
    And feed on their report,

Catching what glimpse an Ulcombe yields
To strangers loitering in her fields.

I go where form has ne'er unbent
   The sameness of its sway;
Where iron rule, stern precedent,
   Mistreat the graceful day;
To pine as prisoner in his cell,
And yet be thought to love it well.

Yet so His high dispose has set,
   Who binds on each his part;
Though absent, I may cherish yet
   An Ulcombe of the heart;
Calm verdant hope divinely given,
And suns of peace, and scenes of heaven;—

A soul prepared His will to meet.
   Full fix'd His work to do;
Not laboured into sudden heat,
   But inly born anew.—
So living Nature, not dull Art,
Shall plan my ways and rule my heart.

Ulcombe.
September, 1826.

VI.

INTRODUCTION

TO AN ALBUM.

I AM a harp of many chords, and each
Strung by a separate hand;—most musical
My notes, discoursing with the mental sense,
Not the outward ear. Try them, they will reply
With wisdom, fancy, graceful gaiety,
Or ready wit, or happy sentiment.
  Come, add a string to my assort of sounds;
Widen the compass of my harmony;
And join thyself in fellowship of name
With those, whose courteous labour and fair gifts
Have given me voice, and made me what I am.

Brighton.
April, 1827.

VII.

SNAPDRAGON.

A Riddle

FOR A FLOWER BOOK

I AM rooted in the wall
Of buttress'd tower or ancient hall;
Prison'd in an art-wrought bed,
Cased in mortar, cramp'd with lead;
Of a living stock alone
Brother of the lifeless stone.

Else unprized, I have my worth
On the spot that gives me birth;
Nature's vast and varied field
Braver flowers than me will yield,
Bold in form and rich in hue,
Children of a purer dew;
Smiling lips and winning eyes
Meet for earthly paradise.

Choice are such,—and yet thou knowest
Highest he whose lot is lowest.
They, proud hearts, a home reject
Framed by human architect;
Humble-I can bear to dwell
Near the pale recluse's cell,
And I spread my crimson bloom,
Mingled with the cloister's gloom.

Life's gay gifts and honours rare,
Flowers of favour! win and wear!
Rose of beauty, be the queen
In pleasure's ring and festive scene.
Ivy, climb and cluster, where
Lordly oaks vouchsafe a stair.
Vaunt, fair Lily, stately dame,
Pride of birth and pomp of name.
Miser Crocus, starved with cold,
Hide in earth thy timid gold.
Travell'd Dahlia, freely boast
Knowledge brought from foreign coast.
Pleasure, wealth, birth, knowledge, power,
These have each an emblem flower;
So for me alone remains
Lowly thought and cheerful pains.

Be it mine to set restraint
On roving wish and selfish plaint;
And for man's drear haunts to leave
Dewy morn and balmy eve.
Be it mine the barren stone
To deck with green life not its own.
So to soften and to grace
Of human works the rugged face.
Mine, the Unseen to display
In the crowded public way,
Where life's busy arts combine
To shut out the Hand Divine.

Ah! no more a scentless flower,
By approving Heaven's high power,
Suddenly my leaves exhale
Fragrance of the Syrian gale.
Ah! 'tis timely comfort given
By the answering breath of Heaven!

May it be! then well might I
In College cloister live and die.

Ulcombe.
October 2, 1827.

VIII.

THE TRANCE OF TIME.

"Felix, qui potuit rerum cognoscere causas,
Atque metus omnes, et inexorabile fatum
Subjecit pedibus, strepitumque Acherontis avari!"

IN childhood, when with eager eyes
   The season-measured year I view'd,
      All garb'd in fairy guise,
         Pledged constancy of good.

Spring sang of heaven; the summer flowers
   Bade me gaze on, and did not fade;
      Even suns o'er autumn's bowers
         Heard my strong wish, and stay'd.

They came and went, the short-lived four;
   Yet, as their varying dance they wove.
      To my young heart each bore
         Its own sure claim of love.

Far different now;—the whirling year
   Vainly my dizzy eyes pursue;
      And its fair tints appear
         All blent in one dusk hue.

Why dwell on rich autumnal lights,
   Spring-time, or winter's social ring?
      Long days are fire-side nights,
         Brown autumn is fresh spring.

Then what this world to thee, my heart?
  Its gifts nor feed thee nor can bless.
    Thou hast no owner's part
      In all its fleetingness.

The flame, the storm, the quaking ground.
  Earth's joy, earth's terror, nought is thine,
    Thou must but hear the sound
      Of the still voice divine.

O priceless art! O princely state!
  E'en while by sense of change opprest,
    Within to antedate
      Heaven's Age of fearless rest.

Highwood.
October, 1827.

IX.

CONSOLATIONS IN BEREAVEMENT.

DEATH was full urgent with thee, Sister dear,
　And startling in his speed;—
Brief pain, then languor till thy end came near—
　Such was the path decreed,
　　The hurried road
To lead thy soul from earth to thine own God's abode.

Death wrought with thee, sweet maid, impatiently:—
　Yet merciful the haste
That baffles sickness;—dearest, thou didst die,
　Thou wast not made to taste
　　Death's bitterness,
Decline's slow-wasting charm, or fever's fierce
　　distress.

Death came unheralded:—but it was well;
　For so thy Saviour bore
Kind witness, thou wast meet at once to dwell
　On His eternal shore;
　　All warning spared,
For none He gives where heart are for prompt
　　change prepared.

Death wrought in mystery; both complaint and cure
　To human skill unknown:—
God put aside all means, to make us sure
　It was His deed alone;
　　Lest we should lay

Reproach on our poor selves, that thou wast caught
　　away.

Death urged as scant of time:—lest, Sister dear,
　　We many a lingering day
Had sicken'd with alternate hope and fear,
　　The ague of delay;
　　　　Watching each spark
Of promise quench'd in turn, till all our sky was
　　dark.

Death came and went:—that so thy image might
　　Our yearning hearts posses,
Associate with all pleasant thoughts and bright,
　　With youth and loveliness;
　　　　Sorrow can claim,
Mary, nor lot nor part in thy soft soothing name.

Joy of sad heart, and light of downcast eyes!
　　Dearest thou art enshrined
In all thy fragrance in our memories;
　　For we must ever find
　　　　Bare thought of thee
Freshen this weary life, while weary life shall be.

Oxford.
April, 1828.

X.

A PICTURE.

"The maiden is not dead, but sleepeth."

SHE is not gone;—still in our sight
    That dearest maid shall live,
In form as true, in tints as bright,
    As youth and health could give.

Still, still is ours the modest eye;
    The smile unwrought by art;
The glance that shot so piercingly
    Affection's keenest dart;

The thrilling voice, I ne'er could hear
    But felt a joy and pain;—
A pride that she was ours, a fear
    Ours she might not remain;

Whether the page divine call'd forth
    Its clear, sweet, tranquil tone,
Or cheerful hymn, or seemly mirth
    In sprightlier measure shown;

The meek inquiry of that face,
    Musing on wonders found,
As 'mid dim paths she sought to trace
    The truth on sacred ground;

The thankful sigh that would arise,
    When aught her doubts removed,
Full sure the explaining voice to prize,
    Admiring while she loved;

The pensive brow, the world might see
    When she in crowds was found;
The burst of heart, the o'erflowing glee
    When only friends were round;

Hope's warmth of promise, prompt to fill
    The thoughts with good in store,
Match'd with content's deep stream, which still
    Flow'd on, when hope was o'er;

That peace, which, with its own bright day,
    Made cheapest sights shine fair;
That purest grace, which track'd its way
    Safe from aught earthly there.

Such was she in the sudden hour
    That brought her Maker's call,—
Proving her heart's self-mastering power
    Blithely to part with all,—

All her eye loved, all her hand press'd
    With keen affection's glow.
The voice of home, all pleasures best
    All dearest thoughts below.

From friend-lit hearth, from social board,
    All duteously she rose;
For faith upon the Master's word
    Can find a sure repose.

And in her wonder up she sped,
  And tried relief in vain;
Then laid her down upon her bed
  Of languor and of pain,—

And waited till the solemn spell,
  (A ling'ring night and day,)
Should fill its numbers, and compel
  Her soul to come away.

Such was she then; and such she is,
  Shrined in each mourner's breast;
Such shall she be, and more than this,
  In promised glory blest;

When in due lines her Saviour dear
  His scatter'd saints shall range,
And knit in love souls parted here,
  Where cloud is none, nor change.

Oxford.
August, 1828.

XI.

MY LADY NATURE
AND HER DAUGHTERS.

LADIES, well I deem, delight
    In comely tire to move;
Soft, and delicate, and bright,
    Are the robes they love.
Silks, where hues alternate play,
Shawls, and scarfs, and mantles gay,
Gold, and gems, and crispèd hair,
Fling their light o'er lady fair.
'Tis not waste, nor sinful pride,
—Name them not, nor fault beside,—
But her very cheerfulness
Prompts and weaves the curious dress
While her holy[1] thoughts still roam
Mid birth-friends and scenes of home.
Pleased to please whose praise is dear,
Glitters she? she glitters there;—
And she has a pattern found her
In Nature's glowing world around her.

Nature loves, as lady bright.
    In gayest guise to shine,
All forms of grace, all tints of light,
    Fringe her robe divine.
Sun-lit heaven, and rain-bow cloud,

---

[1] Vide I Pet. iii. 5; and cf. Gen. xxiv. 22, 28–30.

Changeful main, and mountain proud,
Branching tree, and meadow green,
All are deck'd in broider'd sheen.
Not a bird on bough-propp'd tower,
Insect slim, nor tiny flower,
Stone, nor spar, nor shell of sea.
But is fair in its degree.
'Tis not pride, this vaunt of beauty;
Well she 'quits her trust of duty;
And, amid her gorgeous state,
Bright, and bland, and delicate,
Ever beaming from her face
Praise of a Father's love we trace.
Ladies, shrinking from the view
       Of the prying day,
In tranquil diligence pursue
       Their heaven-appointed way.
Noiseless duties, silent cares, ·
Mercies lighting unawares,
Modest influence working good,
Gifts, by the keen heart understood,
Such as viewless spirits might give,
These they love, in these they live.—
Mighty Nature speeds her through
Her daily toils in silence too:
Calmly rolls her giant spheres,
Sheds by stealth her dew's kind tears;
Cheating sage's vex'd pursuit,
Churns the sap, matures the fruit,
And, her deft hand still concealing,
Kindles motion, life, and feeling.

Ladies love to laugh and sing,
       To rouse the chord's full sound,
Or to join the festive ring
       Where dancers gather round.

Not a sight so fair on earth,
As a lady's graceful mirth;
Not a sound so chasing pain,
As a lady's thrilling strain.—
Nor is Nature left behind
In her lighter moods of mind;
Calm her duties to fulfil,
In her glee a prattler still.
Bird and beast of every sort
Hath its antic and its sport;
Chattering brook, and dancing gnat,
Subtle cry of evening bat,
Moss uncouth, and twigs grotesque,
These are Nature's picturesque.

Where the birth of Poesy?
    Its fancy and its fire?
Nature earth, and sea, and sky,
    Fervid thoughts inspire.
Where do wealth and power find rest,
When hopes have fail'd, or toil oppress'd?
Parks, and lawns, and deer, and trees,
Nature's work, restore them ease.—
Rare the rich, the gifted rare,—
Where shall work-day souls repair,
Unennobled, unrefined,
From the rude world and unkind?
Who shall friend their lowly lot?
High-born Nature answers not.
Leave her in her starry dome.
Seek we lady-lighted home.
Nature 'mid the spheres bears sway,
Ladies rule where hearts obey.

                              Oxford.
                    February 4, 1829.

XII.

OPUSCULUM.

FOR A VERY SMALL ALBUM.

FAIR Cousin, thy page
is small to encage
the thoughts which engage
the mind of a sage,
 such as I am;

'Twere in teaspoon to take
the whole Genevese lake,
or a lap-dog to make
the white Elephant sac-
 -red in Siam.

Yet inadequate though
to the terms strange and so-
-lemn that figures in po-
-lysyllabical row
 in a treatise;

Still, true words and plain,
of the heart, not the brain,
in affectionate strain,
this book to contain
 very meet is.

So I promise to be
a good Cousin to thee,
and to keep safe the se-
cret I heard, although e-
        -v'ry one know it;

With a lyrical air
my kind thoughts I would dare,
and offer whate'er
beseems the news, were
        I a poet.

Brighton.
April, 1829.

XIII.

A VOICE FROM AFAR.

WEEP not for me:—
Be blithe as wont, nor tinge with gloom
The stream of love that circles home,
          Light hearts and free!
Joy in the gifts Heaven's bounty lends;
      Nor miss my face, dear friends!

I still am near,—
Watching the smiles I prized on earth,
Your converse mild, your blameless mirth;
          Now too I hear
Of whisper'd sounds the tale complete,
      Low prayers, and musings sweet.

A sea before
The Throne is spread:—its pure still glass
Pictures all earth-scenes as they pass.
          We, on its shore,
Share, in the bosom of our rest,
      God's knowledge, and are blest.

Horsepath.
September 29, 1829.

XIV.

THE HIDDEN ONES.

HID are the saints of God;—
Uncertified by high angelic sign;
Nor raiment soft, nor empire's golden rod
    Marks them divine.
Theirs but the unbought air, earth's parent sod
    And the sun's smile benign;—
Christ rears His throne within the secret heart,
    From the haughty world apart.

They gleam amid the night,
Chill sluggish mists stifling the heavenly ray;
Fame chants the while,—old history trims his light,
    Aping the day;
In vain! staid look, loud voice, and reason's might
    Forcing its learned way,
Blind characters! these aid us not to trace
    Christ and His princely race.

Yet not all-hid from those
Who watch to see;—'neath their dull guise of earth,
Bright bursting gleams unwittingly disclose
    Their heaven-wrought birth.
Meekness, love, patience, faith's serene repose;
    And the soul's tutor'd mirth,
Bidding the slow heart dance, to prove her power
    O'er self in its proud hour.

These are the chosen few,
The remnant fruit of largely-scatter'd grace,
God sows in waste, to reap whom He foreknew
    Of man's cold race;
Counting on wills perverse, in His clear view
    Of boundless time and space,
He waits, by scant return for treasures given,
    To fill the thrones of heaven.

Lord! who can trace but Thou
The strife obscure, 'twixt sin's soul-thralling spell
And Thy keen Spirit, now quench'd, reviving now?
    Or who can tell,
Why pardon's seal stands sure on David's brow,
    Why Saul and Demas fell?
Oh! lest our frail hearts in the annealing break,
    Help, for Thy mercy's sake!

Horsepath.
September, 1829.

XV.

A THANKSGIVING.

"Thou in faithfulness hast afflicted me."

LORD, in this dust Thy sovereign voice
　　First quicken'd love divine;
I am all Thine,—Thy care and choice,
　　My very praise is Thine.

I praise Thee, while Thy providence
　　In childhood frail I trace,
For blessings given, ere dawning sense
　　Could seek or scan Thy grace;

Blessings in boyhood's marvelling hour,
　　Bright dreams, and fancyings strange;
Blessings, when reason's awful power
　　Gave thought a bolder range;

Blessings of friends, which to my door
　　Unask'd, unhoped, have come;
And, choicer still, a countless store
　　Of eager smiles at home.

Yet, Lord, in memory's fondest place
　　I shrine those seasons sad,
When, looking up, I saw Thy face
　　In kind austereness clad.

I would not miss one sigh or tear,
   Heart-pang, or throbbing brow;
Sweet was the chastisement severe,
   And sweet its memory now.

Yes! let the fragrant scars abide,
   Love-tokens in Thy stead,
Faint shadows of the spear-pierced side
   And thorn-encompass'd head

And such Thy tender force be still,
   When self would swerve or stray,
Shaping to truth the froward will
   Along Thy narrow way.

Deny me wealth; far, far remove
   The lure of power or name;
Hope thrives in straits, in weakness love,
   And faith in this world's shame.

                              Oxford.
                    October 20, 1829.

XVI.

MONKS.

FOR ANOTHER SMALL ALBUM.

(With lines on hinges to fit it.)

WHY, dear Cousin,
                why
Ask for verses,
when a poet's
fount of song is
                dry?
Or, if aught be
                there,
Harsh and chill, it
ill may touch the
hand of lady
                fair.
Who can perfumed waters
                bring
From a convent
                spring
"Monks in the olden
                time,
"They were rhymesters?"—
they were rhymesters,
but in Latin
                rhyme.
Monks in the days of
                old

Lived in secret,
in the Church's
kindly-sheltering
                    fold
No bland meditators
                    they
Of a courtly
                    lay.
"They had visions
                    bright?"—
they had visions,
yet not sent in
slumbers soft and
                    light.
No! a lesson
                    stern
First by vigils,
fast, and penance
theirs it was to
                    learn.
This their soul-ennobling
                    gain,
Joys wrought out by
                    pain.

"When from home they
                    stirr'd,
"Sweet their voices?"—
still, a blessing
closed their merriest
                    word;
And their gayest
                    smile
Told of musings
solitary,

and the hallow'd
                aisle.
"Songsters?"—hark! they answer!
                round
Plaintive chantings
                sound!

Grey his cowlèd
                vest,
Whose strong heart has
pledged his service
to the cloister
                blest.
Duly garb'd is
                he,
As the frost-work
gems the branches
of yon stately
                tree.
'Tis a danger-thwarting
                spell,
And it fits me
                well!

Oxford.
December, 1829.

XVII.

EPIPHANY-EVE.

A BIRTHDAY OFFERING.

BIRTHDAY gifts, with the early year,
Lo! we bring thee, Mary dear!
Prayer and praise upon thy death
Twined together in a wreath,
Grief and gladness, such as may
Suit a solemn holiday.
Christmas snow, for maiden's bloom
Blanched in winter's sudden tomb;
Christmas berries, His red token
Who that grave's stern seal hath broken;
These for thee the faithful heart,
Due mementos, sets apart.

'Twas a fast, that Eve of sorrow,
Herald veil'd of glorious morrow.
Speechless we sat; and watch'd, to know
How it would be; but time moved slow,
Along that day of sacred woe.
Then came the Feast, and we were told
    Bravely of our best to bring.
Myrrh, and frankincense, and gold,
    As our tribute to our King.

Dearest, gentlest, purest, best!
Deep is thy mysterious rest,
Now the solemn hours are over

And the Angels round thee hover,
With the fanning of their wings
Keeping time to one who sings
Of high themes consolatory,
Of the All-loving and His glory,
Of the age that has no ending,
Of the day of thy ascending
From those shades of paradise
To the bright supernal skies.

Thinkest of us, dearest, ever?
Ah! so be it nought can sever
Spirit and life, the past and present,
Still we yield thee musings pleasant.
—God above, and we below;—
So thought ranges, to and fro.
He, in sooth, by tutorings mild,
From the rude clay shaped His child,
Fiery trial, anguish chill,
Served not here His secret will;
But His voice was low and tender,
And so true was thy surrender,
That the work in haste was done,
Grace and nature blent in one.—
Harmless thus, and not unmeet,
To kiss the dear prints of thy feet,
Tracing thus the narrow road
All must tread, and Christ has trod.

Loveliest, meekest, blithest, kindest!
Lead! we seek the home thou findest!
Though thy name to us most dear,
Go! we would not have thee here.
Lead, a guiding beacon bright
To travellers on the Eve of Light.
Welcome aye thy Star before us,

Bring it grief or gladness o'er us;—
Keen regret and tearful yearning,
Whiles unfelt, and whiles returning;—
Or more gracious thoughts abiding,
Fever-quelling, sorrow-chiding;—
Or, when day-light blessings fail,
Transport fresh as spice-fraught gale,
Sparks from thee, which oft have lighted
Weary heart and hope benighted.

I this monument would raise,
Distant from the public gaze.
Few will see it;—few e'er knew thee;
But their beating hearts pursue thee,—
And their eyes fond thoughts betoken,
Though thy name be seldom spoken.
Pass on, stranger, and despise it!
These will read, and these will prize it.

Oxford.
January 5, 1830.

XVIII.

THE WINTER FLOWER.

A BIRTHDAY OFFERING.

(For Music.)

BLOOM, beloved Flower!—
  Unknown;—'tis no matter.
Courts glitter brief hour,
  Crowds can but flatter.

Plants in the garden
  See best the Sun's glory;
They miss the green sward in
  A conservatory.

—PRIZED WHERE'ER KNOWN.—
  Sure this is a blessing,
Outrings the loud tone
  Of the dull world's caressing.

Oxford.
December 30, 1830.

XIX.

KIND REMEMBRANCES.

'TIS long, dear Annie, since we met,
  Yet deem not that my heart,
For all that absence, can forget
  A kinsman's pious part.

How oft on thee, a sufferer mild,
  My kindly thoughts I turn,
He knows, upon whose altar piled
  The prayers of suppliants burn.

I love thy name, admiring all
  Thy sacred heaven-sent pain;
I love it, for it seems to call
  The Lost to earth again.

Can I forget, *she* to thy need
  Her ministry supplied,
Who now, from mortal duty freed,
  Serves at the Virgin's side?

What would'st thou more? Upon thy head
  A two-fold grace is pour'd;—
Both in thyself, and for the dead,
  A witness of thy Lord!

Oxford.
March, 1831.

XX.

SEEDS IN THE AIR.

FOR AN ALBUM.

"Igneus est ollis vigor, et coelestis origo
Seminibus."

COULD I hit on a theme
　To fashion my verse on,
Not long would I seem
　A lack-courtesy person.
But I have not the skill,
　Nor talisman strong,
To summon at will
　The Spirit of song.—
Bright thoughts are roaming
　Unseen in the air;
Like comets, their coming
　Is sudden and rare.
They strike, and they enter,
　And light up the brain,
Which thrills to its centre
　With rapturous pain.
Where the chance-seed
　Is piously nursed,
Brighter succeed
　In the path of the first.—
One sighs to the Muse,
　Or the sweet nightingale,

One sips the night-dews
  Which moon-beams exhale.
All this is a fiction;
  I never could find
A suitable friction
  To frenzy my mind.
What use are empirics?
  No gas on their shelf
Can make one spout lyrics
  In spite of oneself!

Dartington.
July 18, 1831.

XXI.

THE PILGRIM.

FOR AN ALBUM.

THERE stray'd awhile, amid the woods of Dart,
    One who could love them, but who durst not love.
A vow had bound him, ne'er to give his heart
    To streamlet bright, or soft secluded grove.
    'Twas a hard humbling task, onwards to move
His easy-captured eyes from each fair spot,
    With unattach'd and lonely step to rove
O'er happy meads, which soon its print forgot:—
Yet kept he safe his pledge, prizing his pilgrim-lot.

Dartington.
July 21, 1831.

XXII.

HOME.

WHERE'ER I roam in this fair English land,
 The vision of a Temple meets my eyes:
 Modest without; within, all-glorious rise
Its love-encluster'd columns, and expand
Their slender arms. Like olive-plants they stand
 Each answ'ring each, in home's soft sympathies,
 Sisters and brothers. At the altar sighs
Parental fondness, and with anxious hand
Tenders its offering of young vows and prayers.
The same, and not the same, go where I will,
The vision beams! ten thousand shrines, all one.
Dear fertile soil! what foreign culture bears
Such fruit! And I through distant climes may run
My weary round, yet miss thy likeness still.

Oxford.
November 16, 1832.

XXIII.

THE BRAND OF CAIN.

I BEAR upon my brow the sign
  Of sorrow and of pain;
Alas! no hopeful cross is mine,
  It is the brand of Cain.

The course of passion, and the fret
  Of godless hope and fear,—
Toil, care, and guilt,—their hues have set,
  And fix'd their sternness there.

Saviour! wash out the imprinted shame;
  That I no more may pine,
Sin's martyr, though not meet to claim
  Thy cross, a saint of Thine.

Oxford.
November 18, 1832.

XXIV.

ZEAL AND LOVE.

AND would'st thou reach, rash scholar mine,
　　Love's high unruffled state?
Awake! thy easy dreams resign,
　　First learn thee how to hate:—

Hatred of sin, and Zeal, and Fear,
　　Lead up the Holy Hill;
Track them, till Charity appear
　　A self-denial still.

Dim is the philosophic flame,
　　By thoughts severe unfed:
Book-lore ne'er served, when trial came,
　　Nor gifts, when faith was dead.

Oxford.
November 20, 1832.

XXV.

PERSECUTION.

"And the woman fled into the wilderness."

SAY, who is he in deserts seen,
    Or at the twilight hour?
Of garb austere, and dauntless mien,
Measured in speech, in purpose keen,
Calm as in Heaven he had been,
    Yet blithe when perils lower.

My Holy Mother made reply,
    "Dear child, it is my Priest.
The world has cast me forth, and I
Dwell with wild earth and gusty sky;
He bears to men my mandates high,
    And works my sage behest.

"Another day, dear child, and thou
    Shalt join his sacred band.
Ah! well I deem, thou shrinkest now
From urgent rule, and severing vow;
Gay hopes flit round, and light thy brow:
    Time hath a taming hand!"

Oxford.
November 22, 1832.

XXVI.

ZEAL AND PURITY.

"Come with me, and see my zeal for the Lord."

THOU to wax fierce
   In the cause of the Lord,
To threat and to pierce
   With the heavenly sword!
Anger and Zeal,
   And the Joy of the brave,
Who bade *thee* to feel,
   Sin's slave.

The Altar's pure flame
   Consumes as it soars:
Faith meetly may blame,
   For it serves and adores.
Thou warnest and smitest!
Yet Christ must atone
   For a soul that thou slightest—
     Thine own.

Oxford.
November 23, 1832.

XXVII.

THE GIFT OF PERSEVERANCE.

ONCE, as I brooded o'er my guilty state,
   A fever seized me, duties to devise,
   To buy me interest in my Saviour's eyes;
Not that His love I would extenuate,
But scourge and penance, masterful self-hate,
   Or gift of cost, served by an artifice
   To quell my restless thoughts and envious sighs
And doubts, which fain heaven's peace would antedate.
Thus as I tossed, He said:—"E'en holiest deeds
Shroud not the soul from God, nor soothe its needs;
Deny thee thine own fears, and wait the end!"
Stern lesson! Let me con it day by day,
And learn to kneel before the Omniscient Ray,
Nor shrink, when Truth's avenging shafts descend!

Oxford.
November 23, 1832.

XXVIII.

THE SIGN OF THE CROSS.

WHENE'ER across this sinful flesh of mine
  I draw the Holy Sign,
All good thoughts stir within me, and renew
  Their slumbering strength divine;
Till there springs up a courage high and true
  To suffer and to do.

And who shall say, but hateful spirits around,
  For their brief hour unbound,
Shudder to see, and wail their overthrow?
  While on far heathen ground
Some lonely Saint hails the fresh odour, though
  Its source he cannot know.

Oxford.
November 25, 1832.

XXIX.

BONDAGE.

O PROPHET, tell me not of peace,
  Or Christ's all-loving deeds;
Death only can from sin release,
  And death to judgment leads.

Thou from thy birth hast set thy face
  Towards thy Redeemer Lord;
To tend and deck His holy place
  And note His secret word.

I ne'er shall reach Heaven's glorious path;
  Yet haply tears may stay
The purpose of His instant wrath,
  And slake the fiery day.

Then plead for one who cannot pray,
  Whose faith is but despair,
Who hates his heart, nor puts away
  The sin that rankles there.[1]

Iffley.
November 28, 1832.

[1] The last stanza is not as it stood originally. In this and other alterations in these compositions, care has been taken not to introduce ideas foreign to the Author's sentiments at the time of writing.

XXX.

THE SCARS OF SIN.

My smile is bright, my glance is free,
　My voice is calm and clear;
Dear friend, I seem a type to thee
　Of holy love and fear.

But I am scann'd by eyes unseen,
　And these no saint surround;
They mete what is by what has been,
　And joy the lost is found.

Erst my good Angel shrank to see
　My thoughts and ways of ill;
And now he scarce dare gaze on me,
　Scar-seam'd and crippled still.

Iffley.
November 29, 1832.

XXXI.

ANGELIC GUIDANCE.

ARE these the tracks of some unearthly Friend,
  His foot-prints, and his vesture-skirts of light,
  Who, as I talk with men, conforms aright
Their sympathetic words, or deeds that blend
With my hid thought;—or stoops him to attend
  My doubtful-pleading grief;—or blunts the might
  Of ill I see not;—or in dreams of night
Figures the scope, in which what is will end?
Were I Christ's own, then fitly might I call
That vision real; for to the thoughtful mind
That walks with Him, He half unveils His face;
But, when on earth-stain'd souls such tokens fall.
These dare not claim as theirs what there they find,
Yet not all hopeless, eye His boundless grace.

Whitchurch.
December 3, 1832.

XXXII.

SUBSTANCE AND SHADOW.

THEY do but grope in learning's pedant round,
   Who on the fantasies of sense bestow
   An idol substance, bidding us bow low
Before those shades of being which are found,
Stirring or still, on man's brief trial-ground;
   As if such shapes and moods, which come and go,
   Had aught of Truth or Life in their poor show,
To sway or judge, and skill to sane or wound.
Son of immortal seed, high-destined Man!
Know thy dread gift,—a creature, yet a cause:
Each mind is its own centre, and it draws
Home to itself, and moulds in its thought's span
All outward things, the vassals of its will,
Aided by Heaven, by earth unthwarted still.

Falmouth.
December 7, 1832.

XXXIII.

WANDERINGS.

ERE yet I left home's youthful shrine,
  My heart and hope were stored
Where first I caught the rays divine,
  And drank the Eternal Word.

I went afar; the world unroll'd
  Her many-pictured page;
I stored the marvels which she told,
  And trusted to her gage.

Her pleasures quaff'd I sought awhile
  The scenes I prized before;
But parent's praise and sister's smile
  Stirr'd my cold heart no more.

So ever sear, so ever cloy
  Earth's favours as they fade;
Since Adam lost for one fierce joy
  His Eden's sacred shade.

Off the Lizard.
December 8, 1832.

XXXIV.

THE SAINT AND THE HERO.

O AGED Saint! far off I heard
  The praises of thy name;—
Thy deed of power, thy prudent word,
  Thy zeal's triumphant flame.

I came and saw; and, having seen,
  Weak heart, I drew offence
From thy prompt smile, thy simple mien,
  Thy lowly diligence.

The Saint's is not the Hero's praise;—
  This I have found, and learn
Nor to malign Heaven's humblest ways,
  Nor its least boon to spurn.

Bay of Biscay.
December 10, 1832.

XXXV.

PRIVATE JUDGMENT.

POOR wand'rers, ye are sore distress'd
To find that path which Christ has bless'd,
    Track'd by His saintly throng;
Each claims to trust his own weak will,
Blind idol!—so ye languish still,
    All wranglers and all wrong.

He saw of old, and met your need,
Granting you prophets of His creed,
    The throes of fear to swage;
They fenced the rich bequest He made,
And sacred hands have safe convey'd
    Their charge from age to age.

Wand'rers! come home! obey the call!
A Mother pleads, who ne'er let fall
    One grain of Holy Truth;
Warn you and win she shall and must,
For now she lifts her from the dust,
    To reign as in her youth.

Off Cape Ortegal.
December 11, 1832.

XXXVI.

THE WATCHMAN.

(A Song.)

FAINT not, and fret not, for threaten'd woe,
   Watchman on Truth's grey height!
Few though the faithful, and fierce though the foe
   Weakness is aye Heaven's might.

Infidel Ammon and niggard Tyre,
   Ill-fitted pair, unite;
Some work for love, and some work for hire,
   But weakness shall be Heaven's might.

Eli's feebleness, Saul's black wrath,
   May aid Ahithophel's spite;
And prayers from Gerizim, and curses from Gath—
   Our weakness shall prove Heaven's might.

Quail not, and quake not, thou Warder bold,
   Be there no friend in sight;
Turn thee to question the days of old,
   When weakness was aye Heaven's might.

Moses was one, but he stay'd the sin
   Of the host, in the Presence bright;
And Elias scorn'd the Carmel din,
   When Baal would match Heaven's might.

Time's years are many, Eternity one,
    And one is the Infinite;
The chosen are few, few the deeds well done,
    For scantness is still Heaven's might.

At Sea.
December 12, 1832.

XXXVII.

THE ISLES OF THE SIRENS.

CEASE, Stranger, cease those piercing notes,
  The craft of Siren choirs;
Hush the seductive voice, that floats
  Upon the languid wires.

Music's ethereal fire was given
  Not to dissolve our clay,
But draw Promethean beams from Heaven.
  And purge the dross away.

Weak self! with thee the mischief lies,
  Those throbs a tale disclose;
Nor age nor trial has made wise
  The Man of many woes.

Off Lisbon.
December 13, 1832.

XXXVIII.

ABSOLUTION.

O FATHER, list a sinner's call!
Fain would I hide from man my fall—
    But I must speak, or faint—
I cannot wear guilt's silent thrall:
    Cleanse me, kind Saint!

"Sinner ne'er blunted yet sin's goad;
Speed thee, my son, a safer road,
    And sue His pardoning smile
Who walk'd woe's depths, bearing man's load
    Of guilt the while."

Yet raise a mitigating hand,
And minister some potion bland,
    Some present fever-stay!
Lest one for whom His work was plann'd
    Die from dismay.

"Look not to me—no grace is mine;
But I can lift the Mercy-sign.
    This wouldst thou? Let it be!
Kneel down, and take the word divine,
    ABSOLVO TE."

Off Cape St. Vincent.
December 14, 1832.

XXXIX.

MEMORY.

MY home is now a thousand miles away;
   Yet in my thoughts its every image fair
   Rises as keen, as I still linger'd there,
And, turning me, could all I loved survey.
And so, upon Death's unaverted day,
   As I speed upwards, I shall on me bear,
   And in no breathless whirl, the things that were.
And duties given, and ends I did obey.
And, when at length I reach the Throne of Power
Ah! still unscared, I shall in fulness see
The vision of my past innumerous deeds,
My deep heart-courses, and their motive-seeds,
So to gaze on till the red dooming hour.
Lord, in that strait, the Judge! remember me!

Off Cape Trafalgar.
December 15, 1832.

XL.

THE HAVEN.

WHENCE is this awe, by stillness spread
    O'er the world-fretted soul?
Wave rear'd on wave its godless head
While my keen bark, by breezes sped,
Dash'd fiercely through the ocean bed,
    And chafed towards its goal.

But now there reigns so deep a rest,
    That I could almost weep.
Sinner! thou hast in this rare guest
Of Adam's peace a figure blest;
'Tis Eden neared, though not possess'd
    Which cherub-flames still keep.

Gibraltar.
December 16, 1832.

XLI.

A WORD IN SEASON.

O LORD! when sin's close-marshall'd line
   Assails Thy witness on his way,
How should he raise Thy glorious sign,
   And how Thy truth display?

Thy holy Paul, with soul of flame,
    Rose on Mars' hill, a soldier lone;
Shall I thus speak th' Atoning Name,
   Though with a heart stone?

"Not so," He said: "hush thee, and seek,
   With thoughts in prayer and watchful eyes,
My seasons sent for thee to speak,
   And use them as they rise."

                      Gibraltar.
                December 17, 1832.

XLII.

FAIR WORDS.

THY words are good, and freely given,
     As though thou felt them true;
Friend, think thee well, to hell or heaven
     A serious heart is due.

It pains thee sore, man's will should swerve
     In his true path divine;
And yet thou ventur'st nought to serve
     Thy neighbour's weal nor time.

Beware! such words may once be said.
     Where shame and fear unite;
But, spoken twice, they mark instead
     A sin against the light.

Gibraltar.
December 17, 1832.

XLIII.

ENGLAND.

TYRE of the West, and glorying in the name
   More than in Faith's pure fame!
O trust not crafty fort nor rock renown'd
   Earn'd upon hostile ground;
Wielding Trade's master-keys, at thy proud will
To lock or loose its waters, England! trust not still.

Dread thine own power! Since haughty Babel's prime,
   High towers have been man's crime.
Since her hoar age, when the huge moat lay bare,
   Strongholds have been man's snare.
Thy nest is in the crags; ah! refuge frail!
Mad counsel in its hour, or traitors, will prevail.

He who scann'd Sodom for His righteous men
   Still spares thee for thy ten;
But, should rash tongues the Bride of Heaven defy,
   He will not pass thee by;
For, as earth's kings welcome their spotless guest,
So gives He them by turn, to suffer or be blest.

At Sea.
December 18, 1832.

XLIV.

MOSES.

MOSES, the patriot fierce, became
  The meekest man on earth,
To show us how love's quick'ning flame
  Can give our souls new birth.

Moses, the man of meekest heart,
  Lost Canaan by self-will,
To show, where Grace has done its part,
  How sin defiles us still.

Thou, who hast taught me in Thy fear,
  Yet seest me frail at best,
O grant me loss with Moses here.
  To gain his future rest!

At Sea.
December 19, 1832.

XLV.

THE PATIENT CHURCH.

BIDE thou thy time!
Watch with meek eyes the race of pride and crime,
Sit in the gate, and be the heathen's jest,
    Smiling and self-possest.
O thou, to whom is pledged a victor's sway,
    Bide thou the victor's day!

Think on the sin[1]
That reap'd the unique seed, and toil'd to win
Foul history-marks at Bethel and at Dan;
    No blessing, but a ban;
Whilst the wise Shepherd[2] hid his heaven-told fate,
    Nor reck'd a tyrant's hate.

Such loss is gain;
Wait the bright Advent that shall loose thy chain!
E'en now the shadows break, and gleams divine
    Edge the dim distant line.
When thrones are trembling, and earth's fat ones
    quail,
    True Seed! thou shalt prevail!

Off Algiers.
December 20, 1832.

---

[1] Jeroboam.
[2] David.

XLVI.

JEREMIAH.

"O that I had in the wilderness a lodging-place of wayfaring men; that I might leave my people, and go from them!"

"WOE'S me!" the peaceful prophet cried,
  "Spare me this troubled life;
To stem man's wrath, to school his pride,
  To head the sacred strife!

"O place me in some silent vale,
  Where groves and flowers abound;
Nor eyes that grudge, nor tongues that rail,
  Vex the truth-haunted ground!"

If his meek spirit err'd, opprest
  That God denied repose,
What sin is ours, to whom Heaven's rest
  Is pledged, to heal earth's woes?

Off Galita.
December 22, 1832.

XLVII.

PENANCE.

MORTAL! if e'er thy spirits faint,
    By grief or pain opprest,
Seek not vain hope, or sour complaint,
    To cheer or ease thy breast:

But view thy bitterest pangs as sent
    A shadow of that doom,
Which is the soul's just punishment
    In its own guilt's true home.

Be thine own judge; hate thy proud heart;
    And while the sad drops flow,
E'en let thy will attend the smart,
    And sanctify thy woe.

Off Pantellaria.
December 23, 1832.

XLVIII.

THE COURSE OF TRUTH.

"Him God raised up the third day, and showed Him openly,
not to all the people, but unto witnesses chosen before of God."

WHEN royal Truth, released from mortal throes,
Burst His brief slumber, and triumphant rose,
  Ill had the Holiest sued
  A patron multitude,
 Or courted Tetrarch's eye, or claim'd to rule
By the world's winning grace, or proofs from learned
  school.

 But, robing Him in viewless air, He told
 His secret to a few of meanest mould;
  They in their turn imparted
  The gift to men pure-hearted.
 While the brute many heard His mysteries high,
As some strange fearful tongue, and crouch'd, they
  knew not why.

Still is the might of Truth, as it has been:
Lodged in the few, obey'd, and yet unseen.
  Rear'd on lone heights, and rare,
  His saints their watch-flame bear,
 And the mad world sees the wide-circling blaze,
Vain searching whence it streams, and how to
  quench its rays.

        Malta.
      December 24, 1832.

XLIX.

CHRISTMAS WITHOUT CHRIST.

HOW can I keep my Christmas feast
  In its due festive show,
Reft of the sight of the High Priest
  From whom its glories flow?

I hear the tuneful bells around,
  The blessèd towers I see:
A stranger on a foreign ground,
  They peal a fast for me.

O Britons! now so brave and high,
  How will ye weep the day
When Christ in judgment passes by,
  And calls the Bride away!

Your Christmas then will lose its mirth,
  Your Easter lose its bloom:
Abroad, a scene of strife and dearth;
  Within, a cheerless home!

Malta.
December 25, 1832.

L.

SLEEPLESSNESS.

UNWEARIED God, before whose face
　　The night is clear as day,
Whilst we, poor worms, o'er life's scant race
　　Now creep, and now delay,
We with death's foretaste alternate
Our labour's dint and sorrow's weight,
Save in that fever-troubled state
　　When pain or care has sway.

Dread Lord! Thy glory, watchfulness,
　　Is but disease in man;
We to our cost our bounds transgress
　　In Thy eternal plan:
Pride grasps the powers by Thee display'd,
Yet ne'er the rebel effort made
But fell beneath the sudden shade
　　Of nature's withering ban.

Malta.
December 26, 1832.

LI.

ABRAHAM.

THE better portion didst thou choose, Great Heart.
  Thy God's first choice, and pledge of Gentile grace!
  Faith's truest type, he with unruffled face
Bore the world's smile, and bade her slaves depart;
Whether, a trader, with no trader's art,
  He buys in Canaan his last resting-place,—
  Or freely yields rich Siddim's ample space,—
Or braves the rescue, and the battle's smart,
Yet scorns the heathen gifts of those he saved.
O happy in their soul's high solitude,
Who commune thus with God, and not with earth!
Amid the scoffings of the wealth-enslaved,
A ready prey, as though in absent mood
They calmly move, nor reck the unmanner'd mirth.

At Sea.
December 27, 1832.

LII.

THE GREEK FATHERS.

LET heathen sing thy heathen praise,
Fall'n Greece! the thought of holier days
   In my sad heart abides;
For sons of thine in Truth's first hour
Were tongues and weapons of His power
Born of the Spirit's fiery shower,
   Our fathers and our guides.

All thine is Clement's varied page;
And Dionysius, ruler sage,
   In days of doubt and pain;
And Origen with eagle eye;
And saintly Basil's purpose high
To smite imperial heresy,
   And cleanse the Altar's stain.

From thee the glorious preacher came,
With soul of zeal and lips of flame,
   A court's stern martyr-guest;
And thine, O inexhaustive race!
Was Nazianzen's heaven-taught grace;
And royal-hearted Athanase,
   With Paul's own mantle blest.

Off Zante.
December 28, 1832.

LIII.

THE WITNESS.

HOW shall a child of God fufil
His vow to cleanse his soul from ill,
And raise on high his baptism-light,
Like Aaron's seed in vestment white
And holy-hearted Nazarite?

First, let him shun the haunts of vice,
Sin-feast, or heathen sacrifice;
Fearing the board of wealthy pride,
Or heretic, self-trusting guide,
Or where the adulterer's smiles preside.

Next, as he threads the maze of men,
Aye must he lift his witness, when
A sin is spoke in Heaven's dread face.
And none at hand of higher grace
The Cross to carry in his place.

But if he hears and sits him still,
First, he will lose his hate of ill;
Next, fear of sinning, after hate;
Small sins his heart then desecrate;
And last, despair persuades to great.

                              Off Ithaca.
                         December 30, 1832.

LIV.

THE DEATH OF MOSES.

MY Father's hope! my childhood's dream!
  The promise from on high!
Long waited for! its glories beam
  Now when my death is nigh.

My death is come, but not decay;
  Nor eye nor mind is dim;
The keenness of youth's vigorous day
  Thrills in each nerve and limb.

Blest scene! thrice welcome after toil—
  If no deceit I view;
O might my lips but press the soil,
  And prove the vision true!

Its glorious heights, its wealthy plains,
  Its many-tinted groves,
They call! but He my steps restrains
  Who chastens whom He loves.

Ah! now they melt . . . they are but shades.
  I die!—yet is no rest,
O Lord! in store, since Canaan fades
  But seen, and not possest?

Off Ithaca.
December 30, 1832.

LV.

MELCHIZEDEK.

"Without father, without mother, without descent; having
neither beginning of days, nor end of life."

THRICE bless'd are they, who feel their loneliness;
　To whom nor voice of friends nor pleasant scene
　Brings aught on which the sadden'd heart can lean;
Yea, the rich earth, garb'd in her daintiest dress
Of light and joy, doth but the more oppress,
　Claiming responsive smiles and rapture high;
　Till, sick at heart, beyond the veil they fly,
Seeking His Presence, who alone can bless.
Such, in strange days, the weapons of Heaven's grace;
When, passing o'er the high-born Hebrew line,
He moulds the vessel of His vast design;
Fatherless, homeless, reft of age and place,
Sever'd from earth, and careless of its wreck,
Born through long woe His rare Melchizedek.

Corfu.
January 5, 1833.

LVI.

CORCYRA.

I SAT beneath an olive's branches grey,
 And gazed upon the site of a lost town,
 By sage and poet raised to long renown;
Where dwelt a race that on the sea held sway,
And, restless as its waters, forced a way
 For civil strife a hundred states to drown.
 That multitudinous stream we now note down
As though one life, in birth and in decay.
But is their being's history spent and run,
Whose spirits live in awful singleness,
Each in its self-form'd sphere of light or gloom?
Henceforth, while pondering the fierce deeds then
  done,
Such reverence on me shall its seal impress
As though I corpses saw, and walk'd the tomb.

At Sea.
January 7, 1833.

LVII.

TRANSFIGURATION.

"They glorified God in me."

I SAW thee once and nought discern'd
    For stranger to admire;
A serious aspect, but it burn'd
    With no unearthly fire.

Again I saw, and I confess'd
    Thy speech was rare and high;
And yet it vex'd my burden'd breast,
    And scared, I knew not why.

I saw once more, and awe-struck gazed
    On face, and form, and air;
God's living glory round thee blazed—
    A Saint—a Saint was there!

Off Zante.
January 8, 1833.

LVIII.

BEHIND THE VEIL.

BANISH'D the House of sacred rest.
  Amid a thoughtless throng,
At length I heard its creed confess'd,
  And knelt the saints among.

Artless his strain and unadorn'd.
  Who spoke Christ's message there;
But what at home I might have scorn'd.
  Now charm'd my famish'd ear.

Lord, grant me this abiding grace,
  Thy Word and sons to know;
To pierce the veil on Moses' face.
  Although his speech be slow.

At Sea.
January 9, 1833.

LIX.

JUDGMENT.

If e'er I fall beneath Thy rod,
　　As through life's snares I go,
Save me from David's lot, O God!
　　And choose Thyself the woe.

How should I face Thy plagues? which scare,
　　And haunt, and stun, until
The heart or sinks in mute despair,
　　Or names a random ill.

If else . . . then guide in David's path,
　　Who chose the holier pain;
Satan and man are tools of wrath,
　　An Angel's scourge is gain.

Off Malta.
January 10, 1833.

LX.

SENSITIVENESS.

TIME was, I shrank from what was right
    From fear of what was wrong;
I would not brave the sacred fight,
    Because the foe was strong.

But now I cast that finer sense
    And sorer shame aside;
Such dread of sin was indolence,
    Such aim at Heaven was pride.

So, when my Saviour calls, I rise,
    And calmly do my best;
Leaving to Him, with silent eyes
    Of hope and fear, the rest.

I step, I mount where He has led;
    Men count my haltings o'er;—
I know them; yet, though self I dread,
    I love His precept more.

Lazaret, Malta.
January 15, 1833.

LXI.

DAVID AND JONATHAN.

"Thy love to me was wonderful, passing the love of women."

O HEART of fire! misjudged by wilful man,
   Thou flower of Jesse's race!
What woe was thine, when thou and Jonathan
   Last greeted face to face!
He doom'd to die, thou on us to impress
The portent of a blood-stain'd holiness.

Yet it was well:—for so, 'mid cares of rule
   And crime's encircling tide,
A spell was o'er thee, zealous one, to cool
   Earth-joy and kingly pride;
With battle-scene and pageant, prompt to blend
The pale calm spectre of a blameless friend.

Ah! had he lived, before thy throne to stand,
   Thy spirit keen and high
Sure it had snapp'd in twain love's slender band,
   So dear in memory;
Paul, of his comrade reft, the warning gives,—
He lives to us who dies, he is but lost who lives.

Lazaret, Malta.
January 16, 1833.

LXII.

HUMILIATION.

I HAVE been honour'd and obey'd,
   I have met scorn and slight;
And my heart loves earth's sober shade,
   More than her laughing light.

For what is rule but a sad weight
   Of duty and a snare?
What meanness, but with happier fate
   The Saviour's Cross to share?

This my hid choice, if not from heaven,
   Moves on the heavenward line;
Cleanse it, good Lord, from earthly leaven,
   And make it simply Thine.

Lazaret, Malta.
January 16, 1833.

LXIII.

THE CALL OF DAVID.

"And the Lord said, Arise, anoint him, for this is he."

LATEST born of Jesse's race,
Wonder lights thy bashful face,
While the Prophet's gifted oil
Seals thee for a path of toil.
We, thy Angels, circling round thee,
Ne'er shall find thee as we found thee,
When thy faith first brought us near
In thy lion-fight severe.

Go! and mid thy flocks awhile
At thy doom of greatness smile;
Bold to bear God's heaviest load,
Dimly guessing of the road,—
Rocky road, and scarce ascended,
Though thy foot be angel-tended.

Twofold praise thou shalt attain,
In royal court and battle plain;
Then comes heart-ache, care, distress,
Blighted hope, and loneliness;
Wounds from friend and gifts from foe,
Dizzied faith, and guilt, and woe;
Loftiest aims by earth defiled,
Gleams of wisdom sin-beguiled,
Sated power's tyrannic mood,
Counsels shared with men of blood,

Sad success, parental tears,
And a dreary gift of years.

Strange, that guileless face and form
To lavish on the scarring storm!
Yet we take thee in thy blindness.
And we buffet thee in kindness;
Little chary of thy fame,—
Dust unborn may bless or blame,—
But we mould thee for the root
Of man's promised healing Fruit,
And we mould thee hence to rise,
As our brother, to the skies.

Lazaret, Malta.
January 18, 1833.

LXIV.

A BLIGHT.

WHAT time my heart unfolded its fresh leaves
   In springtime gay, and scatter'd flowers around,
   A whisper warn'd of earth's unhealthy ground,
And all that there love's light and pureness
     grieves;
        Sun's ray and canker-worm,
        And sudden-whelming storm;—
But, ah! my self-will smiled, nor reck'd the
     gracious sound.

So now defilement dims life's memory-springs;
   I cannot hear an early-cherish'd strain,
   But first a joy, and then it brings a pain—
Fear, and self-hate, and vain remorseful stings:
        Tears lull my grief to rest,
        Not without hope, this breast
May one day lose its load, and youth yet bloom
     again.

Lazaret, Malta.
January 19, 1833.

LXV.

JOSEPH.

O PUREST Symbol of the Eternal Son!
   Who dwelt in thee, as in some sacred shrine,
   To draw hearts after thee, and make them thine;
Nor parent only by that light was won,
And brethren crouch'd who had in wrath begun,
   But heathen pomp abased her at the sign
   And the hid Presence of a guest divine,
Till a king heard, and all thou bad'st was done.
Then was fulfill'd Nature's dim augury,
That "Wisdom, clad in visible form, would be
So fair, that all must love and bow the knee;"
Lest it might seem, what time the Substance came,
Truth lack'd a sceptre, when It but laid by
Its beaming front, and bore a willing shame.

Lazaret, Malta.
January 20, 1833.

LXVI.

SUPERSTITION.

O LORD and Christ, Thy Children of the South
    So shudder, when they see
The two-edged sword sharp-issuing from Thy
    mouth,
    As to fall back from Thee,
  And cling to charms of man, or heathen rite
To aid them against Thee, Thou Fount of love and
    light!

But I before Thine awful eyes will go
    And firmly fix me there,
In my full shame; not bent my doom to know,
    Not fainting with despair;
  Not fearing less than they, but deeming sure,
If e'en Thy Name shall fail, nought my base heart
    can cure.

Lazaret, Malta.
January 21, 1833.

LXVII.

ISAAC.

MANY the guileless years the Patriarch spent,
 Bless'd in the wife a father's foresight chose;
 Many the prayers and gracious deeds, which rose
Daily thank-offerings from his pilgrim tent.
Yet these, though written in the heavens, are rent
 From out truth's lower roll, which sternly shows
 But one sad trespass at his history's close,
Father's, son's, mother's, and its punishment.
Not in their brightness, but their earthly stains
Are the true seed vouchsafed to earthly eyes.
Sin can read sin, but dimly scans high grace,
So we move heavenward with averted face,
Scared into faith by warning of sin's pains;
And Saints are lower'd, that the world may rise.

Valletta.
January 23, 1833.

LXVIII.

REVERSES.

WHEN mirth is full and free,
Some sudden gloom shall be;
When haughty power mounts high.
The Watcher's axe is nigh.
All growth has bound; when greatest found,
  It hastes to die.

When the rich town, that long
Has lain its huts among,
Uprears its pageants vast,
And vaunts—it shall not last!
Bright tints that shine, are but a sign
  Of summer past.

And when thine eye surveys,
With fond adoring gaze,
And yearning heart thy friend—
Love to its grave doth tend.
All gifts below, save Truth, but grow
  Towards an end.

Valletta.
January 30, 1833.

LXIX.

HOPE.

WE are not children of a guilty sire,
   Since Noe stepp'd from out his wave-toss'd home,
   And a stern baptism flush'd earth's faded bloom.
Not that the heavens then clear'd, or cherub's fire
From Eden's portal did at once retire;
   But thoughts were stirr'd of Him who was to
     come,
   Whose rainbow hues so streak'd the o'ershadowing
     gloom,
That faith could e'en that desolate scene admire.
The Lord has come and gone; and now we wait
The second substance of the deluge type,
When our slight ark shall cross a molten surge;
So, while the gross earth melts, for judgment ripe,
Ne'er with its haughty turrets to emerge,
We shall mount up to Eden's long-lost gate.

Valletta.
February 5, 1833.

LXX.

ST. PAUL AT MELITA.

"And when Paul had gathered a bundle of sticks, and laid them on the fire, there came a viper out of the heat."

SECURE in his prophetic strength,
    The water peril o'er,
The many-gifted man at length
    Stepp'd on the promised shore.

He trod the shore; but not to rest,
    Nor wait till Angels came;
Lo! humblest pains the Saint attest,
    The firebands and the flame.

But, when he felt the viper's smart,
    Then instant aid was given;
Christian! hence learn to do thy part,
    And leave the rest to Heaven.

Messina.
February 8, 1833.

LXXI.

MESSINA.

"Homo sum; humani nil à me alienum puto."

WHY, wedded to the Lord, still yearns my heart
   Towards these scenes of ancient heathen fame?
   Yet legend hoar, and voice of bard that came
Fixing my restless youth with its sweet art,
And shades of power, and those who bore a part
   In the mad deeds that set the world on flame,
   So fret my memory here,—ah! is it blame?—
That from my eyes the tear is fain to start.
Nay, from no fount impure these drops arise;
'Tis but that sympathy with Adam's race
Which in each brother's history reads its own.
So let the cliffs and seas of this fair place
Be named man's tomb and splendid record-stone,
High hope, pride-stain'd, the course without the prize.

Messina.
February 9, 1833.

LXXII.

WARNINGS.

WHEN Heaven sends sorrow,
　　Warnings go first,
　　Lest it should burst
　　With stunning might
　　On souls too bright
　　　　To fear the morrow.

Can science bear us
　　To the hid springs
　　Of human things?
　　Why may not dream.
　　Or thought's day-gleam.
　　　　Startle, yet cheer us?

Are such thoughts fetters,
　　While Faith disowns
　　Dread of earth's tones,
　　Recks but Heaven's call,
　　And on the wall
　　　　Reads but Heaven's letters?

Between Calatafimi and Palermo.
February 12, 1833.

LXXIII.

DREAMS.

OH! miserable power
To dreams allow'd, to raise the guilty past,
And back awhile the illumined spirit to cast
    On its youth's twilight hour;
In mockery guiling it to act again
The revel or the scoff in Satan's frantic train!

Nay, hush thee, angry heart!
An Angel's grief ill fits a penitent;
Welcome the thorn—it is divinely sent,
    And with its wholesome smart
Shall pierce thee in thy virtue's palmy home,
And warn thee what thou art, and whence thy
    wealth has come.

Paestum.
February 26, 1833.

LXXIV.

TEMPTATION.

O HOLY Lord, who with the Children Three
    Didst walk the piercing flame,
Help, in those trial-hours, which, save to Thee
      I dare not name;
Nor let these quivering eyes and sickening heart
Crumble to dust beneath the Tempter's dart.

Thou, who didst once Thy life from Mary's breast
    Renew from day to day,
Oh, might her smile, severely sweet, but rest
      On this frail clay!
Till I am Thine with my whole soul; and fear,
Not feel a secret joy, that Hell is near.

Frascati.
March 28, 1833.

LXXV.

OUR FUTURE.

"What I do, thou knowest not now; but thou shalt know hereafter."

DID we but see,
When life first open'd, how our journey lay
Between its earliest and its closing day,
   Or view ourselves, as we one time shall be,
Who strive for the high prize, such sight would
      break
The youthful spirit, though bold for Jesu's sake.

   But Thou, dear Lord!
Whilst I traced out bright scenes which were to
      come,
Isaac's pure blessings, and a verdant home,
   Didst spare me, and withhold Thy fearful word;
Wiling me year by year, till I am found
A pilgrim pale, with Paul's sad girdle bound.

Tre Fontane.
April 2, 1833.

LXXVI.

HEATHENISM.

'MID Balak's magic fires
The Spirit spake, clear as in Israel;
With prayers untrue and covetous desires
    Did God vouchsafe to dwell;
Who summon'd dreams, His earlier word to bring
To patient Job's vex'd friends, and Gerar's guileless
        king.

    If such o'erflowing grace
From Aaron's vest e'en on the Sibyl ran,
Why should we fear, the Son now lacks His place
    Where roams unchristen'd man:
As though, where faith is keen, He cannot make
Bread of the very stones, or thirst with ashes slake.

Messina.
April 21, 1833.

LXXVII.

TAORMINI.

*"And Jacob went on his way,
and the Angels of God met him."*

SAY, hast thou track'd a traveller's round,
    Nor visions met thee there,
Thou couldst but marvel to have found
    This blighted world so fair?

And feel an awe within thee rise,
    That sinful man should see
Glories far worthier Seraph's eyes
    Than to be shared by thee?

Store them in heart! thou shalt not faint
    'Mid coming pains and fears,
As the third heaven once nerved a Saint
    For fourteen trial-years.

Magnisi.
April 26, 1833.

LXXVIII.

SYMPATHY.

SOULS of the Just, I call not you
　　To share this joy with me,
This joy and wonder at the view
　　Of mountain, plain, and sea;

Ye, on that loftier mountain old,
　　Safe lodged in Eden's cell.
Whence run the rivers four, behold
　　This earth, as ere it fell.

Or, when ye think of those who stay
　　Still tried by the world's fight,
'Tis but in looking for the day
　　Which shall the lost unite.

Ye rather, elder Spirits strong:
　　Who from the first have trod
This nether scene, man's race among,
　　The while you live to God,

Ye see, and ye can sympathise—
　　Vain thought! their mighty ken
Fills height and depth, the stars, the skies,
　　They smile at dim-eyed men.

Ah, Saviour! I perforce am Thine,
   Angel and Saint apart:
Those searching Eyes are all-divine,
   All-human is that Heart.

Agosta.
April 29, 1833.

LXXIX.

RELICS OF SAINTS.

*"He is not the God of the dead, but of the living;
for all live unto Him."*

"THE Fathers are in dust, yet live to God:"—
   So says the Truth; as if the motionless clay
Still held the seeds of life beneath the sod,
   Smouldering and struggling till the judgment-day.

And hence we learn with reverence to esteem
   Of these frail houses, though the grave confines;
Sophist may urge his cunning tests, and deem
   That they are earth;—but they are heavenly shrines.

Palermo.
June 1, 1833.

LXXX.

DAY-LABOURERS.

"And He said, It is finished."

ONE only, of God's messengers to man,
Finish'd the work of grace, which He began;
E'en Moses wearied upon Nebo's height,
    Though loth to leave the fight
With the doom'd foe, and yield the sun-bright land
    To Joshua's armèd hand.

And David wrought in turn a strenuous part,
Zeal for God's house consuming him in heart;
And yet he might not build, but only bring
    Gifts for the Heavenly King;
And these another rear'd, his peaceful son,
    Till the full work was done.

List, Christian warrior! thou, whose soul is fain
To rid thy Mother of her present chain;—
Christ will avenge His Bride; yea, even now
    Begins the work, and thou
Shalt spend in it thy strength, but ere He save,
    Thy lot shall be the grave.

Palermo.
June 2, 1833.

LXXXI.

WARFARE.

"Freely ye have received; freely give."

"GIVE any boon for peace!
Why should our fair-eyed Mother e'er engage
In the world's course and on a troubled stage,
From which her very call is a release?
    No! in thy garden stand,
    And tend with pious hand
    The flowers thou plantest there,
    Which are thy proper care,
O man of God! in meekness and in love,
And waiting for the blissful realms above."

    Alas! for thou must learn,
Thou guileless one! rough is the holy hand;
Runs not the Word of Truth through every land,
A sword to sever, and a fire to burn?
    If blessèd Paul had stay'd
    In cot or learned shade,
    With the priest's white attire,
    And the Saints' tuneful choir,
Men had not gnash'd their teeth, nor risen to slay,
But thou hadst been a heathen in thy day.

Palermo.
June 3, 1833.

LXXXII.

SACRILEGE.

THE Church shone brightly in her youthful days
    Ere the world on her smilled;
So now, an outcast, she would pour her rays
    Keen, free, and undefiled:
Yet would I not that arm of force were mine,
Which thrusts her from her awful ancient shrine.

'Twas duty bound each convert-king to rear
    His Mother from the dust,
And pious was it to enrich, nor fear
    Christ for the rest to trust;
And who shall dare make common or unclean
What once has on the Holy Altar been?

Dear brothers!—hence, while ye for ill prepare,
    Triumph is still your own;
Blest is a pilgrim Church!—yet shrink to share
    The curse of throwing down.
So will we toil in our old place to stand,
Watching, not dreading, the despoiler's hand.

Palermo.
June 4, 1833.

LXXXIII.

LIBERALISM.

"Jehu destroyed Baal out of Israel. Howbeit from the sins of Jeroboam Jehu departed not from after them, to wit, the golden calves that were in Bethel, and that were in Dan."

YE cannot halve the Gospel of God's grace;
　　Men of presumptuous heart! I know you well.
　　Ye are of those who plan that we should dwell,
Each in his tranquil home and holy place;
Seeing the Word refines all natures rude,
And tames the stirrings of the multitude.

And ye have caught some echoes of its lore,
　　As heralded amid the joyous choirs;
　　Ye mark'd it spoke of peace, chastised desires,
Good-will and mercy,—and ye heard no more;
But, as for zeal and quick-eyed sanctity,
And the dread depths of grace, ye pass'd them by.

And so ye halve the Truth; for ye in heart,
　　At best, are doubters whether it be true,
　　The theme discarding, as unmeet for you,
Statesmen or Sages. O new-compass'd art
Of the ancient Foe!—but what, if it extends
O'er our own camp, and rules amid our friends?

　　　　　　　　　　　　　Palermo.
　　　　　　　　　　　　　June 5, 1833.

LXXXIV.

DECLENSION.

WHEN I am sad, I say,
  "What boots it me to strive,
And vex my spirit day by day,
  Dead memories to revive?

"Alas! what good will come,
  Though we our prayer obtain,
To bring old times triumphant home,
  And wandering flocks regain?

"Would not our history run
  In the same weary round,
And service in meek faith begun,
  At length in forms be bound?

"Union would give us strength—
  That strength the earth subdue
And then comes wealth, and pride at length,
  And sloth, and prayers untrue."

Nay, this is worldly-wise;
  To reason is a crime,
Since the Lord bade His Church arise,
  In the dark ancient time.

He wills that she should shine;
So we her flame must trim
Around His soul-converting Sign,
And leave the rest to Him.

Palermo.
June 6, 1833.

LXXXV.

THE AGE TO COME.

WHEN I would search the truths that in me burn,
   And mould them into rule and argument,
A hundred reasoners cried,—"Hast thou to learn
   Those dreams are scatter'd now, those fires are
      spent?"
And, did I mount to simpler thoughts, and try
Some theme of peace, 'twas still the same reply.

Perplex'd, I hoped my heart was pure of guile,
   But judged me weak in wit, to disagree;
But now, I see that men are mad awhile,
   And joy the Age to come will think with me:—
'Tis the old history—Truth without a home,
Despised and slain, then rising from the tomb.

Palermo.
June 9, 1833.

LXXXVI.

EXTERNAL RELIGION.

WHEN first earth's rulers welcomed home
The Church, their zeal impress'd
Upon the seasons, as they come,
The image of their guest.

Men's words and works, their hopes and fears,
Henceforth forbid to rove,
Paused, when a Martyr claim'd her tears,
Or Saint inspired her love.

But craving wealth, and feverish power,
Such service now discard;
The loss of one excited hour
A sacrifice too hard!

And e'en about the holiest day,
God's own in every time,
They doubt and search, lest aught should stay
A cataract of crime.

Where shall this cease? must crosiers fall,
Shrines suffer touch profane,
Till, cast without His vineyard wall,
The Heaven-sent Heir is slain?

Palermo.
June 11, 1833.

LXXXVII.

ST. GREGORY NAZIANZEN.

PEACE-LOVING man, of humble heart and true
　　What dost thou here?
Fierce is the city's crowd; the lordly few
　　Are dull of ear!
Sore pain it was to thee,—till thou didst quit
Thy patriarch-throne at length, as though for
　　power unfit.

So works the All-wise! our services dividing
　　Not as we ask:
For the world's profit, by our gifts deciding
　　Our duty-task.
See in king's courts loth Jeremias plead;
And slow-tongued Moses rule by eloquence of deed!

Yes! thou, bright Angel of the East! didst rear
　　The Cross divine,
Borne high upon thy liquid accents, where
　　Men mock'd the Sign;
Till that cold city heard thy battle-cry,
And hearts were stirr'd, and deem'd a Pentecost
　　was nigh.

Thou couldst a people raise, but couldst not rule:—
     So, gentle one,
Heaven set thee free,—for, ere thy years were full,
     Thy work was done;
According thee the lot thou lovedst best,
To muse upon the past,—to serve, yet be at rest.

Palermo.
June 12, 1833.

LXXXVIII.

THE GOOD SAMARITAN.

OH that thy creed were sound![1]
For thou dost soothe the heart, thou Church of
    Rome,
By thy unwearied watch and varied round
Of service, in thy Saviour's holy home.
    I cannot walk the city's sultry streets,
    But the wide porch invites to still retreats,
Where passion's thirst is calm'd, and care's unthankful
    gloom.

There, on a foreign shore,
The home-sick solitary finds a friend:
    Thoughts, prison'd long for lack of speech, outpour
Their tears; and doubts in resignation end.
    I almost fainted from the long delay
    That tangles me within this languid bay,
When comes a foe, my wounds with oil and
    wine to tend.

Palermo.
June 13, 1833.

---

[1] Of course this is the exclamation of one who, when so writing, was
not in Catholic Communion. The same must be said also of Nos. lxvi.,
lxxviii.

LXXXIX.

REVERENCE.

I BOW at Jesu's name, for 'tis the Sign
Of awful mercy towards a guilty line.
Of shameful ancestry, in birth defiled,
      And upwards from a child
Full of unlovely thoughts and rebel aims
      And scorn of judgment-flames,
How without fear can I behold my Life,
The Just assailing sin, and death-stain'd in the
    strife?
And so, albeit His woe is our release,
Thought of that woe aye dims our earthly peace;
The Life is hidden in a Fount of Blood!
      And this is tidings good
For souls, who, pierced that they have caused
    that woe,
      Are fain to share it too:
But for the many, clinging to their lot
Of worldly ease and sloth, 'tis written "Touch Me
    not."

Off Monte Pellegrino.
June 14, 1833.

XC.

THE PILLAR OF THE CLOUD.

LEAD, Kindly Light, amid the encircling gloom
      Lead Thou me on!
The night is dark, and I am far from home—
      Lead Thou me on!
Keep Thou my feet; I do not ask to see
The distant scene—one step enough for me.

I was not ever thus, nor pray'd that Thou
      Shouldst lead me on.
I loved to choose and see my path, but now
      Lead Thou me on!
I loved the garish day, and, spite of fears,
Pride ruled my will: remember not past years.

So long Thy power hath blest me, sure it still
      Will lead me on,
O'er moor and fen, o'er crag and torrent, till
      The night is gone;
And with the morn those angel faces smile
Which I have loved long since, and lost awhile.

At Sea.
June 16, 1833.

XCI.

SAMARIA.

O RAIL not at our kindred in the North.
  Albeit Samaria finds her likeness there;
A self-form'd Priesthood, and the Church cast forth
    To the chill mountain air.

What, though their fathers sinned, and lost the grace
  Which seals the Holy Apostolic Line?
Christ's love o'erflows the bounds His prophets trace
    In His reveal'd design.

Israel had Seers; to them the Word is nigh;
  Shall not that Word run forth, and gladness give
To many a Shunammite, till in His eye
    The full Seven-thousand live?

Off Sardinia.
June 17, 1833.

XCII.

JONAH.

*"But Jonah rose up to flee unto Tarshish,
from the presence of the Lord."*

DEEP in his meditative bower,
  The tranquil seer reclined;
Numbering the creepers of an hour,
  The gourds which o'er him twined

To note each plant, to rear each fruit
  Which soothes the languid sense,
He deem'd a safe, refined pursuit—
  His Lord, an indolence.

The sudden voice was heard at length,
  "Lift thou the prophet's rod!"
But sloth had sapp'd the prophet's strength,
  He fear'd, and fled from God.

Next, by a feárful judgment tamed,
  He threats the offending race;
God spares;—he murmurs, pride-inflamed,
  His threat made void by grace.

What?—pride and sloth! man's worst of foes!
  And can such guests invade
Our choicest bliss, the green repose
  Of the sweet garden-shade?

Off Sardinia.
June 18, 1833.

XCIII.

FAITH AGAINST SIGHT.

*"As it was in the days of Lot, so shall it be also
in the day of the Son of Man."*

THE world has cycles in its course, when all
    That once has been, is acted o'er again;—
Not by some fated law, which need appal
    Our faith, or binds our deeds as with a chain;
But by men's separate sins, which blended still
        The same bad round fulfil.

Then fear ye not, though Gallio's scorn ye see,
    And soft-clad nobles count you mad, true hearts!
These are the fig-tree's signs;—rough deeds must
        be,
    Trials and crimes: so learn ye well your parts.
Once more to plough the earth it is decreed,
        And scatter wide the seed.

Off Sardinia.
June 18, 1833.

XCIV.

DESOLATION.

O, SAY not thou art left of God,
  Because His tokens in the sky
Thou canst not read: this earth He trod
  To teach thee He was ever nigh.

He sees, beneath the fig tree green,
  Nathaniel con His sacred lore;
Shouldst thou thy chamber seek, unseen,
  He enters through the unopen'd door.

And when thou liest, by slumber bound,
  Outwearied in the Christian fight,
In glory, girt with Saints around,
  He stands above thee through the night.

When friends to Emmaus bend their course,
  He joins, although He holds their eyes:
Or, shouldst thou feel some fever's force,
  He takes thy hand, He bids thee rise.

Or on a voyage, when calms prevail,
  And prison thee upon the sea,
He walks the wave, He wings the sail,
  The shore is gain'd, and thou art free.

Off Sardinia.
June 18, 1833.

XCV.

ZEAL AND PATIENCE.

"I, Paul, the prisoner of the Lord."

O COMRADE, bold of toil and pain!
   Thy trial how severe,
When sever'd first by prisoner's chain
   From thy loved labour-sphere!

Say, did impatience first impel
   The heaven-sent bond to break?
Or, couldst thou bear its hindrance well,
   Loitering for Jesu's sake?

Oh, might we know! for sore we feel
   The languor of delay,
When sickness lets our fainter zeal,
   Or foes block up our way.

Lord! who Thy thousand years dost wait
   To work the thousandth part
Of Thy vast plan, for us create
   With zeal a patient heart.

Off Sardinia.
June 19, 1833.

XCVI.

THE RELIGION OF CAIN.

"Am I my brother's keeper?"

THE time has been, it seem'd a precept plain
  Of the true faith, Christ's tokens to display;
And in life's commerce still the thought retain,
  That men have souls, and wait a judgment-
    day;
  Kings used their gifts as ministers of heaven,
Nor stripp'd their zeal for God, of means which
  God had given.

  'Tis alter'd now;—for Adam's eldest born
    Has train'd our practice in a selfish rule,
  Each stands alone, Christ's bonds asunder torn,
    Each has his private thought, selects his school,
  Conceals his creed, and lives in closest tie
  Of fellowship with those count it blasphemy.

  Brothers! spare reasoning;—men have settled
    long
    That ye are out of date, and they are wise;
  Use their own weapons; let your words be
    strong,

Your cry be loud, till each scared boaster flies
Thus the Apostles tamed the pagan breast,
They argued not, but preach'd; and conscience did
the rest.

Off Sardinia.
June 19, 1833.

XCVII.

ST. PAUL.

I DREAM'D that, with a passionate complaint,
  I wish'd me born amid God's deeds of might;
  And envied those who had the presence bright
Of gifted Prophet and strong-hearted Saint,
Whom my heart loves, and Fancy strives to paint.
  I turn'd, when straight a stranger met my sight,
  Came as my guest, and did awhile unite
His lot with mine, and lived without restraint.
Courteous he was, and grave,—so meek in mien,
It seem'd untrue, or told a purpose weak
Yet, in the mood, he could with aptness speak,
Or with stern force, or show of feelings keen,
Marking deep craft, methought, or hidden pride:—
Then came a voice,—"St. Paul is at thy side."

Off Sardinia.
June 20, 1833.

XCVIII.

FLOWERS WITHOUT FRUIT.

PRUNE thou thy words, the thoughts control
    That o'er thee swell and throng;
They will condense within thy soul
    And change to purpose strong.

But he who lets his feelings run
    In soft luxurious flow,
Shrinks when hard service must be done,
    And faints at every woe.

Faith's meanest deed more favour bears,
    Where hearts and wills are weigh'd,
Than brightest transports, choicest prayers,
    Which bloom their hour and fade.

Off Sardinia.
June 20, 1833.

XCIX.

ZEAL AND MEEKNESS.

CHRIST bade His followers take the sword;
   And yet He chid the deed,
When Peter seized upon His word,
   And made a foe to bleed.

The gospel Creed, a sword of strife,
   Meek hands alone may rear;
And ever Zeal begins its life
   In silent thought and fear,

Ye, who would weed the Vineyard's soil,
   Treasure the lesson given;
Lest in the judgment-books ye toil
   For Satan, not for heaven.

Off Sardinia.
June 20, 1833.

C.

VEXATIONS.

EACH trial has its weight; which, whoso bears
   Knows his own woe, and need of succouring
      grace;
  The martyr's hope half wipes away the trace
Of flowing blood; the while life's humblest cares
Smart more, because they hold in Holy Writ no
      place.

  This be my comfort, in these days of grief,
   Which is not Christ's, nor forms heroic
      tale.
  Apart from Him, if not a sparrow fail,
  May not He pitying view, and send relief
When foes or friends perplex, and peevish thoughts
      prevail?

  Then keep good heart, nor take the niggard
      course
   Of Thomas, who must see ere he would trust.
   Faith will fill up God's word, not poorly just
  To the bare letter, heedless of its force,
But walking by its light amid earth's sun and dust.

Off Sardinia.
June 21, 1833.

CI.

THE CHURCH IN PRAYER.

WHY loiterest within Simon's walls,
  Hard by the barren sea,
Thou Saint! when many a sinner calls
  To preach and set him free?

Can this be he, who erst confess'd
  For Christ affection keen,
Now truant in untimely rest,
  The mood of an Essene?

Yet he who at the sixth hour sought
  The lone house-top to pray,
There gain'd a sight beyond his thought,
  The dawn of Gentile day.

Then reckon not, when perils lour,
  The time of prayer mis-spent;
Nor meanest chance, nor place, nor hour,
  Without its heavenward bent.

Off Sardinia.
June 21, 1833.

CII.

THE WRATH TO COME.

"From His mouth came out a sharp two-edged sword."

WHEN first God stirr'd me, and the Church's word
   Came as a theme of reverent search and fear,
   It little cost to own the lustre clear
Of truths she taught, of rite and rule she stored;
For conscience craved, and reason did accord.
   Yet one there was that wore a mien austere,
   And I did doubt, and, startled, ask'd to hear
Whose mouth had force to edge so sharp a sword.
My mother oped her trust, the holy Book;
And heal'd my pang. She pointed, and I found
Christ on Himself, considerate Master, took
The utterance of that doctrine's fearful sound.
The Fount of Love His servants sends to tell
Love's deeds; Himself reveals the sinner's hell.

Off Sardinia.
June 21, 1833.

CIII.

PUSILLANIMITY.

"I have need to be baptized of Thee, and comest Thou to me?"

HOW didst thou start, Thou Holy Baptist, bid
    To pour repentance on the Sinless Brow!
Then all thy meekness, from thy hearers hid,
    Beneath the Ascetic's port, and Preacher's fire.
Flow'd forth, and with a pang thou didst desire
    He might be chief, not thou.

And so on us at whiles it falls, to claim
    Powers that we dread, or dare some forward part;
Nor must we shrink as cravens from the blame
    Of pride, in common eyes, or purpose deep;
But with pure thoughts look up to God, and keep
    Our secret in our heart.

At Sea.
June 22, 1833.

CIV.

JAMES AND JOHN.

TWO brothers freely cast their lot
    With David's royal Son;
The cost of conquest counting not,
    They deem the battle won.

Brothers in heart, they hope to gain
    An undivided joy;
That man may one with man remain,
    As boy was one with boy.

Christ heard; and will'd that James should
        fall,
    First prey of Satan's rage;
John linger out his fellows all,
    And die in bloodless age.

Now they join hands once more above,
    Before the Conqueror's throne;
Thus God grants prayer, but in His love
    Makes times and ways His own.

At Sea.
June 22, 1833.

CV.

HORA NOVISSIMA.

WHENE'ER goes forth Thy dread command,
  And my last hour is nigh,
Lord, grant me in a Christian land,
  As I was born, to die.

I pray not, Lord, that friends may be,
  Or kindred, standing by,—
Choice blessing! which I leave to Thee
  To grant me or deny.

But let my failing limbs beneath
  My Mother's smile recline;
And prayers sustain my labouring breath
  From out her sacred shrine.

And let the cross beside my bed
  In its dread Presence rest:
And let the absolving words be said,
  To ease a laden breast.

Thou, Lord, where'er we lie, canst aid;
  But He, who taught His own
To live as one, will not upbraid
  The dread to die alone.

At Sea.
June 22, 1833.

CVI.

PROGRESS OF UNBELIEF.

Now is the Autumn of the Tree of Life;
  Its leaves are shed upon the unthankful earth,
Which lets them whirl, a prey to the winds' strife,
  Heartless to store them for the months of dearth.
  Men close the door, and dress the cheerful
    hearth,
Self-trusting still; and in his comely gear
Of precept and of rite, a household Baal rear.

But I will out amid the sleet, and view
  Each shrivelling stalk and silent-falling leaf.
Truth after truth, of choicest scent and hue,
  Fades, and in fading stirs the Angels' grief,
  Unanswer'd here; for she, once pattern chief
Of faith, my Country, now gross hearted grown,
Waits but to burn the stem before her idol's
    throne.

At Sea.
June 23, 1833.

CVII.

CONSOLATION.

"It is I; be not afraid."

WHEN I sink down in gloom or fear.
  Hope blighted or delay'd,
Thy whisper, Lord, my heart shall cheer.
  "'Tis I; be not afraid!"

Or, startled at some sudden blow,
  If fretful thoughts I feel,
"Fear not, it is but I!" shall flow,
  As balm my wound to heal.

Nor will I quit Thy way, though foes
  Some onward pass defend;
From each rough voice the watchword goes,
  "Be not afraid! . . . a friend!"

And oh! when judgment's trumpet clear
  Awakes me from the grave,
Still in its echo may I hear,
  "'Tis Christ; He comes to save."

                              At Sea.
                          June 23, 1833.

CVIII.

UZZAH AND OBED-EDOM.

THE ark of God has hidden strength;
  Who reverence or profane,
They, or their seed, shall find at length
  The penalty or gain.

While as a sojourner it sought
  Of old its destined place,
A blessing on the home it brought
  Of one who did it grace.

But there was one, outstripping all
  The holy-vestured band,
Who laid on it, to save its fall,
  A rude corrective hand.

Read, who the Church would cleanse, and mark
  How stern the warning runs;
There are two ways to aid her ark—
  As patrons, and as sons.

At Sea.
June 24, 1833.

CIX.

THE GIFT OF TONGUES.

ONCE cast with men of language strange
  And foreign-moulded creed,
I mark'd their random converse change,
  And sacred themes succeed.

Oh, how I coveted the gift
  To thread their mingled throng
Of sounds, then high my witness lift
  But weakness chain'd my tongue.

Lord! has our dearth of faith and prayer
  Lost us this power once given
Or is it sent at seasons rare
  And then flits back to heaven?

At Sea.
June 24, 1833.

CX.

THE POWER OF PRAYER.

THERE is not on the earth a soul so base
   But may obtain a place
   In covenanted grace;
So that his feeble prayer of faith obtains
   Some loosening of his chains,
And earnests of the great release, which rise
From gift to gift, and reach at length the eternal
 prize.

All may save self;—but minds that heavenward
 tower
   Aim at a wider power
   Gifts on the world to shower.—
And this is not at once;—by fastings gain'd,
   And trials well sustain'd,
By pureness, righteous deeds, and toils of love,
Abidance in the Truth, and zeal for God above.

          At Sea.
        June 24, 1833.

CXI.

SEMITA JUSTORUM.

WHEN I look back upon my former race,
   Seasons I see at which the Inward Ray
   More brightly burn'd, or guided some new way;
Truth, in its wealthier scene and nobler space
Given for my eye to range, and feet to trace.
   And next I mark, 'twas trial did convey,
   Or grief, or pain, or strange eventful day,
To my tormented soul such larger grace.
So now, whene'er, in journeying on, I feel
The shadow of the Providential Hand,
Deep breathless stirrings shoot across my breast,
Searching to know what He will now reveal,
What sink uncloak, what stricter rule command,
And girding me to work His full behest.

At Sea.
June 25, 1833.

CXII.

THE ELEMENTS.

(A Tragic Chorus.)

MAN is permitted much
　　To scan and learn
　　In Nature's frame;
　Till he well-nigh can tame
　Brute mischiefs and can touch
　Invisible things, and turn
All warring ills to purposes of good.
　　Thus, as a god below,
　　He can control,
And harmonize, what seems amiss to flow
　As sever'd from the whole
　And dimly understood.

　But o'er the elements
　　One Hand alone,
　　One Hand has sway
　What influence day by day
　In straiter belt prevents
　The impious Ocean, thrown
Alternate o'er the ever-sounding shore?
　　Or who has eye to trace
　　How the Plague came?
Forerun the doublings of the Tempest's race?
　　Or the Air's weight and flame
　　On a set scale explore?

Thus God has will'd
That man, when fully skill'd.
Still gropes in twilight dim;
Encompass'd all his hours
   By fearfullest powers
   Inflexible to him.
That so he may discern
   His feebleness.
And e'en for earth's success
   To Him in wisdom turn,
Who holds for us the keys of either home,
Earth and the world to come.

At Sea.
June 25, 1833.

CXIII.

APOSTACY.

FRANCE! I will think of thee as what thou wast,
   When Poictiers show'd her zeal for the true creed;
Or in that age, when Holy Truth, though cast
   On a rank soil, yet was a thriving seed,
Thy schools within, from neighbouring countries chased;
   E'en of thy pagan day I bear to read,
Thy Martyrs sanctified the guilty host,
The sons of blessèd John, reared on a western coast.

I dare not think of thee as what thou art
   Lest thoughts too deep for man should trouble me.
It is not safe to place the mind and heart
   On brink of evil, or its flames to see,
Lest they should dizzy, or some taint impart,
   Or to our sin a fascination be.
And so in silence I will now proclaim
Hate of thy present self, and scarce will sound thy name.[1]

Off the French coast.
June 26, 1833.

[1] Vide note at p. 570.

CXIV.

JUDAISM.

(A Tragic Chorus.)

O PITEOUS race!
  Fearful to look upon,
  Once standing in high place,
    Heaven's eldest son.
    O aged blind
Unvenerable! as thou flittest by,
I liken thee to him in pagan song,
    In thy gaunt majesty,
The vagrant King, of haughty-purposed mind,
  Whom prayer nor plague could bend;[1]
Wrong'd, at the cost of him who did the wrong,
Accursed himself, but in his cursing strong,
  And honour'd in his end.

  O Abraham! sire,
  Shamed in thy progeny;
  Who to thy faith aspire,
    Thy Hope deny.
    Well wast thou given
From out the heathen an adopted heir
Raised strangely from the dead when sin had slain
  Thy former-cherish'd care.
O holy men, ye first-wrought gems of heaven
  Polluted in your kin,

[1] Vide the Œdipus Coloneus of Sophocles.

Come to our fonts, your lustre to regain.
O Holiest Lord! . . . . but Thou canst take no stain
    Of blood, or taint of sin.

    Twice in their day
  Proffer of precious cost
Was made, Heaven's hand to stay
    Ere all was lost.
    The first prevail'd;
Moses was outcast from the promised home,
For his own sin, yet taken at his prayer
    To change his people's doom.
Close on their eve, one other ask'd and fail'd;
    When fervent Paul was fain
The accursèd tree, as Christ had borne, to bear,
No hopeful answer came,—a Price more rare
    Already shed in vain.

Off Marseilles Harbour.
June 27, 1833.

CXV.

SEPARATION OF FRIENDS.

DO not their souls, who 'neath the Altar wait
   Until their second birth,
The gift of patience need, as separate
   From their first friends of earth?
Not that earth's blessings are not all outshone
   By Eden's Angel flame,
But that earth knows not yet, the Dead has won
   That crown, which was his aim.
For when he left it, 'twas a twilight scene
   About his silent bier,
A breathless struggle, faith and sight between,
   And Hope and sacred Fear.
Fear startled at his pains and dreary end,
   Hope raised her chalice high,
And the twin-sisters still his shade attend,
   View'd in the mourner's eye.
So day by day, for him from earth ascends,
   As steam in summer-even,
The speechless intercession of his friends,
   Toward the azure heaven.
Ah! dearest, with a word he could dispel
   All questioning, and raise
Our hearts to rapture, whispering all was well
   And turning prayer to praise.
And other secrets too he could declare,
   By patterns all divine,
His earthly creed retouching here and there,

And deepening every line.
Dearest! he longs to speak, as I to know,
    And yet we both refrain:
It were not good: a little doubt below,
    And all will soon be plain.[1]

Marseilles.
June 27, 1833.

[1] The last twelve lines were added after Feb. 28, 1836, the date of R. Hurrell Froude's death.

CXVI.

THE PRIESTLY OFFICE.

FROM ST. GREGORY NAZIANZEN.

IN service o'er the Mystic Feast I stand;
   I cleanse Thy victim-flock, and bring them near
     In holiest wise, and by a bloodless rite.
     O fire of Love! O gushing Fount of Light!
(As best I know, who need Thy pitying Hand)
   Dread office this, bemired souls to clear
     Of their defilement, and again make bright.

Oxford.
1834.

CXVII.

MORNING.

FROM ST. GREGORY NAZIANZEN.

I RISE and raise my clasped hands to Thee!
Henceforth, the darkness hath no part in me,
    Thy sacrifice this day;
Abiding firm, and with a freeman's might
Stemming the waves of passion in the fight;—
    Ah, should I from Thee stray,
My hoary head, Thy table where I bow,
Will be my shame, which are mine honour now.
Thus I set out;—Lord! lead me on my way!

Oxford.
1834.

CXVIII.

EVENING.

FROM ST. GREGORY NAZIANZEN.

O HOLIEST Truth! how have I lied to Thee!
I vow'd this day Thy festival should be:
   But I am dim ere night.
Surely I made my prayer, and I did deem
That I could keep in me Thy morning beam,
   Immaculate and bright.
But my foot slipp'd; and, as I lay, he came,
My gloomy foe, and robbed me of heaven's flame.
Help Thou my darkness, Lord, till I am light.

Oxford.
1834.

CXIX.

A HERMITAGE.

FROM ST. GREGORY NAZIANZEN.

SOME one whisper'd yesterday,
   Of the rich and fashionable,
Gregory in his own small way
   Easy was and comfortable.

Had he not of wealth his fill
   Whom a garden gay did bless,
And a gently trickling rill,
   And the sweets of idleness?

I made answer:—"Is it ease
   Fasts to keep and tears to shed,
Vigil hours and wounded knees,
   Call you these a pleasant bed?"

Thus a veritable monk
   Does to death his fleshly frame;
Be there who in sloth are sunk,
   They have forfeited the name.

Oxford.
1834.

CXX.

THE MARRIED AND THE SINGLE.

A FRAGMENT FROM ST. GREGORY NAZIANZEN.

As, when the hand some mimic form would paint,
It marks its purpose first in shadows faint,
And next, its store of varied hues applies,
Till outlines fade, and the full limbs arise;
So in the earlier school of sacred lore
The Virgin-life no claim of honour bore,
While in Religion's youth the Law held sway,
And traced in symbols dim that better way.
But, when the Christ came by a Virgin-birth,—
His radiant passage from high heaven to earth,—
And, spurning father for His mortal state,
Did Eve and all her daughters consecrate,
Solved fleshly laws, and in the letter's place
Gave us the Spirit and the Word of Grace,
Then shone the glorious Celibate at length,
Robed in the dazzling lightnings of its strength,
Surpassing spells of earth and marriage vow,
As soul the body, heaven this world below,
The eternal peace of saints life's troubled span,
And the high throne of God, the haunts of man.
So now there circles round the King of Light
A heaven on earth, a blameless court and bright,
Aiming as emblems of their God to shine,
Christ in their heart, and on their brow His Sign,—
Soft funeral lights in the world's twilight dim,
Loving their God, and ever loved by Him.

Ye countless multitudes, content to bow
To the soft thraldom of the marriage vow!
I mark your haughty step, your froward gaze,
Gems deck your hair, and silk your limbs arrays;
Come, tell the gain which wedlock has conferr'd
On man; and then the single shall be heard.

The married many thus might plead, I ween;
Right glib their tongue, full confident their mien:—
"Hear all who live! to whom the nuptial rite
Has brought the privilege of life and light.
We, who are wedded, but the law obey
Stamp'd at creation on our blood and clay,
What time the Demiurge our line began,
Oped Adam's side, and out of man drew man.
Thenceforth let children of a mortal sod
Honour the law of earth, the primal law of God.

"List, you shall hear the gifts of price that lie
Gathered and bound within the marriage-tie.
What taught the arts of life, the truths which sleep
In earth, or highest heaven, or vasty deep?
What fill'd the mart, and urged the vessel brave
To link in one fair countries o'er the wave?
What raised the town? what gave the type and germ
Of social union, and of sceptre firm?
What the first husbandman, the glebe to plough,
And rear the garden, but the marriage vow?

"Nay, list again! Who seek its kindly chain,
A second self, a double presence gain;
Hands, eyes, and ears, to act or suffer here,
Till e'en the weak inspire both love and fear,—
A comrade's sigh, to soothe when cares annoy,
A comrade's smile, to elevate his joy.

"Nor say it weds us to a carnal life,
When want is urgent, fears and vows are rife.
Light heart is his, who has no yoke at home,
Scant prayer for blessings, as the seasons come;
But wife, and offspring, goods which go or stay,
Teach us our need, and make us trust and pray.
Take love away, and life would be defaced,
A ghastly vision on a howling waste,
Stern, heartless, reft of the sweet spells which swage
The throes of passion, and which gladden age.
No child's sweet pranks, once more to make us young;
No ties of place about our heart-strings flung;
No public haunts to cheer; no festive tide
When harmless mirth and smiling wit preside;
A life which scorns the gifts by heaven assign'd,
Nor knows the sympathy of human kind.

"Prophets and teachers, priests and victor kings,
Deck'd with each grace which heaven-taught nature
    brings.
These were no giant offspring of the earth,
But to the marriage-promise owed their birth:—
Moses and Samuel, David, David's Son,
The blessed Tishbite, the more blessed John,
The sacred Twelve in apostolic choir,
Strong-hearted Paul, instinct with seraph fire,
And others, now or erst, who to high heaven aspire
Bethink ye; should the single state be best,
Yet who the single, but my offspring blest?
My sons, be still, nor with your parents strive:
They coupled in their day, and so ye live."

Thus marriage pleads. Now let her rival speak—
Dim is her downcast eye, and pale her cheek;
Untrimm'd her gear; no sandals on her feet;

A sparest form for austere tenant meet.
She drops her veil her modest face around,
And her lips open, but we hear no sound.
I will address her:—"Hail, O child of Heaven,
Glorious within! to whom a post is given
Hard by the Throne where angels bow and fear,
E'en while thou hast a name and mission here,
O deign thy voice, unveil thy brow and see
Thy ready guard and minister in me.
Oft hast thou come heaven-wafted to my breast,
Bright Spirit! so come again, and give me rest."
. . . "Ah, who has hither drawn my backward feet,
Changing for wordly strife my lone retreat?
Where, in the silent chant of holy deeds,
    praise my God, and tend the sick soul's needs;
By toils of day, and vigils of the night,
By gushing tears, and blessed lustral rite.
I have no sway amid the crowd, no art
In speech, no place in council or in mart.
Nor human law, nor judges throned on high.
Smile on my face, and to my words reply.
Let others seek earth's honours; be it mine
One law to cherish, and to track one line,
Straight on towards heaven to press with single bent,
To know and love my God, and then to die content."

. . . .

. . . .

Oxford.
1834.

CXXI.

INTERCESSION OF THE SAINTS.

WHILE Moses on the Mountain lay,
Night after night, and day after day,
   Till forty suns were gone,
Unconscious, in the Presence bright,
Of lustrous day and starry night,
As though his soul had flitted quite
   From earth, and Eden won;

The pageant of a kingdom vast,
And things unutterable, pass'd
   Before the Prophet's eye;
Dread shadows of th'Eternal Throne,
The fount of Life, and Altar-stone.
Pavement, and them that tread thereon,
   And those who worship nigh.

But lest he should his own forget,
Who in the vale were struggling yet,
   A sadder vision came,
Announcing all that guilty deed
Of idol rite, that in their need
He for his flock might intercede,
   And stay Heaven's rising flame.

Oxford.
September 4, 1835

CXXII.

WAITING FOR THE MORNING.

"Quoddam quasi pratum, in quo animæ nihil patiebantur, sed manebant, nondum idoneæ Visioni Beatæ." *Bedae Hist.* v.

THEY are at rest:
We may not stir the heaven of their repose
With loud-voiced grief, or passionate request,
    Or selfish plaint for those
Who in the mountain grots of Eden lie,
And hear the fourfold river, as it hurries by.

    They hear it sweep
In distance down the dark and savage vale;
But they at eddying pool or current deep
    Shall never more grow pale;
They hear, and meekly muse, as fain to know
How long untired, unspent, that giant stream shall flow.

    And soothing sounds
Blend with the neighbouring waters as they glide
Posted along the haunted garden's bounds
    Angelic forms abide,
Echoing, as words of watch, o'er lawn and grove,
The verses of that hymn which Seraphs chant above.

Oxford.
1835.

CXXIII.

MATINS—SUNDAY.[1]

Primo die, quo Trinitas.

TO-DAY the Blessed Three in One
   Began the earth and skies;
To-day a Conqueror, God the Son,
   Did from the grave arise;
We too will wake, and, in despite
Of sloth and languor, all unite,
As Psalmists bid, through the dim night,
   Waiting with wistful eyes.

So may He hear, and heed each vow
   And prayer to Him addrest;
And grant an instant cleansing now,
   A future glorious rest.
So may He plentifully shower,
On all who hymn His love and power,
In this most still and sacred hour,
   His sweetest gifts and best.

Father of purity and light!
   Thy presence if we win,
'Twill shield us from the deeds of night,
   The burning darts of sin;

[1] These Hymns are all free translations, made in 1836–8, from the Roman Breviary, except two which are from the Parisian.

Lest aught defiled or dissolute
Relax our bodies or imbrute,
And fires eternal be the fruit
   Of fire now lit within.

Fix in our hearts, Redeemer dear,
   The ever-gushing spring
Of grace to cleanse, of life to cheer
   Souls sick and sorrowing.
Thee, bounteous Father, we entreat,
And Only Son, awful and sweet,
And life-creating Paraclete,
   The everlasting King.

CXXIV.

MATINS—SUNDAY.

Nocte surgentes.

LET us arise, and watch by night,
　　And meditate always;
And chant, as in our Maker's sight,
　　United hymns of praise.

So, singing with the Saints in bliss.
　　With them we may attain
Life everlasting after this,
　　And heaven for earthly pain.

Grant this, O Father, Only Son,
　　And Spirit, God of grace,
To whom all worship shall be done
　　In every time and place.

CXXV.

MATINS—MONDAY.

Somno refectis artubus.

SLEEP has refresh'd our limbs, we spring
  From off our bed, and rise;
Lord, on Thy suppliants, while they sing,
  Look with a Father's eyes.

Be Thou the first on every tongue,
  The first in every heart;
That all our doings all day long,
  Holiest! from Thee may start.

Cleanse Thou the gloom, and bid the light
  Its healing beams renew;
The sins, which have crept in with night,
  With night shall vanish too.

Our bosoms, Lord, unburthen Thou,
  Let nothing there offend;
That those who hymn Thy praises now
  May hymn them to the end.

Grant this, O Father, Only Son,
  And Spirit, God of grace,
To whom all worship shall be done
  In every time and place.

CXXVI.

MATINS—TUESDAY.

Consors Paterni luminis.

O GOD from God, and Light from Light,
  Who art Thyself the day,
Our chants shall break the clouds of night;
  Be with us while we pray.

Chase Thou the gloom that haunts the mind,
  The thronging shades of hell,
The sloth and drowsiness that bind
  The senses with a spell.

Lord, to their sins indulgent be,
  Who, in this hour forlorn,
By faith in what they do not see.
  With songs prevent the morn.

Grant this, O Father, etc.

CXXVII.

MATINS—WEDNESDAY.

Rerum Creator optime.

WHO madest all and dost control,
    Lord, with Thy touch divine,
Cast out the slumbers of the soul,
    The rest that is not Thine.

Look down, Eternal Holiness,
    And wash the sins away,
Of those, who, rising to confess,
    Outstrip the lingering day.

Our hearts and hands by night, O Lord,
    We lift them in our need;
As holy Psalmists give the word,
    And holy Paul the deed.

Each sin to Thee of years gone by,
    Each hidden stain lies bare;
We shrink not from Thine awful eye,
    But pray that Thou wouldst spare.

Grant this O Father, etc.

CXXVIII.

MATINS—THURSDAY.

Nox atra rerum contegit.

ALL tender lights, all hues divine
    The night has swept away;
Shine on us, Lord, and we shall shine
    Bright in an inward day.

The spots of guilt, sin's wages base,
    Searcher of hearts, we own;
Wash us and robe us in Thy grace,
    Who didst for sins atone.

The sluggard soul, that bears their mark,
    Shrinks in its silent lair,
Or gropes amid its chambers dark
    For Thee, who art not there.

Redeemer! send Thy piercing rays,
    That we may bear to be
Set in the light of Thy pure gaze,
    And yet rejoice in Thee.

Grant this, O Father, etc.

CXXIX.

MATINS—FRIDAY.

Tu Trinitatis Unitas.

MAY the dread Three in one, who sways
    All with His sovereign might,
Accept us for this hymn of praise,
    His watchers in the night.

For in the night, when all is still
    We spurn our bed and rise,
To find the balm for ghostly ill
    His bounteous hand supplies.

If e'er by night our envious foe
    With guilt our souls would stain,
May the deep streams of mercy flow,
    And make us white again;

That so with bodies braced and bright,
    And hearts awake within,
All fresh and keen may burn our light,
    Undimm'd, unsoil'd by sin.

Shine on Thine own, Redeemer sweet!
    Thy radiance increate
Through the long day shall keep our feet
    In their pure morning state.

Grant this, O Father, etc.

CXXX.

MATINS—SATURDAY.

Summae Parens clementiæ.

FATHER of mercies infinite,
  Ruling all things that be,
Who, shrouded in the depth and height,
  Art One, and yet art Three;

Accept our chants, accept our tears,
  A mingled stream we pour;
Such stream the laden bosom cheers,
  To taste Thy sweetness more.

Purge Thou with fire the o'ercharged mind,
  Its sores and wounds profound;
And with the watcher's girdle bind
  The limbs which sloth has bound.

That they who with their chants by night
  Before Thy presence come,
All may be fill'd with strength and light
  From their eternal home.

Grant this, O Father, etc.

CXXXI.

LAUDS—SUNDAY.

Æterne rerum conditor.

FRAMER of the earth and sky,
  Ruler of the day and night,
With a glad variety,
  Tempering all, and making light;

Gleams upon our dark path flinging,
  Cutting short each night begun,
Hark! for chanticleer is singing,
  Hark! he chides the lingering sun.

And the morning star replies,
  And lets loose the imprison'd day;
And the godless bandit flies
  From his haunt and from his prey.

Shrill it sounds, the storm relenting
  Soothes the weary seaman's ears;
Once it wrought a great repenting,
  In that flood of Peter's tears.

Rouse we; let the blithesome cry
  Of that bird our hearts awaken;
Chide the slumberers as they lie,
  And arrest the sin-o'ertaken.

Hope and health are in his strain,
  To the fearful and the ailing;
Murder sheathes his blade profane,
  Faith revives when faith was failing.

Jesu, Master! when we sin,
  Turn on us Thy healing face;
It will melt the offence within
  Into penitential grace:

Beam on our bewilder'd mind,
  Till its dreamy shadows flee;
Stones cry out where Thou hast shined,
  Jesu! musical with Thee.

To the Father and the Son,
  And the Spirit, who in heaven
Ever witness, Three and One,
  Praise on Earth be ever given.

CXXXII.

LAUDS—SUNDAY.

Ecce jam noctis.

PALER have grown the shades of night,
  And nearer draws the day,
Checkering the sky with streaks of light,
  Since we began to pray:

To pray for mercy when we sin,
  For cleansing and release,
For ghostly safety, and within
  For everlasting peace.

Praise to the Father, as is meet,
  Praise to the Only Son,
Praise to the Holy Paraclete,
  While endless ages run.

CXXXIII.

LAUDS—MONDAY.

Splendor Paternæ gloriæ.

OF the Father Effluence bright,
Out of Light evolving light,
Light from Light, unfailing Ray,
Day creative of the day:

Truest Sun, upon us stream
With Thy calm perpetual beam,
In the Spirit's still sunshine
Making sense and thought divine.

Seek we too the Father's face
Father of almighty grace,
And of majesty excelling,
Who can purge our tainted dwelling;

Who can aid us, who can break
Teeth of envious foes, and make
Hours of loss and pain succeed,
Guiding safe each duteous deed,

And infusing self-control,
Fragrant chastity of soul,
Faith's keen flame to soar on high,
Incorrupt simplicity.

Christ Himself for food be given,
Faith become the cup of Heaven,
Out of which the joy is quaff'd
Of the Spirit's sobering draught.

With that joy replenishèd,
Morn shall glow with modest red,
Noon with beaming faith be bright,
Eve be soft without twilight.

It has dawn'd;—upon our way,
Father in Thy Word, this day,
In Thy Father Word Divine,
From Thy cloudy pillar shine.

To the Father, and the Son,
And the Spirit, Three and One,
As of old, and as in Heaven,
Now and here be glory given.

CXXXIV.

LAUDS—TUESDAY.

Ales diei nuntius.

DAY'S herald bird
  At length is heard,
Telling its morning torch is lit,
  And small and still
  Christ's accents thrill,
Within the heart rekindling it.

  Away, He cries,
  With languid eyes.
And sickly slumbers profitless!
  I am at hand,
  As watchers stand,
In awe, and truth, and holiness.

  He will appear
  The hearts to cheer
Of suppliants pale and abstinent
  Who cannot sleep
  Because they weep
With holy grief and violent.

  Keep us awake,
  The fetters break,
Jesu! which night has forged for us;
  Yea, melt the night

To sinless light,
Till all is bright and glorious.

To Father, Son,
And Spirit, One,
To the Most Holy Trinity,
All praise be given
In Earth and Heaven,
Now, as of old, and endlessly.

CXXXV.

LAUDS—WEDNESDAY.

Nox et tenebræ et nubila.

HAUNTING gloom and flitting shades,
   Ghastly shapes, away!
Christ is rising, and pervades
   Highest Heaven with day.

He with His bright spear the night
   Dazzles and pursues:
Earth wakes up, and glows with light
   Of a thousand hues.

Thee, O Christ, and Thee alone,
   With a single mind,
We with chant and plaint would own:
   To Thy flock be kind.

Much it needs Thy light divine.
   Spot and stain to clean;
Light of Angels, on us shine
   With Thy face serene.

To the Father, and the Son,
   And the Holy Ghost,
Here be glory, as is done
   By the angelic host.

CXXXVI.

LAUDS—THURSDAY.

Lux ecce surgit aurea.

SEE, the golden dawn is glowing
While the paly shades are going,
Which have led us far and long,
In a labyrinth of wrong.

May it bring us peace serene;
May it cleanse, as it is clean;
Plain and clear our words be spoke,
And our thoughts without a cloak;

So the day's account, shall stand.
Guileless tongue and holy hand,
Stedfast eyes and unbeguiled,
"Flesh as of a little child."

There is One who from above
Watches how the still hours move
Of our day of service done,
From the dawn to setting sun.

To the Father, and the Son,
And the Spirit, Three and One,
As of old, and as in Heaven,
Now and here be glory given.

CXXXVII.

LAUDS—FRIDAY.

Aeterna cœli gloria.

GLORY of the eternal Heaven,
Blessed Hope to mortals given,
Of the Almighty Only Son,
And the Virgin's Holy One;
Raise us, Lord, and we shall rise
 In a sober mood,
And a zeal, which glorifies
 Thee from gratitude.

Now the day-star, keenly glancing,
Tells us of the Sun's advancing;
While the unhealthy shades decline,
Rise within us, Light Divine!
Rise, and, risen, go not hence,
 Stay, and make us bright,
Streaming through each cleansèd sense,
 On the outward night.

Then the root of faith shall spread
In the heart new fashionèd;
Gladsome hope shall spring above,
And shall bear the fruit of love.
To the Father, and the Son.
 And the Holy Ghost,
Here be glory, as is done
 By the angelic host.

CXXXVIII.

LAUDS—SATURDAY.

Aurora jam spargit polum.

THE dawn is sprinkled o'er the sky,
    The day steals softly on;
Its darts are scatter'd far and nigh,
And all that fraudful is, shall fly
    Before the brightening sun;
Spectres of ill, that stalk at will,
    And forms of guilt that fright,
And hideous sin, that ventures in
    Under the cloak of night.

And of our crimes the tale complete,
    Which bows us in Thy sight,
Up to the latest, they shall fleet,
Out-told by our full numbers sweet,
    And melted by the light.
To Father, Son, and Spirit, One,
    Whom we adore and love,
Be given all praise now and always,
    Here as in Heaven above.

CXXXIX.

PRIME.

Jam lucis orto sidere.

(From the Parisian Breviary.[1])

NOW that the day-star glimmers bright,
   We suppliantly pray
That He, the uncreated Light,
   May guide us on our way.

No sinful word, nor deed of wrong,
   Nor thoughts that idly rove;
But simple truth be on our tongue,
   And in our hearts be love.

And, while the hours in order flow,
   O Christ, securely fence
Our gates, beleaguer'd by the foe,—
   The gate of every sense.

And grant that to Thine honour, Lord,
   Our daily toil may tend;
That we begin it at Thy word,
   And in Thy blessing end.

[1] Vide the Anglo-Norman History of Sir Francis Palgrave (Vol. iii. p. 588), who did the Author the honour of asking him for a translation of this hymn, as also of the Christe Pastorum, *infra*.

And, lest the flesh in its excess
    Should lord it o'er the soul,
Let taming abstinence repress
    The rebel, and control.

To God the Father glory be,
    And to His Only Son,
And to the Spirit, One and Three,
    While endless ages run.

Littlemore.
February, 1842.

CXL.

TERCE.

Nunc Sancte nobis Spiritus.

COME, Holy Ghost, who ever One
Reignest with Father and with Son,
It is the hour, our souls possess
With Thy full flood of holiness.

Let flesh, and heart, and lips, and mind,
Sound forth our witness to mankind;
And love light up our mortal frame,
Till others catch the living flame.

Now to the Father, to the Son,
And the Spirit, Three in One,
Be praise and thanks and glory given
By men on earth, by Saints in heaven.

CXLI.

SEXT.

Rector potens, verax Deus.

O GOD, who canst not change nor fail,
    Guiding the hours, as they roll by,
Bright'ning with beams the morning pale,
    And burning in the mid-day sky,

Quench Thou the fires of hate and strife,
    The wasting fever of the heart;
From perils guard our feeble life,
    And to our souls Thy peace impart.

Grant this, O Father, Only Son,
    And Holy Spirit, God of grace,
To whom all glory, Three in One,
    Be given in every time and place.

CXLII.

NONE.

Rerum Deus tenax vigor.

O GOD, unchangeable and true,
    Of all the Life and Power,
Dispensing light in silence through
    Every successive hour,

Lord, brighten our declining day,
    That it may never wane,
Till death, when all things round decay,
    Brings back the morn again.

This grace on Thy redeem'd confer.
    Father, Co-equal Son,
And Holy Ghost, the Comforter,
    Eternal Three in one.

CXLIII.

VESPERS—SUNDAY.

Lucis Creator optime

FATHER of Lights, by whom each day
  Is kindled out of night,
Who, when the heavens were made, didst lay
  Their rudiments in light;

Thou, who didst bind and blend in one
  The glistening morn and evening pale,
Hear Thou our plaint, when light is gone,
  And lawlessness and strife prevail.

Hear, lest the whelming weight of crime
  Wreck us with life in view;
Lest thoughts and schemes of sense and time
  Earn us a sinner's due.

So may we knock at Heaven's door,
  And strive the immortal prize to win,
Continually and evermore
  Guarded without and pure within.

Grant this, O Father, Only Son,
  And Spirit, God of grace,
To whom all worship shall be done
  In every time and place.

CXLIV.

VESPERS—MONDAY.

Immense cœli conditor.

LORD of unbounded space,
  Who, lest the sky and main
Should mix, and heaven should lose its place,
  Didst the rude waters chain;

Parting the moist and rare,
  That rills on earth might flow
To soothe the angry flame, whene'er
  It ravens from below;

Pour on us of Thy grace
  The everlasting spring;
Lest our frail steps renew the trace
  Of the ancient wandering.

May faith in lustre grow,
  And rear her star in heaven,
Paling all sparks of earth below,
  Unquench'd by damps of even.

Grant it, O Father, Son,
  And Holy Spirit of grace,
To whom be glory, Three on One.
  In every time and place.

CXLV.

VESPERS—TUESDAY.

Telluris alme conditor.

ALL-BOUNTIFUL Creator, who,
　　When Thou didst mould the world, didst drain
The waters from the mass, that so
　　Earth might immovable remain;

That its dull clods it might transmute
　　To golden flowers in vale or wood,
To juice of thirst-allaying fruit,
　　And grateful herbage spread for food;

Wash Thou our smarting wounds and hot,
　　In the cool freshness of Thy grace;
Till tears start forth the past to blot,
　　And cleanse and calm Thy holy place;

Till we obey Thy full behest,
　　Shun the world's tainted touch and breath,
Joy in what highest is and best,
　　And gain a spell to baffle death.

Grant it, O Father, Only Son,
　　And Holy Spirit, God of Grace;
To whom all glory, Three in One,
　　Be given in every time and place.

CXLVI.

VESPERS—WEDNESDAY.

Cœli Deus sanctissime.

O LORD, who, thron'd in the holy height,
　　Through plains of ether didst diffuse
　　　　The dazzling beams of light,
　　　　　In soft transparent hues;

Who didst, on the fourth day, in heaven
　　Light the fierce cresset of the sun,
　　　　And the meek moon at even,
　　　　　And stars that wildly run;

That they might mark and arbitrate
　　'Twixt alternating night and day,
　　　　And tend the train sedate
　　　　　Of months upon their way;

Clear, Lord, the brooding night within,
　　And clean these hearts for Thy abode,
　　　　Unlock the spell of sin,
　　　　　Crumble its giant load.

Grant it, O Father, Only Son,
　　And Holy Spirit, God of Grace,
　　　　To whom all praise be done
　　　　　In every time and place.

CXLVII

VESPERS—THURSDAY.

Magnæ Deus potentiæ.

O GOD, who hast given
    the sea and the sky,
To fish and to bird
    for dwelling to keep,
Both sons of the waters,
    one low and one high,
Ambitious of heaven,
    yet sunk in the deep;

Save, Lord, Thy servants,
    whom Thou hast new made
In a laver of blood,
    lest they trespass and die;
Lest pride should elate,
    or the flesh should degrade,
And they stumble on earth,
    or be dizzied on high.

To the Father and Son
And the Spirit be done,
Now and always,
Glory and praise.

CXLVIII

VESPERS—FRIDAY.

Hominis superne Conditor.

WHOM all obey,—
Maker of man! who from Thy height
Badest the dull earth bring to light
All creeping things, and the fierce might
    Of beasts of prey;—

And the huge make
Of wild or gentler animal,
Springing from nothing at Thy call,
To serve in their due time, and all
    For sinners' sake;

Shield us from ill!
Come it by passion's sudden stress,
Lurk in our mind's habitual dress,
Or through our actions seek to press
    Upon our will.

Vouchsafe the prize
Of sacred joy's perpetual mood,
And service-seeking gratitude,
And love to quell each strife or feud,
    If it arise.

Grant it, O Lord!
To whom, the Father, Only Son,
And Holy Spirit, Three in One,
In heaven and earth all praise be done,
With one accord.

CXLIX.

VESPERS—SATURDAY.

Jam sol recedit igneus.

THE red sun is gone,
  Thou Light of the heart,
Blessed Three, Holy One,
To Thy servants a sun
  Everlasting impart.

There were Lauds in the morn.
  Here are Vespers at even;
Oh, may we adorn
Thy temple new born
  With our voices in Heaven.

To the Father be praise,
  And praise to the Son
And the Spirit always,
While the infinite days
  Of eternity run.

CL.

COMPLINE.

Te lucis ante terminum.

NOW that the day-light dies away,
   By all Thy grace and love,
Thee, Maker of the world, we pray
   To watch our bed above.

Let dreams depart and phantoms fly,
   The offspring of the night,
Keep us, like shrines, beneath Thine eye,
   Pure in our foe's despite.

This grace on Thy redeem'd confer,
   Father, Co-equal Son,
And Holy Ghost, the Comforter,
   Eternal Three in One.

CLI.

ADVENT—VESPERS.

Creator alme siderum.

CREATOR of the starry pole,
   Saviour of all who live,
And light of every faithful soul,
   Jesu, these prayers receive.

Who sooner than our foe malign
   Should triumph, from above
Didst come, to be the medicine
   Of a sick world, in love;

And the deep wounds to cleanse and cure
   Of a whole race, didst go,
Pure Victim, from a Virgin pure,
   The bitter Cross unto.

Who hast a Name, and hast a Power,
   The height and depth to sway,
And Angels bow, and devils cower,
   In transport or dismay;

Thou too shalt be our Judge at length;
   Lord, in Thy grace bestow
Thy weapons of celestial strength,
   And snatch us from the foe.

Honour and glory, power and praise,
  To Father, and to Son,
And Holy Ghost, be paid always,
  The Eternal Three in One.

CLII.

ADVENT—MATINS.

Verbum supernum prodiens.

SUPERNAL Word, proceeding from
    The Eternal Father's breast,
And in the end of ages come,
    To aid a world distrest;

Enlighten, Lord, and set on fire
    Our spirits with Thy love,
That, dead to earth, they may aspire
    And live to joys above.

That, when the judgment-seat on high
    Shall fix the sinner's doom,
And to the just a glad voice cry,
    Come to your destined home;

Safe from the black and yawning lake
    Of restless, endless pain,
We may the face of God partake,
    The bliss of heaven attain.

To God the Father, God the Son,
    And Holy Ghost, to Thee,
As heretofore, when time is done,
    Unending glory be.

CLIII.

ADVENT—LAUDS.

En clara vox redarguit.

HARK, a joyful voice is thrilling,
   And each dim and winding way
Of the ancient Temple filling;
   Dreams, depart! for it is day.

Christ is coming!—from thy bed,
   Earth-bound soul, awake and spring,—
With the sun new-risen to shed
   Health on human suffering.

Lo! to grant a pardon free,
   Comes a willing Lamb from Heaven;
Sad and tearful, hasten we,
   One and all, to be forgiven,

Once again He comes in light,
   Girding each with fear and woe;
Lord! be Thou our loving Might,
   From our guilt and ghostly foe.

To the Father, and the Son,
   And the Spirit, who in Heaven
Ever witness, Three and One,
   Praise on earth be ever given.

CLIV.

THE TRANSFIGURATION—MATINS.

Quicunque Christum quæritis.

O YE who seek the Lord,
　　Lift up your eyes on high,
For there He doth the Sign accord
　　Of His bright majesty.

We see a dazzling sight
　　That shall outlive all time,
Older than depth or starry height,
　　Limitless and sublime.

'Tis He for Israel's fold
　　And heathen tribes decreed,
The King to Abraham pledged of old
　　And his unfailing seed.

Prophets foretold His birth,
　　And witness'd when He came,
The Father speaks to all the earth
　　To hear, and own His name.

To Jesus, who displays
　　To babes His beaming face,
Be, with the Father, endless praise,
　　And with the Spirit of grace. *Amen.*

CLV.

THE TRANSFIGURATION—LAUDS.

Lux alma Jesu.

LIGHT of the anxious heart,
　Jesus, Thou dost appear,
To bid the gloom of guilt depart,
　And shed Thy sweetness here.

Joyous is he, with whom.
　God's Word, Thou dost abide;
Sweet Light of our eternal home,
　To fleshly sense denied.

Brightness of God above!
　Unfathomable grace!
Thy Presence be a fount of love
　Within Thy chosen place.

To Thee, whom children see,
　The Father ever blest,
The Holy Spirit, One and Three,
　Be endless praise addrest. *Amen.*

CLVI.

FOR A MARTYR.

Deus tuorum militum.

O GOD, of Thy soldiers
   the Portion and Crown,
Spare sinners who hymn
   the praise of the Blest;
Earth's bitter joys,
   its lures and its frown,
He scann'd them and scorn'd,
   and so is at rest.

Thy Martyr he ran
   all valiantly o'er
A highway of blood
   for the prize Thou hast given.
We kneel at Thy feet,
   and meekly implore,
That our pardon may wait
   on his triumph in heaven.

Honour and praise
 To the Father and Son
 And the Spirit be done
Now and always. *Amen.*

CLVII.

FOR A CONFESSOR BISHOP.

Christe Pastorum.[1]

O THOU, of shepherds Prince and Head,
　　Now on a Bishop's festal-day
Thy flock to many a shrine have sped
　　　　Their vows to pay,

He to the high and dreadful throne
　　Urged by no false inspirings, prest,
Nor on hot daring of his own,
　　　　But Thy behest.

And so, that soldier good and tried,
　　From the full horn of heavenly grace,
Thy Spirit did anoint, to guide
　　　　Thy ransom'd race.

And he becomes a father true,
　　Spending and spent, when troubles fall.
A pattern and a servant too,
　　　　All things to all.

His pleading sets the sinner free,
　　He soothes the sick, he lifts the low,
Powerful in word, deep teacher, he,
　　　　To quell the foe.

[1] From the Parisian Breviary.

Grant us, O Christ, his prayers above,
  And grace below to sing Thy praise,
The Father's power, the Spirit's love,
  Now and always.

Littlemore.
February 7, 1842.

CLVIII.

ETHELWALD.

From St. Bede's Metrical History of St. Cuthbert.

BETWEEN two comrades dear,
    Zealous and true as they,
Thou, prudent Ethelwald, didst bear
    In that high home the sway.

A man, who ne'er, 'tis said,
    Would of his graces tell,
Or with what arms he triumphèd
    Over the Dragon fell.

So down to us hath come
    A memorable word,
Which in unguarded season from
    His blessed lips was heard.

It chanced, that, as the Saint
    Drank in with faithful ear
Of Angel tones the whispers faint,
    Thus spoke a brother dear:

"Oh, why so many a pause,
    Thwarting thy words' full stream,
Till her dark line Oblivion draws
    Across the broken theme?"

He answered: "Till thou seal
 To sounds of earth thine ear,
Sweet friend, be sure thou ne'er shalt feel
 Angelic voices near."

But then the hermit blest
 A sudden change came o'er;
He shudders, sobs, and smites his breast,
 Is mute, then speaks once more:

"Oh, by the Name Most High,
 What I have now let fall,
Hush, till I lay me down to die,
 And go the way of all!"

Thus did a Saint in fear
 His gifts celestial hide;
Thus did an Angel standing near
 Proclaim them far and wide.

Littlemore.
1844.

CLIX.

CANDLEMAS.

(A Song.)

THE Angel-lights of Christmas morn,
   Which shot across the sky,
Away they pass at Candlemas,
   They sparkle and they die.

Comfort of earth is brief at best,
   Although it be divine;
Like funeral lights for Christmas gone
   Old Simeon's tapers shine.

And then for eight long weeks and more,
   We wait in twilight grey,
Till the high candle sheds a beam
   On Holy Saturday.

We wait along the penance-tide
   Of solemn fast and prayer;
While song is hush'd and lights grow dim
   In the sin-laden air.

And while the sword in Mary's soul
   Is driven home, we hide
In our own hearts, and count the wounds
   Of passion and of pride.

And still, though Candlemas be spent
    And Alleluias o'er,
Mary is music in our need,
    And Jesus light in store.

The Oratory.
1849.

CLX.

THE PILGRIM QUEEN.

(A Song.)

THERE sat a Lady
    all on the ground,
Rays of the morning
    circled her round,
Save thee, and hail to thee,
    Gracious and Fair,
In the chill twilight
    what wouldst thou there?

"Here I sit desolate,"
    sweetly said she,
"Though I'm a queen,
    and my name is Marie:
Robbers have rifled
    my garden and store,
Foes they have stolen
    my heir from my bower.

"They said they could keep Him
    far better than I,
In a palace all His,
    planted deep and raised high.
'Twas a palace of ice,
    hard and cold as were they,
And when summer came,
    it all melted away.

"Next would they barter Him,
        Him the Supreme,
For the spice of the desert,
        and gold of the stream;
And me they bid wander·
        in weeds and alone,
In this green merry land
        which once was my own."

I look'd on that Lady,
        and out from her eyes
Came the deep glowing blue
        of Italy's skies;
And she raised up her head
        and she smiled, as a Queen
On the day of her crowning,
        so bland and serene.

"A moment," she said,
        "and the dead shall revive;
The giants are failing,
        the Saints are alive;
I am coming to rescue
        my home and my reign,
And Peter and Philip
        are close in my train."

The Oratory.
1849.

CLXI.

THE MONTH OF MARY.

(A Song.)

GREEN are the leaves, and sweet the flowers,
　　And rich the hues of May;
We see them in the gardens round,
　　And market-paniers gay:
And e'en among our streets, and lanes,
　　And alleys, we descry,
By fitful gleams, the fair sunshine,
　　The blue transparent sky.

Chorus.

O Mother maid, be thou our aid,
　　Now in the opening year;
Lest sights of earth to sin give birth,
　　And bring the tempter near.

Green is the grass, but wait awhile,
　　'Twill grow, and then will wither;
The flowrets, brightly as they smile,
　　Shall perish altogether:
The merry sun, you sure would say,
　　It ne'er could set in gloom;
But earth's best joys have all an end,
　　And sin, a heavy doom.

Chorus.

But Mother maid, thou dost not fade;
  With stars above thy brow,
And the pale moon beneath thy feet,
  For ever throned art thou.

The green green grass, the glittering grove,
  The heaven's majestic dome,
They image forth a tenderer bower,
  A more refulgent home;
They tell us of that Paradise
  Of everlasting rest,
And that high Tree, all flowers and fruit,
  The sweetest, yet the best.

Chorus.

O Mary, pure and beautiful,
  Thou art the Queen of May;
Our garlands wear about thy hair,
  And they will ne'er decay.

The Oratory.
1850.

CLXII.

THE QUEEN OF SEASONS.

(*A Song for an inclement May.*)

ALL is divine
      which the Highest has made,
Through the days that He wrought,
      till the day when He stay'd;
Above and below,
      within and around,
From the centre of space.
      to its uttermost bound.

In beauty surpassing
      the Universe smiled,
On the morn of its birth,
      like an innocent child,
Or like the rich bloom
      of some delicate flower;
And the Father rejoiced
      in the work of His power.

Yet worlds brighter still,
      and a brighter than those,
And a brighter again,
      He had made, had He chose;
And you never could name
      that conceivable best,
To exhaust the resources
      the Maker possess'd.

But I know of one work
       of His Infinite Hand,
Which special and singular
       ever must stand;
So perfect, so pure,
       and of gifts such a store,
That even Omnipotence
       ne'er shall do more.

The freshness of May,
       and the sweetness of June,
And the fire of July
       in its passionate noon,
Munificent August,
       September serene.
Are together no match
       for my glorious Queen.

O Mary, all months
       and all days are thine own,
In thee lasts their joyousness,
       when they are gone;
And we give to thee May,
       not because it is best
But because it comes first,
       and is pledge of the rest.

The Oratory.
1850.

CLXIII.

VALENTINE TO A LITTLE GIRL.

LITTLE maiden, dost thou pine
For a faithful Valentine?
Art thou scanning timidly
Every face that meets thine eye?
Art thou fancying there may be
Fairer face than thou dost see?
Little maiden, scholar mine,
Wouldst thou have a Valentine?

Go and ask, my little child,
Ask the Mother undefiled:
Ask, for she will draw thee near,
And will whisper in thine ear:—
"Valentine! the name is good;
    For it comes of lineage high,
    And a famous family:
And it tells of gentle blood,
Noble blood,—and nobler still,
    For its owner freely pour'd
Every drop there was to spill
    In the quarrel of his Lord.
Valentine! I know the name,
Many martyrs bear the same;
And they stand in glittering ring
Round their warrior God and King,—
    Who before and for them bled,—
    With their robes of ruby red,
And their swords of cherub flame."

Yes! there is a plenty there,
Knights without reproach or fear,
—Such St. Denys, such St. George,
  Martin, Maurice, Theodore,
  And a hundred thousand more;
  Guerdon gain'd and warfare o'er
By that sea without a surge,
And beneath the eternal sky,
  And the beatific Sun,
    In Jerusalem above,
  Valentine is every one;
Choose from out that company
  Whom to serve, and whom to love.

The Oratory.
1850.

CLXIV.

ST. PHILIP NERI IN HIS MISSION.

(A song.)

In the far North our lot is cast,
    Where faithful hearts are few;
Still are we Philip's children dear,
    And Peter's soldiers true.

Founder and Sire! to mighty Rome,
    Beneath St. Peter's shade,
Early thy vow of loyal love
    And ministry was paid.

The solemn porch, and portal high,
    Of Peter was thy home;
The world's Apostle he, and thou
    Apostle of his Rome.

And first in the old catacombs,
    In galleries long and deep,
Where Martyr Popes had ruled the flock,
    And slept their glorious sleep,

There didst thou pass the nights in prayer,
    Until at length there came,
Down on thy breast, new lit for thee,
    The Pentecostal flame;—

Then, in that heart-consuming love,
    Didst walk the city wide,
And lure the noble and the young
    From Babel's pomp and pride;

And, gathering them within thy cell,
    Unveil the lustre bright,
And beauty of thy inner soul,
    And gain them by the sight.

And thus to Rome, for Peter's faith
    Far known, thou didst impart
Thy lessons of the hidden life,
    And discipline of heart.

And as the Apostle, on the hill
    Facing the Imperial Town,
First gazed upon his fair domain,
    Then on the cross lay down,

So thou, from out the streets of Rome
    Didst turn thy failing eye
Unto that mount of martyrdom,
    Take leave of it, and die.[1]

The Oratory.
1850.

[1] On the day of his death, Philip, "at the beginning of his Mass, remained for some time looking fixedly at the hill of St. Onofrio, which was visible from the chapel, just as if he saw some great vision. On coming to the Gloria in Excelsis, he began to sing, which was a very unusual thing for him, and he sang the whole of it with the greatest joy and devotion," &c.—*Bacci's Life.*

CLXV.

ST. PHILIP IN HIMSELF.

(A Song.)

THE holy Monks, conceal'd from men,
　In midnight choir, or studious cell,
In sultry field, or wintry glen,
　The Holy Monks, I love them well.

The Friars too, the zealous band
　By Dominic or Francis led,
They gather, and they take their stand
　Where foes are fierce, or friends have fled.

And then the unwearied Company,
　Which bears the Name of Sacred might,
The Knights of Jesus, they defy
　The fiend,—full eager for the fight.

Yet there is one I more affect
　Than Jesuit, Hermit, Monk, or Friar,
'Tis an old man of sweet aspèct,
　I love him more, I more admire.

I know him by his head of snow,
　His ready smile, his keen full eye,
His words which kindle as they flow,
　Save he be rapt in ecstasy.

He lifts his hands, there issues forth
   A fragrance virginal and rare,
And now he ventures to our North,
   Where hearts are frozen as the air.

He comes, by grace of his address,
   By the sweet music of his face,
And his low tones of tenderness,
   To melt a noble, stubborn race.

O sainted Philip, Father dear,
   Look on thy little ones, that we
Thy loveliness may copy here,
   And in the eternal kingdom see.

The Oratory.
1850.

CLXVI.

ST. PHILIP IN HIS GOD.

PHILIP, on thee the glowing ray
  Of heaven came down upon thy prayer,
To melt thy heart, and burn away
  All that of earthly dross was there.

Thy soul became as purest glass,
  Through which the Brightness Incarnate
In undimm'd majesty might pass,
  Transparent and illuminate.

And so, on Philip when we gaze,
  We see the image of his Lord;
The Saint dissolves amid the blaze
  Which circles round the Living Word.

The Meek, the Wise, none else is here,
  Dispensing light to men below;
His awful accents fill the ear,
  Now keen as fire, now soft as snow.

As snow, those inward pleadings fall,
  As soft, as bright, as pure, as cool,
With gentle weight and gradual,
  And sink into the feverish soul.

The Sinless One, He comes to seek,
    The dreary heart, the spirit lone,
Tender of natures proud or weak,
    Not less than if they were His own.

He takes and scans the sinner o'er,
    Handling His scholars one by one,
Weighing what they can bear, before
    He gives the penance to be done.

Jesu, to Philip's sons reveal
    That gentlest wisdom from above,
To spread compassion o'er their zeal,
    And mingle patience with their love.

The Oratory.
1850.

CLXVII.

GUARDIAN ANGEL.

MY oldest friend, mine from the hour
  When first I drew my breath;
My faithful friend, that shall be mine,
  Unfailing, till my death;

Thou hast been ever at my side;
  My Maker to thy trust
Consign'd my soul, what time He framed
  The infant child of dust.

No beating heart in holy prayer,
  No faith, inform'd aright.
Gave me to Joseph's tutelage,
  Or Michael's conquering might.

Nor patron Saint, nor Mary's love,
  The dearest and the best,
Has known my being, as thou hast known,
  And blest, as thou hast blest,

Thou wast my sponsor at the font;
  And thou, each budding year,
Didst whisper elements of truth
  Into my childish ear.

And when, ere boyhood yet was gone,
  My rebel spirit fell,
Ah! thou didst see, and shudder too,
  Yet bear each deed of Hell.

And then in turn, when judgments came,
  And scared me back again,
Thy quick soft breath was near to soothe
  And hallow every pain.

Oh! who of all thy toils and cares
  Can tell the tale complete,
To place me under Mary's smile,
  And Peter's royal feet!

And thou wilt hang about my bed,
  When life is ebbing low;
Of doubt, impatience, and of gloom,
  The jealous sleepless foe.

Mine, when I stand before the Judge;
  And mine, if spared to stay
Within the golden furnace, till
  My sin is burn'd away.

And mine, O Brother of my soul,
  When my release shall come;
Thy gentle arms shall lift me then,
  Thy wings shall waft me home.

The Oratory.
1853.

CLXVIII.

THE GOLDEN PRISON.

WEEP not for me, when I am gone,
  Nor spend thy faithful breath
In grieving o'er the spot or hour
  Of all-enshrouding death;

Nor waste in idle praise thy love
  On deeds of head or hand,
Which live within the living Book,
  Or else are writ in sand;

But let it be thy best of prayers,
  That I may find the grace
To reach the holy house of toll,
  The frontier penance-place,—

To reach that golden palace bright,
  Where souls elect abide,
Waiting their certain call to Heaven,
  With Angels at their side;

Where hate, nor pride, nor fear torments
  The transitory guest,
But in the willing agony
  He plunges, and is blest.

And as the fainting patriarch gain'd
   His needful halt mid-way,
And then refresh'd pursued his path,
   Where up the mount it lay,

So pray, that, rescued from the storm
   Of heaven's eternal ire,
I may lie down, then rise again
   Safe, and yet saved by fire.

The Oratory.
1853.

CLXIX.

HEATHEN GREECE.

(A Song.)

WHERE are the Islands of the Blest?
    They stud the Ægean Sea;
And where the deep Elysian rest?
    It haunts the vale where Peneus strong
    Pours his incessant stream along,
    While craggy ridge and mountain bare
    Cut keenly through the liquid air,
    And their own pure tints array'd,
    Scorn earth's green robes which change and fade,
    And stand in beauty undecay'd,
        Guards of the bold and free.

For what is Afric, but the home
    Of burning Phlegethon?
What the low beach and silent gloom,
And chilling mists of that dull river,
Along whose bank the thin ghosts shiver,—
The thin wan ghosts that once were men,—
But Tauris, isle of moor and fen,
Or dimly traced by seamen's ken,
    The pale-cliff'd Albion.

The Oratory.
1856.

CLXX.

A MARTYR CONVERT.

(A Hymn.)

THE number of Thine own complete,
    Sum up and make an end;
Sift clean the chaff, and house the wheat;
    And then, O Lord, descend.

Descend, and solve by that descent
    This mystery of life;
Where good and ill, together blent,
    Wage an undying strife.

For rivers train are gushing still,
    And pour a mingled flood;
Good in the very depths of ill,
    Ill in the heart of good.

The last are first, the first are last,
    As angel eyes behold;
These from the sheep-cote sternly cast,
    Those welcomed to the fold.

No Christian home, no pastor's eye,
    No preacher's vocal zeal,
Moved Thy dear Martyr to defy
    The prison and the wheel.

Forth from the heathen ranks she stept,
    The forfeit crown to claim
Of Christian souls who had not kept
    Their birthright and their name.

Grace form'd her out of sinful dust;
    She knelt a soul defiled,
She rose in all the faith, and trust,
    And sweetness of a child.

And in the freshness of that love
    She preach'd, by word and deed,
The mysteries of the world above,
    Her new-found, glorious creed.

And running, in a little hour,
    Of life the course complete,
She reach'd the Throne of endless power,
    And sits at Jesu's feet.

Her spirit there, her body here,
    Make one the earth and sky;
We use her name, we touch her bier,
    We know her God is nigh.

Praise to the Father, as is meet,
    Praise to the Only Son,
Praise to the Holy Paraclete
    While endless ages run.

                    The Oratory.
                    1856.

CLXXI.

ST. PHILIP IN HIS SCHOOL.

(A Song.)

THIS is the Saint of gentleness and kindness,
　　Cheerful in penance, and in precept winning;
Patiently healing of their pride and blindness,
　　　　　　Souls that are sinning.

This is the Saint, who, when the world allures us,
　　Cries her false wares, and opes her magic coffers,
Points to a better city, and secures us
　　　　　　With richer offers.

Love is his bond, he knows no other fetter,
　　Asks not our all, but takes whate'er we spare him,
Willing to draw us on from good to better,
　　　　　　As we can bear him.

When he comes near to teach us and to bless us,
　　Prayer is so sweet, that hours are but a minute;
Mirth is so pure, though freely it possess us,
　　　　　　Sin is not in it.

Thus he conducts by holy paths and pleasant,
　　Innocent souls, and sinful souls forgiven
Towards the bright palace where our God is
　　present,
　　　　　　Throned in high heaven.

The Oratory.
1857.

CLXXII.

ST. PHILIP IN HIS DISCIPLES.

(A Song.)

I ASK not for fortune, for silken attire,
For servants to throng me, and crowds to admire;
I ask not for power, or for name or success,
These do not content me, these never can bless.

Let the world flaunt her glories! each glittering
    prize,
Though tempting to others, is nought in my eyes.
A child of St. Philip, my master and guide,
I would live as he lived, and would die as he died.

Why should I be sadden'd, though friendless I be?
For who in his youth was so lonely as he?
If spited and mock'd, so was he, when he cried
To his God on the cross to stand by his side.

If scanty my fare, yet how was he fed?
On olives and herbs and a small roll of bread.
Are my joints and bones sore with aches and with
    pains?
Philip scourged his young flesh with fine iron
    chains.

A closet his home, where he, year after year,
Bore heat or cold greater than heat or cold here;
A rope stretch'd across it, and o'er it he spread
His small stock of clothes; and the floor was his
    bed.

One lodging besides; God's temple he chose,
And he slept in its porch his few hours of repose;
Or studied by light which the altar-lamp gave,
Or knelt at the Martyr's victorious grave.

I'm ashamed of myself, of my tears and my tongue,
So easily fretted, so often unstrung;
Mad at trifles, to which a chance moment gives
    birth,
Complaining of heaven, and complaining of earth.

So now, with his help, no cross will I fear,
But will linger resign'd through my pilgrimage
    here.
A child of St. Philip, my master and guide,
I will live as he lived, and will die as he died.

The Oratory.
1857.

CLXXIII.

FOR THE DEAD.

(A Hymn.)

HELP, Lord, the souls which Thou hast made,
　　The souls to Thee so dear,
In prison for the debt unpaid
　　Of sins committed here.

Those holy souls, they suffer on,
　　Resign'd in heart and will,
Until Thy high behest is done,
　　And justice has its fill.
For daily falls, for pardon'd crime,
　　They joy to undergo
The shadow of Thy cross sublime,
　　The remnant of Thy woe.

Help, Lord, the souls which Thou hast made,
　　The souls to Thee so dear,
In prison for the debt unpaid
　　Of sins committed here.

Oh, by their patience of delay,
　　Their hope amid their pain,
Their sacred zeal to burn away
　　Disfigurement and stain;

Oh, by their fire of love, not less
    In keenness than the 'flame,
Oh, by their very helplessness.
    Oh, by Thy own great Name,

Good Jesu, help! sweet Jesu, aid
    The souls to Thee most dear,
In prison for the debt unpaid
    Of sins committed here.

The Oratory.
1857.

CLXXIV.

TO EDWARD CASWALL.

*(A gift for the new year
in return for his volume of Poems.)*

ONCE, o'er a clear calm pool,
The fulness of an over-brimming spring,
I saw the hawthorn and the chestnut fling
Their willing arms, of vernal blossoms full
And light green leaves: the lilac too was there,
The prodigal laburnum, dropping gold,
While the rich gorse along the turf crept near,
Close to the fountain's margin, and made bold
To peep into that pool, so calm and clear:—
As if well pleased to see their image bright
Reflected back upon their innocent sight;
Each flower and blossom shy
Lingering the live-long day in still delight,
Yet without touch of pride, to view,
Yea, with a tender, holy sympathy,
What was itself, yet was another too.
So on thy verse, my Brother and my Friend,
—The fresh upwelling of thy tranquil spirit,—
I see a many angel forms attend;
And gracious souls elect,
And thronging sacred shades, that shall inherit
One day the azure skies,
And peaceful saints, in whitest garments deck'd;
And happy infants of the second birth:—

These, and all other plants of paradise,
Thoughts from above, and visions that are sure,
And providences past, and memories dear,
In much content hang o'er that mirror pure,
And recognize each other's faces there,
And see a heaven on earth.

The Oratory.
January 1, 1858.

CLXXV.

THE TWO WORLDS.

UNVEIL, O Lord, and on us shine
　　In glory and in grace;
This gaudy world grows pale before
　　The beauty of Thy face.

Till Thou art seen, it seems to be
　　A sort of fairy ground,
Where suns unsetting light the sky,
　　And flowers and fruits abound.

But when Thy keener, purer beam
　　Is pour'd upon our sight,
It loses all its power to charm,
　　And what was day is night.

Its noblest toils are then the scourge
　　Which made Thy blood to flow;
Its joys are but the treacherous thorns
　　Which circled round Thy brow.

And thus, when we renounce for Thee
　　Its restless aims and fears,
The tender memories of the past,
　　The hopes of coming years,

Poor is our sacrifice, whose eyes
    Are lighted from above;
We offer what we cannot keep,
    What we have ceased to love.

The Oratory.
1862.

CLXXVI.

ST. MICHAEL.

(A Hymn.)

THOU champion high
Of Heaven's imperial Bride,
For ever waiting on her eye,
Before her onward path, and at her side,
In war her guard secure, by night her ready guide!

To thee was given,
When those false angels rose
Against the Majesty of Heaven,
To hurl them down the steep, and on them close
The prison where they roam in hopeless unrepose.

Thee, Michael, thee,
When sight and breathing fail,
The disembodied soul shall see;
The pardon'd soul with solemn joy shall hail,
When holiest rites are spent, and tears no more
    avail.

And thou, at last,
When Time itself must die,
Shalt sound that dread and piercing blast,
To wake the dead, and rend the vaulted sky.
And summon all to meet the Omniscient Judge on
    high.

The Oratory.
1862.

CLXXVII.

THE DREAM OF GERONTIUS.

I.

GERONTIUS.

JESU, MARIA—I am near to death,
  And Thou art calling me; I know it now.
Not by the token of this faltering breath,
  This chill at heart, this dampness on my brow.—
(Jesu, have mercy! Mary, pray for me!)
  'Tis this new feeling, never felt before,
(Be with me, Lord, in my extremity!)
  That I am going, that I am no more.
'Tis this strange innermost abandonment,
  (Lover of souls! great God! I look to Thee,)
This emptying out of each constituent
  And natural force, by which I come to be.
Pray for me, O my friends; a visitant
  Is knocking his dire summons at my door,
The like of whom, to scare me and to daunt,
  Has never, never come to me before;
'Tis death,—O loving friends, your prayers!—'tis
    he! . . .
As though my very being had given way,
  As though I was no more a substance now,
And could fall back on nought to be my stay,
  (Help, loving Lord! Thou my sole Refuge, Thou,)
And turn no whither, but must needs decay
  And drop from out the universal frame

Into that shapeless, scopeless, blank abyss,
    That utter nothingness, of which I came:
This is it that has come to pass in me:
    Oh, horror! this it is, my dearest, this;
So pray for me, my friends, who have not strength
        to pray.

ASSISTANTS.

Kyrie eleïson, Christe eleïson, Kyrie eleïson.
Holy Mary, pray for him.
All holy Angels, pray for him.
Choirs of the righteous, pray for him.
Holy Abraham, pray for him.
St. John Baptist, St. Joseph, pray for him.
St. Peter, St. Paul, St. Andrew, St. John,
All Apostles, all Evangelists, pray for him.
All holy Disciples of the Lord, pray for him.
All holy Innocents, pray for him.
All holy Martyrs, all holy Confessors,
All holy Hermits, all holy Virgins,

GERONTIUS.

Rouse thee, my fainting soul, and play the man;
    And through such waning span
Of life and thought as still has to be trod,
    Prepare to meet thy God.
And while the storm of that bewilderment
    Is for a season spent.
And, ere afresh the ruin on me fall,
    Use well the interval.

ASSISTANTS.

Be merciful, be gracious; spare him, Lord.
Be merciful, be gracious; Lord, deliver him.
From the sins that are past;
    From Thy frown and Thine ire;
        From the perils of dying;
        From any complying
        With sin, or denying
        His God, or relying
On self, at the last;
    From the nethermost fire;
From all that is evil;
From power of the devil;
Thy servant deliver,
For once and for ever.

By Thy birth, and by Thy Cross,
Rescue him from endless loss;
By Thy death and burial,
Save him from a final fall;
By Thy rising from the tomb,
    By Thy mounting up above,
    By the Spirit's gracious love,
Save him in the day of doom.

GERONTIUS.

Sanctus fortis, Sanctus Deus,
    De profundis oro te,
Miserere, Judex meus,
    Parce mihi, Domine.
Firmly I believe and truly
    God is three, and God is One;
And I next acknowledge duly
    Manhood taken by the Son.

And I trust and hope most fully
　　In that Manhood crucified;
And each thought and deed unruly
　　Do to death, as He has died.
Simply to His grace and wholly
　　Light and life and strength belong,
And I love, supremely, solely,
　　Him the holy, Him the strong.
Sanctus fortis, Sanctus Deus,
　　De profundis oro te,
Miserere, Judex meus,
　　Parce mihi, Domine.
And I hold in veneration,
　　For the love of Him alone,
Holy Church, as His creation,
　　And her teachings, as His own.
And I take with joy whatever
　　Now besets me, pain or fear,
And with a strong will I sever
　　All the ties which bind me here.
Adoration aye be given,
　　With and through the angelic host,
To the God of earth and heaven,
　　Father, Son, and Holy Ghost.
Sanctus fortis, Sanctus Deus,
　　De profundis oro te,
Miserere, Judex meus,
　　Mortis in discrimine.

I can no more; for now it comes again,
That sense of ruin, which is worse than pain,
That masterful negation and collapse
Of all that makes me man; as though I bent
Over the dizzy brink
Of some sheer infinite descent;
Or worse, as though

Down, down for ever I was falling through
The solid framework of created things,
And needs must sink and sink
Into the vast abyss. And, crueller still,
A fierce and restless fright begins to fill
The mansion of my soul. And, worse and worse,
Some bodily form of ill
Floats on the wind, with many a loathsome curse
Tainting the hallow'd air, and laughs, and flaps
Its hideous wings,
And makes me wild with horror and dismay.
O Jesu, help! pray for me, Mary, pray!
Some Angel, Jesu! such as came to Thee
In Thine own agony. . . . .
Mary, pray for me. Joseph, pray for me. Mary,
    pray for me.

ASSISTANTS.

Rescue him, O Lord, in this his evil hour,
As of old so many by Thy gracious power:—
    (Amen.)
Enoch and Elias from the common doom;
    (Amen.)
Noe from the waters in a saving home;
    (Amen.)
Abraham from th' abounding guilt of Heathenesse;
    (Amen.)
Job from all his multiform and fell distress;
    (Amen.)
Isaac, when his father's knife was raised to slay;
    (Amen.)
Lot from burning Sodom on its judgment-day;
    (Amen.)
Moses from the land of bondage and despair;
    (Amen.)

Daniel from the hungry lions in their lair;
      (Amen.)
And the Children Three amid the furnace-flame;
      (Amen.)
Chaste Susanna from the slander and the shame;
      (Amen.)
David from Golia and the wrath of Saul;
      (Amen.)
And the two Apostles from their prison-thrall;
      (Amen.)
Thecla from her torments;
      (Amen:)

               —so to show Thy power,
Rescue this Thy servant in his evil hour.

GERONTIUS.

Novissima hora est; and I fain would sleep.
The pain has wearied me . . . Into Thy hands,
O Lord, into Thy hands. . . .

THE PRIEST.

Proficiscere, anima Christiana, de hoc mundo!
Go forth upon thy journey, Christian soul!
Go from this world! Go, in the Name of God
The Omnipotent Father, who created thee!
Go, in the Name of Jesus Christ, our Lord,
Son of the living God, who bled for thee!
Go, in the Name of the Holy Spirit, who
Hath been pour'd out on thee! Go, in the name
Of Angels and Archangels; in the name
Of Thrones and Dominations; in the name
Of Princedoms and of Powers; and in the name
Of Cherubim and Seraphim, go forth!

Go, in the name of Patriarchs and Prophets;
And of Apostles and Evangelists,
Of Martyrs and Confessors; in the name
Of holy Monks and Hermits; in the name
Of Holy Virgins; and all Saints of God,
Both men and women, go! Go on thy course;
And may thy place to-day be found in peace,
And may thy dwelling be the Holy Mount
Of Sion:— through the Same, through Christ, our
    Lord.

2.

SOUL OF GERONTIUS.

I went to sleep; and now I am refresh'd,
A strange refreshment: for I feel in me
An inexpressive lightness, and a sense
Of freedom, as I were at length myself,
And ne'er had been before. How still it is!
I hear no more the busy beat of time,
No, nor my fluttering breath, nor struggling pulse;
Nor does one moment differ from the next.
I had a dream; yes:—some one softly said
"He's gone;" and then a sigh went round the
    room.
And then I surely heard a priestly voice
Cry "Subvenite;" and they knelt in prayer.
I seem to hear him still; but thin and low,
And fainter and more faint the accents come,
As at an ever-widening interval.
Ah! whence is this? What is this severance?
This silence pours a solitariness
Into the very essence of my soul;
And the deep rest, so soothing and so sweet,
Hath something too of sternness and of pain.

For it drives back my thoughts upon their spring
By a strange introversion, and perforce
I now begin to feed upon myself,
Because I have nought else to feed upon.—

Am I alive or dead? I am not dead,
But in the body still; for I possess
A sort of confidence which clings to me,
That each particular organ holds its place
As heretofore, combining with the rest
Into one symmetry, that wraps me round,
And makes me man; and surely I could move,
Did I but will it, every part of me.
And yet I cannot to my sense bring home
By very trial, that I have the power.
'Tis strange; I cannot stir a hand or foot,
I cannot make my fingers or my lips
By mutual pressure witness each to each,
Nor by the eyelid's instantaneous stroke
Assure myself I have a body still.
Nor do I know my very attitude,
Nor if I stand, or lie, or sit, or kneel.

So much I know, not knowing how I know,
That the vast universe, where I have dwelt,
Is quitting me, or I am quitting it.
Or I or it is rushing on the wings
Of light or lightning on an onward course,
And we e'en now are million miles apart.
Yet . . . is this peremptory severance
Wrought out in lengthening measurements of space
Which grow and multiply by speed and time?
Or am I traversing infinity
By endless subdivision, hurrying back
From finite towards infinitesimal,
Thus dying out of the expansive world?

Another marvel: some one has me fast
Within his ample palm; 'tis not a grasp
Such as they use on earth, but all around
Over the surface of my subtle being,
As though I were a sphere, and capable
To be accosted thus, a uniform
And gentle pressure tells me I am not
Self-moving, but borne forward on my way.
And hark! I hear a singing; yet in sooth
I cannot of that music rightly say
Whether I hear, or touch, or taste the tones.
Oh, what a heart-subduing melody!

ANGEL.

My work is done,
        My task is o'er
                And so I come,

                Taking it home,
For the crown is won,
        Alleluia,
For evermore.

My Father gave
        In charge to me
                This child of earth
                E'en from its birth,
To serve and save,
        Alleluia,
        And saved is he.

This child of clay
        To me was given,
                To rear and train

By sorrow and pain
In the narrow way,
Alleluia,
From earth to heaven.

SOUL.

It is a member of that family
Of wondrous beings, who, ere the worlds were
    made,
Millions of ages back, have stood around
The throne of God:—he never has known sin
But through those cycles all but infinite,
Has had a strong and pure celestial life,
And bore to gaze on the unveil'd face of God,
And drank from the everlasting Fount of truth,
And served Him with a keen ecstatic love.
Hark! he begins again.

ANGEL.

O Lord, how wonderful in depth and height,
    But most in man, how wonderful Thou art!
With what a love, what soft persuasive might
    Victorious o'er the stubborn fleshly heart,
  Thy tale complete of saints Thou dost provide,
  To fill the thrones which angels lost through pride!

He lay a grovelling babe upon the ground,
    Polluted in the blood of his first sire,
With his whole essence shatter'd and unsound,
    And coil'd around his heart a demon dire,
  Which was not of his nature, but had skill
  To bind and form his op'ning mind to ill.

Then I was sent from heaven to set right
    The balance in his soul of truth and sin,
And I have waged a long relentless fight,
    Resolved that death-environ'd spirit to win,
    Which from its fallen state, when all was lost,
    Had been repurchased at so dread a cost.

Oh, what a shifting parti-colour'd scene
    Of hope and fear, of triumph and dismay,
Of recklessness and penitence, has been
    The history of that dreary, life-long fray!
    And oh, the grace to nerve him and to lead,
    How patient, prompt, and lavish at his need!

O man, strange composite of heaven and earth!
    Majesty dwarf'd to baseness! fragrant flower
Running to poisonous seed! and seeming worth
    Cloking corruption! weakness mastering power!
    Who never art so near to crime and shame,
    As when thou hast achieved some deed of name;—

How should ethereal natures comprehend
    A thing made up of spirit and of clay,
Were we not task'd to nurse it and to tend,
   Link'd one to one throughout its mortal day?
More than the Seraph in his height of place,
The Angel-guardian knows and loves the ransom'd
    race.

SOUL.

Now I know surely that I am at length
Out of the body; had I part with earth,
I never could have drunk those accents in,
And not have worshipp'd as a god the voice

That was so musical; but now I am
So whole of heart, so calm, so self-possess'd,
With such a full content, and with a sense
So apprehensive and discriminant,
As no temptation can intoxicate.
Nor have I even terror at the thought
That I am clasp'd by such a saintliness.

ANGEL.

All praise to Him, at whose sublime decree
  The last are first, the first become the last;
By whom the suppliant prisoner is set free,
  By whom proud first-borns from their thrones
    are cast;
Who raises Mary to be Queen of heaven,
While Lucifer is left, condemn'd and unforgiven.

3.

SOUL.

I will address him. Mighty one, my Lord,
My Guardian Spirit, all hail!

ANGEL.

   All hail, my child!
My child and brother, hail! what wouldest thou?

SOUL.

I would have nothing but to speak with thee
For speaking's sake. I wish to hold with thee

Conscious communion; though I fain would know
A maze of things, were it but meet to ask,
And not a curiousness.

ANGEL.

You cannot now
Cherish a wish which ought not to be wish'd

SOUL.

Then I will speak. I ever had believed
That on the moment when the struggling soul
Quitted its mortal case, forthwith it fell
Under the awful Presence of its God,
There to be judged and sent to its own place.
What lets me now from going to my Lord?

ANGEL.

Thou art not let; but with extremest speed
Art hurrying to the Just and Holy Judge:
For scarcely art thou disembodied yet.
Divide a moment, as men measure time,
Into its million-million-millionth part,
Yet even less than the interval
Since thou didst leave the body; and the priest
Cried "Subvenite." and they fell to prayer;
Nay, scarcely yet have they begun to pray.

For spirits and men by different standards mete
The less and greater in the flow of time.
By sun and moon, primeval ordinances—
By stars which rise and set harmoniously—

By the recurring seasons, and the swing,
This way and that, of the suspended rod
Precise and punctual, men divide the hours,
Equal, continuous, for their common use.
Not so with us in the immaterial world;
But intervals in their succession
Are measured by the living thought alone,
And grow or wane with its intensity.
And time is not a common property;
But what is long is short, and swift is slow,
And near is distant, as received and grasp'd
By this mind and by that, and every one
Is standard of his own chronology.
And memory lacks its natural resting-points
Of years, and centuries, and periods.
It is thy very energy of thought
Which keeps thee from thy God.

SOUL.

                    Dear Angel, say,
Why have I now no fear at meeting Him?
Along my earthly life, the thought of death
And judgment was to me most terrible.
I had it aye before me, and I saw
The Judge severe e'en in the Crucifix.
Now that the hour is come, my fear is fled;
And at this balance of my destiny,
Now close upon me, I can forward look
With a serenest joy.

ANGEL.

                    It is because
Then thou didst fear, that now thou dost not fear,

Thou hast forestall'd the agony, and so
For thee the bitterness of death is past.
Also, because already in thy soul
The judgment is begun. That day of doom,
One and the same for the collected world,—
That solemn consummation for all flesh,
Is, in the case of each anticipate
Upon his death; and, as the last great day
In the particular judgment is rehearsed,
So now, too, ere thou comest to the Throne,
A presage falls upon thee, as a ray
Straight from the Judge, expressive of thy lot.
That calm and joy uprising in thy soul
Is first-fruit to thee of thy recompense,
And heaven begun.

4.

SOUL.

But hark! upon my sense
Comes a fierce hubbub, which would make me fear
Could I be frighted.

ANGEL.

We are now arrived
Close on the judgment-court; that sullen howl
Is from the demons who assemble there.
It is the middle region, where of old
Satan appeared among the sons of God,
To cast his jibes and scoffs at holy Job.
So now his legions throng the vestibule,
Hungry and wild, to claim their property,
And gather souls for hell. Hist to their cry.

SOUL.

How sour and how uncouth a dissonance!

DEMONS.

Low-born clods
    Of brute earth
        They aspire
To become gods,
    By a new birth,
And an extra grace,
    And a score of merits,
        As if aught
Could stand in place
            Of the high thought,
        And the glance of fire
    Of the great spirits,
The powers blest,
    The lords by right,
        The primal owners,
            Of the proud dwelling
    And realm of light,—
Dispossess'd
Aside thrust,

                Chuck'd down
    By the sheer might
    Of a despot's will,
                Of a tyrant's frown,
        Who after expelling
        Their hosts, gave,
    Triumphant still,
And still unjust,
                Each forfeit crown
        To psalm-droners,

And canting groaners,
To every slave,
And pious cheat,
And crawling knave,
Who lick'd the dust
Under his feet.

ANGEL.

It is the restless panting of their being;
Like beasts of prey, who, caged within their bars,
In a deep hideous purring have their life,
And an incessant pacing to and fro.

DEMONS.

The mind bold
And independent,
The purpose free,
So we are told,
Must not think
To have the ascendant.
What's a saint?
One whose breath
Doth the air taint
Before his death;
A bundle of bones,
Which fools adore,
Ha! Ha!
When life is o'er;
Which rattle and stink,
E'en in the flesh.
We cry his pardon!
No flesh hath he;
Ha! ha!

For it hath died,
'Tis crucified
Day by day,
Afresh, afresh,
          Ha! Ha!
That holy clay,
          Ha! Ha!
This gains guerdon,
So priestlings prate,
          Ha! ha!
Before the Judge,
          And pleads and atones
For spite and grudge,
          And bigot mood,
And envy and hate,
          And greed of blood.

SOUL.

How impotent they are! and yet on earth
They have repute for wondrous power and skill;
And books describe, how that the very face
Of the Evil One, if seen, would have a force
Even to freeze the blood, and choke the life
Of him who saw it.

ANGEL.

In thy trial-state
Thou hadst a traitor nestling close at home,
Connatural, who with the powers of hell
Was leagued, and of thy senses kept the keys,
And to that deadliest foe unlock'd thy heart.
And therefore is it, in respect of man,
Those fallen ones show so majestical.

But, when some child of grace, Angel or Saint,
Pure and upright in his integrity
Of nature, meets the demons on their raid,
They scud away as cowards from the fight.
Nay, oft hath holy hermit in his cell,
Not yet disburden'd of mortality,
Mock'd at their threats and warlike overtures;
Or, dying, when they swarm'd, like flies, around,
Defied them, and departed to his Judge.

DEMONS.

Virtue and vice,
  A knave's pretence,
    'Tis all the same;
    Ha! Ha!
      Dread of hell-fire,
    Of the venomous flame,
        A coward's plea.
Give him his price,
      Saint though he be,
Ha! ha!
   From shrewd good sense
      He'll slave for hire
   Ha! ha!
     And does but aspire
To the heaven above
    With sordid aim.
And not from love.
     Ha! ha!

SOUL.

I see not those false spirits; shall I see
My dearest Master, when I reach His Throne?

Or hear, at least, His awful judgment-word
With personal intonation, as I now
Hear thee, not see thee, Angel? Hitherto
All has been darkness since I left the earth;
Shall I remain thus sight-bereft all through
My penance-time? If so, how comes it then
That I have hearing still, and taste, and touch,
Yet not a glimmer of that princely sense
Which binds ideas in one, and makes them live?

ANGEL.

Nor touch, nor taste, nor hearing hast thou
        now;
Thou livest in a world of signs and types,
The presentations of most holy truths,
Living and strong, which now encompass thee.
A disembodied soul, thou hast by right
No converse with aught else beside thyself;
But, lest so stern a solitude should load
And break thy being, in mercy are vouchsafed
Some lower measures of perception,
Which seem to thee, as though through channels
        brought,
Through ear, or nerves, or palate, which are
        gone.
And thou art wrapp'd and swathed around in
        dreams,
Dreams that are true, yet enigmatical;
For the belongings of thy present state,
Save through such symbols, come not home to
        thee.
And thus thou tell'st of space, and time, and
        size,
Of fragrant, solid, bitter, musical,
Of fire, and of refreshment after fire;

As (let me use similitude of earth,
To aid thee in the knowledge thou dost ask)—
As ice which blisters may be said to burn.
Nor hast thou now extension, with its parts
Correlative,—long habit cozens thee,—
Nor power to move thyself, nor limbs to move.
Hast thou not heard of those, who after loss
Of hand or foot, still cried that they had pains
In hand or foot, as though they had it still?
So is it now with thee, who hast not lost
Thy hand or foot, but all which made up man.
So will it be, until the joyous day
Of resurrection, when thou wilt regain
All thou hast lost, new-made and glorified.
How, even now, the consummated Saints
See God in heaven, I may not explicate;
Meanwhile, let it suffice thee to possess
Such means of converse as are granted thee,
Though, till that Beatific Vision, thou art blind;
For e'en thy purgatory, which comes like fire,
Is fire without its light.

SOUL.

His will be done!
I am not worthy e'er to see again
The face of day; far less His countenance,
Who is the very sun. Natheless in life,
When I looked forward to my purgatory,
It ever was my solace to believe,
That, ere I plunged amid the avenging flame,
I had one sight of Him to strengthen me.

ANGEL.

Nor rash nor vain is that presentiment;
Yes,—for one moment thou shalt see thy Lord.
Thus will it be: what time thou art arraign'd
Before the dread tribunal, and thy lot
Is cast for ever, should it be to sit
On His right hand among His pure elect,
Then sight, or that which to the soul is sight,
As by a lightning-flash, will come to thee,
And thou shalt see, amid the dark profound,
Whom thy soul loveth, and would fain approach,—
One moment; but thou knowest not, my child,
What thou dost ask: that sight of the Most Fair
Will gladden thee, but it will pierce thee too.

SOUL.

Thou speakest darkly, Angel; and an awe
Falls on me, and a fear lest I be rash.

ANGEL.

There was a mortal, who is now above
In the mid glory: he, when near to die,
Was given communion with the Crucified,—
Such, that the Master's very wounds were stamp'd
Upon his flesh; and, from the agony
Which thrill'd through body and soul in that
      embrace,
Learn that the flame of the Everlasting Love
Doth burn ere it transform. . . .

5.

                              . . . Hark to those sounds!
They come of tender beings angelical,
Least and most childlike of the sons of God.

FIRST CHOIR OF ANGELICALS.

Praise to the Holiest in the height,
    And in the depth be praise:
In all His words most wonderful;
    Most sure in all His ways

To us His elder race He gave
    To battle and to win,
Without the chastisement of pain,
    Without the soil of sin.

The younger son He will'd to be
    A marvel in His birth:
Spirit and flesh his parents were;
    His home was heaven and earth.

The Eternal bless'd His child, and arm'd,
    And sent him hence afar,
To serve as champion in the field
    Of elemental war.

To be His Viceroy in the world
    Of matter, and of sense;
Upon the frontier, towards the foe
    A resolute defence

ANGEL.

We now have pass'd the gate, and are within
The House of Judgment; and whereas on earth
Temples and palaces are form'd of parts
Costly and rare, but all material,
So in the world of spirits nought is found,
To mould withal, and form into a whole,
But what is immaterial; and thus
The smallest portions of this edifice,
Cornice, or frieze, or balustrade, or stair,
The very pavement is made up of life—
Of holy, blessed, and immortal beings,
Who hymn their Maker's praise continually.

SECOND CHOIR OF ANGELICALS.

Praise to the Holiest in the height,
   And in the depth be praise:
In all His words most wonderul;
   Most sure in all His ways!

Woe to thee, Man! for he was found
   A recreant in the fight;
And lost his heritage of heaven,
   And fellowship with light.

Above him now the angry sky,
   Around the tempest's din;
Who once had Angels for his friends,
   Had but the brutes for kin.

O man! a savage kindred they;
   To flee that monster brood
He scaled the seaside cave, and clomb
   The giants of the wood.

With now a fear, and now a hope,
  With aids which chance supplied,
From youth to eld, from sire to son,
  He lived, and toil'd, and died.

He dreed his penance age by age;
  And step by step began
Slowly to doff his savage garb,
  And be again a man.

And quicken'd by the Almighty's breath,
  And chasten'd by His rod,
And taught by angel-visitings,
  At length he sought his God;

And learn'd to call upon His Name,
  And in His faith create
A household and a father-land,
  A city and a state.

Glory to Him who from the mire,
  In patient length of days,
Elaborated into life
  A people to His praise!

SOUL.

The sound is like the rushing of the wind—
The summer wind—among the lofty pines;
Swelling and dying, echoing round about,
Now here, now distant, wild and beautiful;
While, scatter'd from the branches it has stirr'd,
Descend ecstatic odours.

THIRD CHOIR OF ANGELICALS.

Praise to the Holiest in the height,
    And in the depth be praise:
In all His words most wonderful;
    Most sure in all His ways!

The Angels, as beseemingly
    To spirit-kind was given,
At once were tried and perfected,
    And took their seats in heaven.

For them no twilight or eclipse;
    No growth and no decay:
'Twas hopeless, all-ingulfing night,
    Or beatific day.

But to the younger race there rose
    A hope upon its fall;
And slowly, surely, gracefully,
    The morning dawn'd on all.

And ages, opening out, divide
    The precious, and the base,
And from the hard and sullen mass
    Mature the heirs of grace.

O man! albeit the quickening ray,
    Lit from his second birth,
Makes him at length what once he was.
    And heaven grows out of earth;

Yet still between that earth and heaven—
    His journey and his goal—
A double agony awaits
    His body and his soul.

A double debt he has to pay—
    The forfeit of his sìns:
The chill of death is past, and now
    The penance-fire begins.

Glory to Him, who evermore
    By truth and justice reigns;
Who tears the soul from out its case,
    And burns away its stains!

ANGEL.

They sing of thy approaching agony,
Which thou so eagerly didst question of:
It is the face of the Incarnate God
Shall smite thee with that keen and subtle pain;

And yet the memory which it leaves will be
A sovereign febrifuge to heal the wound;
And yet withal it will the wound provoke,
And aggravate and widen it the more.

SOUL.

Thou speakest mysteries; still methinks I know
To disengage the tangle of thy words:
Yet rather would I hear the angel voice,
Than for myself be thy interpreter.

ANGEL.

When then—if such thy lot—thou seest thy Judge,
The sight of Him will kindle in thy heart
All tender, gracious, reverential thoughts.

Thou wilt be sick with love, and yearn for Him,
And feel as though thou couldst but pity Him,
That one so sweet should e'er have placed Himself
At disadvantage such, as to be used
So vilely by a being so vile as thee.
There is a pleading in His pensive eyes
Will pierce thee to the quick, and trouble thee.
And thou wilt hate and loathe thyself; for, though
Now sinless, thou wilt feel that thou hast sinn'd,
As never thou didst feel; and wilt desire
To slink away, and hide thee from His sight:
And yet wilt have a longing aye to dwell
Within the beauty of His countenance.
And these two pains, so counter and so keen,—
The longing for Him, when thou seest Him not;
The shame of self at thought of seeing Him,—
Will be thy veriest, sharpest purgatory.

SOUL.

My soul is in my hand: I have no fear,—
In His dear might prepared for weal or woe.
But hark! a grand, mysterious harmony:
It floods me like the deep and solemn sound
Of many waters.

ANGEL.

We have gain'd the stairs
Which rise towards the Presence-chamber; there
A band of mighty Angels keep the way
On either side, and hymn the Incarnate God.

ANGELS OF THE SACRED STAIR.

Father, whose goodness none can know, but they
     Who see Thee face to face,
By man hath come the infinite display
     Of thy victorious grace;
But fallen man—the creature of a day—
     Skills not that love to trace.
It needs, to tell the triumph Thou hast wrought,
An Angel's deathless fire, an Angel's reach of
     thought.

It needs that very Angel, who with awe,
     Amid the garden shade,
The great Creator in His sickness saw,
     Soothed by a creature's aid,
And agonized, as victim of the Law
     Which He Himself had made;
For who can praise Him in His depth and height,
But he who saw Him reel amid that solitary fight?

SOUL.

Hark! for the lintels of the presence-gate
Are vibrating and echoing back the strain.

FOURTH CHOIR OF ANGELICALS.

Praise to the Holiest in the height,
     And in the depth be praise:
In all His words most wonderful;
     Most sure in all His ways! ·

The foe blasphemed the Holy Lord,
     As if He reckon'd ill,

In that He placed His puppet man
    The frontier place to fill.

For, even in his best estate,
    With amplest gifts endued
A sorry sentinel was he,
    A being of flesh and blood.

As though a thing, who for his help
    Must needs possess a wife,
Could cope with those proud rebel hosts
    Who had angelic life.

And when, by blandishment of Eve,
    That earth-born Adam fell,
He shriek'd in triumph, and he cried,
    "A sorry sentinel;

"The Maker by His word is bound,
    Escape or cure is none;
He must abandon to his doom,
    And slay His darling son."

ANGEL.

And now the threshold, as we traverse it,
Utters aloud its glad responsive chant.

FIFTH CHOIR OF ANGELICALS.

Praise to the Holiest in the height
    And in the depth be praise:
In all His words most wonderful;
    Most sure in all His ways

O loving wisdom of our God!
   When all was sin and shame,
A second Adam to the fight
   And to the rescue came.

O wisest love! that flesh and blood
   Which did in Adam fail,
Should strive afresh against the foe,
   Should strive and should prevail;

And that a higher gift than grace
   Should flesh and blood refine,
God's Presence and His very Self,
   And Essence all-divine.

O generous love! that He who smote
   In man for man the foe,
The double agony in man
   For man should undergo;

And in the garden secretly,
   And on the cross on high,
Should teach His brethren and inspire
   To suffer and to die.

6.

ANGEL.

Thy judgment now is near, for we are come
Into the veilèd presence of our God.

SOUL.

I hear the voices that I left on earth.

ANGEL.

It is the voice of friends around thy bed,
Who say the "Subvenite" with the priest.
Hither the echoes come; before the Throne
Stands the great Angel of the Agony,
The same who strengthen'd Him, what time He
    knelt
Lone in that garden shade, bedew'd with blood.
That Angel best can plead with Him for all
Tormented souls, the dying and the dead.

ANGEL OF THE AGONY.

Jesu! by that shuddering dread which fell on Thee;
Jesu! by that cold dismay which sicken'd Thee;
Jesu! by that pang of heart which thrill'd in Thee;
Jesu! by that mount of sins which crippled Thee;
Jesu! by that sense of guilt which stifled Thee;
Jesu! by that innocence which girdled Thee;
Jesu! by that sanctity which reign'd in Thee;
Jesu! by that Godhead which was one with Thee;
Jesu! spare these souls which are so dear to Thee;
Souls, who in prison, calm and patient, wait for
    Thee;
Hasten, Lord, their hour, and bid them come to
    Thee.
To that glorious Home, where they shall ever gaze
    on Thee.

SOUL.

I go before my Judge. Ah!. . . .

ANGEL.

. . . . Praise to His Name!
The eager spirit has darted from my hold,
And, with the intemperate energy of love,
Flies to the dear feet of Emmanuel;
But, ere it reach them, the keen sanctity,
Which with its effluence, like a glory, clothes
And circles round the Crucified, has seized,
And scorch'd, and shrivell'd it; and now it lies
Passive and still before the awful Throne.
O happy, suffering soul! for it is safe,
Consumed, yet quicken'd, by the glance of God.

SOUL.

Take me away, and in the lowest deep
　　　　There let me be.
And there in hope the lone night-watches keep,
　　　　Told out for me.
There, motionless and happy in my pain,
　　　　Lone, not forlorn,—
There will I sing my sad perpetual strain,
　　　　Until the morn.
There will I sing, and soothe my stricken breast,
　　　　Which ne'er can cease
To throb, and pine, and languish, till possest
　　　　Of its Sole Peace.
There will I sing my absent Lord and Love:—
　　　　Take me away,
That sooner I may rise, and go above,
And see Him in the truth of everlasting day.

7.

ANGEL.

Now let the golden prison ope its gates,
Making sweet music, as each fold revolves
Upon its ready hinge. And ye, great powers,
Angels of Purgatory, receive from me
My charge, a precious soul, until the day,
When, from all bond and forfeiture released,
I shall reclaim it for the courts of light.

SOULS IN PURGATORY.

1. Lord, Thou hast been our refuge: in every generation;
2. Before the hills were born, and the world was: from age to age Thou art God.
3. Bring us not, Lord, very low: for Thou hast said, Come back again, ye sons of Adam.
4. A thousand years before Thine eyes are but as yesterday: and as a watch of the night which is come and gone.
5. The grass springs up in the morning: at evening tide it shrivels up and dies.
6. So we fail in Thine anger: and in Thy wrath are we troubled.
7. Thou hast set our sins in Thy sight: and our round of days in the light of Thy countenance.
8. Come back, O Lord! how long: and be entreated for Thy servants.
9. In Thy morning we shall be filled with Thy mercy: we shall rejoice and be in pleasure all our days.
10. We shall be glad according to the days of our humiliation: and the years in which we have seen evil.

11. Look, O Lord, upon Thy servants and on Thy work: and direct their children.

12. And let the beauty of the Lord our God be upon us: and the work of our hands, establish Thou it.

Glory be to the Father, and to the Son: and to the Holy Ghost.

As it was in the beginning, is now, and ever shall be: world without end. Amen.

ANGEL.

Softly and gently, dearly-ransom'd soul,
    In my most loving arms I now enfold thee,
And, o'er the penal waters, as they roll,
    I poise thee, and I lower thee, and hold thee.

And carefully I dip thee in the lake,
    And thou, without a sob or a resistance,
Dost through the flood thy rapid passage take,
    Sinking deep, deeper, into the dim distance.
Angels, to whom the willing task is given,
      Shall tend, and nurse, and lull thee, as thou
        liest;
And masses on the earth, and prayers in heaven,
      Shall aid thee at the Throne of the Most,
        Highest.

Farewell, but not for ever! brother dear,
    Be brave and patient on thy bed of sorrow;
Swiftly shall pass thy night of trial here,
    And I will come and wake thee on the morrow.

The Oratory.
January, 1865.

APPENDIX I.

In honorem Sancti Philippi Nerii, Patris mei.

I.

AD VESPERAS.

FREQUENTAT antra rupium
Domosque subterraneas,
Ubi prisca gens fidelium
Quievit in Deo suo,—

Ubi martyrum vis ignea
Adhuc in ossibus viget,—
Amoris inde spiritum
Philippus hausurus sibi.

Nec mortuorum supplicem
Fefellit intercessio,
Neque juvenili pectori
Non rite respondet Deus.

Nam lucido tandem globo,
Festis diebus in suis.
Clientis in sinum memor
Illabitur Paraclitus.

Et tecta dum mortalia
Vehemens subit Divinitas,

727

Confringit ardescens latus,
Et cordium compaginem.

Exinde, tanto debile
Jam corpus impar muneri,
Et Martyr et miraculum
Amoris elanguet rogo.

Æterna laus et gloria
Patri sit atque Filio,
Et igneis Paracliti
Virtutibus per sæcula. Amen.

II.

AD LAUDES.

POMPÂ relictâ sæculi,
Philippus antra martyrum
Noctu celebrat et die,
Pro Christo anhelans emori.

Frustra! cruentans ungula
Clavique non manent tibi.
Sed Martyri genus novum
Nova emeretur charitas.

En ipse tortoris vices
Almus subit Paraclitus,
Et gestientis victimæ
Transverberat Præcordia.

O cor beatum vulnere,
Plagâ æstuans septemplici,
Te dulcis Hospes occupat
Mirisque rimatur modis.

O cor, Joannis æmule!
Jesu sacrum cor exprimens!
Te Concremator Spiritus
Nobis in exemplum edidit.

Te deprecamur supplices.
Proles et hæredes tui,
Nos in figuram da patris
Amoris esse martyres.

Æterna laus et gloria
Patri sit atque Filio,
Et igneis Paracliti
Virtutibus per sæcula. Amen.

APPENDIX II.

I.

PROLOGUS IN PHORMIONEM.

QUOD Atticissans edidit Terentius,
Id ore nostro balbutimus barbari;
Quod ethnicorum coetui protulit ethnicus,
Id castis loquimur auribus Fidelium;
Hoc nomine de poetâ jam benemeriti
Quòd, ille quae tam pulchrè nobis tradidit,
Nos emendando pulchriora fecimus.

   Felices, quibus in omni re haec usu venit
Illâ Terentianâ arte ars sublimior,
Bona amplectendi, non amplectendi mala;
Dubiam ut vitaï percurrentibus viam,
Amittat terra id omne quod terram sapit,
Et plus quàm proprio vestiatur lumine!

   Quod amplius est dicendum, populares mei,
Breviter dicetur;—ad histriones attinet
Tenellas animas, corda palpitantia,
Partes virorum ausos puerorum viribus,
Qui primi[1] hìc intra Catholicorum limites
Inducere aggrediuntur veterum fabulas.
His vos favete, haud sordida affectantibus.
Siquid præclarè fit, vos manibus plaudite,

---

[1] Viz. 1864.

Si claudicat quid, adesto vostra humanitas.
  Satis jam prologi: Davus huc nunc prodeat,
Et ritè præbeat aurem, dum loquitur Geta.

The Oratory.
1864.

TRANSLATION OF THE ABOVE.

What Attic Terence wrote of old for Rome,
We in our northern accents lisp to-night;
What heathen Terence spoke to heathen ears,
We speak with Christian tongues to Christian
    men:
Doing the while this service to the Bard,
That the rare beauty of his classic wit
We by our pruning make more beautiful.

O happy art, which Terence never knew,
But they have learned, who aim in every thing
To choose the good, and pass the evil by!
These, as they pace the tangled path of life,
Cleanse from this earth its earthly dross away,
And clothe it with a pure supernal light.

Neighbours and friends, what I have more to
    say,—
It is not much,— concerns our actors here,
Fresh tender souls, and palpitating hearts,
Boys, who, tho' boys, essay the parts of men,
And are the first within this Catholic fold
To represent a classic comedy.
Be kind,—they strive with no inglorious aim;
Where they do well, applaud; and, if in aught
They shall come short, be mild and merciful.

Prologue enough; let Davus enter now.
And lend his ear, while Geta tells his tale.

The Oratory.
1864.

II.

PROLOGUS IN PINCERNAM.

Sɪ quis miretur speciem habere hanc fabulam
Recentiorum non dissimilem temporum,
Meminerit ille, passim quæ nunc assolent,
Ea vi naturæ etiam accidisse in Græcia.
Nihil est quod in poeta reprobes, si volet
Senem Rhodiensem uxorem ducere, tunc mori;
Viduam ex marito mortuo ditescere;
Argutam porro et pulchram esse et mutabilem
Migrare Athenas; ibi amatores plurimos
Allicere, quos suspensos languide tenet,
—Ecquem rejiciat, ecquem denique præferat,—
Superbientis animi blandula mora.

Hoc vero in Thaïde nostra sat laudabile est,
Quod illa sua favoris inclinatio
Hinc in Thrasonem, et illinc rursum in Phaedriam,
Non id inhumanioris vitium est ingenî,
Sed ex ratione fit, et ex benevolentia.
Cupientis nimium, virginem, amissam diu,
Ægre repertam, fratri salvam tradere.

Quod si spem Thaïdis audax resecat Chaerea,
Modo ambiendi sponsam non satis Attico,
At Sparta tales genuit virginum procos,
Et vi Sabinas petiit Roma conjuges.

Boni itaque sitis, quotquot convenistis huc,
Nec compositoris menda jam moremini,
In reficiendis partibus hujus fabulae,
Modo, ad actionem tandem cum proceditur,
Partes hodie illæ sustineantur sedulo.

The Oratory.
1866.

III.

PROLOGUS IN ANDRIAM.

NON actuosam, Spectatores, fabumam,
Non gestis, non personis non vi comica
Illustrem, hac nocte vobis exhibebimus;
Qualem in Pincerna, qualem in Aulularia,
Et qualem in Phormione dedimus antehac.
Fatemur ultro:—at Andriæ manet tamen
Laus singularis, et honos revera suus.
Namque in sermone castus et simplex nitor,
Bene cogitata bonis expressa vocibus,
Modus in ludendo, mores depicti probe,
Colloquia concinna, aptæ dramatis vices,
Hæc si scripturam faciunt melioris notæ,
Hæc si sibi nostra jure vindicat suo,
Tum Plautus nec Terentius ipse tradidit
Præstantiorem fabulam ullam hac Andria.
Non de poeta, Spectatores optimi,
Non, sed de nobis ipsis hic timendum erit;
Ne nos, qui fuimus acriores fabulas
Jam fauste aggressi, nequeamus persequi
Cum laude venam hanc doctioris ingenî.

Vos ideo, amici, nunc scenam ingredientibus
Concedite. ut soletis, sed mage quam prius,
Namque opus impense est, vestram benevolentiam.

The Oratory.
1870.

INDEX OF FIRST LINES

Appendix I

Appendix II